P9-DXL-889

THINK IN PUBLIC

Public Books Series

Public Books Series

Sharon Marcus and Caitlin Zaloom, Editors

Founded in 2012, *Public Books* is required reading for anyone interested in what scholars have to say about contemporary culture, politics, and society. The monographs, anthologies, surveys, and experimental formats featured in this series translate the online experience of intellectual creativity and community into the physical world of print. Through writing that exemplifies the magazine's commitment to expertise, accessibility, and diversity, the Public Books Series aims to break down barriers between the academy and the public in order to make the life of the mind a public good.

THINK IN PUBLIC

A PUBLIC BOOKS READER

Edited by

SHARON MARCUS
CAITLIN ZALOOM

COLUMBIA UNIVERSITY PRESS
NEW YORK

Columbia University Press
Publishers Since 1893
New York   Chichester, West Sussex
cup.columbia.edu

Library of Congress Cataloging-in-Publication Data

Names: Marcus, Sharon, 1966– editor of compilation. | Zaloom, Caitlin,
    editor of compilation.

Title: Think in public : a Public books reader / edited by Sharon Marcus
    and Caitlin Zaloom.

Other titles: Public books (Online journal)

Description: New York : Columbia University Press, [2019] |
    Series: Public books series | Includes bibliographical references and
    index.

Identifiers: LCCN 2018054003 (print) | LCCN 2019007204 (ebook) |
    ISBN 9780231548717 (e-book) | ISBN 9780231190084 (cloth : alk. paper) |
    ISBN 9780231190091 (pbk. : alk. paper)

Classification: LCC AC5 (ebook) | LCC AC5 .T355 2019 (print) |
    DDC 081—dc23

LC record available at https://lccn.loc.gov/2018054003

∞

Columbia University Press books are printed on permanent and durable
acid-free paper.
Printed in the United States of America

Cover design: Julia Kushnirsky
Cover image: Ourit Ben-Haim
Book design: Lisa Hamm

CONTENTS

PART II. THINK IN PUBLIC

PART III. READ IN PUBLIC

THINK IN PUBLIC

INTRODUCTION

SHARON MARCUS AND CAITLIN ZALOOM

I n an age of ignorance, how do we learn to think? Who protects old ideas from extinction? How do new ideas emerge and take flight?

One short answer to all these questions: books. Thanks to their durability as physical objects, books connect people and ideas across space and time. Books stimulate and preserve inconvenient truths and inspire new ways of thinking. At their best, books require slow research, careful argument, and immersed engagement. The independent, the unorthodox, and the solitary have long turned to books to fuel their imaginations.

Another short answer: universities. Universities preserve old insights and foster new ones. They are social laboratories where students experiment with politics and expression. At their best, universities gather people from around the world and encourage them to challenge received wisdom, advance knowledge, and overturn established hierarchies.

Our answer is *Public Books*. A digital magazine that unites the best of the university with the openness of the internet, *Public Books* celebrates the power of books to spread research, pioneer new ways of thinking, and introduce ideas into our lives. Our site puts readers and writers in deep conversation with books past and present—serious books, popular books, good books, and even bad books that can teach us something important when examined seriously.

Public Books is a gathering place for those who seek, as our motto and the title of this collection put it, to "think in public." Our contributors know their subjects deeply and use their knowledge to wrestle with complex problems, confront urgent issues, and offer insight into problems old and new. Our readers value knowledge and arguments that challenge us to think differently.

Today we think of a scholar as an authoritative specialist who teaches and writes. But the original meaning of "scholar" was a student: someone who learns and reads. *Public Books* exists to nurture public scholars: professors who want to speak to the broadest possible audience and readers who want to learn more about ideas both timeless and timely. Our contributors are public scholars—and our readers are, too.

■ ■ ■

We founded *Public Books* in 2012 on these precepts: That publics are thirsty for knowledge. That those who devote their lives to mastering their subjects need to be heard. That expertise and authority are not confined to white, straight, cisgender men. That it is desirable for academics to speak to a broader audience and exciting for readers outside the academy to debate what academics have to say. Most importantly, that boundaries between disciplines and ways of knowing deserve to be bridged—and barriers between the academy and the public deserve to be broken.

Academia, for too long, has excelled at building walls: walls between colleagues and specialties, walls between the corridors of research and the world outside. And now, to the benefit of public scholars and ideas, these walls are tumbling down. Whole generations of graduate students, unable to secure employment in the ivory tower, are flooding the public square. Union drives have humanists uniting with ethnographers and lab scientists. Competing universities join forces to fend off attacks by partisan politicians who want to defund knowledge. All the while, young people fighting for commonsense gun laws and humane immigration policies find themselves embracing theories of intersection and solidarity. All signs point toward a future for knowledge based on unification, not division.

It's time to embrace this new openness, to look broadly for inspiration and interconnection, to speak out widely and wisely.

Academics can no longer stay in cloistered enclaves, reassuring themselves that universities and colleges will always provide a secure oasis for books and ideas, for informed answers and clear thinking. We cannot sit back, assuming that the value of knowledge speaks for itself and that we can focus exclusively on dissertations, conferences, and publications geared toward specialists in our subfields.

To make the life of the mind a public good, academics need to join with critics, artists, activists, and readers everywhere. To fight for the policies and budgets and norms that support the thinking life, we must make our hard-earned knowledge part of debates in the world at large. We must build bridges both within the academy and beyond it if we want to preserve what is essential and expand our collective sense of what is possible.

▪ ▪ ▪

As the editors of *Public Books*, we have worked to create a place where the latest knowledge is accessible and open to all, where public scholars can draw on the power of books and create new ideas. Kate is an anthropologist who studies finance and loves to read contemporary fiction. Sharon is a literature professor who in another life almost became a scientist. In 2011, we started talking about how difficult it was to find writing that brought academic depth to discussions of contemporary books, television, and politics. Instead of watered-down versions of ideas, we craved articles by experts who could present complicated ideas clearly, accessibly, and accurately. We knew many of our friends outside the academy were curious about the ideas generated within it. Like them, we wanted to read pieces that were erudite without being esoteric, by authorities who could make cutting-edge ideas interesting to non-specialists without talking down to them.

We decided to be the change we wanted to see in our corner of the world, and the idea for *Public Books* was born. Our mission was simple: to create an open-access online magazine that would invite readers everywhere to delve into cutting-edge essays about important ideas. Our credo: anything properly understood can be explained to anyone. Our ground rules for authors: no jargon; no unexplained allusions; never take the reader's interest and attention for granted. We don't all know what "free indirect discourse" means, what the "ontological turn" might be, or why "prospect theory" has been revolutionary. But all of us could understand those concepts if someone broke them down for us. Once we understand them, those ideas just might change how we see the world.

To fulfill the *Public Books* mission, we set about creating a new cohort of scholarly writers. We brainstormed about all the academics and deeply knowledgeable artists, activists, and thinkers we knew who could write smart, engaging essays about contemporary ideas and politics. We drafted a list of potential contributors and came up with names of people young, old, and all over the map in terms of race, gender, and sexuality. At that point, few of them had been tapped to write for a broad public.

Our authors draw on expertise they've honed for years, sometimes decades. Our writers have spent years immersed in a topic; they know the evidence, collect the data, unearth new primary sources. They use that knowledge to examine today's most pressing social, political, and cultural developments. In the process, they turn academic expertise into public scholarship and engage readers who become public scholars by engaging seriously with ideas. Our writers and readers venerate research and use it to raise questions about why we think we know what we do and how we can understand what we don't. We use knowledge to confront the world and to provide direction for where we should go next.

Like all good research, public scholarship aims to be timeless. But public scholars also aim to be timely, to take up important issues of the day. *Public Books* contributors do this by discussing recently published books. But unlike ordinary book reviewers, our authors draw on knowledge and interpretative techniques that have evolved over centuries and that they have dedicated their careers to mastering.

Scholarly values undergird everything we do at *Public Books*. Our magazine's mission is to invite contributors and readers to view current problems through the lens of academic ideas that have not yet entered the mainstream. To take only a few examples from the forty-five pieces anthologized here: Destin Jenkins shows us that we can't blame the twentieth century's housing segregation on either racism or the government but instead on a wholly distinct force—racial capitalism. Lily Irani argues that we must recognize the human labor hidden within artificial intelligence. Imani Perry investigates how "black memoirs" speak to the contradictions of the Obama era. And Haruo Shirane examines a book concerned with centuries-old literary writing in Japan to critique and rethink English's current global dominance.

In these and in all our *Public Books* pieces, we've asked our writers to reckon with the world and to showcase leading-edge developments in research and theory. Making scholarship public matters because we are all part of the same society. When academics separate themselves from the realities of their fellows thousands of miles or only a few blocks away, scholarship is impoverished, and any gains won by knowledge a mirage. When general readers lose access to experts who devote their lives to mastering disciplines, they are deprived of a perspective that could offer more than sound bites. When these worlds are kept separate, we all suffer.

■ ■ ■

Books can be vehicles of exploration, reexamination, and resistance. That's why *Public Books* is devoted to books and why it is now here, for the first time, manifested as a book for you.

This book—our first—brings together some of the most cherished, ambitious, and far-ranging articles of our first six years of life. This collection is a monument to that period's achievements and to its anxieties, loves, fears, and hopes. Taken singly, each of the pieces collected here offers a chance to learn from a brilliant thinker about a compelling work. Taken together, they provide a compact introduction to some of the most exciting academic thinking guiding recent debates about our culture, politics, and economy. We hope that this anthology, along with future books in this series, will serve as a handbook for those who engage with public scholarship, both as readers and as writers. Each of these essays offers an exemplary model for how to communicate complex ideas; how to cherish what is worthy in a book, film, or television series; and how to fight and dream for a more just and beautiful world by stepping out of the towers and into the public square.

The book is divided into three parts. Part 1, "Ask in Public," contains essays on major debates about technology, climate change, race, money, cities, historical memory, morality, religion, and geopolitics. Part 2, "Think in Public," draws on one of the most inspiring features of academic life: the space that it affords people to reflect on thought itself. This section contains interviews with and essays by scholars about how they got their start and about how artists and activists—including the former Black Panther Lynn French, the artist Ramiro Gomez, and the novelists James Hannaham and Ursula K. Le Guin—use images, words, and stories to think about power, labor, and freedom. Finally, part 3, "Read in Public," offers thoughtful, nimble takes on contemporary literature. You will find essays here on such major authors of the twenty-first century as Roberto Bolaño, Elena Ferrante, Anne Carson, and Marilynne Robinson.

We hope that these essays will allow readers to experience what all scholarship offers at its best: the joy of discovering ideas, making connections, communing with great minds, and pondering questions with no easy answers. If you find yourself craving more, you can find it for free at www.publicbooks.org. Read on! ▮

PART I

Ask in Public

ON ACCELERATIONISM

FRED TURNER

What is to be done? In 1901, when Lenin posed this now-canonical question, the answer was a communist revolution. Today, twenty-five years since the internet went public, the answer has come to seem to many on the Left to be a technological one. In the 1990s, it was right-wing libertarians such as John Perry Barlow who claimed to know what to do with the information system. In the future, they wrote, we would leave our bodies behind and dive headlong into a glorious pool of universal mind called cyberspace. In the early 2000s, the builders of social media, some of whom subscribed to the tech-left ideals of open-source software and copyleft reproduction rights, sold the public a new utopia. But instead of the world of technology-enabled interpersonal intimacy they promised, social media have become a series of commercially sponsored stages on which to preen for selfies and spin off data to be mined by states and corporations. During the Arab Spring uprisings of 2011, pundits on the Right and the Left even declared that cell phones and the internet were becoming tools of political revolution. Yet today the authoritarian leaders of Egypt are if anything more entrenched than their predecessors were.

In their new book, *Inventing the Future: Postcapitalism and a World Without Work*, based on their widely circulated 2013 "Manifesto for an Accelerationist Politics," British cultural theorists Nick Srnicek and Alex Williams argue that all of this needs to change. At a time when the future seems to belong to Chicago-school economists and the internet to Google and the NSA, Srnicek and Williams have courageously drafted a call to reimagine left politics from top to bottom. Nonetheless, the alternative vision of the Left they propose in fact owes a great deal to the neoliberal imagination it aims to challenge. Srnicek and Williams believe that emerging technologies have laid the foundation for the kind of egalitarian social world once promised by Lenin himself. To bring that world into being, they argue, we need not to resist but to *accelerate* the development of new technologies and the spread of capitalism. And they are not alone. In the last two years, a vigorous debate has bubbled up in England, where Srnicek and Williams live, and spilled over into the tech-savvy enclaves of the United States. To visit that debate may be to catch a glimpse of a new New Left emerging—or, in the view of some of the movement's more strident critics, the final triumph of techno-libertarianism.

One thing that Srnicek and Williams make abundantly clear is that the tactics the Left has inherited from the social movements of the 1960s and 1970s no longer work. The antiglobalization actions of the 1990s, various student uprisings in Europe and North Africa, and, above all, the Occupy Movement in the United States—Srnicek and Williams argue that all have failed because of the Left's preoccupation with what they call, with the hint of a sneer, "folk politics." This mode emerged in the late 1960s and early 1970s, they write, from roots in anarchism, autonomism, and various forms of communism. In their view, the last fifty years have seen "the collapse of the traditional organizations of the left, and the simultaneous rise of an alternative new left predicated upon critiques of bureaucracy, verticality, exclusion and institutionalization." This new New Left loathes all forms of top-down power, revels in consensus decision making, and believes in direct action. Above all, it hopes that its own local democratic processes might be a model for a new, more democratic social order at scale.

As Srnicek and Williams note, such an ethos has produced relatively little in the way of lasting change—at least in social structure. The case of Occupy is particularly instructive. Many participants have described how gathering together in public squares, debating public issues, and shouting together in the Human Megaphone made them feel politically powerful, often for the first time. And few would deny that the Occupier's famous phrase— "We are the 99 percent!"—shaped public debate for months to come. But where are the structural changes that Occupy has wrought? What congressmen are beholden to the Occupiers in the way that so many are to the Tea Party?

According to Srnicek and Williams, the logic of folk politics has prevented movements like Occupy from evolving into something more than a string of ephemeral protests. A faith in horizontal organizations, local action, and the transformative potential of immediacy is all well and good, they write, but almost by definition, it prevents the emergence of large-scale, well-organized forces that claim and hold institutional and financial territory. Folk politics also reflects a failure to accept a series of truths about capitalism and modernity, they argue. The first of these is that capitalism is omnivorous. Srnicek and Williams note that, as Marx pointed out, capitalism devours almost all social forms in its way. This means that efforts to create local enclaves of, say, ethical consumerism or horizontal, extramarket social relations are ultimately bound to fail. For all their emphasis on bottom-up reform, such efforts can do little to prevent the commodification of experience, the expansion of inequality, and the ever-extended need to turn social life toward financially profitable ends.

Anyone who has visited the cheese boutiques of San Francisco will recognize the truth of this critique. Even as the city hosts an ever-growing flock of charcuteries, hipster barbershops, and artisanal groceries, the rich young technologists who use them have been steadily pushing the poor out of their apartments. But this is where Srnicek and Williams take an unexpected turn. Rather than try to resist the forces of technology and capitalism, they urge us to embrace them. Or, more specifically, they argue that in fact the only way to escape the maw of the consumer society is to accelerate the engines driving it. The Left must do what the neoliberal Right has done: it must celebrate the liberating tendencies of capitalism; it must take advantage of the ever-more-social affordances of new technologies; and it must help the world imagine both as sources of social improvement.

Given the failures of conventional left movements in recent years, Srnicek and Williams's call to imitate the tactics of the far more successful New Right makes a certain amount of sense. As they note, capitalism is a complex global phenomenon, a creature of banks and states, digitized financial flows, global transportation networks, and transcontinental media systems, all defended by border police of various kinds. Thanks largely to the work of the Mont Pelerin Society, a network of economists and fellow travelers first convened by Friedrich Hayek in 1947, the neoliberal Right has built a coherent ideological framework that takes into account the full range of capitalist activity. In other words, they explain, neoliberalism *scales*. In the hands of neoliberal ideologues, for instance, Schumpeter's notion of "creative destruction" becomes something that individuals can do (as entrepreneurs), that companies can do (through innovation), and that even whole economies experience (in cycles of growth and recession). Neoliberalism seems to "work" at every level of individual and collective experience. To match its power, Srnicek and Williams argue, the Left will need to build its own version of the Mont Pelerin group and spread its own alternative vision of the future.

Imitating neoliberal tactics is one thing; arguing that commerce and technology will bring about utopia is another. Srnicek and Williams want both. And they don't think conventional politics is the way to get it. Instead, they hope to build "a post-work society" by "fully automating the economy, reducing the working week, implementing a universal basic income, and achieving a cultural shift in the understanding of work." For Srnicek and Williams, the central problem with capitalism is not the inequality it produces nor the ways it intersects with longstanding patterns of racism and nationalism but rather the hoary problem of labor. For generations, they write, the Left has "sought to liberate humanity from the drudgery of work, the dependence on wage labor, and submission of our lives to a boss." New technologies allow us to build "a postcapitalist and post-work platform upon which multiple ways of living could emerge and flourish."

Here Srnicek and Williams resurrect the ancient ghost of romanticism and marry it to a Marxist critique of labor in a way that would be quite familiar to the American counterculture of the 1960s. First, they describe virtually all labor as a species of spiritual subjection. We have authentic selves, they argue, and to work for wages, we must leave our authentic desires at home. Such a view also animated the American communards of the 1960s. After all, the point of a commune was to bridge work and home so as to make it possible to be "authentic" at all times. Second, Srnicek and Williams misinterpret an important aspect of contemporary labor. They note that a 2013 Gallup poll showed that only 13 percent of workers worldwide find their work "engaging." In their view, the survey provides evidence of global alienation. Yet

Gallup conducted the survey for a group of CEOs who were quite likely seeking to make work more engaging precisely so as to draw out and monetize ever more of their workers' inner selves. Today, levels of engagement at work measure not so much workers' ability to achieve psychological authenticity on the job as they do the ability of employers to integrate the psychological needs of employees into the work process. Employers *want* their employees to be authentic at work. The more work feels like home, the more and better work employees will do.

Oddly enough, Srnicek and Williams seem quite comfortable with top-down management. In one of their book's strangest passages, they invoke the computerized management system known as "Cybersyn" as an emblem of the future they hope for. Cybersyn was designed and partially built for Salvador Allende's socialist government in Chile in the early 1970s.[1] It featured a command center that resembled the bridge of the Star Trek *Enterprise*. Like Captain Kirk and his officers, leaders were to sit together watching information stream in from around the nation and to act on what they saw. Srnicek and Williams see today's digital technologies as tools with similar potential. In order to free our individual desires, they claim, we need to automate all the work we can, manage that automation together using systems like Cybersyn, and so build a flexible postcapitalist economy in which we work when we want to, love when we want to, and, all in all, "create new modes of being."

If this sounds more than a little like a marketing campaign for Uber, it should. This is the same logic that drives the rhetoric of the sharing economy. And that should make us nervous. New digital platforms really are making work patterns more flexible and automation really is replacing (some) drudgery. Yet, marketers' claims notwithstanding, they have hardly brought us a new era of social sharing. Instead, they've marketized ever smaller segments of time and transformed formerly private resources (such as your car) into potential sources of profit. You of course bear the responsibility for capitalizing those resources (buying and maintaining the car) and getting the training to use them (learning to drive). For all their vaunted computer power, companies like Uber, Airbnb, and TaskRabbit are essentially traditional service brokers. And the vision of sharing that underlies them belongs more to the legacy of Friedrich Hayek than of Karl Marx.

Srnicek and Williams are blinded by their faith in all things digital. To consider automation only in terms of its ability to replace onerous labor is wondrously naive. Who will build the machines? Manage them? Say we succeed in building a new Cybersyn. Who will sit in the armchairs of command? As the current rage for Donald Trump reminds us, leaders need hardly be rational, disinterested public servants. And what will become of those who never reach the centers of command? Or should I say, what will become of us? How will we speak back to power? Will we become the political equivalent of Uber drivers, communicating with central powers only through the data our work throws off?

Some of Srnicek and Williams's future is indeed enticing, particularly the notion of a universal basic income. And their willingness to crack open the door of left theory to embrace the sometimes liberating power of capitalism does offer an alternative to the folk politics they rightly critique. Yet, as two other important volumes point out, that door has been opened before, and not always with liberating results.

Robin Mackay and Armen Avanessian's #Accelerate reprints two dozen essays and book sections written between the mid-nineteenth century and today. In a wide-ranging introduction, the editors make the case that contemporary accelerationists belong to a long-neglected left intellectual tradition. "Accelerationism is a political heresy," they write. "The insistence that the only radical political response to capitalism is . . . to accelerate its uprooting, alienating, decoding, abstractive tendencies" would seem, they suggest, to violate the founding principles of left politics. But that would be wrong, according to Mackay and Avanessian, who cite and reprint Marx's "Fragment on Machines" from the *Grundrisse* in reply. There Marx describes a process by which capital, embodied in the machines of production, draws the living labor of workers into itself. In Marx's account, automated machines work on behalf of capital to turn men into mere prostheses. Mackay and Avanessian take this to be a good thing. For Mackay and Avanessian, the best way to supersede capitalism is to become one with its machines.

The "Fragment on Machines" notwithstanding, Marx might well have taken issue with their view. In *Das Kapital* he argues that the centralization of capital and of production will come into conflict with the social relations that support them and capitalism will crumble from there.[2] In the Marx of *Das Kapital*, conflicts among men, machines, and money pave the road for revolution; in Mackay and Avanessian's introduction, the fusion of men and machines into something new *is* the revolution. In many ways Mackay and Avanessian's vision of accelerationism's postcapitalist effects derives from the readings of two bodies of philosophy. The first emerged in France in the early 1970s, when theorists like Deleuze and Guattari and Lyotard aimed to synthesize Marx and Freud. These critics sought to escape Marxist dialectics and to suggest that, in Mackay and Avanessian's words, "emancipation from capitalism be sought . . . by way of the polymorphous perversion set free by the capitalist machine itself." The machine, these critics wrote, would free us to create what Mackay and Avanessian call "a new fluid social body."

As Mackay and Avanessian note, such work helped set the stage for Donna Haraway's celebration of the feminist cyborg in the

United States and for the autonomist Marxism of Antonio Negri and Tiziana Terranova in Italy. But it also helped give rise to the reveries of Nick Land and the Cybernetic Culture Research Unit (CCRU) at the University of Warwick in England, which Land founded with cybertheorist Sadie Plant. In the mid-1990s, Land and Plant played an ecstatic prose accompaniment to the rise of the public internet. A random sample, from the CCRU collective's essay "Swarmachines," which Mackay and Avanessian reprint: "Jungle rewinds and reloads conventional time into silicon blips of speed and slowness that combust the slag-heaps of historical carbon-dating."

This was the kind of thing that seemed to make sense about the time *Wired* magazine first appeared on corporate coffee tables. It was also quite right wing. "The past is passed," wrote the CCRU collective. "The eternally deferred eschatologies of the left are consigned to the white trash-can of the future and leave a present tense with synthetic possibilities." Clumsy wordplay aside, the writers of the CCRU saw in the emerging digital matrix much what John Perry Barlow did: a new frontier on which they could leave their fleshy bodies and even politics itself behind. They dismissed not only folk politics but all left politics. They embraced the logic of creative destruction—not only as an economic project but as an aesthetic and, in raves at least, as a lifestyle too.

To British cultural theorist Benjamin Noys, the members of the CCRU had fallen under the spell of "Deleuzian Thatcherism." Noys is widely credited with having coined the term "accelerationism" in his 2010 volume of critical philosophy, *The Persistence of the Negative*. His recent *Malign Velocities* presents a sustained and stinging rereading of the history mapped out by Mackay and Avanessian. Like them, Noys points to nineteenth- and early-twentieth-century Marxism and Futurism and to early 1970s French philosophy as key sources of accelerationist ideals. Yet he reads both very differently. He reminds us that Lenin himself embraced the management theories of Frederick Taylor and dreamed of a world in which productivity gains would free workers to relax. Noys notes that such policies resulted not in universal leisure but in the Kafka-esque machinations of Soviet bureaucracy. Returning to the reveries of the Italian Futurists, their love of speed and the automobile, Noys reminds his readers of their deep misogyny and their affection for fascism.

As Noys points out, these first accelerationists did much more than fail to spark a populist revolution; they actually helped legitimate the technologies of domination in place today. Noys saves his harshest criticism for the French theorists of the 1970s and for the CCRU. In the social unrest of 1968, he argues, the French Left saw its hopes for an anticapitalist revolution raised and dashed. In response, thinkers such as Baudrillard, Lyotard, and Deleuze and Guattari turned their frustration into celebration. They not only accepted their inability to escape capitalism; they reveled in it. They dreamed of individuals who could melt into the libidinal slipstream of media spectacles and consumer delights. Like the Marx of the "Fragment on Machines," they dreamed of human beings who could become one with their tools.

In the 1990s, Nick Land and Sadie Plant promoted the same dreams, writes Noys, this time to a techno beat. Noys is not content to attack accelerationism as a philosophy. He also takes its aesthetics to task. Land and Plant wrote at the same moment that Kraftwerk and Detroit techno could be heard from London to Berlin. Such artists seduced listeners into a fantasy of becoming one with machine systems, of giving over their agency and taking pleasure in complete submission, argues Noys. Like the essays of the CCRU, the music appeared to herald an "exit from feeling and consciousness," and this, writes Noys, is the true promise underpinning accelerationism. For all its talk of a technology-enabled socialist utopia, accelerationism actually offers little more than a steep dive down a nihilist rabbit hole.

Here Noys picks up on an essential paradox of accelerationism and in fact of many ostensibly left-leaning, technology-embracing social movements. The same devices that are slowly choking off our ability to act in the world without their help have also offered us extraordinary pleasures. With our iPhones in our pockets, we can find out almost anything, instantly. We can summon the sounds of Muddy Waters and Django Reinhardt alongside Devo and Talking Heads. We see pictures of places whose names we've only just heard. And we can send them to people we've only just met. Much as the Italian Futurists did when they first drove off in cars, we have every reason to marvel at the new speed in the world.

Yet as the Futurists themselves have taught us, the dream of machines that will speed us away from everyday life can just as easily open the road to fascism as to democracy. In their rush to celebrate the benefits of automation, Srnicek and Williams have forgotten this history. Lenin may have turned to Taylorism to ease the lives of peasants, and the founders of the CCRU may have embraced Schumpeterian creative destruction in order to experience a technocentric form of ecstasy. Yet neither approach substantially improved the prospects for a more egalitarian social world. On the contrary, one set the stage for Stalin, and the other helped legitimate Margaret Thatcher.

To their credit, Srnicek and Williams do not ask us to dissolve into digital ones and zeros, as John Perry Barlow once did. Their call for a universal basic income makes a kind of grounded sense that has eluded earlier accelerationists. So too does their critique of folk politics. Yet the problem of politics writ large remains. How can we build a more just, more egalitarian society when our devices already surround us with so many of the personalized delights we might want such a society to offer? Meetings are boring. Talking to people unlike ourselves is hard. How can we turn away from the mediasphere long enough to rediscover the pleasures of that difficult work? And how can we sustain it when we do?

To these kinds of questions, the accelerationists have no answers.

NOTES

1. See Eden Medina, *Cybernetic Revolutionaries: Technology and Politics in Allende's Chile* (Cambridge, MA: MIT Press, 2011).
2. Karl Marx, *Das Kapital*, chap. 32, quoted in Steven Shaviro, *No Speed Limit: Three Essays on Accelerationism* (Minneapolis: University of Minnesota Press, 2015), 43.

JUSTICE FOR DATA JANITORS

LILLY IRANI

S cience fiction author Arthur C. Clarke famously declared that any sufficiently advanced technology becomes indistinguishable from magic. Today, the likes of Google, Amazon, and Facebook appear determined to sell us the dream that machines—drones, self-driving cars, and one-click shopping services—can almost miraculously fulfill users' desires. But what is at stake in hiding the delivery people, stockroom workers, content moderators, and call-center operators laboring to produce the automated experience?

Between 2003 and 2007, I worked as a "user experience designer" at Google, a company celebrated for being a creative, perk-filled information factory. Once, as I worked in my cubicle, an Oprah camera crew rolled by, filming my stickered laptop and whiteboards covered with scribbles. Every so often, company founders Larry Page and Sergey Brin would lead policy makers, including Bill Clinton and Colin Powell, around the campus, conjuring visions of Silicon plenty and showing off the engineers, designers, and product managers who would build them.

Another Google presented itself after hours, at the edges of campus, in the marginalia of product talks, and beyond journalists' and policy makers' view. Watching a "tech talk," I saw an engineer present a machine for turning the pages of rare books under a scanning camera. The patented machine housed a worker who flipped the pages in time to a rhythm-regulated soundtrack. Later, I worked on an advertising project to partially automate the process of sanitizing Google ad results. Indian workers I never met checked ads to filter out porn, alcohol, and violence. The partial automation reduced their work but could not replace it completely.

These moderators and scan workers never showed up in the lavish, celebrated spaces where Googlers drank, ate, and brainstormed. They didn't ride the Google shuttle, eat the Google food, or attend beer-filled all-hands Friday meetings. In fact, Google's abundantly productive, nonhierarchical, and playful workplace seemed to rely on hidden layers of human data work: subcontractors who were off the books, out of sight, and safely away from both central campus and technological entrepreneurship's gleaming promise of job creation.

The human-fueled automations I saw at Google are also largely out of sight in current international debates about the relationship between digital technology and the future of work. Will technology produce new jobs, new industries, and new forms of comparative advantage? Or will technology take away jobs and concentrate wealth among those who own the machines? As the United States and Europe grapple with austerity policies, the threat to employment is deepened by the boom in machine learning, robotics, and drones, as two recent books show.

Erik Brynjolfsson and Andrew McAfee's *The Second Machine Age* offers a tour through corporate visions of spectacular automation, and well-meaning advice about how to stave off the future inequality such visions might generate. Simon Head's *Mindless* redirects our gaze: business automation has already spread far and wide, he demonstrates, and its dire effects on workers' wages and souls lie in the here and now. In examining computerization futures—whether in terms of abundance or of alienation—neither book recognizes the profits and pleasures of pretending technology is magic. That magic always relies on invisible labors.

The Second Machine Age opens with a roller coaster ride through the promised future of artificial intelligence (AI) and its threat to replace human labor. Once incredulous about AI's reach, the authors have become AI faithful, and here they march out one killer demo after another. They open the book with a ride in Google's self-driving car. The vehicle drives them around the Mountain View campus and surrounding roads with nary a bump or a hard brake. Google has named the driving software Chauffeur. Chauffeur symbolically promises middle-class drivers relief from drudgery and suggests automated access to the lifestyles of the rich and famous. Chauffeur represents just one of legion labor-replacing automations around the corner, the authors prophesy. Why hire a living person when a learning robot can work quickly, quietly, and without breaks, demands, or opinions?

There are lots of reasons managers won't fully automate workforces. The cost of research and development (R&D) for automations like Chauffeur can be staggering.[1] Far from simply realizing a dream of GoogleLabs, Google's Chauffeur project builds on decades and untold millions of dollars of military investment in research on autonomous cars. The military's on-the-ground autonomous warfare initiatives have produced and shaped an ecology of careers, techniques, infrastructures—including that of Chauffeur leader Sebastian Thrun. Complex automation, then, is not something many companies can develop on their own, even with dedicated effort.

But could AI and robotics companies do the R&D and sell automation technologies to other companies? To the extent that companies constrain their operations to meet robots' limitations, yes. But even still, human labor is necessary to configure, calibrate, and adjust automation technologies to adapt to a changing world, whether those changes are a differently shaped product or a bird that flies into the factory. Brynjolfsson and McAfee lump together a wide swath of AI applications and predict that the successes among them portend the more general expansion of automated work. But in doing so they overlook the enormous amounts of behind-the-scenes, domain-specific labor that makes AI possible in the first place. Google's self-driving car doesn't simply go anywhere its passengers please. For this car to drive "itself," a human worker has to drive around, scan, and map the car's world—including everything from curb heights to intersection angles. Machine-learning algorithms that partially automate data processing still need to be trained for every new form or every new kind of topic the algorithm might deal with. Other robots profiled in *The Second Machine Age* will learn the movements of shop-floor workers and then replace them, until the next tune-up or calibration is necessary. Such work of alignment is not a bug—it is the condition of possibility for keeping humans and automation working in the same world. *The Second Machine Age* leans heavily on the accounts of corporate executives promising fantastic new horizons of tech profit, but it's undeniable that for those pursuing customers and venture capital for automation, there's good money to be had in hiding these headaches.

This care for and feeding of artificial intelligence suggests a much bigger oversight in Brynjolfsson and McAfee's argument. Automation doesn't replace labor. It displaces it. Historian Ruth Schwartz Cowan famously showed how the invention of the washing machine mainly increased the standards of cleanliness domestic workers (paid and unpaid) had to meet. Shoshana Zuboff's 1988 book *In the Age of the Smart Machine* described how factory automation created text-based labor, displacing workers who smelled and felt wood pulp with those who could read screens and meters and tend to the machines. Hamid Ekbia and Bonnie Nardi call these managerially advantageous human-machine configurations "heteromation."[2]

The emergence of the digital microwork industry to tend artificial intelligence shows how labor displacement generates new kinds of work. As technology enterprises attempt to expand the scope of culture they mediate, they have had to grapple with new kinds of language, images, sounds, and sensor data. These are the kinds of data that flood Facebook, YouTube, and mobile phones—data that digital microworkers are then called on to process and classify. Such microworkers might support algorithms by generating "training data" to teach algorithms to pattern-match like a human in a certain domain. They might also simply process large volumes of cultural data to prepare it to be processed in other ways. These cultural data workers sit at computer terminals, transcribing small audio clips, putting unstructured text into structured database fields, and "content moderating" dick pics and beheadings out of your Facebook feed and Google advertisements.[3]

Computers do not wield the cultural fluencies necessary to interpret this kind of material, but people do.[4] This is the hidden labor that enables companies like Google to develop products around AI, machine learning, and big data. The New York Times calls this "janitor work," labeling it the hurdle, rather than the enabling condition, of our big data futures.[5] The second machine age doesn't like to admit it needs help.

These cultural data workers are central to the political economy of computing, from the free labor of AOL chat-room moderators to the organized but invisible labor of paid content moderators.[6] Since the early 2000s, Google has relied on data workers to tune and train its algorithms. The company constantly refines its search algorithms in a war for higher rankings with other search optimizers and spammers. How do Google engineers figure out if their new algorithm produces high-quality results? They have to rely on workers called "raters"—contractors often working from home—to judge the search result pages and rate them; workers can label resulting pages as "vital," "useful," "slightly relevant," or even "maybe spam."[7] Google engineers then feed these worker-generated ratings back into their algorithm so the algorithm can learn to see more like the rating workers.

Twitter also relies on cultural data workers to help its search engine cope with breaking news and instances of sudden linguistic change. Think of when Mitt Romney impressed the nation with his diversity strategies, including "binders full of women." The gaffe set Twitter afire with satire, but Twitter's algorithms didn't know the difference between "binders full of women" and binders on sale at Office Depot for ninety-nine cents. Such differences matter for Twitter's search results, for its ad placements, and for its famed trend detection. Because terms like these spike and go away very quickly, Twitter engineers can't train algorithms fast enough. To fill the gap, Twitter deploys an army of cultural data workers to sort and classify tweets in real time.[8]

In response to demand for this cultural labor, several companies have sprung up to match workers to engineers who need them. The most famous of these is Amazon Mechanical Turk (AMT), the data-work clearinghouse that Twitter relied on to power the search engine described above. Amazon launched AMT to allow programmers to issue data-processing calls directly from their computer code. Rather than other code answering the call, thousands of workers wait at their computers, ready to perform cognitive piecework on demand. AMT workers choose among tasks like transcription, content moderation, and image classification, getting paid per piece of data processed. They might work for ten employers in the span of a day. Amazon sends the data work to the employer, structures the market that enables the microcontracts, and, should the employer choose to pay, transmits payment to the worker.

Work conditions for these data workers are what "the market," or workers, will tolerate. As contractors, AMT workers are excluded from the protections of minimum-wage laws. Amazon also allows employers to decide whether or not they want to pay. The intention is to let employers set standards. The effect is that unscrupulous AMT users steal wages. Although workers share information to avoid these thieves, they report that Amazon will very rarely step in to arbitrate disputes when an employer and worker disagree about work quality or where the fault lies for bad work.

New companies, and even a subfield of computer science, have sprung up to develop research and applications around algorithmically managed "human computation." History repeats itself. Originally, "computers," until their calculations were automated in the mid-twentieth century, were women.[9] Today's hierarchy of data labor echoes older gendered, classed, and raced technology hierarchies. What's new is the way AMT and similar crowdsourcing platforms democratize outsourcing to any employer with a computer and credit card.

Such necessary and low-paid data work has no place in *The Second Machine Age*. McAfee and Brynjolfsson readily admit that AI will not replace all jobs. They quote Steven Pinker: "The main lesson of thirty-five years of AI research is that the hard problems are easy and the easy problems are hard. . . . [I]t will be the stock analysts and petrochemical engineers and parole board members who are in danger of being replaced by machines. The gardeners, receptionists, and cooks are secure in their jobs for decades to come." First, this all depends on how one defines "secure," since those irreplaceable workers often earn little and work on precarious terms. Second, McAfee and Brynjolfsson ignore the labor of cultural data workers, as if algorithms trained, tuned, and augmented themselves, like magic.

■ ■ ■

Undazzled by AI fantasies, journalist Simon Head looks closely at the semiautomated work we've been living with for decades. In particular, Head details how computing business systems (CBSs) have shaped work conditions at warehouses, banks, and call centers. CBSs are massive networked data-management systems that underpin the operations of most very large financialized organizations, from Goldman Sachs to public universities. The systems are built, sold, and maintained by high-tech behemoths, some famous, some that operate below the radar: IBM, PeopleSoft, Sales-Force, and SAP, just to name a few. Head, citing Brynjolfsson and McAfee's earlier research, points out that enterprise resource-planning systems—systems that automate and control organizational data processing—comprised 75 percent of all U.S. corporate IT investment in 2001.

These routine technologies rarely make the nightly news, but, unheralded, they allow managers tight control over workers. Managers use algorithms to steer employee workflows. They can track workers' typing at their keyboards and their movements through body-worn GPS. They can monitor fulfillment rates or success at sales and cut workers who cannot meet targets. By manipulating information screens, managers never have to confront workers, who might push back, or observe workers' circumstances.

Head describes Amazon's warehouses as a prime example of such grueling, semiautomated management. Amazon's algorithms take incoming orders and develop scripts to direct a worker around the warehouse. The worker has to follow the script, gathering items into carts and meeting travel times set at management whim. Like with AMT, employers set the script and workers have to meet it or leave. Warehouse workers are hired on as temps, so management can let go those who cannot keep the pace: older workers, sick workers, or just tired workers.

Call-center workers, ticket agents, and delivery people all work under similar scripts and under comparable surveillance. The CBS-enabled workplace has become the factory floor of the service economy. CBS control, Head argues, forces people into skill-stripped jobs that satisfy corporate thirst for transparency and control, heightening the effects of earlier strategies of scientific management and assembly-line factory organization. The scripts allow service workers, like their warehouse counterparts, little latitude to express judgment, creatively problem-solve, or leverage their built-up, on-the-job wisdom. Instead, managers retain control so they can swap one worker for another and keep wages low.

CBSs organize the systems we all have to live with as consumers, enabling the production of complex financial instruments, insurance plans, and health-care systems—systems that shape our lives but operate in mysterious, seemingly nonnegotiable ways. Head even argues that the financial crisis is a consequence of CBSs run amok. Banks like Goldman Sachs script their bankers to sell financial products—complex informational commodities—at a speed and scale that prohibits individual, human judgment from interrupting fast capitalism's flow.

For Head, a better digital workplace is possible. The Treuhand workshop in Chemnitz, Germany, presents one possibility. The shop uses advanced machining systems to manufacture components, but strong trade unions facilitate worker control over their labor. Managers send specifications to workers trained in craft-apprentice traditions, and those workers decide how to use machine tools to design the component. Managers check for quality only just before shipment. The Treuhand workers augment their craft with technology without falling under managerial microcontrol from a distance. We might call this approach *specify and enable.*

Head then compares the German shop with two others that use the same technologies: Caterpillar in Peoria, Illinois, and John Deere in Waterloo, Iowa. In the American shops, managers act as engineers, specifying both parts and process in detail. They plan how to machine a component. Machinists then execute the plan. Little collaboration transpires between machinists, who know the machines intimately, and the managers who detail the work. When machining the materials inevitably reveals design problems, the distance between workers and managers stymies resolution. With their command-and-control structure, the American workshops do not meet the design and quality standards German companies achieve with empowered machinists.

Automation itself is not to blame, Head argues. The problem lies with the ways automation entrenches command-and-control relationships between managers and workers. This is a deep and valuable insight of the book. Such insight could have led Brynjolfsson and McAfee to more productive questions. They might still ask if and how automation may augment productivity, but they should also ask: What exactly is being produced? And, what is its quality? Command-and-control automation strips away the "the human factor," as Head calls it. Such a wide range of accumulated human ability and wisdom can generate more subtle kinds of value than that which top management can predict. Head's subtitle, "why smarter machines are making dumber humans," sounds like catchy technological determinism, and yet the book actually tells a more subtle story about machines and social power.

In fact, Head's analysis of CBS systems answers a question that effectively haunts Brynjolfsson and McAfee's book: What are the implications of digital technologies for the growing gap between rich and poor? *The Second Machine Age* notes that wage stagnation parallels another economic trend; its authors argue that owners of physical capital today keep a far larger portion of their profits than in the past five decades. (Their argument assumes but does not demonstrate that businesses more dependent on human capital such as talent or skill distribute profits more equally.) Unwilling to question free-market ideas, the authors argue that digital bounty replaces some workers' skills; it also creates rock stars, who gather in the lion's share of profit, by delivering their superior talent to bigger markets. This conventional explanation effaces the struggles over control, craftsmanship, and the value of worker labor that Head details so well. Such different diagnoses of inequality lead to starkly differing prescriptions.

Brynjolfsson and McAfee believe machines produce digital abundance; humans, therefore, must become entrepreneurial masters of the machines or peacefully coexist with them. This leads them to personal and policy recommendations that focus on individualized human capital enhancement. They argue, for example, that massive open online courses (MOOCs) and revamped universities can reskill soon-to-be-redundant workforces. Machines, Brynjolfsson and McAfee argue, are great at processing data but can't generate new ideas. To race against the machine, workers should become creative entrepreneurs. Still, they argue, the digital playing field will produce irrationalities and require some forms of redistribution. Brynjolfsson and McAfee advocate for high taxes on top earners, recognizing that those who control platforms or brands often charge more because they can (part of what economists call rent seeking). More radically, the authors suggest funding basic income guarantees (BIG) to sustain lives and consumer demand during capitalism's periodic crises.

Head, on the other hand, would improve the quality of life and work. He calls for a coalition among those squeezed by CBSs—white-collar workers, like middle managers and nonelite professionals, and low-income workers—to press for higher-paying, more highly skilled jobs. CBSs, he argues, should supplement worker expertise rather than replace it. Head calls on governments to reinvest in educational institutions that can prepare workers for these more highly valued jobs. Brynjolfsson and McAfee, on the other hand, take the CEO perspective on the world, assuming that skill and talent concentrate at the top, with mediocrity increasingly predominant as one descends the ladder of success. The authors of both these books agree that the lower rungs of production are low-skill, whether by repression in *Mindless* or absence of need in *The Second Machine Age*. Neither book displays an awareness of how the likes of Google, Twitter, and Amazon already rely on low-status workers' smarts to power the companies' seemingly miraculous algorithms and information systems. Of course, the magic depends on a slight of hand that obscures the humans and their minds inside the machines.

In the early years of AMT, I saw programmers excitedly explain the system to one another. They could write code as they always did, and call upon Amazon's processors with data crunching requests. When they sent their requests to Amazon's servers, the described how it was "like magic"—the servers answered the call. The magic, however, was Turk workers' handiwork. With workers hidden in the technology, programmers can treat workers like bits of code and continue to think of themselves as builders, not managers. Anthropologist Lucy Suchman has argued that much technology enchants in precisely this way—by masking the labors of production.[10] Technologies like AMT, then, do not make dumber humans but rather channel the human factor into forms pleasurable for programmers.

The aesthetics of service magic pervade many businesses launched by technologists. Google Express (formerly Google Shopping Express) enables customers in pilot cities to click a few buttons on the web to receive their Chapstick, board games, and other items from brick-and-mortar stores. A subcontractor courier, directed and paid by Google, will deliver the items to customers' front doors. Another company, Hointer, allows mall shoppers to walk up to products, scan them, and have robots and invisible workers drop the right-sized jeans and sweaters into a dressing room. The company, started by an early Amazon employee, makes shopping without salespeople possible. In all these cases, workers are not only complementing automation; they are employed to simulate it.

What is at stake here? Google, Hointer, and AMT all work to "disintermediate" consumption, to remove obstacles between the user and her desires. With workers and distribution infrastructures out of sight, consumers can focus on and value the brand, the product, and the platform. Disintermediation liberates consumers from troublesome or awkward labor encounters and accountabilities.

The stakes of technological magic are also financial. Companies able to pose as "technology" companies can also command higher market valuations than those with lots of labor on the books. This became clear to me at a technology industry conference when a venture capitalist explained that he saw crowdsourcing companies as technology companies rather than labor companies. Technology companies invest lots in up-front research but then scale to serve large volumes of customers—and make large volumes of profit—with relatively little increase in operating costs. Labor-intensive companies, on the other hand, increase their labor expenditures as their revenue increases. Venture capitalists love to invest money up front and then collect massive returns. Technology companies enjoy soaring market valuations when they make their non-R&D labor force as low-cost and low-risk as possible.[11]

The global distribution of information work reveals a racial politics to hiding the workers as well. Responding to customers' preference to hear voices like their own, Avatar Technologies has devised software that allows overseas operators to "speak" American English; at their stations in Asia, workers click buttons that trigger prerecorded voices.[12] A Mexican call center capitalizes on deportees from the United States to offer American-accented services to U.S. clients.[13] In his 2008 film, *Sleep Dealer*, screenwriter and director Alex Rivera deftly depicts the transnational politics of American service work. His protagonist, Memo Cruz, labors in an *infomaquila* where he uses a networked telepresence system to control construction robots across the US border. "We give the United States what they always wanted," Cruz explains of his remote labors, "all the work, without the workers."

Subcontracted work powers technological magic, just out of consumer sight and off the company's payroll. Google page raters work for outsourcing companies. Google Express is powered by subcontracted courier companies.[14] AMT workers are all self-employed contractors. The U.S. Equal Employment Opportunity Commission tracks labor-force diversity with the employer information report EEO-1. Google's EEO-1, released reluctantly in 2013, lists only managers, technicians, sales, and professional workers.[15] Their report suggests they employ almost no laborers, service workers, or operatives. These workers power the tech industry yet are out of sight and out of mind in the press and policy on diversifying the tech workplace. The diversity is there. It's just subcontracted and paid poorly.

These workers excel in doing what machines cannot. They have won the race against the machine, but they do not always even make minimum wage. Should they lean in, take MOOCs, and be more creative? Among the most active AMT workers, nearly 58 percent already have a bachelor's degree or higher. (An AMT worker, clickhappier, generated this statistic by cross-tabulating data from NYU professor Panos Ipeirotis.)[16] Many do the work because the cost of saying no is too high when bills come due. Their employers, situated in universities, start-ups, and tech companies, have more powerful forms of human capital that enable them to take advantage of AMT workers' diverse skills and talents.

The pleasures and conveniences of human-powered technology will continue to fuel a growing market for technology's hidden laborers. Employers, driven by profit margins and stock prices, have great incentives to keep these workers off the books and out of sight. Inside the machines, inequality will persist. Unless, that is, we discredit and challenge the industry's hierarchies of value that grant managers and programmers rock star status and wealth, while confining data workers to a life of underpayment and insecurity.

How can workers withdraw their essential labors to demand fair work conditions? Despite the shortcomings of their analysis, Brynjolfsson and McAfee propose a weapon that could strengthen the hidden workers of the digital age: a basic income guarantee (BIG). The guarantee provides all citizens with a lump sum; the programs can make up the cost of money outlays by cutting government institutions focused on administering, disciplining, and monitoring welfare recipients—a redistribution strategy compatible with neoliberal economic theories that attempt to separate the market from the social.[17] The state of Alaska already has such a guarantee in the form of oil-income disbursements. Brynjolfsson and McAfee frame the BIG as a support for those who cannot produce value in an automated economy; we might also see it as a means to strengthen opposition to coercion. Today's hidden data contractors often must work to maintain their livelihoods—strikes prove difficult in online work when anyone with a computer and a bill coming due can break the picket line. An income guarantee would allow workers to walk away, or at least starve the algorithms of their data until managers shape up.

NOTES

1. See, e.g., Hamid Ekbia and Bonnie Nardi, "Heteromation and Its (Dis)contents: The Invisible Division of Labor Between Humans and Machines," *First Monday* 19, no. 6 (2014), https://firstmonday.org/ojs/index.php/fm/article/view/5331.

2. Ekbia and Nardi, "Heteromation and Its (Dis)contents."

3. See Adrian Chen, "The Laborers Who Keep Dick Pics and Beheadings Out of Your Facebook Feed," *Wired*, October 23, 2014, https://www.wired.com/2014/10/content-moderation/.

4. See Terry Winograd and Fernando Flores, *Understanding Computers and Cognition: A New Foundation for Design* (Addison-Wesley, 1987).

5. Steve Lohr, "For Big-Data Scientists, 'Janitor Work' Is Key Hurdle to Insights," *New York Times*, August 17, 2014, https://www.nytimes.com/2014/08/18/technology/for-big-data-scientists-hurdle-to-insights-is-janitor-work.html. My essay's title is a tribute to the SEIU "Justice for Janitors" campaigns that won Silicon Valley janitors contracts and improved working conditions.

6. For a discussion of how unpaid communicative work powers the digital economy, see Tiziana Terranova, "Free Labor: Producing Culture for the Digital Economy," *Social Text* 18, no. 2 (2000): 33–58.

7. See Laureen Miles Brunelli, "Work at Home Job Profile: Google Ads Quality Rater," About.com (accessed December 22, 2014), https://www.thebalancecareers.com/google-ads-quality-rater-job-profile-3542817; and Andrew Orlowski, "Revealed: Google's Manual for Its Unseen Humans Who Rate the Web," *Register*, November 27, 2012, https://www.theregister.co.uk/2012/11/27/google_raters_manual/.

8. See Christopher Williams, "Twitter's Machines Call on Low-Paid Humans in Battle to Keep Up with Hashtags," *Telegraph* (UK), January 9, 2013, https://www.telegraph.co.uk/technology/twitter/9791091

/Twitters-machines-call-on-low-paid-humans-in-battle-to-keep-up -with-hashtags.html.

9. See Jennifer S. Light, "When Computers Were Women," *Technology and Culture* 40, no. 3 (1999): 455–83. See also Lilly Irani, "The Cultural Work of Microwork," *New Media & Society* (2013).

10. Lucy Suchman, *Human-Machine Reconfigurations: Plans and Situated Actions* (Cambridge: Cambridge University Press, 2006), 245.

11. Irani, "The Cultural Work of Microwork," 9.

12. See Alexis Madrigal, "Almost Human: The Surreal, Cyborg Future of Telemarketing," *The Atlantic*, December 20, 2013, https://www.theatlantic .com/technology/archive/2013/12/almost-human-the-surreal-cyborg -future-of-telemarketing/282537/.

13. The call center is featured in episode 520 of the radio program *This American Life*, "No Place Like Home," aired March 14, 2014, https://www .thisamericanlife.org/520/no-place-like-home.

14. See Cyrus Farivar, "Google Shopping Express Expands Old Formula: Take Orders, Deliver Stuff (Mostly)," *Ars Technica*, September 25, 2013, https://arstechnica.com/information-technology/2013/09/google -shopping-express-expands-old-formula-take-orders-deliver-stuff -mostly/.

15. See Caroline Fairchild, "Why Google Voluntarily Released Dismal Diversity Numbers," *Fortune*, May 29, 2014, http://fortune.com/2014/05 /29/why-google-voluntarily-released-dismal-diversity-numbers/.

16. Clickhappier, "Demographics of Mechanical Turk," post 20, Mturkgrind .com, July 28, 2014, http://www.mturkgrind.com/threads/26341-Demo graphics-of-Mechanical-Turk.

17. See Michel Foucault, *The Birth of Biopolitics: Lectures at the Collège de France, 1978–1979*, trans. Graham Burchell (London: Palgrave Macmillan, 2008), 202–3.

ANTHROPOCENE AND EMPIRE

STACEY BALKAN

n the autumn of 1839, an unusually strong tropical storm devastated coastal communities along the Bay of Bengal in what was then the English East India Company's premier settlement. A decade later, company merchant and sometime scientist Henry Piddington coined the term "cyclone" to describe this climatological phenomenon, taking a cue from the seaborne storm's circular movement and eerily hollow center, or "eye." So common are cyclones in that part of the world that when a tornado—a typically smaller, terrestrial storm—ravaged the land-locked city of New Delhi in 1978, local newspapers erroneously identified the storm as a cyclone.

Amitav Ghosh was a graduate student at the time of the tornado and recounts its aftermath in a new monograph entitled *The Great Derangement: Climate Change and the Unthinkable.* His first book-length work of nonfiction in decades, *The Great Derangement* began as a series of lectures delivered last autumn at the University of Chicago. Focused in part on fictional representations of climate change, the author begins by addressing the bewildering absence of such storms from what he calls the "mansions" of "serious" fiction—an egregious oversight, he argues, given the proliferation of similarly catastrophic storms like Hurricane Sandy.

Ultimately, he asks: "Is climate change [simply] too wild a stream to be navigated in the accustomed barques of narration?"

This may strike a familiar chord: ecocritics in the humanities, philosophers, natural scientists, economists, and geographers have devoted a great deal of attention to the question of climate change, its causes, and its consequences. In acknowledging such causes as industrialized agriculture they have achieved something like a consensus around the concept of the Anthropocene—a term coined to describe the period within the Cenozoic Era (approximately 66 million years ago to the present) during which human beings became "geological agents."[1]

Many have also begun to argue that it is not humanity as such that is the primary engine of climate change but rather historic modes of capital accumulation. But Ghosh's argument casts a much wider net than conventional rebukes of capitalism. Indeed, more than an indictment of capital or a critique of popular fiction, *The Great Derangement* folds questions about empire, colonialism, and ecological imperialism into an otherwise familiar discussion of the Anthropocene.

Readers of Ghosh's magisterial Ibis Trilogy—a fictional saga of the nineteenth-century Opium Wars and the English East India Company's rapacious poppy program—will recognize this critique, although the author's pronouncements about fiction and climate may seem somewhat quizzical.[2] While the impact of human development may in fact be "too wild a stream" for some, it is surely not "too wild" for Ghosh. In the Ibis novels, for instance, he reveals the savage nature of colonial-era agricultural programs that relied on monoculture. A central motif is the destruction of local ecosystems for the purpose of planting poppy, a cash crop that consumed some 25,000 acres of arable land in Bengal.[3]

But the sorts of slow violence that Ghosh documents in these novels resonate rather differently than, say, a category three storm of the sort that struck Delhi. As Ghosh admits early on in *The Great Derangement*, "It is certainly true that storms, floods, and unusual weather events do recur in my books . . . [but] oddly enough, no tornado has ever figured in my novels."

While his historical novels offer important critiques of the colonial-imperial project and the environmental destruction that it wrought, conjuring tornadoes, much to his own dismay, is not so easy. Climate change, or what Ghosh calls the "environmental uncanny," to refer to statistically improbable weather events, seems to be the province of "cli-fi"—a "generic outhouse," he derisively remarks, "made up mostly of disaster stories." A notable example is the 2004 film *The Day After Tomorrow* in which the anomalous weather events of recent years somehow all coalesce into a single cataclysmic horror. Of course, to be fair, environmental violence is notoriously spectacle-deficient. Surely Ghosh's portraits of beleaguered poppy farmers are less titillating for mass audiences than packs of feral wolves terrorizing the New York Public Library, the latter among several absurdist tropes of the film. Hence the author's remarks that "the climate crisis is also a crisis of culture, and thus of imagination." This imaginative failure, he goes on to explain, has been many decades in the making.

The disaster films and novels that constitute "cli-fi" in fact signal a grave crisis—a "great derangement," Ghosh argues, midwifed by the emergence of literary realism and its accompanying intellectual traditions. In the first chapter of *The Great Derangement*, entitled "Stories," Ghosh traces the contemporaneous development of the modern novel, nineteenth-century theories of probability, and Freud's concept of the "uncanny," which he defines as "an irreducible element of mystery" well-suited to describing the bizarre weather events of recent years. Ghosh attributes our current inability to see, represent, and understand environmental crisis to a probabilistic worldview that emerged in the nineteenth century and made no room for such "uncanny" weather phenomena as freak tornadoes. Indeed, he argues that "the uncanny intimacy of our relationship with the nonhuman" would only be tolerated in the realm of the supernatural, in the ghost stories of Charles Dickens or Henry James.

In this sense, what the author terms "derangement" is both an imaginative as well as an epistemological crisis, a crisis born, unfortunately, at the same moment that the "accumulation of carbon in the atmosphere was rewriting the destiny of the earth." The uncertainty of climate, he argues, was anathema to the "uniformitarian expectations" of the era. And the modern novels of writers like Jane Austen would succor those "expectations" by "offering the kind of narrative pleasure compatible with the new regularity of bourgeois life."[4]

Ghosh, though, is less interested in the novel's birth than in the "bourgeois order" that it engendered. The thrust of "Stories" is primarily an argument about form: about the way that we ought to tell stories at a moment when the "Anthropocene has reversed the temporal order of modernity." He begins by recounting the 1978 Delhi tornado. After documenting its absence from his own work, Ghosh turns to the omission of less spectacular forms of climate violence, mounting a compelling argument for the role of fiction in the great derangement. "When we see a green lawn that has been watered with desalinated water, in Abu Dhabi or Southern California," he remarks, "we are looking at an expression of a yearning that may have been midwifed by the novels of Jane Austen."

Also speaking to the imperial hubris that might account for Elizabeth Bennett's verdant backyard, Ghosh addresses a series of post-Enlightenment construction projects that are equally troubling: the development of port cities like Mumbai, Hong Kong, and New York. As we have seen lately, the consequences of such imperialist schemes have proven catastrophic. As a case in point, we might look to coastal areas like New Orleans, another colonial city, whose architects once mused that the port should never be inhabited.[5] The most striking illustration of this phenomenon is Mumbai's formerly estuarine landscape: a class four or five cyclone could bring irrevocable devastation to millions of its citizens.

Nevertheless, bar the occasional cyclone—in *Sea of Poppies* or *The Hungry Tide*, both of which occurred in the storm-prone Bay of Bengal—Ghosh's novels are a far cry from cli-fi. His fictional worlds instead offer searing portraits of ecological imperialism, intervening radically into a discourse that too often ignores the role of empire in anthropogenic climate change. With some noteworthy exceptions—among them, Mike Davis's 2001 book *Late Victorian Holocausts: El Niño Famines and the Making of the Third World* and Ashley Dawson's 2016 *Extinction: A Radical History*—even the most well-meaning critics often dismiss the uneven history of development, opting instead for indictments of the entire species. But, as Davis and Dawson also make clear, not all nations are equally culpable for the ravages of global capitalism.

We cannot ignore the coincidence of European imperialism and the so-called great acceleration in greenhouse gases like carbon dioxide. At the same time as Britain's premier trading company acquired an exclusive writ of free trade for the purpose of growing and selling opium, Western imperialist projects became increasingly reliant on new modes of transport and production. This includes, of course, plantation agriculture. The cultivation of cotton, for example, would far outstrip the impact of poppy production: even beyond the American South, Manchester's Cotton Supply Association was laying the groundwork for the horrors we are now witnessing in India's cotton belt.[6] Since 1998, approximately 250,000 Indian cotton farmers have committed suicide because of debt incurred from free-trade policies between the Indian government and agricultural companies like Monsanto. It is worth mentioning that sugar would also play a critical role. Sidney Mintz's 1985 *Sweetness and Power* offers a remarkable glimpse into its destructive path.[7]

Ghosh argues, therefore, that we should expand our indictment of "capitalism"—a common protagonist "on which the narrative [of the Anthropocene] turns"—to include "an aspect of the Anthropocene that is of equal importance: empire and imperialism." Indeed, he notes, the uneven effects of climate change are the "result of systems that were set up by brute force to ensure that poor nations remained always at a disadvantage in terms of both wealth and power."

The burden of the book's two shorter chapters, "History" and "Politics," is to demonstrate just this. In "History," Ghosh offers an exhaustive portrait of the material impact of our modern worldview. With a nod to his 2000 novel *The Glass Palace*, he begins with a critique of the petroleum industry, citing Burma (now Myanmar) and not Titusville, Pennsylvania, as the site of its prodigious birth. He then links the above-mentioned epistemological shifts to economic models that also emerged during the colonial era and that laid the groundwork for what former World Bank president Larry Summers would call an "impeccable economic logic."[8] In a shockingly explicit endorsement of accumulation by dispossession, Summers actually suggested that it made perfect economic sense to sacrifice the Third World for the prosperity of the First. As if responding directly to Summers, Ghosh notes quite rightly that "the patterns of life that modernity engender[ed could] only be practiced by a small minority of the population." He then cautions: if "every family in the world" acquired "two cars, a washing machine, and a refrigerator," we'd all be asphyxiated.

In "Politics," he traces the ideological roots of Summers's perverted "logic." He locates its origin in the social contracts of the eighteenth century, which Ghosh describes as "grotesque fictions designed to secure exactly the opposite of [their] professed ends." As Ghosh and others have pointed out, political thinkers like Jean-Jacques Rousseau were far more interested in theorizing abstract liberties than in the survival of Europe's many colonial subjects—Rousseau's 1762 *Social Contract* giving a name to Enlightenment-era notions of human rights, which then and now made no provisions for a vast majority of the world.[9] Summers is but a neoliberal instantiation of Rousseau, insofar as the World Bank (and other Bretton Woods institutions like the International Monetary Fund) purports to advocate on behalf of a global majority when in fact their ideas only benefit a handful of rich nations.

Notably, in the final chapter, Ghosh also comments on the recent Paris Agreement on climate change. In Ghosh's view, the Paris Agreement is similarly grotesque when we consider that the agreed upon threshold for increases in carbon dioxide amounts to a death sentence for many African and Asian nations. Ghosh favors Pope Francis's 2015 encyclical *Laudato Si'*. The encyclical, unlike the Paris Agreement, attends to the economic, social, and ecological legacy of empire.

Pace Pope Francis, Ghosh's dual focus on colonialism and ecological imperialism tells a very different story. And it is a story that comes across in his fiction as well: *The Glass Palace* offers a stunning critique of petro-imperialism, and his 2004 novel *The Hungry Tide* centers (in part) on the violent eviction and murder of refugees (in the West Bengal region of India in 1979), delivering a commentary on development models that hinge on dispossession.[10] It is, however, in his recent Ibis Trilogy that Ghosh most fully elaborates the connection among empire, climate, and the forms of economic thinking left over from the Enlightenment.

The first novel of the trilogy, *Sea of Poppies*, opens in 1839 on the eve of the first Opium War. Hailed by critics as the first subaltern history of British rule in the region, the novels' unlikely heroes include poppy farmers, lascars, opium addicts, fishermen, and sepoys (the name given to Indian soldiers forced into British service). Illustrating the economic origins of contemporary forms of ecological imperialism like Monsanto's cotton trade, the trilogy offers a commentary on the establishment of free trade in the region, the concomitant enclosure of peasant land, and such instances of epistemological violence as the cooptation of local language systems.

The novels likewise attend to the impact of imperialism on local flora, a logical correlate of the opium and cotton trades. In *River of Smoke*, Ghosh creates a series of fictional botanists who regard plants as no different than "doorknobs, or sausages, or any other object that could be sold for a price on the market." *Sea of Poppies* bears witness to the human cost of free trade—as poppy farmers are forced from their land and onto Indian Ocean slavers—while the second novel depicts a veritable ecocide. One character goes so far as to liken the East India Company's botanical gardens to the hull of a slave ship. The final novel takes a slightly different tack: in *Flood of Fire*, readers are introduced to the company's cavalry—an uncomfortable reminder that current multinationals differ only in their inability to marshal their own armies.

Perhaps Ghosh devotes the bulk of *The Great Derangement* to stories and narration because novels like *Sea of Poppies* achieve something rather different than even the best economic histories. If works such as Ranajit Guha's 1963 *A Rule of Property for Bengal* introduced readers to the economics of land seizure, Ghosh offers us the oft-forgotten voices of actual farmers.[11] As with the humanities more generally, his stories offer us rich glimpses into seemingly distant lives, glimpses too often proscribed by the narrow limits of bourgeois realism.

Narrow to a fault, our greatest derangement seems to be one of scale. Throughout the book, Ghosh returns again and again to

John Updike's infamous definition of the novel as an "individual moral adventure"—a phrase coined in Updike's damning review of Abdul Rahman Munif's 1984 *Cities of Salt*, in which the author refers to the novel as "insufficiently westernized." Pointing out the surfeit of "Western novels" that foreground what Ghosh terms "men in the abstract," among them *War and Peace* and *Moby-Dick*, Ghosh mounts an exquisite argument for the collective both politically and aesthetically. He contests the primacy of the individual at a moment when hope resides only in those abstract masses who have long "pose[d] a powerful challenge to the idea that the free pursuit of individual interests always leads to the general good."

Ghosh skewers American individualism and its toxic political fruit.[12] He then reminds his readers that the "Pentagon devotes more resources to the study of climate change than any other branch of the U.S. government," a fact that ought to ignite political engagement among voters with a seemingly unshakable faith in the wisdom of our military. Unfortunately, the populace is routinely paralyzed by the latest cli-fi blockbuster—terror quickly transformed into inertia.

I wonder, though, what to make of such films: 2015 was the hottest year on record; there were, for the first time in history, as many cyclones in the Arabian Sea as there were in the Indian Ocean; and the proliferation of "unprecedented" weather events has made it so that the very word "unprecedented" is starting to sound a bit foolish. Perhaps such dystopian stories are appropriate responses to the nightmare of global climate change.

Ghosh, though, arrives at a different conclusion. Arguing against any fantasies about state-level intervention, he turns to the sacred. Perhaps, he suggests, religious communities are our last resort. Their transnational frameworks offer us potential models for collective political action. While I would disagree with Ghosh's assertion that "religious worldviews . . . do not partake of economistic ways of thinking," it is in fact in the realm of religion that we find an "acceptance of limits and limitations," and an embrace of a power beyond ourselves. In any case, before any real change can occur, we must first be able to imagine a possibility beyond the limited horizon of our deranged imaginations.

NOTES

1. Dipesh Chakrabarty, "The Climate of History: Four Theses," *Critical Inquiry* (Winter 2009): 197–222.
2. The trilogy contains *Sea of Poppies* (2008), *River of Smoke* (2011), and *Flood of Fire* (2015).
3. See Carl A. Trocki's *Opium, Empire, and the Global Political Economy: A Study of the Asian Opium Trade* (London: Routledge, 1999) for a discussion of poppy cultivation in eighteenth- and nineteenth-century Bengal.
4. Franco Moretti, *The Bourgeois* (London: Verso, 2013), 380.
5. Craig E. Colten, *An Unnatural Metropolis: Wresting New Orleans from Nature* (Baton Rouge: Louisiana State University Press, 2006).
6. For a discussion of the eighteenth-century cotton trade established by Manchester's Cotton Supply Association, see Mike Davis's *Late Victorian Holocausts: El Niño Famines and the Making of the Third World* (London: Verso, 2002).
7. Sidney Mintz, *Sweetness and Empire: The Place of Sugar in Modern History* (New York: Penguin, 1985).
8. Jim Vallette, "Larry Summers's War Against the Earth," *Counterpunch*, June 15, 1999.
9. See also Lisa Lowe's *The Intimacies of Four Continents* (Durham, NC: Duke University Press, 2015).
10. Ghosh discusses *The Glass Palace* in "History," making note of the role of the petroleum industry in the great derangement. See also his review of Abdel Rahmam Munif's novel *Cities of Salt*, called "Petrofiction," *New Republic*, March, 2, 1992.
11. Ranajit Guha, *A Rule of Property for Bengal: An Essay on the Idea of Permanent Settlement* (1963; reprint, Durham, NC: Duke University Press, 1996).
12. In describing the pathological nature of American individualism, Ghosh relies in part on Christian Parenti's concept of an "armed lifeboat" from his *Tropic of Chaos: Climate Change and the New Geography of Violence*

(New York: Nation Books, 2011). Parenti's "armed lifeboat" is a dark riff on U.S. border policy and its treatment of migrants and refugees. In a disturbingly literal version of Parenti's argument, the recent cli-fi blockbuster *San Andreas* (2015) features Dwayne "The Rock" Johnson driving an actual armed lifeboat.

CHANGING CLIMATES OF HISTORY

J. R. McNEILL

Neither Thucydides, Gibbon, von Ranke, nor Braudel ever cited a paper appearing in *Geophysical Research Letters*. They did not worry themselves about fluctuations in the Siberian High or the Southern Oscillation. The vast majority of more recent historians also remained untroubled by such concerns. However, in the past five years, a handful of highly distinguished historians have come out with new books that put climate at the center of historical explanation. What on Earth is going on?

Perhaps a historiographical wheel is turning. A century ago, historians and other scholars of human affairs often felt quite comfortable turning to climate as explanation for both broad patterns and twists and turns in history. Those who saw in climate adequate explanation for the vigor of some peoples and the stupor of others followed in the intellectual traditions of Montesquieu, Ibn Khaldun, and Aristotle. They looked to climatic regimes to help make sense of the diverse fortunes of nations. This outlook was deeply ahistorical: the climate that allegedly made people in southern China listless a century ago is very much the same as it is today, when the people of southern China are among the most economically dynamic around. Arnold Toynbee, writing in the 1930s, believed that the bracing climate accounted for the economic vivacity of the north of England, whereas the softer climate of London and the home counties did not provide sufficient stimulus in the south, which lagged behind. This looks silly eighty years later, not least because it's the north of England that lags behind today. Toynbee also thought the challenging climate of New England explained the domination of U.S. history, as he saw it, by New Englanders.[1] Such views, emphasizing the power of climatic regimes in human affairs, were never universally held—Hegel, among others, objected strenuously to them—but nonetheless made sense to many leading lights of the historical profession before the mid-twentieth century.

Climate change, on the other hand, never seemed quite as useful to historians. Some geographers, most famously perhaps Ellsworth Huntington, argued that pulses of drought accounted for the folk migrations of various pastoral peoples across Asia. His argument was taken up here and there, and others like it occasionally found favor among historians. But by and large, climate change did not figure prominently in historical explanation. No doubt this was in part because no one knew enough about past climate to make much use of it. And few people, whether historians or not, supposed that climates *did* change very much, or fast enough, to make much difference to human history. As late as the 1960s, the great French historian Emmanuel Le Roy Ladurie supported this position when, after a decade of careful study of the question, he concluded that climate change had mattered little in European history in the centuries since 1000 CE. In the English translation of his big book on climate history, he put it this way: "The human consequences of climate seem to be slight, perhaps negligible, and certainly difficult to detect."[2] (He now freely admits he thought climate more important than he allowed but trimmed his sails for fear of the response from his senior colleagues in the French academic firmament.)

By the 1960s, the sciences of historical climatology and paleo-climatology had just begun to reveal the mutability of climate on historical time scales (as opposed to geological ones). Not only might ice ages come and go, but volcanic eruptions could bring a string of very cold years around the world. Droughts, especially those related to the El Niño Southern Oscillation might not only be severe but could affect several large regions of the world at once. Evidence from European history piled up in favor of the proposition that the centuries between 1250 and 1850 were colder than those immediately preceding or following. This evidence inspired scholars to conceive of a Little Ice Age, a term first used in 1939 and in routine use among historians by the 1970s.

Since the 1980s, anxiety about contemporary climate change has inspired research that has brought a cavalcade of new evidence about past climate. New scientific techniques have emerged providing "proxy" evidence for past climate, allowing increasingly lengthy and detailed reconstructions of global, regional, and local climates. Every year the numbers of tree ring, fossil pollen, and ice core oxygen isotope analyses grows. For more than a decade now, new evidence from Antarctic and Greenland ice cores has provided a fair record of earthly climate going back more than 400,000 years. For anyone interested in the subject, these are heady times. It is easy to feel like a kid in a candy shop, with endless morsels of new data there for the grabbing.

Nonetheless, historians on the whole have resisted temptation. They are ill at ease assigning agency to anything other than people, whether individually or in groups. They may delight in arguments about the role of culture or economic structures or the agency available to the dispossessed or subaltern, but they are usually unwilling to take seriously arguments that attribute historical agency to animals, plants, rocks, or changes in any of the Earth systems, climate included. Arguments that embrace such nonhuman agents are routinely dismissed as environmental determinism, which since 1945 has carried a faint whiff of the biological determinism of the Nazis. No wonder historians sought to distance themselves from it.

■ ■ ■

Historical arguments and understandings that entirely omit climate change are of course often right to do so. Depending on a historian's subject, climate shifts might indeed be entirely irrelevant. Intellectual historians, for example, might not see any use for climate data. When studying the origins of Maoism it might not seem particularly relevant. Equally, the hordes of historians focusing on the years between 1815 and 1980, have chosen a period in which climate change was slow, extreme climate events comparatively few, and nonclimatic changes dramatic—in other words, an era in which neglect of climate is minimally problematic.

But earlier periods are another matter, and it is here that a new literature foregrounding climate is taking hold. While junior scholars are wading in fearlessly, as they are expected to do, it is more remarkable that established historians are taking a climate turn. Among those eager to seize on the new evidence about old climates is Richard Bulliet. He is a distinguished historian of the Middle East who has written reams of respected work on medieval Iran, on Islamicization, on technology, and, not least, on camels.[3] Bulliet, now emeritus at Columbia University, has long been attracted by new methods and built his reputation partly on innovative study of biographical dictionaries and the evidence provided by names therein.

In his *Cotton, Climate, and Camels in Early Islamic Iran: A Moment in World History*, he offers an elaborate if tentative argument to explain the rise and fall of an urbanized, commercialized, cotton-based economy in Iran from the ninth through the twelfth centuries. Using the extremely slender evidence from medieval Iran, especially the names of a few hundred religious scholars, Bulliet argues for an irrigation-fed cotton boom in northern Iran in the ninth and tenth centuries, initiated mainly by immigrant Arab Muslim entrepreneurs. The cotton boom fueled urbanization and export trade and undergirded an era of prosperity in Iran. But, employing relevant snippets of medieval Arabic texts and tree-ring analyses from western Mongolia, Bulliet identifies a century-long cold snap, beginning early in the eleventh century, which he calls the Big Chill. Caused by a high-pressure cell usually anchored over Siberia that connects the climates of Mongolia and Iran, the Big Chill, according to Bulliet, undercut the cotton economy and "triggered" the southward migration of Turkic herders from western steppe lands into Iran. In making the migration argument, Bulliet returns to his knowledge of camels and camel history, arguing that colder times made northern Iran less hospitable to the one-humped dromedary familiar in Arabia and more suited to two-humped, shaggy, Bactrian camels (or to two types of hybrid camels that were also cold-resistant) native to the steppes. He finds implications of the Big Chill and the decline of cotton that include the exodus of many Persian literati, shifting the cultural centers of Islam westward from Iran and Iraq and spreading Persian influence far and wide. In this case, at least, if one believes Bulliet, intellectual history *did* have a component of climate change history to it.

Building on Bulliet's analysis, Ronnie Ellenblum, of Hebrew University in Jerusalem, also invests great significance in climate shifts in the history of the medieval Middle East. Ellenblum has written admired books on Crusader castles and Frankish settlement in the medieval Levant.[4] Now, in *The Collapse of the Eastern Mediterranean: Climate Change and the Decline of the East,*

950–1072, he finds the political and economic history of the region driven by climate, specifically by drought. He uses many of the same Arabic-language chronicles as Bulliet, buttressed by many more in Hebrew, Greek, and other tongues. Despite an undergraduate education in geology, which presumably shows some sympathy for the natural sciences, he does not delve far into the abundant proxy evidence on climate or its mechanics. Nonetheless, Ellenblum advances a sweeping argument.

In his view, the decline of agrarian states and urban culture in the Middle East and corresponding upsurge in regime instability, famine, and nomadic incursions, arose from a series of prolonged and severe droughts beginning in the mid-tenth century that worsened in the eleventh, peaking in the 1050s. Drought is common in the Middle East and often disastrous for farmers already operating at the margins of dryland agriculture. But it is mercifully rare that drought affects southwest Asia and the Nile Valley at the same time because the Nile's water comes mainly from Ethiopian rainfall, governed by an entirely different weather system than Anatolia, Syria, Mesopotamia, and Iran's. Thus, throughout the long history of agrarian states and regional trade in the Middle East, when harvests failed in one place, grain could normally be imported from another. Usually it was Egypt that could bail out the rest of the eastern Mediterranean. This insurance against drought helps explain the success of large states in the region. Ellenblum explains the depth of disaster in the tenth and eleventh centuries by claiming that, especially in the 1050s, droughts brought harvest failure for years on end both in Southwest Asia and in Egypt, something that, he says, happens on such a scale only once every thousand years or so.

This perfect storm of simultaneous droughts undermined dynasties in Cairo, Baghdad, and Constantinople. Crops failed throughout the region. States could not collect enough grain and taxes to pay their soldiers and bureaucrats, who rose in rebellion just as desperate herders began riding in from the desert or steppes, searching for food. Urban riots, persecution of minorities, sectarian violence, and refugee movements, among other crises, overwhelmed the struggling states. When the Crusaders showed up in 1099, the region was still recovering from over 120 trying years of famine, rebellion, plunder, and chaos.

Historians of medieval Western Europe, familiar with what used to be called the Medieval Warm Period, but is now more often termed the Medieval Climate Anomaly (or MCA), will recognize that Ellenblum is arguing for a radically different trajectory in the eastern and western parts of the Mediterranean, and Europe generally. For medievalists attuned to the MCA, its warmth and longer growing seasons help to explain the rising prosperity of Western Europe between 900 and 1250. The contrast with the eastern Mediterranean could not be starker. Ellenblum draws another contrast as well. He claims that medievalists of the western realms need only Latin to read their sources, whereas those of the eastern realms need Arabic, Persian, Greek, Turkish, and Hebrew at a minimum. The linguistic challenges, he says, account for why scholars so far have missed the central role of climate shifts in the political tumult of the medieval Middle East. Chained to their own specializations, he says, based on hard-won linguistic competence, they have not been able to assemble the data from the various chronicles that refer to drought and starvation across the region.

At the other end of Eurasia, climate also helped to drive political and economic history, according to Timothy Brook of the University of British Columbia. Brook spent most of his professional life at universities such as Stanford, Toronto, and Oxford, writing about China from the Yuan (Mongol) Dynasty to the present. His most distinguished works deal with the proto-globalization of the seventeenth century as revealed in the paintings of Johannes Vermeer, the social and cultural life in the late Ming, and the Japanese occupation of China, 1937–45.[5] In 2010, Brook published an overview of the Yuan (1271–1368) and Ming (1368–1644) dynasties, *The Troubled Empire: China in the Yuan and Ming Dynasties*, that found bad climate luck played a big part in explaining Chinese history. Brook's book is more of an overview than Bulliet's or Ellenblum's, with less pointed argument. It takes up all the main themes of Chinese history over the four centuries it covers and focuses much less resolutely on climate. He is not interested in patterns of atmospheric circulation or volcanic eruptions that might explain climate shifts.

Nevertheless, given that there are so many other ways to present Chinese history of the time, Brook puts an astonishing emphasis on climate. As he notes, he kept coming across references in his sources to famines, floods, droughts, tornadoes, and other natural disasters and was driven to the conclusion that the Yuan and Ming dynasties form a single period, coinciding with some of the colder parts of the Little Ice Age, and should be seen as such. The warmer and wetter weather of earlier centuries, which had helped the Song oversee rising prosperity, turned colder and drier as the Mongols took over. Everyone struggled to survive and adjust, and this is the unifying theme of his book. Spells of bad weather lasting three to seven years, together with other natural disasters, "shaped life and memory during these dynasties as strongly as any other factor."

Using texts and paintings as his sources, Brook finds cold and dry times, beginning around 1270, that recurred on and off until the mid-seventeenth century. In China, the effects of bad weather were not limited to bad harvests, hunger, and perhaps starvation. When cold enough, the canals on which transport depended would freeze for longer periods, making it harder to relieve famine in one place with food shipped in from another. Chinese concepts of the "mandate of heaven," furthermore, made the weather a divine performance review for emperors. Prolonged drought or cold implied a lack of heavenly support for the emperor. The extremely poor weather and harvests of the late 1630s and early 1640s thus made the survival of the Ming unlikely, for both material and ideological reasons. Brook also finds world-historical implications in his story. The struggle to survive and adjust to the climate (and other) shocks during the Ming pushed the Chinese into ever-greater webs of exchange and interaction, helping to bring about proto-globalization.

Brook allows that "the weather on its own does not explain the rise of the Yuan or the fall of the Ming, still less everything that occurred between. . . . But the history of these four centuries cannot be understood without taking into account the pressure of weather on society and the state." In other words, what other historians have long been content to do is not enough.

Why the Mongols even ruled China, in the form of the Yuan dynasty, may also have a component of climate behind it. Recently, Nicola di Cosmo, of the Institute for Advanced Study in Princeton, has joined forces with dendrochronologists (who study past climate as revealed in tree rings) to explore the role of climate in the rise of the Mongols. Di Cosmo is a historian of China and its steppe neighbors whose previous work concerned military matters and cross-frontier relationships in Inner Asia. But lately he is coauthoring papers in unusual places for a historian, such as the *Proceedings of the National Academy of Sciences*.[6] Using new tree-ring evidence from central Mongolia, di Cosmo and his colleagues argue that the sudden rise of the Mongol Empire under Jingiz Khan in the early thirteenth century corresponds with an extraordinary moment in the climate history of the Inner Asian steppe. In Mongolia, until recently, the number of people depended on the number of grazing animals, which depended on the abundance of grass, which depended on the amount of rain. Aware of this general situation, some historians had earlier proposed that drought had set desperate Mongols on the move.

Di Cosmo and his colleagues, however, posit exactly the opposite. The tree rings indicate that only once in the past 1,112 years have there been 15 consecutive years of above-average rainfall in central Mongolia, and that those 15 years fell just as Jingiz was starting to build the largest land empire in history. As they see it, plentiful rain begat plentiful grass, which begat abundant flocks and herds, which allowed far more Mongols to survive to adulthood than normal, and they set about conquering their neighbors in every direction. A rare climate anomaly led to a unique political anomaly. These arguments are preliminary, but there's a good chance we'll hear more of them in years to come.

Geoffrey Parker's arguments, though, are anything but preliminary. For the better part of twenty years, Parker has labored on the nexus of climate change, economic distress, and political violence in the seventeenth century. The result, *Global Crisis: War, Climate Change, and Catastrophe in the Seventeenth Century*, is 845 pages in length and 3.2 lbs in weight. Parker, a professor at Ohio State University, made a distinguished career writing about early-modern Europe, mainly Spain and the Netherlands, and became one of the world's leading voices on the theme of the military revolution.[7] He gave scant sign in these earlier works of an interest in climate or climate change.

But in *Global Crisis*, Parker advances the argument that the several seemingly disparate crises in the seventeenth century were, in fact, connected, and that the main connection was adverse climate change. He finds fifty revolts, revolutions, and civil wars in the decades between 1618 and 1688, and no shortage of interstate wars, either. He links this worldwide spate of violence to the climatic challenges presented by the Little Ice Age, the product of unusually large and numerous volcanic eruptions, which created dust veils in the atmosphere that reduced the amount of sunshine reaching the Earth, and of a decline in the sun's energy output (called the Maunder Minimum). Its deepest and most frequent cold spells and droughts came disproportionately in the years 1610–1690. Parker, like Bulliet, does not hesitate to delve into the geophysical mechanics of climate shifts.

Parker has amassed detail on the climate history of the seventeenth century around the world, using all manner of sources. He collected several dozen quotations from seventeenth-century authors noting unprecedented cold, drought, hunger, or violence. He sketches seemingly endless crop failures, famines, bread riots, uprisings, tax revolts, revenue crises, state collapses, and civil wars and tries to show how they all fit together. In every case, extraordinary and recurrent bad weather lay at the root of the troubles.

Parker is well aware that he will ruffle historians' feathers by emphasizing nonhuman causation and climate change in particular. But he does not pull his punches and repeatedly offers summary statements of complex political turmoil, such as his claim that "even the Sun King was no match for the Little Ice Age." Parker's book amounts to a heady challenge for all historians of the early-modern world, none of whom has put as much stock in climate variables and few of whom can write about the big picture with the authority that he brings.

Finally, there is the new portrait of the human experience by John Brooke, also at Ohio State. Brooke is a prize-winning historian of colonial America and the early republic. His prior work principally featured comparatively small spaces over modest spans of time.[8] In his latest book, *Climate Change and the Course of Global History: A Rough Journey,* Brooke throws caution to the solar wind, offering a 631-page global history of humankind that spans a quarter of a million years. (Full disclosure: this book appears in a series that I coedit). Brooke's central proposition is that for the great majority of human history, our ancestors struggled (and sometimes failed) to adjust to the many ups and downs in climate. Without modern technology, coping with climate was harder than it is now, and climate surprises were sometimes far greater than anything we've experienced in the last couple of centuries. Few, if any, societies, up until the last 200 years, ran into trouble for purely endogenous reasons such as population growth, despite the views of Malthus and those influenced by him. Rather, societies were routinely buffeted by changing climate and epidemic disease—exogenous shocks. Brooke dove deeply into the climate science, and includes over twenty graphs of the sort one finds in articles in *Geophysical Research Letters*.

The latter part of Brooke's tome deals with recent centuries, in which climate shocks have played a lesser role and humankind has, in effect, been taking revenge on the Earth. Now humankind affects climate more than vice-versa. He ends with a plea for more careful conduct on the part of our species.

Brooke betrays no fear, despite taking positions that other historians will surely denounce as environmental or climatic determinism. He, too, does not pull his punches. On page 279, for example, he lays out a scheme by which to understand the last 12,200 years of human history, a periodization based chiefly on climate shifts, and accepts "the risk of being labeled an environmental determinist."

■ ■ ■

Historians are not alone in their recourse to climate change as an explanatory variable. Archaeologists, historical geographers, and paleoscientists of all stripes are climbing on the same bandwagon.

For the deeper past, it sometimes seems that the less we know, the more climate change seems to matter. When there is abundant evidence, scholars can fashion explanations for whatever they observe from social forces, without invoking climate change—which is not to say they are always right to do so. For Brook and Parker, especially, evidence abounds, and generations of historians have found it easy enough to account for the ups and downs of the Yuan and Ming, or the seventeenth century crises, without mentioning climate. And yet Brook and Parker still put it front and center.

For the most part, these five senior historians use climate change to discuss economic and political history. Unexpected climate shifts, or brief climate shocks, brought crop failure, hunger, unrest—these arguments appear time and again in these five books. In particular, climate shifts help explain economic distress and political violence. They are not, generally, quite as ready to explain good economic times or enduring political stability as deriving from benign climate change. That could be because these authors are affected by the current climate anxiety, in which climate change is expected to be a bad thing. But it might also be a reflection of a historical reality: if societies, and especially their crops and animals, are accustomed to a given climate regime, sharp change of any sort is likely to be bad, whether it becomes hotter or colder, drier or wetter. For the moment, at least, climate shifts do not seem to illuminate social, cultural, and intellectual history to the same extent that, in these authors' hands, they now do economic and political history.

Bulliet, Ellenblum, Brook, Parker, and Brooke are all senior historians, all comfortably ensconced in the higher strata of their respective fields. All are conversant in conventional explanations for the various rises and falls, crises and expansions that pepper their pages. Up to this point, all have contented themselves by tinkering with those conventional explanations, offering new ideas within the traditional comfort zone of professional historians, where human affairs change because of human initiatives, arranged as social and political forces. So why are they all writing differently now, challenging readers to consider climate shifts as central to the course of history?

Perhaps it is the availability of new evidence from the natural sciences. Perhaps it is the current general anxiety over climate change. Perhaps, as senior figures with robust reputations, they all felt free to say what others fear to, as Le Roy Ladurie feared to speak his mind in the 1960s. Perhaps the charge of "environmental determinist" does not seem so odious today as it once did. Or perhaps it is mere coincidence that five major historians came out with such books in the last five years; after all, thousands of other history books were published in the same span that ignored climate altogether. Time will tell whether this quintet, and others working in a similar vein, represents a new intellectual climate in the historical profession or just a passing shower.

NOTES

1. Arnold Toynbee, *A Study of History*, 12 vols. (Oxford: Oxford University Press, 1934–1961), 2:60–73.
2. Emmanuel Le Roy Ladurie, *Times of Feast, Times of Famine* (New York: Doubleday, 1971), 119. Le Roy Ladurie has since changed his mind: see his *Histoire humaine et comparée du climat*, 3 vols. (Paris: Fayard, 2004–10).
3. Richard Bulliet, *Conversion to Islam in the Medieval Period: An Essay in Quantitative History* (Cambridge, MA: Harvard University Press, 1979); Bulliet, *The Camel and the Wheel* (Cambridge, MA: Harvard University Press, 1975).
4. Ronnie Ellenblum, *Frankish Rural Settlement in the Latin Kingdom of Jerusalem* (Cambridge: Cambridge University Press, 1997); Ellenblum, *Crusader Castles and Modern Histories* (Cambridge: Cambridge University Press, 2007).

5. Timothy Brook, *The Confusions of Pleasure: Commerce and Culture in Ming China* (Berkeley: University of California Press, 1998); Brook, *Collaboration: Japanese Agents and Local Elites in Wartime China* (Cambridge, MA: Harvard University Press, 2005); and Brook, *Vermeer's Hat: The Seventeenth Century and the Dawn of the Global World* (London: Bloomsbury, 2007).

6. Neil Pederson, Amy Hessl, Nachan Bataarbileg, Kevin Anchukaitis, and Nicola di Cosmo, "Pluvials, Droughts, the Mongol Empire, and Modern Mongolia," *PNAS* 111 (2014): 4,375–79.

7. Geoffrey Parker, *The Army of Flanders and the Spanish Road, 1567–1659* (Cambridge: Cambridge University Press, 1972); Parker, *The Military Revolution: Military Innovation and the Rise of the West, 1500–1800* (Cambridge: Cambridge University Press, 1988); and Parker, *The Grand Strategy of Philip II* (New Haven, CT: Yale University Press, 1998), among many others.

8. John Brooke, *The Heart of the Commonwealth: Society and Political Culture in Worcester County Massachusetts, 1713–1861* (Cambridge: Cambridge University Press, 1989); Brooke, *The Refiner's Fire: The Making of Mormon Cosmology, 1644–1844* (Cambridge: Cambridge University Press, 1994); and Brooke, *Columbia Rising: Civil Life on the Upper Hudson from the Revolution to the Age of Jackson* (Chapel Hill: University of North Carolina Press, 2010).

THE YEAR OF BLACK MEMOIR

IMANI PERRY

My first week as a college freshman, in 1990, I sat in W. L. Harkness Hall and listened to Professor Robert Stepto lecture on African American literature. He began with the slave narratives, in particular the one by the man referred to as the father of African American literature, the abolitionist Frederick Douglass. Professor Stepto described how, at its inception, freedom was sought in movement and literacy. Running away "down the freedom road" and learning to read both violated slave law. They were also means of self-creation and self-emancipation and became treasured motifs across generations of Black American art and culture.

But in 2011, Professor Kenneth Warren declared there was no longer any such thing as African American literature. The first Black president was in the White House. Coming around the corner was a combustion of outrage in American cities at the persistence of racial inequality. Warren famously (or infamously, depending on your perspective) stated further that the slave narratives weren't even African American literature. To the extent that African American literature had been something, it was essentially a literature of appeal and protest in response to Jim Crow that began in the 1890s and ended some time in the 1960s or '70s. That era was no more.

Despite Warren's pronouncements, Black writing is still a big deal and not simply because there are so many extraordinary Black American writers working today. Black life continues to be an important subject in this vexing, separate, and unequal nation. This is evidenced by the way Ta-Nehisi Coates's *Between the World and Me* has captivated readers. It stands in the Black literary tradition, as do others in the most recent crop of Black memoirs, including Margo Jefferson's *Negroland*, Clifford Thompson's *Twin of Blackness*, and Rosemary Freeney Harding and Rachel Harding's *Remnants: A Memoir of Spirit, Activism, and Mothering*.

Memoir, the offspring of the slave narrative, is not simply a form within the Black literary tradition; it has thoroughly shaped that tradition. From personal essays to bildungsromans, stories of becoming and remembering are essential to it. Following the path laid by those running to freedom and living to tell about it, Black memoirists continue to use the motifs of movement and literacy as markers of emancipation. However, in the current landscape, when Black life is so varied and complex, no memoir can stand as a singular representation of Black life, regardless of how compelling it might be. They stand in a tradition but the world is not the same.

Ta-Nehisi Coates's work has been likened to James Baldwin, but he is the son of Richard Wright. His title is borrowed from Richard Wright's harrowing lynching poem. The chapters are structured as a nod to Wright's *Native Son* three sections, "Fear," "Flight," and "Fate." And though his fate is distinct from Bigger Thomas's, like Wright's, this book nearly jumps with the palpable feelings of danger, isolation, and displacement. Coates is a young man under constant threat, from other young Black men, from police, from a neglectful school system. His parents are present: a father who was a university librarian and a mother who pushed him constantly to be a critical thinker. He reminds us toward the end that he was loved, but poor and urban Baltimore seems to be his closest companion in youth, and it is a cruel one.

His flight, or first running toward emancipation, takes place when he ventures an hour away from Baltimore to Howard University, known colloquially as "the Mecca." Coates's world opens up at the historically Black research university. It is an intoxicating microcosmic diaspora. Three women from three places, the last of whom becomes his wife, are vehicles for his development, leading him away from a self-described flat-footed Black nationalism and towards more liberal and expansive ideas about race, gender, and sexuality. One of the most moving parts of the text is when he describes his Chicago-born wife's travel to Paris and how she returned with photographs of doors of all sizes and colors—"deep blue, ebony, orange, turquoise, and burning red doors. I examined the pictures of these giant doors in our small Harlem apartment. I had never seen anything like them. It had never even occurred to me that such giant doors could exist, could be so common in one part of the world and totally absent in another." His wonder enchants the reader who hopes that he will follow in her footsteps there, and he does. Through those doors, in Paris, he finds something closer to freedom.

That the book is a letter to his son makes readers think of Baldwin's letter to his nephew, but the comparison is not particularly apt for several reasons. Coates is concerned primarily with making sure his son has a life outside of the confines he was born into as a young person. He is teaching his son about class mobility, gifting him with middle-class comforts, including a relative freeness of spirit when he navigates the world. Baldwin's lesson to his nephew, in contrast, was a mode of interpreting the injustice of the society without belittling himself, as well as a demand that the son maintain sensitivity toward his father, a man who was beaten down by America's racism. Be gentle with one who may have failed you, Baldwin cautions. Be attentive beyond your suffering. Coates, though critical of American racism, is not particularly invested in such sensitivities. The interior lives of those in his neighborhood in Baltimore are not his literary concern. Nor is the entrenched racism confronting Algerians and other descendants of empire in the Paris where he finds some freedom. This is his story.

And that is the rub. The possessiveness of memoir can be problematic when it comes to the subject of race. American philosopher William James, in his lecture on *The Varieties of Religious Experience*, wrote: "I do not see how it is possible that creatures in such different positions and with such different powers as human individuals are, should have exactly the same functions and the same duties. No two of us have identical difficulties, nor should we be expected to work out identical solutions. Each, from his peculiar angle of observation, takes in a certain sphere of fact and trouble, which each must deal with in a unique manner."

James's essay is useful for thinking about these memoirs generally. Today we acknowledge the widely ranging experiences of Black people across lines of class, gender, identity, region, education, sexuality, and ethnicity. Add to that range the reality that each person out of the trouble and fact of their particular lives makes interpretive choices about the world in which they reside, ones that elude any fiction of objective truth. Telling one's story is one's story. The varieties of our racial experience are one thing, and the sense we make of them is yet another narrowing distinction. Yet the sense one individual Black writer makes of his or her life, from the perch of our wounds, our aspirations, our bourgeois frames of reference, are often read as saying much more than they actually can about the broader experiences and thoughts of Black people. That is dangerous.

Clifford Thompson paints a very different portrait than Coates of growing up in the lower-middle class of the upper South, the region of Frederick Douglass's enslavement. Thompson's account of coming of age in Washington, DC, is filled with intimacy, multigenerational attachments, laughter, chatter, family, friendship, rituals, and so much music. There are a few unpleasant racist episodes and dangers, but they don't define his youth.

Perhaps this difference has something to do their ages: Coates came of age squarely in the midst of the Reagan era, deindustrialization, and the rise of crack cocaine and mass imprisonment. And although he doesn't dwell on it, students of American urban history are well aware of the consequences of the 1980s for Black communities. But it is not as though Thompson, born in 1963, completely escaped these impacts. The difference between the two depictions seems to be largely one of the meaning drawn from the stuff of each one's life, the particulars of each one's situatedness.

They are each outsiders to Black life in their own way. Coates is an atheist; Thompson, a Catholic. Hence, neither finds comfort in what we call "the Black Church." They see the world they come from, and depart from, differently. Thompson finds jazz and Oberlin; Coates, hip-hop and Howard. They are voracious in their pursuits. And while Coates and Thompson write a great deal about what Black communities lack, they both have their imaginations set afire by the creative abundance of Black communities.

Thompson and Coates would probably each balk at being so likened. They are politically at odds. Whereas Thompson decries Black Power, Coates feels a sense of loss about its departure. Thompson sings "Kumbaya" about racial reconciliation; Coates is Derrick Bell–like in his insistence that race isn't going anywhere. What they share most is a sense of being "different" from the others around them. While this may be a literary conceit generally demanded of personal narratives (the writer must be set apart in some way), it threatens to leave the racial stereotypes of the places from which they hail intact. They emerge unique out of neighborhoods that remain a large and undifferentiated scene rather than testifying to the truth that complex human beings are everywhere, even and especially in "the hood."

I cannot refute Thompson's claim that he was called "white boy" by his peers. That was and is his trouble and fact. I can, however, read and cite the dozens of studies that say Black children in general value academic achievement and do not think of doing well in school as "acting white." But the power of narrative hits the heart and mind harder than that of social science. Stories teach us how to think more than data does, for better or worse.

Thompson's memoir is as much assertion as reflection. He finds his emancipation journeys leading him to Oberlin College, Spain, and New York. Emancipation from what, exactly, is a little inchoate. It has something to do with Blackness and his transition as an adult from an intimate and loving Black family life to a life in which his intimate associations are largely with White people. He preaches a gospel of interracial unity, acknowledging racism but telling Black people who hate White people that they have failed morally. Thompson surprisingly deploys Baldwin to authorize his perspective. He cites early Baldwin, the Baldwin before he became despondent about the assassination of Martin Luther King Jr., before he saw the post-Movement backlash against Black people. But Thompson also seems to neglect the distinction Baldwin always drew between individual White people with whom he had close, loving relationships, and Whiteness itself. Thompson instead reads Baldwin as distinguishing racist White people from his White friends. That is a very different sort of distinction. Baldwin's capacity to love White people, as individuals, never countervailed his rage at Whiteness writ large as an ideological project, as work that causes suffering across the globe, among both those suffering from the wrath of White supremacy and those who believed in it.

Methinks Thompson protests too much and Coates perhaps not enough. Whereas Thompson tries to convince us that he is indeed Black enough to count as Black or that it doesn't really matter whether he is Black, Coates doesn't try to convince us of enough regarding how we ought to respond to the condition of Blackness under the thumb of American racism. Coates echoes H. Rap Brown: Racism is American as Cherry Pie. And it is trenchant, and terrible. And what? Yes, Howard is the Mecca, but what of the dire financial straits it finds itself in now, despite its extraordinary history of service to the nation? What ought we do about it? What of the political mobilization we are witnessing among young people in Baltimore in response to Freddie Gray's murder? What is our responsibility to his hometown, to the many other places like his hometown?

I say this and yet I know it is not fair to ask for a different book than the one he chose to write. The frustration I share should not be set at Coates's front door but issued instead to those who have chosen to make the book a singular guidepost on race today. It doesn't respond to those most pressing questions of race and shouldn't be approached as if it did. Nor do, or should, the others.

So how does the Black writer refuse being caught up in the logic of racism in the midst of efforts to find and share his or her voice? There are cringe-worthy moments in these works that reveal the sticky web they navigate, such as when Coates describes a victim of American racism: "His manner was like all the powerless black people I'd ever known, exaggerating their bodies to conceal a fundamental plunder that they could not prevent," or when he describes "a philosophy of the disembodied, of a people who control nothing, who can protect nothing, who are made to fear not just the criminals among them but the police who lord over them with all the moral authority of a protection racket." It sounds faintly like a culture of poverty claim about Black people rather than railing against injustice. When Thompson generalizes from a single boy who asked him, disdainfully, "Why you read?" he implies that reading was generally frowned upon in Black Washington, DC. But the works beg the question: How does it feel to be an exception? Writers stand apart. They are "different." And yet Black writers are caught in a web in which "different and therefore superior, and superior and therefore different" is applied to most Black achievement. This has sharpened in the Obama era with the juxtaposition between an idealized vision of Black excellence in the Obama family and a reckless trafficking in images of Black decadence and deviance on everything from reality television to popular music and the evening news. Attainment is supposed to put you in the former camp, to make life a little easier. And yet that attainment also becomes a tool used against those who don't make it, to say "look at these exceptional Black people. If they can do it you have no excuse."

But more than that, in the moments in which the reader is forced to recognize that being elite doesn't protect one from racism, exclusion, or even violence in response to one's Blackness, it isn't clear what sense we are to make of that reality. Perhaps it allows the reader to have selective outrage for the type of elite Black people who seemingly ought to be able to escape such ravages. Or perhaps it is a way of demonstrating the sense of linked fate that persists amongst Black Americans despite our varying lives. As Coates writes elegantly: "We have made something down here. We have taken the one-drop rules of Dreamers and flipped them. They made us into a race. We made ourselves into a people." I hope it is the latter, but can't be sure.

Margo Jefferson's story is distinguished from Coates and Thompson in that she was born to be an exception. The strict rules of her bourgeois upbringing reveal that membership in the middle class is hardly a panacea for restrictions on individual expression, notwithstanding the impression we might get from the other two. She describes "Negroland" as "my name for a small region of Negro America where residents were sheltered by a certain amount of privilege and plenty." Its residents "thought of ourselves as the Third Race, poised between the masses of Negroes and all classes of Caucasians. Like the Third Eye, the Third Race possessed a wisdom, intuition, and enlightened knowledge the other two races lacked. Its members had education, ambition, sophistication, and standardized verbal dexterity" and lived by dictates of propriety and decorum, exclusive institutions and rituals of exclusion and affirmation. Jefferson, born in 1947, is a full generation older than Coates. Her coming of age is a desegregation-generation story, a story of feminist awakening, and one of movement from her world of Black elites, through the '60s, to an adulthood in which she too is told by a friend "she thinks she's a white woman."

But Jefferson teases. Her pen is clever, ironic, and sarcastic, self-deprecatingly suggesting that "maybe they're right." She reveals that she feels the death of Audrey Hepburn more acutely than that of Thurgood Marshall and spends several pages debating James Baldwin's criticism of the sentimentalism of nineteenth-century White women writers. While she adores Baldwin, she loves Louisa May Alcott, too. "Femininity" and its privileges, oft held away from working-class Black women, are part of her inheritance. She speaks achingly of her cheerleader try-outs and her formal dresses. While she is raised to admire matronly Black heroines with darker skin, broader features, and kinkier hair, like Mary McLeod Bethune and Marian Anderson, it is clear she does not want to ever *be* like them.

Jefferson's relationship to being a member of the Black elite is hard to untangle. She is unquestionably critical of their colorism, elitism, and conservatism, and yet at other turns she echoes those flaws, and not unwittingly. When she describes how young women of her group chose to be traitors to their class and mix with regular Black folks in the midst of the '60s, she says, "Naturally, errors were made. The doctor's daughter studying architecture married a man with suspected ties to the drug trade: within the year, she was shot in the head from behind and left beside her murdered husband, a large pool of blood widening in what *Jet* magazine called their 'affluent South Side home.'" And she sounds as though she finds regular Black folks as dangerous as her antecedents did. But then again, she is not trying to be an ideal character.

One flaw of the work, and this returns to the problems memoirs create for thinking about race, is that Jefferson attributes virtually everything of value done by Black people to the Black elite. The book begins as a collective biography of vignettes about great Black members of "Negroland." If Coates missteps by saying that Howard had a "near-monopoly on Black talent" in the Jim Crow era (simply false, given both the number of other Black colleges and university communities, such as Tuskegee University, alma mater of Albert Murray and Ralph Ellison, for example, and those who weren't formally educated, those who nevertheless made rhythm and blues, rock 'n' roll, and whose number included Baldwin himself), Jefferson missteps by naming the Black elite as a world apart and then claiming all accomplished Black people as part of it. This is simply wrong. College-educated teachers, for example, who taught in rural Jim Crow communities and served as community leaders were not of the ilk she described, with wavy hair, exclusive club memberships, and doctor husbands. And though she attended the elite University of Chicago Laboratory Schools, there were also laboratory schools that also drew from John Dewey's educational philosophy that served Black students in the Deep South. They were not the exclusive province of the talented tenth.

Jefferson's departure then, is less apparent than the others. She doesn't transform much in terms of how she sees herself. Rather, she pulls back the curtain on her polished facade, shows the seams, as it were, and, in the process, reveals her own struggles with depression.

This form of departure exists throughout African American women's literature. As she notes in the book, we see it in Harriet Jacobs's despair in the slave narrative *Incidents in the Life of a Slave Girl*. This despair breaks Jacobs and Jefferson both out of the sentimentalist conventions. We see it further in the writings of Marita Bonner, Alice Walker, and Toni Morrison. The departure from the performance of composed strength in Black women's literary traditions usually operates as an argument about the importance of communities of women who heal each other from the ravages of the world.

The relative solitude in Jefferson's memoir, however, has its purposes. She captures the feelings of isolation that are characteristic of this moment in history, in which people are more connected digitally but less so in the flesh. It depicts a reality worthy of note even as it is not an argument for anything in particular.

And maybe this is because argument is not seen as necessary in the way it once was for African American memoir. Instead, "revelations" take on a larger role. The memoirists are telling you about something you don't know about, whether it is a set of experiences or feelings or a group of people. In so doing, they speak primarily to White audiences, but people of color, too, on another, quieter register and with somewhat different messages: "know your history," "venture beyond your neighborhoods," and "please don't judge me for being different." Somewhat pedagogical, sometimes condescending, mostly they are appeals for the writers to be understood as individuals.

Rosemarie Freeney and Rachel Elizabeth Harding's *Remnants* does something quite different, however. Coauthored by Rachel and her late mother, it is in its very composition both intimate and collaborative. Rosemarie Freeney Harding was the child of migrants from southwest Georgia to Chicago. Whereas Jefferson's Chicago community looked askance at Deep South migrants, seeing them as low-status and unsophisticated, Harding's story honors their resilience and cultural practices while acknowledging the wounds that pushed them north.

Harding returns to the South with her husband Vincent: two rare Black members of the Mennonite church during the Civil Rights Movement. They become activists in the various branches of the southwest Georgia movement and then lifelong social-justice workers and educators. Although the story is written with a keen sense of circumstance—we hear stories of ancestors who worked the land, cleaned houses, struggled mightily for literacy and then of subsequent generations with advanced degrees and philosophical training—the lines of class are not sharply drawn. In this work, the life of the mind and spirit are understood as inheritances that carried those who were enslaved and Jim Crowed through the most adverse of conditions, and must continue to be embraced in the present. Mother and daughter, as their mothers before them, are ecumenical in their approaches to life, drawing on Eastern spirituality, global indigenous traditions, and the traditions of both West Africa and the Black Protestant church in the United States.

It is a book of returning to the source as a resource for the future and present. There are lessons about human connection and resilience and our capacities to be better to one another. Out of the particulars of these two lives, a window opens into Black life more broadly, in all of its complexity and interconnectedness with the vast networks of humanity.

In this sense it brings us back to the ring shout, a spiritual practice that we see depicted in many early works of African American literature, from the *Narrative of the Life of Frederick Douglass* to Harriet Jacobs's *Incidents in the Life of a Slave Girl* and the writings William Wells Brown. It is elliptical rather than escapist. In the ring shout, worshippers shuffling in a circle keep time with one another. The individual spirit leaps out with a blue note, a cry, wail, or holler. The others respond to the call, or simply keep time while it reverberates. At one point in her memoir, Harding recalls how Bob Moses told

> a story of a woman he knew in the Movement. Somebody in Mississippi who had been through so much pain, so much loss, she just fell to her knees in despair, one day. She fell on the floor of her kitchen, cradling bad news or pushing away a fresh memory, and from nowhere anybody could see, a sound rose up. It was within her someplace between her waist and her lungs, a vast place more guttural than the throat, a sacred place. And it was a deep haunting sound. Not shrill. But it rose and was full. The tone rose up out of this woman's body on the floor, on her knees, and when she was done, everything was alright. She was alright. She had made a road.

If indeed Black memoir, and Black literature, are to be methods for us to understand race in America today in all of its messiness, then each should be understood as one cry in the ring, a small piece of a mosaic, vast and ever changing. They should be set amidst other forms of knowledge and considered carefully rather than treated with simplistic adulation. And at best we hope they open a road.

POP JUSTICE

FRANCES NEGRÓN-MUNTANER

Sonia Sotomayor is not the first Supreme Court justice with a good story to tell. The tales of Thurgood Marshall or Clarence Thomas are, in some ways, no less dramatic. Sotomayor, however, may be unique in viewing the promotion of her story as her most essential mission *as* a Supreme Court justice: "It is my great hope that I'll be a great justice, and that I'll write opinions that will last the ages," Sotomayor told journalist Jodi Kantor. "But . . . it's only one measure of meaning in life. To me, the more important one is my values and my impact on people who feel inspired in any way by me." Consistently, this idea is at the heart of the justice's first memoir, *My Beloved World*, which in selling thousands of copies and making it to the top of the *New York Times* best-seller list, has consolidated Sotomayor's status as the nation's first "pop" justice.

The "pop" here works on several levels. Like a Katy Perry song, *My Beloved World* aims to uplift; its overt objective, as the book's preface indicates, is to show "people who live in difficult circumstances . . . that happy endings are possible." Detailing her ascent from Puerto Rican diabetic working-class kid to tough-talking Supreme Court justice, the book upholds the familiar American Dream fable that there are no overwhelming obstacles to success in the United States for those who work hard and stay positive. Or as Sotomayor writes, "Call it what you like: discipline, determination, perseverance, the force of will. . . . If only I could bottle it, I'd share it with every kid in America."

Sotomayor's literary self has a superhero feel to her: she is a feisty if cerebral figure who, in response to her father's death and a working mother who is too busy to take care of her, develops enormous talents of reason that she repeatedly and successfully uses to meet multiple challenges. True, as noted by most reviewers, Sotomayor admits to making mistakes, to being afraid and even lonely. But no matter how daunting the obstacle—poverty, illness, alcoholism—Sotomayor strikes back with cool rationality and controlled prose to reassure the reader that at the end everything will be all right.

Sotomayor's pop ambition was likewise evident in the book's promotional tour. She often appeared alongside celebrities and made history by being the first Supreme Court justice to be a guest on both Jon Stewart's *Daily Show* and *The View*. On the road, Sotomayor was no less pop: the topics of discussion were sometimes quite risqué, particularly for a sitting justice. In an emblematic conversation with actress Rita Moreno, for instance, the *Washington Post* reported that Sotomayor engaged in a detailed exchange about "Moreno's hot love affair with Marlon Brando." And in her heart-to-heart interview with the ultimate talk show diva of our time, Sotomayor asked Oprah for help in finding a date.

That Sotomayor would become the court's first pop justice is not, however, surprising. She became a household name during her gripping televised 2009 confirmation hearings, which made her a bona fide TV personality. Moreover, her pop status was recognized immediately by the media: in trying to envision Sotomayor as part of American culture, commentators on all sides compared her not to other Latino jurists or intellectuals—who are largely absent from the public sphere—but to popular-culture figures like Jennifer Lopez. Fittingly, while conservative bloggers like Debbie Schlussel tried to diminish Sotomayor's intellectual abilities by calling her "Justice J-Lo," the Latino cultural entrepreneur Orlando Plaza hailed her as the "real Jenny from the block" in a *New York Times* interview.

Equally important, Sotomayor's response to the relentless objections voiced by conservatives to the 2001 Berkeley speech in which she asserted that "a wise Latina woman with the richness of her experiences would more often than not reach a better conclusion than a white male who hasn't lived that life" turned the future justice into a star for millions of Latinos, particularly women. In tribute to Sotomayor's steely determination not to be emotionally destabilized by what many thought were racist and sexist remarks, her image and words began to appear en masse on T-shirts, posters, bumper stickers, and coffee mugs. If since the beginning of motion pictures Latinas have demanded to see themselves on the small and big screens playing roles other than maids, hot tamales, and *beautiful señoritas*, Sotomayor finally delivered on these aspirations, becoming only the second mass-media Latina to be famous for her brains—after the cartoon character Dora the Explorer.

Yet the justice's "popness" is not solely about how she embodies the American Dream or the desires of Latinas for more nuanced representation. It is also a literary choice. In Sotomayor's memoir, popular culture provides a public language to relate the pain of family life made triply invisible for being Puerto Rican, Spanish-speaking, and poor. So, to describe how her father's personality soured when he drank, Sotomayor turns to the movies: "It was like being trapped in a horror film, complete with his lumbering Frankenstein walk." And once her father dies, Sotomayor notes that while Frankenstein may have left the building, a new undead creature now lives among them: her mother, Celina, who serves dinner "like a zombie, hardly saying a word."

Although many scholars—myself included—often criticize the mass media and popular fiction for their exclusion or stereotyping of Latinos, Sotomayor's narrative credits both with opening up worlds of possibility for her. According to Sotomayor, the path to another existence began "with me in Nancy [Drew]'s shoes." Later, she states, "Even though it is fiction, I knew such a world did exist." Similarly, once Sotomayor is told that she cannot aspire to be a detective due to her diabetes, it is the Perry Mason show that provides her with a new prospect: to be a judge, one who "called the shots" and "decided whether [a motion] was 'over-ruled' or 'sustained' when a lawyer said 'Objection!'"

In other words, given the dearth of well-stocked libraries and flesh-and-blood role models in the hood, popular culture nurtured the imagination and kept hope alive. Yet at this point in Sotomayor's career, the deployment of these cultural allusions is likely to be more strategic than nostalgic. At one level, by relating herself through pop references, Sotomayor is able to fashion a widely accessible narrative that seeks to deliver a degree of media justice to others who share her origins and propel a sympathy revolution for Latinas, especially Latinas who do not look like Sofía Vergara. At another level, by calling attention to her humble origins and unlikely rise through a pop culture repertoire, Sotomayor suggests that balanced judgment and knowledge are not only the province of elite education and good breeding.

The pop strategy, however, is not without costs. In pursuing a feel-good story, Sotomayor's tale largely avoids politics and intellectual debate. Moreover, when tackling complex issues like Puerto Rico's political status, the book's commentary can at times verge on the nonsensical. An early example in the memoir is when she explains the island's colonial history as the result of "poor governance . . . compounded by bad luck." Later she makes the inexplicable assertion that Nuyoricans have a lot to learn from Puerto Ricans because islanders "took it for granted that they were fully American: American citizens born to American parents on American territory."

In an attempt to accentuate individual agency over social constraints, Sotomayor also dismisses the idea that racism and sexism are systemic or structural. Rather, she proposes that bigotry is simply "narrow-mindedness" and "a matter of old habits dying hard." Steep differences of class and wealth are likewise naturalized through domestic metaphors. "What mattered most of all," writes Sotomayor, after noting the tremendous affluence of her corporate clients the Fendis, "was that they became family." In addition, Sotomayor understands Latino identity as narrowly cultural, not political, suggesting that what Latinos primarily seek is ethnic "accommodation," to be allowed to salsa dance instead of two-step to the top.

Sotomayor goes out of her way to distance herself from leftist "militant[s]" and "Marxist[s]." The issue here is not that she should be a radical or that radicals cannot be foolish. It is that although the reader is invited to see the privileged—whether they are rich, male, and/or white—as complex individuals, Sotomayor tends to offer reductive portraits of Latino activists. Declaring that "being a rabble-rouser did not appeal to me," the justice at times displays an edgy hostility for those who publicly holler to challenge the status quo.

A key example is a passage in the memoir's final pages where Sotomayor recounts the arguments she had in high school with a black "Hispanic girl who identified herself as a Marxist" and accused the future justice of having "no principles." Despite acknowledging that she is haunted by the accusation, Sotomayor nevertheless chooses to portray radicals as inflexible beings who place "principle above even reason" while "abdicating the respon-sibilities of a thinking person." Significantly, in *My Beloved World*, it is the rejection of left-wing—not right-wing—politics that defines Sotomayor's own more balanced temperament, even if it was the hard labor of many leftists that made her career possible.

Fortunately, despite Sotomayor's avowed need to appear com-pletely rational and in control, her writing cannot entirely redress all of her journey's wounds. Although critics have overlooked this aspect of the book, *My Beloved World* is not solely about inspiring readers to achieve. It is also about a struggle to come to terms with the fact that upward mobility has not come without a price; in climbing so high, Sotomayor may have irrevocably yanked her own roots from the ground, leaving her unanchored.

This anxiety is manifest throughout, but is particularly obvi-ous in the book's title, which comes from a poem by the nineteenth-century Puerto Rican poet José Gautier Benítez. In Gautier's text, the poetic voice declares he is an exile and asks readers to allow him the "sweetness" of returning again to his "beloved world." While Sotomayor asserts that she "moved easily between different worlds," in invoking Gautier, she seems to view the fulfillment of her lifelong dream to become a Supreme Court justice as a form of exile from her beloved Nueva York. Sotomayor's memoir thus articulates the classic problem of exile: it is as impossible to return home as it is to be at home anywhere.

The memoir also cannot help but be a restless—if not outright vengeful—plot against her mother, Celina. The ways that Soto-mayor wrestles with perhaps the greatest emotional injury of her life—the lack of maternal affection—brings to mind writer Colm Tóibin's recent book *New Ways to Kill Your Mother: Writers and Their Families*. In this text, Tóibin elaborates on the longstanding feminist argument that nineteenth-century female authors like Jane Austen could only narrate the autonomous self through the creation of fictional universes that "killed" their mothers by rendering them irrelevant and/or making them absent (dead or missing).

In *My Beloved World*, Sotomayor metaphorically kills her mother in at least two creative ways. First, by writing a widely loved memoir of familial reconciliation, Sotomayor proves that she is nothing like the mother she describes as cold and detached, "perfectly dressed and made up, like a movie star, the Jacqueline Kennedy of the Bronxdale Houses, refusing to pick me up and wrinkle her spotless outfit." Second, she makes the painful claim that, given Celina's unreliability as a caretaker, she had to mother herself. What Tóibín wrote about Austen's heroines could, then, equally be said of Sotomayor's presentation of her younger self: "Power arises from the quality of her own intelligence. It is her own ability to be alone, to move alone, to be seen alone, to come to conclusions alone, that sets her apart."

Ultimately, *My Beloved World* is a carefully crafted tale about a disciplined and hard-working girl who grew up to inspire others into productive citizenry. For those who want more from (our) justice, this narrative may not be enough. In fact, while reading the book, I found myself more drawn to Sotomayor's aloof mother, who, despite her movie-star glamour, might be the story's most compelling character. Unlike Sotomayor, Celina is often impulsive and vulnerable and broken in ways that can never be repaired—not even by writing. She embodies a truth that the memoir cannot entirely embrace but is nevertheless inescapable: that despite professional success or upward mobility, we may still hurt from a ride that no one, not even the nation's chief pop justice, could ever fully control. This may be the best reason to read *My Beloved World*.

A BLACK POWER METHOD

N. D. B. CONNOLLY

A half century ago this week, "Black Power" entered America's mass consciousness. In early June 1966, James Meredith launched his "March Against Fear," a one-man demonstration down the 220 miles of road between Memphis, Tennessee, and Jackson, Mississippi. Meredith hoped to inspire black men to exercise their voting rights or at least to join him in a defiant trek across the Mississippi Delta. Just two days in, the demonstration seemed abruptly ended when a white sniper shot and hospitalized Meredith while he was walking alone. Some 15,000 demonstrators—men and women—resolved to complete the march, with Meredith following the events from his hospital bed. When the march reached Jackson nearly three weeks later, black activists had not just crossed the Delta and renounced a general fear of white supremacy in the South. They had adopted "Black Power" in place of "We Shall Overcome" as the national rallying cry of the black freedom struggle.

This year will no doubt see plenty of fitting and necessary commemorations of Black Power's importance in American history. Still, fiftieth anniversaries seem as good a time as any to clear up enduring confusions. "Black Power" is not some dusty or even hallowed slogan trapped in the past. It resides in the here and now as a set of living political and civic commitments. It includes a healthy suspicion of white-run institutions and an enduring desire for black ownership and other forms of self-determination. It also includes a hope that an unapologetic love of black people can, indeed, become a site of interracial political consensus. Chicago's Black Youth Project 100, Baltimore's Leaders of a Beautiful Struggle, and scores of #BlackLivesMatter activists and their affiliates around the country represent but a handful of the groups that sharply echo the most militant political practices of the last half century.

Not unlike Meredith's marchers, courageous men and women over the last fifty years have also kept alive a certain intellectual fearlessness, advancing what one could fittingly call a Black Power method. A Black Power method remains both antiracist and, often, antiliberal in its interpretive and archival practice. Interpretively, it refuses to caricature black radicalism as doomed for failure. It also remains attentive to racism's class and gendered dimensions even if, like historical Black Power, it is not uniformly or even necessarily "progressive" on either. Projections of black unity, as Elsa Barkley Brown recently reminded, often require silencing. Thus, it still takes real intellectual work to prioritize the stories of working-class people, queer people, and women who might otherwise be erased from the historical record, either by white-supremacist history making or black bourgeois responses to it.

In even more fundamental, archival terms, a Black Power method moves to destabilize or interrogate dominant white perspectives in mainstream media outlets, government records, and in the very definition of what constitutes a credible source. For any history book addressing black subject matter, its first challenge is usually dealing with white power in the archive. *Who* gets to become an archivist, *how* archives get organized, and even what *counts* as an archive have a profound racial impact on what endures as valued historical research. Expansive, digital archives can still be locked behind paywalls or library turnstiles at elite universities. Brick-and-mortar archives stand in racially segregated parts of town. In the most concrete ways possible, racial politics determine how we locate the past.

Thankfully, a Black Power method has historically been productive, one could even argue cumulative, by pointing successive generations of scholars toward an ever-expanding archive. During the 1970s and 1980s, the first generation of writers and publishers to chronicle the fervor of Black Power politics were the activists themselves. Keepers of Black Power's flame included Angela Davis, Huey Newton, Paul Coates, George Jackson, and many others, some of whose names we'll never know. They carried out the critical early work of archival reclamation and antiracist theorization. They worked under the most modest conditions and, not infrequently, from behind bars. Through the political winter of the Reagan era, these thinkers countered the vilification and erasure of black radical history, thereby laying the foundation for the arrival of Black Power as a "legitimate" topic of academic study in the 1990s and its eventual mainstreaming in the early 2000s.

We enjoy, today, a rich collection of Black Power books. But, as with any other aspect of black culture gone mainstream, preserving Black Power's insurgent *scholarly* politics demands a measure of inventiveness and deliberate, often courageous effort.

One signal example of such courage is Dan Berger's impressive account of black prison activism, *Captive Nation: Prison Organizing in the Civil Rights Era*. Berger compels readers to place black prisoners at the center of the history of social movements and the intellectual history of America in the late twentieth century. "The history of black radicalism," Berger maintains, "can be thought of as a long opposition to confinement." Echoing the Black Panther Party's early invocations of the Declaration of Independence,

Berger takes as his analytic starting point the notion that black people do indeed possess inalienable rights. But rather than argue for the gradual expansion of black citizenship by way of liberal reform, he focuses on the imposition of "rightlessness," or "a state sponsored deprivation of group rights and political action." For the formerly enslaved and the currently incarcerated, the history of America is the history of rights taken, not granted. Thus, organizing *within* prisons, Berger argues, represented "less a claim to expand rights than it was a critique of rights-based frameworks."

As prisoners themselves did (and do), Berger uses the thinking, writing, and public protest of American inmates to challenge the absoluteness of the cage. If twentieth-century liberalism in the United States conveyed its benefits largely on the basis of white belonging and property ownership, then prisons served as containers for liberalism's discarded, the place where rights and people, quite literally, went to die. In Berger's able hands, however, we see how prisoners have long refused to yield to the cage's designs. "Prisoners and their allies reasoned that if the prison's power lay in its invisibility"—its ability to disappear people—"then exposure constituted a means of resistance." By simply making their thoughts and actions public, prisoners could, in effect, turn confinement against itself.

Berger makes a similar move, using the prison, as an archive, to undermine white supremacy's silencing power. Prison officials collected and generated paper as part of their particular brand of administrative violence and surveillance. But Berger uses these records to foreground how black people experienced and evidenced state oppression. He takes prisoner manuscripts, smuggled antiprison pamphlets, inmate interviews, and even confiscated love letters between Angela Davis and George Jackson to reveal a rich genealogy of black abolitionist thought.

Berger also challenges the presumed intellectual origins of the antiprison movement by detailing how even the most revered European theorist of prisons, Michel Foucault, remained indebted to black thought-work. Foucault's 1975 tome, *Discipline and Punish*, which famously theorized the relationship among state violence, intimacy, and the self, first emerged as part of a prison-reform group, of which Foucault was a member. The group studied George Jackson's *Soledad Brother* and corresponded with the American prison movement. The famed French philosopher, Berger points out, makes no acknowledgment of Jackson's influence. Berger has no interest in branding Foucault a white supremacist. He recognizes fully, however, that Foucault's European pedigree and his at times impenetrable prose have long helped white academe police and indeed racialize the boundary between who counts as a credible "theorist" of prisons and who doesn't. "While Foucault emphasized the eighteenth-century European prisoner as the normative carceral subject," Berger writes, "his arguments about the constrictions of regulatory power could be found in Black Panther writings generally and *Soledad Brother* particularly." Even if we chose to ignore an oversight in Foucault's footnotes, Berger's broader point remains unequivocal and clear: black thought mattered.

Drawing black thought from the archive remains critical to countering dominant white narratives and, thus, critical to a Black Power method. And perhaps the most durable post–Civil Rights myth about black people concerns their seeming predilection for crime. At some vaguely determined historical moment, usually "the sixties," as the story goes, African Americans got free from white supremacy and instead fell victim to their own discernible "culture of poverty." Fattened by the Great Society and emboldened by urban rebellions, Black America became (or perhaps always was) less interested in hard work, more committed to welfare, and predisposed, when not sharply checked, to criminal behavior.

In *The Black Silent Majority: The Rockefeller Drug Laws and the Politics of Punishment*, Michael Javen Fortner seeks to dispel what we might call, for shorthand, this "Fox News" rendering of Black America. He foregrounds those "invisible black victims" who deserve "a fair hearing," those African Americans who worked hard, who feared drug dealers and thieves, and who demanded expanded law enforcement and incarceration. Focusing on 1970s Harlem, Fortner argues that African Americans, motivated by what he calls "indigenous values," pushed ever further for greater personal responsibility among black Americans and harsher law-and-order approaches from white officials. Fortner maintains that, in spite of our collective memory of a fiery black Left, everyday black people during the Black Power era preserved a deep-seated antipathy for crime and a commitment to working through established modes of governance. He contends that, if we're to contextualize properly African American gains after the Civil Rights Movement—to understand Black Power in its ideological fullness—we should include the establishment of the highly punitive Rockefeller drug laws of 1973, what Fortner calls the black silent majority's "greatest legislative victory."

Fortner's book represents brilliantly the contours and costs of bourgeois Black Power as a scholarly approach. Repeatedly, he professes disdain for white liberal "do-gooders" (his term). One gets the impression from Fortner, in fact, that white sympathy represented a greater threat to black people than state violence. Even more substantively, Fortner casts black anticrime politics as proof of "indigenous values." This term proves central to the book's projection of black respectability and to its deeper aim of rescuing "Black America's" reputation from the taint of poverty culture. To be sure, it remains a matter of considerable debate whether there *is* a "Black America," at all. There can be no argument, though, that projections of a black "we" have long served as a defining feature of black nationalism in general and Black Power in particular.

Its apparent Black Power politics aside, Fortner's book makes several "mainstream" and, indeed, liberal interpretive moves. First, there is no radical Harlem to speak of in Fortner's account. The only blacks with a structural understanding of poverty stand no further to the left than Kenneth Clark or William Julius Wilson. Even when observers occasionally link vice in black communities to mafia activity or absentee landlording, Fortner privileges those black voices that choose to reduce crime to normative explanations about individual dysfunction. In ways quite comforting to the average viewer of Fox News, Fortner's black New York makes no excuses for its bad behavior.

As a final point on *The Black Silent Majority*, both the book's nationalist and liberal tendencies flow from its archival dependence on the black press. Black newspapers could not credibly be considered "white" sources, of course. They were, however, businesses. As such, black papers, especially the longer-lived ones like the *New York Amsterdam News*, tended to veer toward bourgeois visions of black community. In the realpolitik of interracial America, black newspaper owners colluded routinely with white powerbrokers to secure much-needed resources for working- and middle-class African Americans. That collusion almost always included assertions of bourgeois black unity, a condemnation of the black poor, and a professed commitment to those forms of state violence white Americans most widely found acceptable. In this way, excessive force in black-on-black policing is no byproduct of the 1970s; it's as old as segregation itself.

A more persuasive treatment of black politics and culture animates two other books that also explore the black 1970s: Russell Rickford's *We Are an African People: Independent Education, Black*

Power, and the Radical Imagination and Gayle Wald's *It's Been Beautiful: Soul! and Black Power Television.* Black autonomy, we learn from these works, flourishes and fails in equal measure through its fractures.

Rickford shows how an array of black independent schools brought distinct approaches to "decolonize" the minds of black children. Liberation schools explained the continuity between the struggles against Jim Crow and those against police brutality. They also linked subpar public education to the housing and infrastructural failures plaguing black communities. Whether run by cultural or revolutionary nationalists, Pan-Africanists or Marxists, the schools sought to prove, in Rickford's words, "that black people could develop alternatives to the oppressive social institutions that dominated their lives."

With an unshakable grip on materialist analysis, Rickford casts Black Power as a discourse used to solve the material problems of white racism. To merely survive economically, Pan-Africanist schools, in particular, needed to encourage cooperative economics and incentivize donations by trafficking in cultural fictions, or what Rickford describes as "Tropes of Negritude and African Personality." Schools had to "reclaim a homogeneity that never existed," he explains. Certain philosophies of Black Power belonging in schools began to replicate elements of European thought; they prescribed, as Rickford succinctly puts it, "cultural and behavioral solutions for structural maladies."

Through a mastery of Black Power as an *analytic*, not just a topic, Rickford historicizes what Michael Fortner simply takes for granted. He writes about the schools as "indigenous structures." But for Rickford, "indigenous" is a claim to unity—to essence—not a state of being. Indigeneity served as an argument meant to protect black institutions from discriminatory zoning, predatory policing, and any number of white attacks on the schools' bottom line.

Understanding the precarity of Black Power institutions means, in effect, being able to balance and detail structural factors alongside individual and group dynamics. It also means valuing and giving sustained scholarly attention to what might seem to be fleeting moments. In *It's Been Beautiful*, Gayle Wald explores the history *Soul!*, a little-known Black Power news and entertainment program that lasted for five seasons on public television. *Soul!*'s guests brought viewers a wide variety of black political thought and creative arts. It featured the talents of Latin@ performers and intellectuals as well as gay artists and writers, two groups not usually associated with popular renderings of Black Power.

The creative genius of *Soul!* flowed, first, from its creator and host, Ellis Haizlip. Equally important was the show's freedom from corporate sponsorship. As a public-television program, *Soul!* could have Haizlip, who was openly gay, make sexual orientation an acceptable part of black politics in public. One hour-long show, featuring a spritely, thirty-something Louis Farrakhan, included asking the minister very pointed questions about the role of secular black professionals in bringing about the Nation of Islam's distinct vision of an independent black country. Haizlip followed up his question, even more remarkably, with a second query about the place of homosexuality within the Nation, particularly as it related to the organization's prison ministry. Rather than spoil the exchange (which is available on YouTube),[1] I'll only point out that this and so many other conversations on the show provide for Wald and her readers a truly revelatory window into an era that even Black Power experts thought they knew. Wald, an eminent scholar in the field of African American literature, confesses her own surprise at learning that even black nationalism was forced to answer to "emerging queer and feminist critiques."

Soul! offers Wald and the show's viewers what the author calls a "powerfully affecting archive." From file footage she opens up an unseen side of the '70s. Not only is Black Power (and really nationalism of any color) far suppler that we thought, but, through Wald's handling of *Soul!*, it becomes clear that the vagaries of funding for television have had a profound impact on our very memory of "the Movement." We recall *Soul Train*, *The Jeffersons*, and *Good Times* from '70s TV because, with their commercial backing, their reach remained broad, their place on television more secure. Their message, by virtue of that same sponsorship, however, was less imaginative and certainly not, despite our nostalgia, revolutionary.

The public funding of *Soul!* gave Haizlip the power to exercise his creative autonomy, but it also meant subjugation to what Wald simply calls, "the racial state." Haizlip's experiment in revolutionary television eventually succumbed to defunding from the Corporation for Public Broadcasting, attacks from the Nixon administration's broader efforts to undermine public-affairs programming, and undue pressure from white critics concerned about black militancy elsewhere on *Soul!*'s host network. In spite of the show's eventual cancellation, Haizlip's attempt to create a viable black counter-public raised for Wald powerful questions that affirm the value of *Soul!* as an archive. What good are black shows, Wald asks, if "the visibility of black people on television has no necessary or stable relation to social change?" For a brief moment, it seems, the Revolution *might well have been* televised.

Blackness in the public view can be a tricky thing to historicize, but in describing his book as "an act of recovery," Peniel Joseph, in *Stokely: A Life*, tries to do just that. Joseph argues that, as perhaps America's most visible Black Power icon, Stokely Carmichael belonged to an imagined succession of charismatic black male leaders that included Adam Clayton Powell, Martin Luther King, and, most notably, Malcolm X. As Joseph details, Carmichael seemed to inflate his own importance. And, as often happens with "movement" men, Stokely's critics in the media and federal law enforcement took such inflations even further. Carmichael fanned myths about his own influence to advance his at times noble political aims. White observers, in turn, heightened public and police paranoia about Carmichael to justify the time and resources spent monitoring his movements and public statements. Carmichael's importance, Joseph suggests, rarely extended beyond the symbolic. But that, the author contends, is historically significant in its own right.

Stokely may have suffered from a chronic shortage of economic resources, constituents, and discernible political victories, but he was also, in Joseph's words, "the last icon of the racial and political revolutions . . . associated with the 1960s." Joseph's recognition of Carmichael as symbol spurs the author to bear down on Stokely's own inspirations, his shifting sense of purpose, and his complicated, if at times opportunistic alliances with prominent figures. Mirroring Manning Marable's biography of Malcolm X, Joseph's book exhibits a keen awareness of Carmichael's manufactured public persona. Casting Carmichael as what one critic described as "a peculiar kind of literary invention" and "an activist who lacked the political support and organizational backing of everyone except the media," *Stokely*, as a book, provides one of the strongest accounts, to date, of the making and unmaking of a Black Power celebrity.

The book also offers, however, a shining example of what can happen when one elects *not* to employ a Black Power method. Its declarations about "recovery" notwithstanding, Joseph's book lets archival white supremacy overwhelm the work's more subversive potential. Even as it attempts to interrogate Carmichael's star status, *Stokely* relies too heavily on the policing and news sources most responsible for Carmichael's outsized public image. The result is a profoundly imbalanced story. Just two years of Carmichael's life, 1966 and 1967, take up eight of the book's sixteen chapters. When the American surveillance state and the white press stop paying as much attention to Carmichael, Joseph essentially follows suit. The author reduces the last thirty years of, now, Kwame Ture's life to a single chapter.

Stokely Carmichael, unlike Martin Luther King Jr. or Malcolm X, was not assassinated in the late 1960s, but, at times in *Stokely*, it feels he may well have been. Joseph's reliance on government and corporate news sources forces him to deny readers the chief benefits of biography as a genre, namely the chance to understand, largely through aging, the unseen universality of a figure widely considered iconic. For Carmichael's closing decades, much of the world lying beyond the white gaze remains unseen. Describing Stokely's attendance at Fannie Lou Hamer's funeral in 1977, for instance, Joseph explains that "Carmichael's respect and love for Hamer . . . remained a hidden feature of his legacy, as did the deference he paid to scores of anonymous black women and men in Mississippi, Alabama, and . . . Africa." These are precisely the kinds of personal and, indeed, *political* details a book like *Stokely* is meant to explore in depth, but doesn't. Even more curiously, Joseph describes Carmichael's silence around Sékou Touré's jailing and the torturing of dissidents in postindependence Guinea as "[carrying] long-term costs that could only be judged by history." Such an accounting should be, by definition, the task of the historian.

Through a preoccupation with marketable individuals, so-called Black Power studies has, to various degrees, abandoned key elements of Black Power's insurgent methodology. It has made the black Left increasingly at home in the world of trade publishing and made shows of nonwhite "diversity" integral to the corporate multiculturalism of elite foundations and higher education. The late Manning Marable's centrist treatment Malcolm X or

Joseph's *Stokely* stand in for our broader political moment. We live in a time when an actress in blackface could play Nina Simone or when Pauli Murray's name gets added to one Yale residential college just so John C. Calhoun's doesn't have to get removed from another.

Today's market engagement with Black Power feels, on one level, like earlier commitments to black capitalism. But given that this commodification is now overwhelming parts of the historical narrative itself, we are bearing witness to an even more dramatic domestication of black radicalism. In spite of the great work by Wald, Rickford, Berger, and others, our struggle with corporate history teeters on the edge of erasing the queer, female, incarcerated, and non-English-speaking people from our common history of black nationalism. If capital has anything to say about it, we can plausibly expect *Stokely!*, a summer blockbuster starring Will Smith. Such calamities, and worse, are indeed possible under white supremacy.

But take heart. We can avoid the hazards that have accompanied the mainstreaming of black radicalism by resolving to incorporate those people who usually fall out of liberal and conservative imaginaries about Black Power. In *Concrete Demands: The Search for Black Power in the 20th Century*, Rhonda Williams attests that "for all those who became icons, there are many more who have contributed to the struggle." *Concrete Demands* offers a synthetic account of the movement as a whole, starting over a decade before James Meredith's march and highlighting strains of Black Power politics among working-class women, government employees, underworld gamblers, and others. Whether shouting "Black Power" in the streets or whispering it in the quiet halls of the American workplace, Black Power's adherents, Williams explains, "placed less faith in white goodwill and paid more attention to the structures of power." This attentiveness to structure inspired black nationalists of every stripe and degree to make every manner of American institution more attentive to black interests. Echoing the work of Alondra Nelson on hospitals, Joyce Bell on social work, Martha Biondi on colleges, and other experts on Black Power's afterlife, Williams avoids treating black nationalism as the dark underside of white nationalism. It suffers none at all from myths about "indigenous" autonomy or rugged individualism. Rather, as Williams explains, "self determination" meant, at least in part, refusing to release "government from its responsibility to black people and communities."

It's a lesson James Meredith could have used long before he ever got shot. Hoping to prove the courage of a lone black man and releasing the government, at least symbolically, from its protective responsibility, Meredith took to the road by himself. Thankfully, he survived and, thankfully, he was wrong. Fifty years ago, it took not one but many fearless thousands—men and women, queer and straight—to march against fear. They forced the White House to deploy armed registrars to the South for the first time since Reconstruction and, ultimately, they gave us Black Power. We will only get to keep it by exercising similar commitments. Collective courage and collective action, of both the scholarly *and* political kinds: history has rarely been made or, for that matter, written any other way.

NOTE

1. Ellis Haizlip interviews Louis Farrakhan, *Soul!* (1972), https://www.youtube.com/watch?v=37fykZ8xwPY.

SOFT ATHEISM

MATTHEW ENGELKE

I t's not easy being new. It doesn't last long. Sometimes it isn't even an apt characterization in the first place.

Take "New Atheism," the label applied to a body of writings by such figures as Richard Dawkins, Christopher Hitchens, and Daniel Dennett. New Atheism is typically understood to have emerged in the first years of the twenty-first century, after 9/11 and after a series of prominent advances by creationists in schools, especially in the United States (but also in the United Kingdom). For one thing, though, as with many labels, it is not wholly owned by the people it is meant to describe. (I know a lot of atheists who are inspired by Dawkins, who *love* his work; none of them refer to themselves as "new atheists.") For another thing, what's "new" in this atheism has some observers wondering; John Gray, for one, thinks "most of the present atheists are not sufficiently familiar with the history of thought to recognize the fact that they've revived [a] slightly atavistic type of 19th-century atheism."[1]

All the same, the label sticks. And in the stereotyped version, what it refers to is a nasty form of atheism, nasty in the sense that its critiques of religion are biting, mocking, and relentless. But it's not all negative. Much is celebrated in new atheism, above all, the power of Reason (definitely capital-R) and its handmaiden, the scientific method.

New atheism—however one wants to cast or define it—is nevertheless alive and well. Yet almost as soon as it took hold—sometime around 2006—other kinds of atheists (often more likely to refer to themselves in the first instance as humanists or secular humanists) tried to shake it loose. In 2011, I was in the audience, as an anthropological observer, at the British Humanist Association's annual conference in Manchester. Julian Baggini, the atheist, humanist, and philosopher, was at the podium trying to convince fellow BHA members that maybe the idea of transcendence had something going for it. There were sharp intakes of breath by some, but he wasn't thrown off stage. The next year, Alain de Botton published *Religion for Atheists*, premised on the idea that we shouldn't throw the baby out with the bathwater. Religion has some things going for it (community, etc., etc.), and we ought to hold on to that, even as we get rid of the silly and sometimes dangerous stuff. In the United States, not far from Daniel Dennett's redoubt at Tufts University, Greg Epstein was appointed the first humanist chaplain at Harvard University. Epstein's appointment came a year (2005) before the new atheist watershed (2006, when both Dawkins's *The God Delusion* and Dennett's *Breaking the Spell* appeared), but it wasn't until 2010, when he published his own book, *Good Without God: What a Billion Nonreligious People Do Believe*, that this more obviously positive version started gaining some significant attention.

Of course, nasty is often more noisy—and certainly more notable in the public sphere. It has taken a few years for the new-atheist din to subside enough for us to hear what else is being said—and, crucially, done. The "nice atheism" is often very much committed to doing things, to building community. The British Humanist Association, which I have been studying for over four years now, conducts close to nine thousand "nonreligious" funerals every year. It has a lot of these nice atheists (many say they are atheists, yes, but prefer to emphasize their humanism because it's more positive and constructive: like Epstein would have it, they emphasize what they *do* believe). Back in 2011, I accompanied the CEO of the BHA to a prison, where he was hoping to pilot a humanist chaplaincy project for interested inmates; this has now grown into a much wider effort and includes hospitals. Humanism is care for others. In 2013, not far from the BHA's headquarters in London, two British comedians launched the "Sunday Assembly," often dubbed church for atheists, the motto for which is "live better, help often, wonder more." There are now Sunday Assemblies throughout the world, attracting tens of thousands of people. Even Dawkins, it must be said, has gone on, in books after *The God Delusion*, to wax poetic about the wonder and beauty of the (natural) world; he also loves Bach's St. Matthew Passion. Dawkins has a nice side, too.

To this mix we can now add Philip Kitcher's *Life After Faith: The Case for Secular Humanism*, a work of major erudition, clarity, and stimulating arguments. This is the nice atheism or, as he prefers to call it, *soft atheism*. "The atheist movement today often seems blind to the apparently irreplaceable roles religion and religious community play in millions, if not billions, of lives," he writes. "The central purpose of this book is to show how a thoroughly secular perspective can fulfill many of the important functions religion, at its best, has discharged."

Kitcher grew up in England and in the Church of England; he was a choirboy and attended Christ's Hospital, a very Christian, very establishment school. At school his faith waxed and waned until it finally "disappeared for good." He kept singing, though, and "neither as an undergraduate at Cambridge nor as a graduate student at Princeton did it seem to me necessary to abandon the

music I loved simply because I no longer believed the words."
(Dawkins was a choirboy, too.)

It's a long-standing joke that the Church of England is well
known for its atheists. Like all jokes there's something in this one.
Long before Kitcher came along, this established church could be
known to inculcate the paradoxical mix of godless minds and god-
filled bodies: people for whom "religion" was about sensibilities
and practices—not doctrines or, still less, literal readings of scripture. Yet Kitcher's prefatory personal remarks in the book—which
are distinct from the less personal but no less personable disquisition that follows—go halfway to betraying one of his central
insights: that the "atheist movement today" has been too insistent
on doctrines and beliefs as the bedrock of religion. Indeed,
throughout the book, Kitcher works to disentangle "religion" from
doctrines and show how its articulation of values and community
(and activities like singing) are what need to be owned.

Kitcher has a penchant for telling his readers what things are
really about. In this way, like his new-atheist cousins, he appeals
to enlightenment to dispel the shadows and misperceptions of
social thought and life. Death is nothing to be frightened of, he
reasons, and we don't need an afterlife to console ourselves;
immortality would surely be unbearable: "We cannot, I think,
fully imagine what it would be like to be the kind of being for
which immortality was a condition of eternal joy. If my diagnosis
is correct, distress at the prospect of not being is founded in a
confusion." And speaking of joy—of fulfillment—secular humanists can have plenty of it. Charles Taylor is smart, sure, but he is,
for Kitcher, wrong; exclusive humanism, as Taylor calls it, doesn't
"flatten" life out. Uplift and fullness are available to all: "There
should be no automatic presumption," Kitcher writes, "that religious believers are especially predisposed to having their lives
transformed for the better. Indeed, once it is appreciated that the

central issue concerns the enduring positive effects of a type of experience available to religious and secular subjects alike, it should be clear that a large number of empirical questions are in danger of being begged."

If Kitcher nonetheless appeals to enlightenment and science to help discern what *really* matters and what the *real* issues are, he does so in a much more pragmatic style than some other contemporary atheists and humanists. I mean pragmatic in two overlapping but distinct senses. Above all, this is a practical, realistic mode—one pursued with accommodation and collaboration in mind. Secular humanists should recognize that some believers—those of what he calls "real faith" (i.e., who aren't held under the sway of literalism)—are kith and kin, especially when it comes to certain political and social commitments. Again: don't throw the baby out with the bathwater. More specifically, though, Kitcher's pragmatism is inspired by Pragmatism. Kitcher may be an Anglican choirboy, but he's become a child of John Dewey, too. By combining Dewey's line of thinking with some of the key insights of Wittgenstein's *Philosophical Investigations*, Kitcher approaches "truth" not in some absolute, capital-T sense, but, rather, in terms of the "aptness" of the language in which it is expressed. A myth is not a literal truth, but it can be understood to be "true" if it expresses a purpose worth striving for. (This is part of how Kitcher makes room for some believers—those who bridle at fundamentalism as much as he and his fellow humanists do.) Progress in life, then, and for society and for the world has to be driven not by some distant object on or just beyond the horizon. Reason is a chimera, the same as divinity. So it's not, as he puts it, "progress to," but rather "progress from" that should drive the ethical project. We should be wholly immanent in this sense, fully aware of the fact that the ground we stand on, and the past we share, is all there is until we create (*not* discover) something more.

Ethics shoots through every chapter of Kitcher's book, every aspect of what it must mean to be human. (He has explored this more fully in another recent book, *The Ethical Project*.) In the service of framing what he calls, with wit, the "always already" character of ethics, Kitcher provides a story (his word) of human nature and evolution, as well as some attendant normative claims to help us make progress from now. His starting point, which draws from findings in primatology, evolutionary psychology, and related fields, is that hominids want to be kind and get along with one another but sometimes haven't or don't. We have what he calls "limited responsiveness." Ethics, Kitcher reasons, emerged from a "social technology" to help humans achieve what they really want: "pleasure in the company of their fellows." Rudimentary proto-ethics then becomes marked by "directives to share resources and to avoid unprovoked violence." To be sure, this is not, for Kitcher, ethics proper. But it is the staging ground for the emergence of the "progress from" that characterizes his commitments.

One of the strands of the story of human evolution and the ethical project that most seems to grip Kitcher is the loss of egalitarianism (and here the origins of agriculture are seen as just as important as the origins of organized religion; a soft atheist has to admit we can't blame it all on the shamans grabbing power for themselves). It's not that Kitcher wants us to become hunter-gatherers again. Denmark, rather, is where we are—where we've got to—and where we should work from. There is too much suffering, too much inequality, too much violence, and we could do worse than what the Scandinavian model has tried to deliver. "Through demanding that all people be provided with the preconditions for choosing and pursuing lives of genuine worth, my proposal insists on a redistribution of the material resources collectively owned by our species, a redistribution sufficient to support the material and social bases whose current absence dooms many of the world's people to want and ill-health and ignorance and oppression and lack of choice."

For someone concerned with "socioeconomic justice across the human species," however, the absence of "the world's people" niggled at me while reading this book—the absence, really, of anything beyond northern Europe and North America when it came to the resources, ideas, and traditions from which Kitcher draws and with which he understands and defines "religion." To be fair, Kitcher is a philosopher; notwithstanding the quote above about how the world ought to look, *Life After Faith* is a book of arguments in relation to the history of ideas. It is not sociology, anthropology, or social policy. But if we shouldn't expect the "world's people" to appear in a more grounded, empirical, case-study sense, couldn't we reasonably expect some of those people's philosophers, poets, or even shamans to figure in the philosophical investigations? To nuance and historicize what "religion" is? Fanon and Gandhi are mentioned on the penultimate page, Buddhism is mentioned a few times, and there is a reference to Australian aborigines and dreamtime. But there is a distinct limit to the range of traditions of thought underpinning *Life After Faith*. Culture is not part of Kitcher's case for secular humanism.

To my mind, attention to the cultural elements and assumptions of both "religion" and "secular humanism" has to be a next step in the progress from where we are. Because where we are is not only (certain armchairs) in New York, London, Oxford, Medford, or Königsberg. The importance of this can be seen by considering the key assumptions of Kitcher's project. This is ironic in light of Kitcher's understandings, not least because his views of human sociality give the lie to some of the more hackneyed claims about what Western modernity produces. Take the common claim that life becomes all about individualism—all about nicely packaged and privatized, rights-bearing persons. (This is connected to what Taylor calls "the buffered self," for those who care to make comparisons.) Kitcher doesn't undo this, but he shows how secular humanism is as much about community and relations as individuals and the principles of autonomy. And it is not only that he wants the kind of fellowship and community that religious traditions have often provided. It's that "lives matter when they touch others"; it is such normative claims that open up avenues for considering non-Western ways of thinking and being. Often, reading Kitcher, I was reminded of the descriptions we have of personhood among Melanesians—often called "relational" or "dividual" by my fellow anthropologists—rather than among Europeans.

One of Kitcher's first and foremost claims, which is both descriptive and normative, is that "secular humanism begins in doubt," and not just any doubt, but "about religion, of course." In keeping with his logic of illumination, though, Kitcher also tells us that doubt about religion is *really* doubt about transcendence, that "religions are distinguished by their invocation of something beyond the mundane physical world, some 'transcendent' realm . . . [that] is radically different in kind from mundane reality." His use of scare quotes around the term *transcendent* is a rare rhetorical device in the book; Kitcher is admirably averse to hedging his prose. In this case, though, it is necessary not because he wants to complicate his own usage but because the term is "as vague as it is popular."

Just so. However, the vagueness is a weak link in terms not only of what defines "religion" but also of Kitcher's line of argumentation. As the ethnographic record makes clear, "transcendence" is *not* the lowest common denominator of what gets called religiosity. This is not to say transcendence or something like it—however wispy—plays no role in what other people do and what other people believe that we then dub "religion." But there are many anthropologists who would argue against the aptness of the term *transcendent* to describe what religion is all about. And this is not only some recent, postmodern shattering of essentialism. At one point, drawing from Émile Durkheim, Kitcher talks about religion's "commitment to the transcendent." Yet Durkheim never speaks of the transcendent in *The Elementary Forms of Religious Life* (1912), and he explicitly rules out both "the supernatural" and "the divine"—good candidates for examples of the transcendent—as necessary elements of religiosity.

What Durkheim speaks of is the sacred and the profane. And the sacred is that which is set apart. This isn't quite the same thing as the transcendent. There is not room here for a proper discussion of Durkheim, nor do I want to engage in further anthropological nit-picking with a philosopher. My point here is simply to question the logic of offering a transhistorical definition of religion in the first place. In this, Kitcher ends up limiting the perspectives and insights of his hard-won pragmatism in the service of an awkward and unhelpful essentialism.

Secular humanism may well begin with doubt—"about religion, of course." But it ought to end with doubt, too—about itself, about its own structures, presuppositions, and sufficiency. *Life After Faith* is a welcome contribution to the current god debate. Even more importantly, it is a sophisticated, sensitive, and thought-provoking social and philosophical vision. But this soft atheism needs to give way to a yet more self-reflexive and other-aware one. For when it comes to critique, nothing should be sacred.

NOTE

1. "The New Atheism: Where Has It Come From and Where Is It Going?" (lecture, Theos Think Tank, London, June 16, 2008).

WHERE DO MORALS COME FROM?

PHILIP GORSKI

The social sciences have an ethics problem. No, I am not referring to the recent scandals about flawed and fudged data in
psychology and political science.[1] I'm talking about the failure of the social sciences to develop a satisfactory theory of ethical life. A theory that could explain why humans are constantly
judging and evaluating and why we care about other people and
what they think of us. A theory that could explain something so
trivial as the fact that social scientists care about data fudging.

This is not to say that we have *no* theories. It's just that they're
bad theories. Consider evolutionary game theory.[2] It says that ethical life results from individual rationality. How so? Assume a
population of self-interested actors. (A big assumption!) Have them
play a one-on-one, zero-sum game with each other, over and over
again. (Prisoner's dilemma, anyone?) The winning strategy will be
something called "tit-for-tat." The rules of TFT are as follows: 1)
be nice in the first round; 2) copy your partner on all subsequent
rounds. In other words, if they are mean, you should be mean back;
if they act nice, you should, too. In the long run, individuals who
follow the TFT strategy will be better off than people who follow
a mean strategy. Or so the computer simulations tell us.

This theory is morally satisfying. Nice guys don't finish last after all! But it is not intellectually satisfying. Human evolution didn't really work this way. Early *homo sapiens* was not modern *homo economicus*. Our ancestors were not isolated monads. They lived in small groups. They were social animals. A good theory would start with good assumptions—realistic ones. Ethical life just doesn't feel like game theory. Often, it's hot emotion, not cool calculation. It's filled with anger and sorrow, love and joy, not minimizing and maximizing. Finally, a good theory would have to account for why we have moral emotions in the first place. In particular, it would have to account for "niceness" itself.

Of course, evolutionary game theory never got much traction outside economics. In anthropology and sociology, the usual response to the question of ethical life has been a blend of cultural relativism and social constructionism.[3] The standard account goes something like this: Once upon a time, we thought there were moral universals. ("We" meaning our poor, unenlightened predecessors.) Then we discovered cultural diversity. ("We" here meaning clever social scientists.) We saw that what is forbidden in one culture may be enjoined in another. (Cannibalism, anyone?) We realized that there is no moral law within us, much less in the starry skies above us. (Take that, Immanuel!) We concluded that all laws are ultimately arbitrary. They are the product of power, not reason, be it human or divine. We understood that human beings are just blank slates on which cultural systems inscribe their moral codes. Or so Nietzsche and his acolytes tell us.

This theory may be intellectually satisfying. It makes us feel very worldly and cosmopolitan. But it is morally unsatisfying. To begin, human moral cultures are not really as diverse as the theory implies. Values and virtues like fairness and generosity are well-nigh universal, even if the concepts and conventions we use to name and express them are variable. What's more, our own relativism is rarely as radical as the theory requires. Who would now deny that the Holocaust was evil? Or that abolition was good? Finally, as anyone who has raised a child well knows, the slates are not exactly blank, and the codes are rarely clear. If they were, child rearing would be much easier than it is. In short, we can't be complete relativists in our everyday lives. There is no escaping ethical life.[4]

Still, for all their faults, the rationalist and relativist accounts are not so easily dismissed either. A good social-scientific theory of ethical life would need to be compatible with both our current understanding of human evolution and the brute fact of cultural diversity. It would need to show how natural selection could give rise to human ethics. And it would need to show how human history could lead to variation and change in ethical life. It would somehow have to square universalism and historicism. That is a tall order, but that is the aim of Webb Keane's *Ethical Life*.

Keane's book is in three parts. The first focuses on recent developments in moral psychology, where two strands of work are especially important for Keane. One concerns laboratory studies of child development. Here's an example of the kind of research Keane focuses on. In a fascinating series of laboratory experiments, my colleagues Karen Wynn and Paul Bloom have repeatedly shown that young babies have a moral sense.[5] In each version of the experiment, small infants watched a brief puppet show. One puppet exhibits a positive moral behavior (e.g., sharing, helpfulness, or kindness). Another exhibits a negative one (e.g., selfishness, hindering, meanness). The infants were then given the opportunity to reward and/or punish one or both of the puppets. The majority consistently preferred the nice puppet to the mean one. Keep in mind that these are prelinguistic babies, some only three months old. These results are awfully hard to square with a rationalist account, which presumes that human beings in the "state of nature" are self-interested monads. And they are also hard to square with the relativist account, which treats moral values as cultural constructions. If either of these theories were right, then little babies would not have a moral sense.

But where does this moral sense come from? The second strand of work that Keane considers provides the beginnings of an answer. In an ongoing series of books, Michael Tomasello has sought to explain human cognition in evolutionary terms.[6] In his recent work, he puts especial emphasis on what he calls "joint attention." By this he means the capacity of two or more human beings to focus on a shared project, such as gathering food. Tomasello argues that our primate cousins lack this capacity. Great apes forage collectively, he says, but not cooperatively. Out there in the jungle, it's every chimp for herself. Human beings, however, evidence a capacity for joint attention from a very early age. Perhaps you've seen a young child call an adult's attention to an object by pointing at it and looking at the adult. That's the beginning of joint attention.

Tomasello thinks that joint attention conferred evolutionary advantages. To see why, imagine two individuals who both wish to harvest fruit from the upper branches of a tree. Knowing that there are predators about, they are hesitant to do so. Climbing the tree might expose them to attack. If the individuals in question were chimpanzees, they would likely give up. They are capable of imitation but not cooperation, at least not of this sort. But if the individuals in question were early hominids, they could have established a simple division of labor, with one individual standing guard and the other collecting fruit. They probably would not have needed language to do this. Pointing and pantomiming might have been enough. Tomasello speculates that joint attention might have coevolved with collective foraging. It would have enabled early humans to exploit ecological niches—high-hanging fruit—that their rivals could not.

By now, you might be wondering what joint attention could possibly have to do with human ethics. The answer is a lot, according to Keane, because it requires that we be capable of taking the perspective of another person. And once we have done that, we can also see ourselves through their eyes. In other words, the capacity for joint attention presumes a capacity for second- and third-person perspectives. And this lays the cognitive foundations for moral reasoning. Ego's ability to put herself in alter's shoes gives rise to notions of basic equity. And ego's ability to "observe" her own behavior from "outside" gives rise to feelings of moral obligation vis-à-vis others. In short, no collective foraging, no categorical imperative.

To be clear, Keane is not arguing that the relationship between joint attention and human ethics is a simple one of cause and effect, where one automatically follows the other in lawlike fashion. It is one of "affordance." Consider a chair. It is designed for humans to sit on. But it can also be used for other purposes for which it was not designed: to stand on, to block a door, as firewood, and so on. And it can be used by nonhumans, too—a cat, for instance. Now consider a rock. It is not "designed" for humans or for anything at all. But it can also be used as a chair if it has a large enough and flat enough surface (smaller if you're a cat) or, if it is small and heavy, as a doorstop. Let me put this formally: an affordance "A" is a relationship between two entities "X" and "Y" such that X can use Y to do A even though Y was not designed for X to do A and A is not its evolutionary function, either.

Now we can see how joint attention creates what Keane calls "ethical affordances." Joint attention was not designed to enable human ethics, nor was that its original function. If Tomasello is right, the original function of joint attention was to enable collective foraging. But the second- and third-person perspectives that are required for joint attention can also be employed for ethical reasoning. Is my partner foraging as diligently as I am? Is the fruit being divided evenly? Keane argues that the basic structures of human interaction provide a variety of "ethical affordances" like this.

As a linguistic anthropologist, Keane is especially interested in the ethical affordances created by human language. He puts particular stress on abstraction and generalization. Like joint attention, language probably first evolved as a means of coordinating action, rather than labeling things. But the one afforded the other. And once humans began labeling, they were already on the road to generalizing. Labeling requires categorizing, after all. But, again, what does this have to do with ethics? A lot, Keane argues. The capacity for generalizing via language can also be applied to ethics. It can be used to formulate rules, maxims, and codes of behavior. This is important, because ethics is often implicit. Much of our "moral reasoning" doesn't involve conscious reasoning at all. It is driven by moral emotions such as anger and disgust or sympathy and benevolence. And it is expressed through habitual responses such as headshaking or handshaking. We can also be called to account for our responses. Often, we can even give a rational explanation of these responses after the fact. Once we have done so, however, that explanation may be subject to dispute. For example, we may be told that we were wrong to feel disgusted or angry when we saw two men holding hands on the street. We can imagine various responses depending on the context. "There's nothing wrong with being gay!" "In the Middle East, holding hands is just an expression of male friendship." And so on. The point is that once an ethical response has been made explicit, it is subject to discussion and debate. And discussion and debate might lead us to monitor our habitual responses. Eventually, it might even bring about a change in our emotional responses. Seeing two men holding hands might bring a smile to our faces instead of a grimace. Indeed, that has been one of the greatest ethical transformations in contemporary Western societies in recent decades.

This is how ethical transformation often happens, namely, through conceptual redescription. Keane gives the example of "consciousness raising" in the feminist movement of the 1960s and 1970s. Women learned to redescribe their life experiences with new concepts such as "patriarchy" and "sexual harassment." And this changed their emotional responses to these experiences—from melancholy to anger. Consciousness raising led to policy demands such as equal pay for equal work, but it also led to interactional demands, e.g., for nonsexist language. And inevitably so, says Keane, because ethics is not just a matter of impersonal rules; it is also entwined with personal interactions. Ethics is second-personal as well as third-personal.

But how is ethical life stabilized? By means of "semiotic forms" and "historical objects," says Keane. We are accustomed to conceptualizing culture with immaterial terms (e.g., "ideas," "codes," "binaries," "discourses," and so on). But culture—and ethics—also has material instantiations. These may be human artifacts, such as icons or books. Or they may be human practices, such as gestures or rituals. We may contest the meanings of semiotic forms. We can even contest their very meaningfulness. But we cannot create and sustain meaning without them. Historical objects are complex assemblages of semiotic objects. Icons, books, gestures, and rituals may be assembled into that complex object know as a "liturgy," for example. Add a few more ingredients—a cloister and some robes—and you have a "monastery." Of course, liturgies can be altered or even abolished, just as monastic orders can be reformed or even dissolved. But this will involve material as well as mental work. That is why culture and ethics are not as pliable or fragile as strong forms of cultural constructionism imply.

Now, let's take a step back and look at the theoretical machinery that undergirds Keane's analysis. Keane tacitly distinguishes at least four levels of social reality. Let's call them the physiological, the psychological, the sociological, and the anthropological. Each emerges out of the other. Human culture emerges out of human interactions; human interactions depend on psychic capacities; psychodynamics are rooted in our bodily makeup. Contra the current rage for reduction, in which all the action is bottom-up, Keane assumes that higher levels can exert "downward causation" on lower ones. Cultural change (e.g., the success of feminism) can lead to interactive change (e.g., nonsexist styles of interaction), which can lead to emotional change (anger about "patriarchy" replaces resignation to "male superiority") and even physiological change (gender goes from binary to fluid). In technical terms, Keane's framework is "ontologically stratified."[7] It presumes that there really are different levels of social reality, not just in the analyst's mind but out in the world.

Importantly, Keane understands the relationship between these levels as one of affordance rather than determinism. Some of the affordances are "bottom-up." For example, the human capacity for linguistic abstraction affords the creation of ethical systems (e.g., utilitarian and Kantian). Others are "top-down." Ethical values such as equality and inclusion afford critiques of sexist interactions. In technical terms, the various levels of social reality are "loosely coupled" rather than tightly conjoined.

To this social ontology, Keane adds a moral phenomenology. Ethical life has three moments. Let's call them "I," "thou," and "me." The "I" moment is unthinking action where consciousness is submerged in doing. The "thou" moment is empathic projection where ego imagines the perspective of alter. And the "me" moment is critical observation of the self where ego looks at herself through eyes of the generalized other. Perhaps we should also add a fourth moment, a historical moment in which ego considers past actions, interactions, and selves as a prelude to further action. We could call that the "we."

In his magisterial essay, "Religious Rejections of the World and Their Directions," the German sociologist Max Weber painted a tragic picture of our ethical situation.[8] In the premodern world, he lamented, life and the world were of a piece. Abraham could die in peace, knowing that he had lived a life in full. He had been blessed with wives, progeny, and property. There was nothing more to want. But "cultural beings" (*Kulturmenschen*) such as ourselves can never experience this sense of completion. There is always more to know and experience. Nor is that the end of the tragedy. We also live in a world of multiple and competing "value spheres": religious, economic, political, aesthetic, erotic, and intellectual, among others. Each sphere is held together by a particular value, an "ultimate value" that demands our total devotion: salvation, success, power, beauty, pleasure, truth, and so on. What to do? Some would be dilettantes, flitting from one experience to another, collecting stories along the way. That is perhaps the dominant ethos of the present age: "YOLO!" But that was not Weber's creed. He longed for the unity of life that Abraham had enjoyed. The only way to achieve this, he believed, was to devote one's life to a single god, the "daemon" that seized the very fibers of one's being. Not monotheism, the worship of the one true god, then, but monolatry, devotion to one's *own* true god—that was Weber's ethos.

What is Keane's? He, too, paints an arresting picture of our ethical predicament, albeit a less tragic one than Weber. Where Weber saw multiple and competing "value spheres," Keane sees multiple and competing cultural worlds, both past and present. Once upon a time, these worlds were separate. Some chose to visit other worlds; others did not. No more. Now, one cultural world bleeds into the next, sometimes quite literally, but more often via the global flow of people, artifacts, and ideas. We are all anthropologists now. What are we to do? Stay home? Go native? Be hybrid? Keane does not venture an answer to these questions.

However we answer these questions for ourselves, we cannot escape the phenomenological tension between the first-, second-, and third-person perspectives on ethical life. Some will seek refuge in the first person. They will seek to be "true to themselves," to "listen to their inner voice," and they will respond to challenges with a mix of apology and indignation. Others will immerse themselves in the second person. They will value loyalty to the "tribe," and respond to "outsiders" with a mix of indifference and hostility. Still others—intellectuals, mostly—will take shelter in the third person. They will place a high value on toleration and acceptance, and they will respond to challenges with a phlegmatic aloofness. The problem is that none of us can stand still in any perspective for very long. The affordances of our minds and our languages, and the demands of social cooperation and interaction, will not permit it for long. We cannot escape ethical life. Nor can we find peace in it, either. That, for Keane, is our predicament.

NOTES

1. Jesse Singal, "The Case of the Amazing Gay-Marriage Data: How a Graduate Student Reluctantly Uncovered a Huge Scientific Fraud," *New York Magazine*, May 29, 2015, https://www.thecut.com/2015/05/how-a-grad-student-uncovered-a-huge-fraud.html; Nicholas Wade, "Harvard Finds Scientist Guilty of Misconduct," *New York Times*, August 20, 2010, https://www.nytimes.com/2010/08/21/education/21harvard.html; Monya Baker, "First Results from Psychology's Largest Reproducibility Test," *Nature*, April 30, 2015, https://www.nature.com/news/first-results-from-psychology-s-largest-reproducibility-test-1.17433.

2. Robert Axelrod and William Donald Hamilton, "The Evolution of Cooperation," *Science* 211, no. 4,489 (1981).

3. Sophisticated defenses of moral relativism include David B. Wong, *Natural Moralities: A Defense of Pluralistic Relativism* (Oxford: Oxford University Press, 2006); and Carol Rovane, *The Metaphysics and Ethics of Relativism* (Cambridge, MA: Harvard University Press, 2013). Within the social sciences, the most influential forms of relativism and constructionism are rooted in the work of Franz Boas and Michel Foucault. See especially Franz Boas, *Anthropology and Modern Life* (New York: Norton, 1932); and Michel Foucault, *The History of Sexuality*, trans. Robert Hurley, 3 vols. (London: Pantheon, 1978–86).

4. Perhaps the most trenchant version of this argument can be found in the introduction to Charles Taylor, *Sources of the Self: The Making of the Modern Identity* (Cambridge, MA: Harvard University Press, 1989).

5. For an overview of this research, see Paul Bloom, *Just Babies: The Origins of Good and Evil* (New York: Crown, 2013).

6. Michael Tomasello, *Why We Cooperate* (Cambridge, MA: MIT Press, 2009); Tomasello, *The Cultural Origins of Human Cognition* (Cambridge, MA: Harvard University Press, 2009).

7. This concept is taken from Roy Bhaskar, *The Possibility of Naturalism: A Philosophical Critique of the Contemporary Human Sciences* (New York: Routledge, 1998).

8. Max Weber, "Religious Rejections of the World and Their Directions," in *From Max Weber: Essays in Sociology*, ed. and trans. H. H. Gerth and C. Wright Mills (New York: Routledge, 1948).

THE ALCHEMY OF FINANCE

KIM PHILLIPS-FEIN

For a few years in the late 1990s, the myth of a New Economy was everywhere. The old economy, with its pesky booms and busts, was a thing of the past, replaced by a new era of infinite prosperity powered by globalization, the internet, and—most of all—the stock market. Lured on by the promise of a market that would never fall, Americans played at becoming day traders, invested in mutual funds, piled into 401(k) plans. At the time, the idea of "risk," popularized by economist Peter Bernstein's 1996 book, *Against the Gods*, was ubiquitous. Risk made the free ride of the market into a sign of your own virtue and perspicacity. Even though it still had a bit of the frisson of gambling, success in the market wasn't mere chance: if you were clever enough, picked the right mix for your portfolio, held onto the options just the right amount of time, you, too, could become wealthy beyond your wildest dreams.

Of course, the downside of risk became evident just a few years later when the tech bubble crashed; suddenly, the 401(k) plans of Enron's employees looked a lot less appealing than a boring old pension with regular payouts. But its allure did not disappear, either for bankers or for people eager to hold onto (or attain) a middle-class life—a proposition that seemed more and more of a long shot. The draw of risk reappeared with the expansion of mortgage lending in the early 2000s, following the tech-bubble crash. This time, it was accompanied by the promise of security. Investors in mortgage-backed securities sought to "pool" economic dangers, making it easier and safer to make home loans by spreading out the risk of default. And for the people buying and refinancing their homes, the purchase represented a way to hedge against the risks of life by owning a valuable financial asset—one that doubled as a dwelling place. Yet, as we all now know, these efforts to manage risk wound up making the economy as a whole far more unstable and dangerous.

Subprime mortgages, mutual funds, and 401(k) plans are all relatively recent financial inventions. So, too, is the idea that the model for an individual life should be that of the stock-market entrepreneur. But the story of risk, as Jonathan Levy shows us in *Freaks of Fortune: The Emerging World of Capitalism and Risk in America*, is anything but new. Levy traces the evolution and popularization of the idea of "risk" from the early nineteenth century, which he sees as the origin point of our contemporary American entanglement with finance.

At the start of the nineteenth century, risk was primarily associated with marine trade, the unpredictable, chaotic world of the seas. By its end, the idea that being a responsible, free individual meant assuming your own financial risk had penetrated all parts of American society. As Levy puts it, the new economic order of rising capitalism was as uncertain and dangerous as the world of the oceans once had been, fraught with instability, recession, panics, and booms. To cope, people sought out ways of managing risk. New financial instruments were created—insurance, futures contracts, profit sharing—and new ideas of selfhood came about as people began to understand themselves as individual financial agents navigating a dangerous though exciting world.

In contrast to older histories of capitalism that focus on changes in property ownership, the class structure, or the expansion of the market, Levy deals with financial institutions and the rise of a network of financial relationships. His interest in these, though, is not so much their economic function as their cultural and intellectual influence. The question is not how futures contracts changed the economy but how they both invented and were part of a new way of thinking about time and about material reality. Insurance is interesting to him as a way of understanding how people came to consider their lives and labors as assets—commodities to be insured. The interlocking history of the rise of accounting and the abolitionist movement suggests something important about new ideas of freedom. Levy's purpose is to think about and take apart the daily reality and underlying assumptions of life and selfhood under capitalism and to show the history that lies beneath our most mundane conceptions of ourselves. "Analyzing the nitty-gritty details of new financial practices demonstrates how risk burrowed into popular consciousness," as he puts it.

In this way, *Freaks of Fortune* is an excellent example of the recent move in American historiography toward writing the "history of capitalism," which promises to jettison the divisions among labor, economic, and business history, offering instead an expansive vision of how to write about the political, cultural, and intellectual meaning of the economy. These histories seek to undo the economist's image of the market as a space that transcends history, in which categories such as "risk" are essentially timeless, by showing how much of what we take for granted as natural today is in fact the product of historical change. *Freaks of Fortune* is not just an important book in its own right but a model of a new kind of scholarship—and accordingly it offers a chance to think about both the insights afforded and the questions raised by this new approach.

■ ■ ■

The story of the rise of capitalism in the United States over the course of the nineteenth century—the transformation of the United States from a rural, agricultural backwater to an industrial behemoth—is one of the great narratives of American history. It can be told from the right, as a triumph of commercial ingenuity and can-do Yankee spirit, or from the left, as a declension narrative of the fall away from a democratic past. Either way, it is one of the central themes of American history.

But the familiar narrative appears new in Levy's telling because of his emphasis on finance. His central concern is less with inequality than with the instability and rapid fluctuations of the new commercial order, the way that it opened up the future and made it a realm of uncertainty, and the myriad efforts of nineteenth-century Americans to seek some material security within the chaotic new economy. The Industrial Revolution is not at the center of his story, which is focused to a surprisingly large extent on the transformation of the agricultural economy by finance. And in contrast to historians such as Jackson Lears and Ann Fabian, who have explored the obsession with risk and chance in the late nineteenth century by examining the cultural fascination with gambling, so apparently out of step with the sober morality of the commercial ethos, Levy offers a different way of thinking about economic culture—one that is grounded in legal decisions and financial relationships rather than art and literature, the mainstream instead of the underground. What readers may find surprising is that, for Levy, finance emerges as a tool to contain the turbulence of the market. The book, he suggests, tells the story of a "countermovement" against the rise of market society. On one level, many people were drawn to "the existential thrill of taking a risk." The tantalizing prospect of self-invention, the idea that one's social status was determined by one's own actions instead of inherited from the past, seemed to open up a new landscape in which the distribution of economic resources reflected individual virtues.

The assumption of risk came to be freighted with moral meaning, a "liberal ideal of self-ownership" according to which people were essentially responsible alone for their futures—the "master of their own personal destiny." Yet this isolation, while bracing, was also terrifying. Desperate to find security, some people stepped outside the marketplace: to the hierarchies and mutual obligations of the family, to the religious idea that the world unfolded according to the plans of God rather than human choice, a divine Providence that shaped people's ends and guided their lives. Levy sees the dream of landed independence as an effort to find a form of security that could transcend the new "economic chance-world." Even slavery appears to him a "hedge" against the market. Although these preceded the nineteenth-century world, Levy suggests that they were transformed by the new insecurities of life in the fully commercial society.

But even as some people tried to retreat from the market, others began to seek ways to regulate and contain their risks within the new financial order itself—by purchasing insurance, taking out a mortgage on the farm, or trading futures on agricultural crops. All these seem to Levy to be efforts to manage the inevitable insecurity of life under capitalism by using the tools and instruments of finance. Yet these financial instruments also tend to facilitate speculation, and so they ultimately undermine collective long-term security, even as individual fortunes may be won (or lost).

Freaks of Fortune begins with the slave trade. The merchant capitalists of the eighteenth century, Levy argues, developed multiple techniques for coping with the financial uncertainty that accompanied long-distance commerce. Traders could purchase insurance to cover the costs of various kinds of losses that came from doing business on the waters—the "perils of the seas," the storms, floods, or other acts of God that could ruin the cargo while it was in transit. But slavery posed a special problem: how to think about slave revolt? Was this a risk that could be insured against, and, if so, how could one admit the possibility of rebellion while at the same time insuring the human cargo aboard the ship? Looking at the legal arguments made by insurance companies after an 1841 slave mutiny, Levy shows that the insurers tried to argue that in the act of rebellion, slaves were reclaiming their own "risks"—their own futures, which made it impossible for them to be considered property (and which meant that the insurer didn't need to pay).

In this way, among others, slavery came to be the institution against which freedom would be defined in the late nineteenth century. Yet, with a focus on risk, freedom would not be seen so much in terms of landed independence, self-sufficiency, or even control over one's own labor; rather, freedom came to be a question of the ability to shape a future life for oneself. Being free was at heart a question of the individual's relationship to time and to the uncertainty of the unknown.

The book then moves through the tumultuous history of the nineteenth century, through a series of chapters that read a bit like independent meditations on the theme of risk and on the role of finance in both managing risk and at the same time opening people up to it in new and unexpected ways. We learn the story of Elizur Wright, an American abolitionist who helped bring life insurance to the United States. We see Reconstruction through the story of the Freedmen's Bank, a savings bank where freed slaves were encouraged to deposit their new earnings (it failed in 1874, brought down by the panic and depression of the previous year, shortly after none other than Frederick Douglass assumed its presidency). The ability to save would demonstrate that the former slaves had truly taken control of their lives and futures. As the first president of the bank put it, "Slavery prevented all forecasting of thought," but with emancipation "a change has come." What was more, many in the North hoped that financial independence would replace the freedmen's dream of landed autonomy based on potential government redistribution of the planters' lands.

Levy explores the westward expansion of the country by looking at the story of the mortgages that underwrote new farms and the "mortgage-backed securities"—long predating those that drove the financial crisis of 2008—that helped to finance the move west. (He also suggests that the new life-insurance companies played a major role in financing this move; thus, again he links the financial innovations of the east to those that drove the market into every aspect of western farm life.) He looks at the fraternal societies of the late nineteenth century, which he argues were a working-class rejection of the actuarial science of insurance. And he writes about Progressivism through the figure of George Perkins, a vice president at the House of Morgan who proselytized in the early twentieth century on behalf of profit-sharing plans, or what Levy calls "finance-led, corporate socialism." Through owning stocks, American workers could buy into the risks that their companies pursued. By World War I, however, even Perkins had turned his eyes toward the federal government as the one institution that could effectively manage risk.

Perhaps the best chapter in the book deals with the fierce controversy at the end of the nineteenth century over the Chicago futures markets, which were initially seen as vehicles for speculation and faced many legal challenges. None other than Justice Oliver Wendell Holmes ultimately wrote the ruling that legitimized them. The new markets in "futures" transformed the very meaning of the economy itself—turning thoughts about prices into financial products to be bought and sold, echoing the intellectual revolution of Pragmatism, in which ideas about the world came to be as important as some kind of objective, external reality: "The uncertainty of a particular financial transaction modeled the fundamental metaphysical uncertainty of the universe."

Taken as a whole, *Freaks of Fortune* reveals a nineteenth-century world that is eerily reminiscent of our own. There is the same sharp ambivalence about finance and debt, the same longing for wealth mixed with a sense of the unpredictability and unfairness of the marketplace, the same entanglement of aspiration and anxiety. The phrase that provides Levy with his title—"freaks of fortune," often used in the mid-nineteenth century to describe people who seemed able to capitalize on the chance to become phenomenally wealthy or, conversely, who lost all their money through little fault of their own but simply because of the vicissitudes of the market—captures the underlying nineteenth-century uncertainty about the moral legitimacy of capitalism. In this new economic order, "the freaks defied every possible moral explanation for why an individual might become very rich or very poor." There was a morality to risk, an ethical imperative to take responsibility for oneself in an uncertain world, not to mention a sheer excitement to flinging oneself into the gears of chance. But at the same time, the very riskiness of capitalism made it seem random, unpredictable, inherently perilous and amoral. Faith and certitude drained out of the world; several of the people whose stories Levy tells begin as evangelicals and wind up as atheists.

In his epilogue, Levy compares the nineteenth-century world of the "freaks of fortune" with our contemporary economy. Coming directly after the Great Crash, the New Deal (especially through Social Security) sought to tame the ferocity of the market: "It stumbled towards constituting the nation as a risk community, thereby making baseline economic security a fundamental right of American citizenship." Postwar American capitalism was much less tumultuous than that of the nineteenth century, characterized by steady growth and mass consumption. But then, in the 1970s, that changed. And even before the recession of that decade heralded the end of the postwar economic order, there had been hints of hostility toward managed capitalism throughout the postwar years from people across the political spectrum—from C. Wright Mills to George Gilder—who yearned for "a reinvigoration of the old link among freedom, self-ownership, and the personal assumption of risk." The era of the "freaks of fortune" was not past, but prologue.

■ ■ ■

Freaks of Fortune is a compelling book, one that uncovers a vast amount of primary material and offers a new interpretation of the nineteenth century. Yet the very strengths of the book raise questions about what it means to write the "history of capitalism" and how this new approach differs from older ways of thinking about political economy. In a way, Levy's very focus on risk reflects the historical changes he touches on in the book's epilogue, namely, the transformation of the American economy that took place in the 1970s and 1980s: the deindustrialization of the Northeast and Midwest and the simultaneous explosion of finance as a source of profit, as described by sociologist Greta Krippner. Our fascination with the idea of risk and our sense of its centrality in contemporary capitalism reflect these shifts in the structure of economic life, as do the decline of collective forms of security and the sense that each of us is on our own. Risk feels relevant because the economic landscape today seems so unstable, built as it is on consumer debt that papers over underlying inequalities, powered by speculative bubbles and profits generated through finance alone, with the markets seen as being at least as powerful as the state.

The scholarly turn that has produced the new "history of capitalism" has a similar historical source. Just as it is difficult to think of risk having its resurgence without the euphoric rise of the financial markets that followed the fall of the Berlin Wall, it is hard to imagine the idea of the "history of capitalism" emerging before the end of the Cold War. The crumpling of the Soviet Union led to a new celebration of capitalism and the free market in the West, the utopianism of which simultaneously opened up the category anew as a subject for study and critique. Historians, sociologists, anthropologists, and even scholars of literature began to write about political economy, seeking to rescue it from economists who approached it in the narrowest possible way. They sought to bring the perspective of history to the study of capitalism, to view it as an evolving social order instead of one universal timeless market, as the economists would have it. Yet, at the same time, in their hands the very category of capitalism has been less polemical and acutely political than it was in those of an earlier generation of Marxian scholars, for whom the central story of capitalism was class conflict. In a way, for at least some of these historians, capitalism is becoming a category the way that modernity is—not something to be for or against, to oppose or to celebrate, but rather the world in which everything operates, the social air we all breathe, whether we like it or not.

Seen this way, Levy's book models a particular way of writing capitalism's history. For him, capitalism appears a mode of being in the world, a new conceptual infrastructure, as much as it is a set of class relationships or an economic order defined by private property and the quest for profit. The central problem with capitalism is not so much exploitation or inequality but rather the "generative insecurity and radical uncertainty" that make the system work. In this, Levy's major influence is Karl Polanyi, who suggested that all society would come to revolt against the instability of the free market, instead of Karl Marx, who saw the social classes divided against each other. His major concern is the bizarre, surreal nature of the process of commodification—the way that the market comes to treat life, the land, and even time itself, none of which are "true" commodities, as though they can simply be bought and sold, and the impact that this has on social relationships. Although Levy is keenly aware that the transformations he describes were facilitated by (and made possible) the rise of powerful financial corporations, his emphasis is not really on the banks, the elites who operate them, or the politicians who give them leeway but rather the small farmers who buy the mortgages, the freedmen who invest their savings, and occasionally the vice president who devises the profit-sharing plan. These characters do not freely choose the social language of finance invented by the insurance companies, futures traders, and banks all operating within a new set of legal rules, but all become participants in the alchemy of commodification; all are destabilized and transformed by it. For to live under capitalism means learning to think of the self, of the family, of time and life itself in ways radically different from the past. To historicize this social order—which claims to be the most natural imaginable, to flourish because it corresponds so perfectly to innate human nature—is to reintroduce history into a world that constantly seems to cast it away.

This analysis of the culture of capitalism from within helps to illuminate the way that the pyrotechnics of finance, rather than being the machinations of distant elites, become part of the way that we all see the world. And yet the virtual absence from *Freaks of Fortune* of the world of the Industrial Revolution and its class relationships (which are present here primarily as a backdrop, the source of the uncertainty that risk managers sought to hedge against) makes the past too easily comparable to the present: as historian Steve Fraser has argued, the turn to finance in the nineteenth century accompanied the rise of the United States as an industrial power, in contrast to the hollowing out of the manufacturing economy today. It also raises the question of whether the worldview of risk was really as widely accepted as Levy suggests. Is risk an experience that floats free of class? And does it make sense to write about risk without also exploring as deeply the changes in class structure—especially the rise of a new working class and the creation of an elite on a national scale (and international à la J. P. Morgan)—that were central to the late nineteenth century? For many in the nineteenth century, to say nothing of today, individual risk taking never amounted to real security. One could make the case that the increasing reliance on financial instruments in the late nineteenth century reflected the weakness of workers in the marketplace more than an embrace of the principle of risk, just as the turn to credit today is the result of decades of economic stagnation. Viewed this way, finance seems not so much a way of managing risk but a technique for distributing corporate ownership and economic power (as journalist Doug Henwood argued in his 1997 book, *Wall Street*). And risk is a very particular way of talking about the world, a rhetorical stance that helps transform the domain of politics into one of individual choices and calculations.

Both the late nineteenth century and the present day are characterized by an economic volatility that seems to go hand in hand with the ossification of social inequality. There is the dazzling inventiveness of the markets, the gripping drama of the upswing and the plunge. Yet at the same time there is stasis: the wild ride never seems to unsettle the static divisions of wealth and power. *Freaks of Fortune* implicitly raises the question of how we should think about the connection between "risk"—both as a social fact and as a way of thinking about the world—and this social gulf. All the tumult of capitalism and the market in recent economic history has not led to some great upheaval in the social order; on the contrary, it has been accompanied by a solidification of wealth and power at the top. It is as though we assume all the downside risks, while they take the upside ones. Chance may seem to have "the last featuring blow at events," as Levy quotes Herman Melville in his epigraph. But on another level, risk is a fiction, too, and the insecurities of capitalism, like so much else, are distributed far more to some of us than they are to others.

HOW GENTRIFIERS GENTRIFY

MAX HOLLERAN

his past spring a new French restaurant opened in the Bedford-Stuyvesant neighborhood of Brooklyn. Located on Malcolm X Boulevard, directly across the street from a Crown Fried Chicken, the restaurant—with a menu that includes frog legs and a bottle of Bordeaux that sells for $2,000—is an incongruous new addition to an area of Brooklyn where the median household income is below $35,000. It is named L'Antagoniste, ostensibly for its celebration of the contrarian French personalities pictured on its walls, but neighbors might interpret the name differently.

In Brooklyn the opening of a Francophile farm-to-table restaurant in a neighborhood where many bodegas still have bulletproof glass now follows a well-worn path. Yet if or, more likely, when the restaurant's patrons move into the neighborhood, they will face off against long-term residents for control. How do gentrifiers take over a place culturally, racially, and socioeconomically different from themselves? In *Good Neighbors: Gentrifying Diversity in Boston's South End*, Sylvie Tissot examines how new neighborhood antagonists come to wield local power.

Writing on gentrification has generally taken two very different approaches: the bird's-eye view (popular in critical geography), in which gentrifiers are cogs in an unequal economy that manifests itself in disputes over city space, and the ground-level focus on the cultural trappings of newcomers: flat white coffee, vintage T-shirts, artisanal beer, and vegan cupcakes. *Good Neighbors* brings together culture and politics to show how such tastes can lead to political power for gentrifiers, creating a wedge with which they penetrate neighborhood organizations and assume authority over others. The process of forming a neighborhood elite in Boston's South End happened, according to Tissot, not always through the often-colorful world of the city's democratic politics but through voluntary associations that, despite being private, wielded considerable power—interior design or park conservation is not just a hobby. Drawing on Pierre Bourdieu's analysis of how groups use cultural capital for social advancement, Parisian sociologist Tissot shows how wealthier newcomers used city boards and nonprofits to mold Boston's South End in their own image and to actively exclude those who lived there before them from decision making and positions of power.

Through such benign-sounding activities as philanthropy, historic preservation, and serving on committees for parks and liquor licenses, gentrifiers solidified their position in the community and began to erase the cultural presence of those who preceded them. Tissot draws on years of ethnographic fieldwork and interviews, as well as historical material on the South End (much of which appears in fascinating boxed-text asides), to demonstrate how culture was used as a cudgel in a protracted battle of neighborhood realpolitik.

Newcomers—armed with more time, education, connections, and "cultural authority"—professionalized the community groups they joined in ways that discouraged broad participation while extolling the virtues of involvement. Under the banner of community improvement and civic-mindedness, gentrifiers were able to concentrate on issues they found important, often over the objections of long-term residents. These issues included: opposing "high density" housing (understood here as a euphemism for public housing but also for apartment buildings in areas where single-family homes are the norm), more space for dogs, quality-of-life crackdowns on noise and public drinking, and more support for the carefully supervised renovation of Victorian homes. Tissot implies that these gentrifiers, in prioritizing upper-middle-class, white prerogatives, did not just disagree over the proper uses of public spaces but were specifically drawn to concerns that privileged their cultural knowledge and maintained them in a position of prominence.

Historic preservation of Boston's uniquely large stock of old homes is the key to the book's cultural argument. In a series of lively accounts of home renovation, Tissot shows how neighborhood boards concerned with scrupulous Victorian "authenticity" for rehabbed houses often alienated community members through conversations littered with arcane architectural terms. That exclusionary discourse, Tissot argues, became the norm across many kinds of organizations and historic preservation itself became the paramount neighborhood issue. Not only did poorer long-term residents have less of a stake in this conversation—because they were less frequently homeowners—but the importance of properly restoring lintels and Doric columns often failed to move those among them living paycheck to paycheck. Tissot makes clear that this new community concern was not just an innocent refocus, based on gentrifiers' group interests, but a deliberate ordering of what culture matters at the expense of less "worthy" subjects like rent control and subsidized preschool.

Good Neighbors powerfully demonstrates how gentrifiers often fixate on the old (homes) and the marginally political (green-markets) so that they do not have to think about the displacement involved in neighborhood change and their own role in it.

Newcomers endeavor to project a relaxed and egalitarian nature by working through civic groups rather than more formal channels of institutional and state power (although these are always there if they need them). Yet within these groups they create many barriers for participation: from inconvenient meeting times to all-but-mandatory large donations and discussions held in a language of corporate-speak and legalese. Tissot, using a web of informants, makes the deliberateness of this exclusion clear and she apparently cannot help but acidly lampoon the cultural pretensions of her subjects. At times, her dismissal of some of her informants' sincere Francophilia or complaints about meeting them in restaurants that charge more than ten dollars for a glass of wine betrays an authentic loathing for the cappuccino-and-pug culture they have created. But Tissot transcends a mere chronicling of the totems of yuppiness by showing that when these cultural symbols are mobilized as evidence of virtue they can help to confer real neighborhood power. Something that can't be bought in a coffee shop.

SYRIA'S WARTIME FAMINE AT 100

"Martyrs of the Grass"

NAJWA AL-QATTAN

I n the days leading up to the Muslim holiday of the Feast of Sacrifice (*Eid al-Adha*) in October 2013, several Syrian clerics issued
a fatwa (a religious opinion or responsum) allowing—in several
besieged and starved suburbs of Damascus—the consumption of
cats, dogs, and donkeys killed in bombings. The fatwa, publicly
announced from mosques and uploaded on YouTube, came in the
context of war- and siege-induced food scarcities and starvation.[1]
It was not the first; over the previous year, similar fatwas had been
issued in other besieged areas, including Aleppo, Homs, and Yarmouk, the largest Palestinian refugee camp in Syria. But there was
poignancy to the timing of this fatwa: on this holiest of Muslim
*eid*s, believers all over the world celebrate the end of the Hajj, in
part by the slaughtering of a sacrificial animal (and sharing its
meat with the needy) in homage to the Prophet Abraham. But in
this war, as was the case a century ago, it is the Syrian civilians that
are being sacrificed.

In the centenary of the Great War, and amid the plethora of
publications, conferences, and memorials that this has engendered,
we may also want to remember the lost and almost forgotten hundreds of thousands of civilian casualties who, in Ottoman Syria
(including Lebanon), perished amid the upheavals of that war.

Across the world from the place where the trenches devoured Europe's youth, in Lebanon and Syria people devoured grass. One of Lebanon's most renowned poets, Beshara al-Khouri, penned a poem titled "1914," in which he described his war-ravaged countrymen as "beggars and the desperate / People dispersed by hunger, they eat grass."[2]

One hundred years ago, civilians in Syria and Lebanon experienced the Great War as a "starvation war." As starvation spreads in Syria today, it might be instructive to consider the similarities as well as the differences between the two. Needless to say, the Syrian civil war is a more politically complex event, involving a larger number of local, regional, and international actors, and has brought to Syria's cities and towns the kind of military brutalization that was not part of the Syrian home experience during the Great War. And unlike soldiers on the Western Front—and civilians in Syria today—Ottoman Syrian civilians were spared the agonies of poison gas. But they were spared nothing else. Like most civilians on other home fronts of the Great War, the Syrian population experienced deprivation and death but did so more intensely: according to most estimates, some 300,000 people perished during the war, the vast majority dying of starvation.

The famine, which became acute by 1915, had several natural as well as political causes, which in conjuncture led to catastrophic loss. The war years brought unusually cold and snowy winters that closed the mountain passes to the wheat-growing regions, leading to widespread shortages of bread, a staple in the local diet. In 1915 and again in 1916, much of the area was swarmed by locusts that "devoured everything green, including our grass, so we started eating them."[3] In Ottoman Palestine, the year 1915 would be recalled as "the year of the locusts."[4] Famine, the historical handmaid of disease, enabled the spread of malaria, typhoid, typhus, and the plague.

Yet, unsurprisingly, the impact of nature's wrath might have been softened had it not been for the politics of the historical moment. Following the Ottoman decision to join the war—and through the peace talks in Versailles in 1919—the Entente Powers blockaded the eastern Mediterranean. This prevented the arrival of foodstuffs by sea, as well as much needed remittances from immigrants in America (after the United States declared war in 1917). At the same time, Ottoman wartime policies of forced conscription depleted the work force, particularly of peasant labor, and—together with requisition, currency devaluation, corruption, and inefficiency—compounded the economic crisis and social dislocation. The confluence of these events and the myriad diseases that spread brought civilian life to the edge of catastrophe. By 1916, Syria's civilians were hardly surviving on a diet of cats, dogs, trash, and grass.

In 2014, "the martyrs of the grass" was the name given by the people of Yarmouk to the men and women who had been shot dead by snipers while foraging for a meal of grass in a no-man's-land on the edge of the starving camp.[5] In its elegance and simplicity, the name captures both the tragic and the ironic meanings of this kind of dying. Interestingly, the name also coveys, albeit reluctantly, the mantle of martyrdom that was withheld from their forebears who had died from starvation a century ago. Instead, those who were remembered and memorialized in postwar Syria and Lebanon were the few dozen men who were hanged by the Ottoman government for their wartime nationalist politics. Because of their sacrifices for the nation, they were (and are) celebrated on Martyrs' Day and have city squares in Damascus and Beirut named after them. Although the death of civilians was deeply mourned in the literature and memoirs of the times, it was not deemed worthy of public historical remembrance, let alone of martyrdom. Writing from the safety of distant exile in North

America in 1916, the Syrian poet Nasib Arida, regarding the events unfolding in his country, went so far as to declare:

> Shroud them,
> Bury them,
> Lay them in coffins down the deep grave.
> Then leave at once without weeping,
> For they are dead and will not wake.[6]

Today we are weeping, as we should. In fact, the agony of the people of Yarmouk became iconic, if only for a short time in January 2014, thanks to a widely circulated photograph of thousands of men, women, and children lining up to receive aid from the UN Relief and Works Agency.[7] A month after reports of massive starvation made international headlines, a few scores of people in New York and Tokyo came together to march in solidarity with the starving. By that time, two years had passed since reports of civilian death by starvation had started to leak out. Today, over five years into the Syrian civil war, news of civilian hunger continues. Voicing incredulity that the unimaginable was taking place, one eyewitness interviewed in Yarmouk said, "Maybe the people can eat each other. I don't know. I don't know. I can't imagine. Before, no one can imagine that a family can just cook a cat. Now it's happened."[8] The urgency speaks of horrors that have little to do with the *sharia*.

Like many *sharia* rules, the prohibition against the consumption of cats and dogs, as opposed to pork or wine (or donkeys), for example, is not necessarily the object of legal consensus. My sense is that, historically, the prohibition has not been tested often enough for it to have become a significant part of *sharia* discourse. (In addition, all four of the major Muslim legal schools allow the consumption of forbidden foods if survival hangs in the balance.)

What is explicit in *sharia* is the prohibition against the consumption of animals not ritually slaughtered (as is normally the case of animal casualties of war). The flesh of such animals—"dead meat"—is not permissible (*halal*) because the animals had not been ritually slaughtered. These traditional distinctions have been overturned by the recent fatwa. It is ironic that now such animals, when killed as a result of bombing, become in death the food that saves human life; war's burnt offerings, made *halal* by brutal force and need.

It may be argued that, technically speaking, this was not a fatwa as it was not articulated in response to a specific inquiry regarding Islamic law. Rather, it was expressed by multiple religious authorities, who were responding to the reality, as well as the rumors, that starving people were already consuming such animals. In other words, the fatwa was an act of legal intervention driven by the compassionate necessity to accommodate actual (and apparently public) practices. Additionally, according to the clerics, the fatwa was intended to be "a symbolic cry for help and an appeal for compassion in the Muslim and larger world."[9] There is an interesting inversion at play here: if the consumption of forbidden foods is only permissible in cases of life-threatening starvation, then permitting such consumption becomes a signal for and a symbol of a humanitarian crisis. But technicalities matter little in such situations. As succinctly expressed by a Yarmouk resident: "this is no longer a fatwa; it is the only choice," adding that the "scepter of starvation is more dangerous than war."[10] He might have well said that starvation is war by other means.

The year 1916 is the year of Sykes-Picot: the British-French wartime agreement on the postwar colonial division and remapping of the Middle East, including Syria. Sandwiched between the Hussein-McMahon Correspondence of 1915–1916 and the Balfour Declaration of 1917 in the nationalist discourses of the twentieth-century Middle East, the Sykes-Picot Agreement is considered the cause and indeed the exemplar of the destructive influence of the West, including the drawing of modern borders. Sykes-Picot still resonates despite, or perhaps because of, the horrors of the Syrian present. Over the past five years, millions of Syrians have streamed over the country's borders with Lebanon and Jordan, in unintended but symbolic mockery of the postwar colonial arrangements and borders. At the same time, as ISIS-controlled territory expanded from Iraq into Syria in the centenary of the Great War, a road sign at the trampled border proudly announced the end of Sykes-Picot. While ISIS violently dissolves colonial borders, the government is bringing Syrian society itself to a horrific dissolution.

Although neither snow nor locusts have a role in the starvation of the present, it is noteworthy that the drought-induced agricultural failures in Syria (as of 2008) and the failure of the Assad regime in dealing with subsequent food shortages had a role in the Syrian Arab Spring. That "the martyrs of the grass" lost their lives rummaging in the Ghouta—the agricultural belt surrounding the city of Damascus and, historically, its breadbasket—adds poignancy to their story. But food is not merely an indirect cause of popular uprising; it has become a lethal weapon in this war's deadly arsenal.

The starvation in present-day Syria, like the majority of starvation episodes in modern times, is primarily the product of war and politics. For four years now, the Assad regime has had in place a policy of imposing choking sieges in order to starve areas of resistance into submission. Although at times used by antiregime resistance groups (Islamist and other), the government has used food as a weapon in calculated, cruel, and fatal ways. Rather than a coastal blockade like the one that cut off Ottoman shores in the

Great War, the blockades in Syria today are inland and mobile, encircling different areas as the war progresses.

Yet despite their differences, the two famines share one defining characteristic: the unimaginable suffering that is the experience of starvation. Whereas the Great War is most often recalled as the time when deprivation was shared across the population, the civil war today is saturated with sectarian bloodshed. Still, the hunger is the same. Pictures of emaciated people, particularly children, may be worth a thousand words. But in the year 2016, as various armies battle it out in Syria, it is apt to remember the words of a Lebanese historian, Jirjis al-Maqdisi, who wrote about the Great War as it was unfolding. He speaks of a different kind of army: "an army of beggars"—the civilians of the region. He writes that

> the war managed, albeit temporarily, to erase sectarian differences; instead, there were two kinds of people: those who were mobile and able to rummage for and eat banana and lemon peels and even carrion, and others too weak to move or even speak. But the hardest sights were of children twisted by hunger sitting in the laps of mothers too exhausted to move. And God protect us from such horrific sights.[11]

NOTES

1. Sebastian Usher, "Clerics Rule Besieged Damascus Residents May Eat Dogs," *BBC News*, October 15, 2013, https://www.bbc.com/news/world-middle-east-24532793; "Eid in Besieged Damascus," *Rozana Radio*, October 21, 2013, https://rozana.fm/en/home/media/4/advance-contents/7418/advance_contentname.

2. Beshara al-Khouri, *Shir al-Akhtal al-Saghir: Beshara Abdallah al-Khouri* (Garden Grove, CA: Dar al-Kitab al-Arabi, 1972), 342–50. This and all the translations in this essay are mine.

3. Mamduh Udwan, *Safarbarlik o: Ayyam al-ju* (Majallat al-Hayat, 1994), 13, 20.

4. Salim Tamari, *Year of the Locusts: A Soldier's Diary and the Erasure of Palestine's Ottoman Past* (Berkeley: University of California Press, 2011), 5.

5. Ann Curry, "People Eating Cats as Starvation and Deaths Plague Syrian Camp," *NBC News*, February 3, 2014, https://www.nbcnews.com/news/world/people-eating-cats-starvation-deaths-plague-syrian-camp-n21016; Samira Said, "Palestinian Refugees Starving to Death in Syrian Camp, Human Rights Groups Say," CNN, January 25, 2014, https://www.cnn.com/2014/01/15/world/meast/syria-palestinian-refugees-starving/.

6. Nasib Arida in *Mukhtarat min al-shir al-hadith*, ed. Mustafa Badawi (Beirut: Dar al-Nahar li'l-Nashr, 1969), 111–12.

7. Jonathan Steele, "How Yarmouk Refugee Camp Became the Worst Place in Syria," *Guardian*, March 5, 2015, https://www.theguardian.com/news/2015/mar/05/how-yarmouk-refugee-camp-became-worst-place-syria.

8. Curry, "People Eating Cats as Starvation and Deaths Plague Syrian Camp."

9. Usher, "Clerics Rule Besieged Damascus Residents May Eat Dogs"; "Eid in Besieged Damascus."

10. "Eid in Besieged Damascus."

11. Jirjis al-Maqdisi, *Jirjis al-Maqdisi, Azam harb fi al-tarikh* (al-Matbaa al-Ilmiyya, 1918), 68–69.

THE MORTAL MARX

JEREMY ADELMAN

n the mid-1860s, as an anxious and ailing Karl Marx worked on the thirty-page essay that would billow into *Das Kapital*, his daughter Eleanor—"Tussy"—would play under his desk. With her dolls, kittens, and puppies, Tussy turned the sage's study into her playroom. Occasionally, Marx would take a break from his "fat book" (as the family friend and patron, Friedrich Engels, called the growing pile of pages) to work on a children's story to recite to his daughter. It featured an antihero, Hans Röckle, who became Tussy's favorite character, a dark-eyed, bearded magician devoted to creating marvels in his chaotic toyshop. Years later, Eleanor would recognize Röckle's struggles as her father's own and see the child's tale as a send-up of his unorthodox life. Röckle's magic was also a parable about making value out of things and accumulating capital out of debt, the fictive version of what Marx was determined to demystify in *Das Kapital*.

Yet Karl Marx has come down to us as a systems thinker; as the curtain rose on the age of capital, Marx supposedly sought timeless explanations for capitalism's ravaging success—and inevitable demise. He lashed the laws of History to the rise and fall of an economic system.

In the end, it was not capitalism but communism that toppled. So, with the spread of market forces, the sage of revolution has been downsized. Historians have packed him away into a nineteenth-century world of wistful romantics—closer to the magician Röckle than to the pseudoscientific Stalin. Francis Wheen, his first biographer after the fall of the Berlin Wall, gave us Marx the adventurer and engagé journalist. Jonathan Sperber went one step further, turning the architect of twentieth-century scientific socialism into a starry-eyed rebel, a utopian descendant of French Revolutionaries.[1]

Gareth Stedman Jones's long-awaited new book continues this trend. Stedman Jones makes Marx a man in his time, forever reading, revising, and yearning to puzzle out his emerging global present. *Karl Marx: Greatness and Illusion* is a majestically important book about an intellectual struggling to make sense of a rapidly integrating world; it is also a fascinating portrait of that world seen through one mind's eye. Finally, *Karl Marx* is a story of failure, specifically the failure to come up with a universal idea of development—one that might equip a revolutionary cause.

This makes sense. When neoliberalism parades itself as the only game in town, it is hard to imagine alternatives, never mind an economic utopia. In an age of stripped-down expectations, it is no surprise to find a redimensioned Marx.

And yet if Marx was so wrong about some things, he seemed to get some others right. Since the financial meltdown of 2008 and the runaway success of Thomas Piketty's *Capital in the Twenty-First Century* (2013), there has been, along with increased awareness of the widening gap between the haves and the have-nots, a renewed fascination with the man that historians have locked away into a vault of the past. Seething discontent and globalization fatigue pose the question: Is it hopeless to imagine a Marx who speaks to us now? If so, which Marx? Stedman Jones offers some clues. But to find them, you have to see Marx as the first to admit the limits of his own creed.

In a sense, Marx was the first post-Marxist.

Marx or Engels

If Marx is to speak to us now, it is important to be clear about who he was and was not. For over a century, he has been ventriloquized by some of his followers. No one did more to create the myth of Marx as *Homo sistematicus* than Marx*ists*. And no one made Marx into Marx*ism* more than Friedrich Engels.

To immortalize Marx for a scientific breed of socialism, Engels delivered a famous and widely disseminated eulogy at his graveside. On March 17, 1883, as Marx's coffin was being lowered into a grave in Highgate Cemetery, Engels told the coterie of mourners that "just as Darwin discovered the law of development of organic nature, so Marx discovered the law of development of human history: the simple fact, hitherto concealed by an overgrowth of ideology, that mankind must first of all eat, drink, have shelter and clothing, before it can pursue politics, science, art, religion, etc." What is more, Marx had "discovered the special law of motion governing the present-day capitalist mode of production." This was the scientific Marx, fascinated by electricity, not poetry.

Dead, Marx got repurposed by Engels, the Russian Georgi Plekhanov, and others for a twentieth-century struggle over the soul of the planet. Now, as we look back, a generation after the Cold War commitments for which Marx had been summoned, the origins of his creed look quite different. Drained of heroic clarity, they are more hesitant and ambivalent.

For starters, literature and political economy were not far apart for Karl Marx. He had wooed his wife, Jenny, as an aspiring poet. He taught himself English (thanks to Jenny's urgings) by reading Shelley and Shakespeare. He would recite by heart long passages from the Elizabethan bard to Tussy. There was a set-piece tragic quality to Marx's accounts of the failed uprisings of 1848 and his polemic in "The Civil War in France" about the massacre of the Communards. By the time he was writing "The Civil War" with Engels, behind the scenes Marx was in full retreat, literally returning to some of his original obsessions and parting ways with Engels. One might say that Marx had been retreating for decades.

Pariah Within

Marx was quicker to see the failure of his theories than his followers were. The question of whether there could be a general explanation for the world's advancement dogged Marx from early on, starting with his early ruminations on the Jewish Question. To recover this Marx, Stedman Jones begins with the fitful emancipation of Rhineland Jewry. Born in Trier of converted Jewish parents (his grandfather was the town's rabbi), Marx went to the local *Gymnasium*, where he imbibed "the sacred belief in progress and moral ennoblement" and learned the canon of neoclassical and humanist culture of German schooling.

The background is important. Marx's father, Heinrich, né Herschel Mordechai, a lawyer, had the predicament of all Rhineland Jews emancipated in the wake of the French Revolution but stripped of rights when the region got swept under Protestant Prussian rule after 1815. Faced with the prospect of losing his civic rights (which included the right to practice law), he became a

Lutheran the year before Karl was born in 1818. The shadow of that choice loomed over Marx, though Stedman Jones resists the biographical temptation of reducing everything thereafter to that one, arduous moment. The Jewish son, nonetheless, was the heir to involuntary conformity. Though he later called capitalism the greatest homogenizer of them all, he did nurture the possibility there was a way to avoid the human blender of commodification. By the 1870s, one finds an aging Karl wondering whether everyone was doomed to submit. In a letter to the Russian magazine *Otetchestvennye Zapitsky*, he warned its editors against a misreading of *Das Kapital*: historical materialism was not some theory "of the *marche generale* [general path] imposed by fate upon every people, whatever the historic circumstances in which it finds itself."[2]

From Trier, Marx went to university in Bonn to become a lawyer like his father. After learning that his son was boozing and partying his way through studies, Heinrich sent the young Karl to the sobriety of Berlin. There, it was philosophy, not law, that gave Marx the means to imagine a world without illusions, to clear the way for a future governed by reason, not religion. Following the Young Hegelians, Marx turned to—some would say against—his own kind. He has been seen as a self-hating Semite and the author of bilious words about his ancestors. But he had a problem on his hands: what to do about particular communities in the rationalizing current of History? Did Jews, like others, have to step to the *marche generale*? This, it turns out, was a preoccupation that runs like a seam through Marx's oeuvre. It was the source of some of his most blistering prose; it would also motivate his most profound doubts.

The case of the Jews illustrated the plight of self-estrangement. The bourgeois era put Jews in a spot: political and civic rights were still denied while their financial power, tied to banking and commerce, was on the rise. The dilemma of a people that were publicly excluded while privately ascending was disturbing enough; what rankled Marx was Jews' profiting as capitalist "hucksters" while obeying old lifeways. It was the worst fusion imaginable, a kind of double alienation: godless reverence of money mixed with godly backwardness.

"On the Jewish Question" (1844) and its awful passages about Jewish backwardness and opportunism would later become a touchstone for Stalin's crusade against "rootless cosmopolitans." But often forgotten is how Marx insisted that Jews should not have to renounce their faith as a condition for political emancipation. The question for him was: Could pariahs ever be fully emancipated as humans while holding on to their community ways? If at times he answered with unambiguous certainty—no—there was more going on. As feudal enclosures and walled cities gave way to industrial societies, "On the Jewish Question" addressed the fate of people consigned to a partial and unfair place in the flow of history. For many, community was the way to handle and resist the risks, not to say ruin, of capitalism.

Marx was always more attentive to this ambiguity than the certainty seekers would ever admit. His early radical idealism probed different ways of imagining how a "communal nature of man" might emerge from the "interdependence of civil society." It also strove to avoid basic deterministic ways of thinking. Stedman Jones portrays a Marx yearning to reconcile idealism and materialism, "incorporating nature and mind without assigning primacy to one or the other." The posthumous campaign to make him the author of a "materialist theory of history" has had to either erase all of this early style or wave it off as immature speculation.

In Stedman Jones's view, Marx carried these traits forward. Trying to reconcile dichotomies, thinking about freedom as more than deliverance from necessity, insisting that humans were social creatures with a deep need to belong—these became substrata of his thinking. But by 1844 Marx was turning to a new source of viewing the world: political economy. Marx's concern shifted from consciousness of the mind to human activity.

Fighting Words

Turning to political economy also directed Marx away from a boring academic existence and toward his lifelong career as a journalist. It was as a journalist that the pariah became an exile.

In the short-lived *Rheinische Zeitung,* Marx and his pals published some scabrous articles about religion and the pietistic hypocrisies of the Russian tsar, who stood in as an icon of fanatical despotism. Under pressure from St. Petersburg and uneasy about where all this inflammatory talk was going, the Prussian government shut down the paper and drove its last editor, Marx, into exile. He moved to Paris, where he lasted for about a year, until he got driven out again, this time to Brussels. It was there that he would team up with Engels and write the book that would make him the sage of revolution that we now know—*The Manifesto of the Communist Party.* (It was originally titled, just to remind us of the enduring appeal of spiritual imagery, "communist confession of faith.")

After that, the Belgians threw him out. Marx went briefly to Cologne, to resume his editorship of another newspaper. That lasted a year, until the Prussian government sent him packing again. He went back to Paris for a few months, only to become a persona non grata there once more, and then finally to England, where he would settle down—though he was always denied citizenship and would live out his years as a stateless denizen, not

unlike his parents' parents. It was in these pinball years that religion ceased to be his obsession, making way for the "bourgeois
system." Industry, factory life, smokestacks, money men: a whole
new set of props and a new cast of characters took Marx's literary
stage. For all his curiosity, he developed some striking blind spots.
As Stedman Jones makes clear, there was little about the events of
the late 1840s and early 1850s that Marx got right. He read the
events of 1848 through the prism of 1789 and a fantasy about
revolution.

One of those realities was the beginnings of mass consumption.
Another was the rise of free trade. In an insight that had zero effect
on either of them, Engels wrote to Marx from Manchester that "the
free traders here are exploiting the prosperity or semi-prosperity
to buy the proletariat."[3] Among the even more important shifts,
according to Stedman Jones, were the democratization of the state,
the rise of electoralism, and the formation of competitive party
systems that enlivened political life. While Marx and his followers decried the falsehoods of ballot casting and treated elections
as shambolic ceremonies, they missed completely the significance
of the political process and its consequences for the alienated.
Marx's was "a static and anachronistic picture," Stedman Jones
concludes. Marx labored to understand the political and economic
forces behind Europe's upheavals, to the point of misunderstanding them completely.

This had enormous consequences for his leadership in the fledgling communist movement; Marx never reckoned with the
importance of making alliances and coalitions, skills fundamental to democratic politics. The result was some spectacular swinging from optimism and euphoria to desolation and despair, followed by finger-pointing among revolutionary factions.

And yet Marx was on to something. Being an exiled journalist
for a newspaper in another country gave him a perch that few

others had or chose to occupy. Marx became a reporter of the world; he poured his sarcasm and his relentless drive to connect disparate events into a regular stream of articles. All the while, information about the world poured into London. In 1851, a submarine cable linked Dover to Calais. The Atlantic got cabled in 1858. Just before then, as the Crimean War raged, the Channel Cable Company laid a cable from the British military headquarters at Balaklava on the Crimean Peninsula to Bulgaria. The frenzy of anti-Russian reporting reached its acme in the pages of the *London Illustrated News*, only reinforcing Marx's die-hard Russophobia. Marx lapped all this up, at a moment in which London was the hub of not just finance and trade but also news and information.

Marx must have known that this was a gold mine. Exploiting it led to some profound insights into global economic integration. For all his political blind spots, the stateless journalist wrote some perceptive essays about the world economy as it was coming into being, the role of finance capital in the fall of the East India Company, the influence of free trade in the Taiping Rebellion. He also recycled some of his notorious biases, especially in his views of the "Hindoostan" peasantry and what he thought was the impending crisis of the Russian aristocracy (in fact, the Russian empire was expanding at a clip that rivaled the United States and struck fear into the heart of Lord Palmerston's paranoid ministry).

Globalization and *Das Kapital*

As a global interpreter, Marx saw the need for a new kind of political economy, one that could explain not just the rise of industrialism and bourgeois society but its expansion and growth. It was not just that capitalism (a word coined by Louis Blanc and

Pierre-Joseph Proudhon and used rarely by Marx himself) was replacing earlier "systems." It was that it had an unbridled ability to grow and absorb. It went global—which called for a different sort of theory than *The Communist Manifesto*'s self-assured "stagism," which predicted that socialism would eclipse capitalism as surely as capitalism eviscerated feudalism. From the Crimean War until early 1868, explaining global growth became Marx's mission. From that came *A Contribution to the Critique of Political Economy* (1859) and, eight years later, *Das Kapital*.

Seen over the long arc of Marx's lifework, this was a relatively short, furtive, and anxiety-ridden moment. But it had lasting consequences for how Marx would be remembered. In fact, much of what he wrote is now forgotten or consigned to misty debates between insiders about what Marx actually meant. In my collegiate days, many hours were spent poring over Marx's syntax, searching for clues to the mystery of the real Röckle's prose. When I arrived at Oxford as a graduate student in the mid-1980s, Gerald Cohen was streamlining Marx's theory of history as a story about the growth of productive power. Jon Elster made a valiant effort to bring some clarity to our exuberant debates with *Making Sense of Marx* (1985), with the premise that it *could* make basic sense—if we could only purge Marx of his Hegelianisms and replace them with the elegance of methodological individualism. The irony, of course, was that while we debated the cleansing virtues of "analytical Marxism"—a.k.a. "no-bullshit Marxism"—real world actors were tearing down the remnants of Bolshevism, which left us puzzled: Was there anything left of Marxism but bullshit?

But two pieces from this moment of Marx's life stand out. The first is his preface to the *Critique*, which begins, as Stedman Jones notes, with one of the most cited passages in the Marxist canon: "The mode of production of material life conditions the general process of social, political and intellectual life. It is not the consciousness of men that determines their existence, but their social existence that determines their consciousness." Ever since, Marxists have agonized over the meaning of that choice of cryptic verbs. What does it mean "to condition?" What does "determine" do? Stedman Jones, whose career has illuminated the power of language and rhetoric in class consciousness, finds in this passage a lot of muddled thinking and, thus, misguided politics about collective action and social change.

The second was his "fat book." But *Das Kapital* made things even murkier by tangling the reader up in tortuous formulae about how money turns into capital, from C-M-C to M-C-M (with *C* as code for commodities and *M* for money). Plugging the formulae into big theories of History turned the passage of time into a wind-up toy marching down the capitalist road to some apotheosis.

Ironically, while witnessing the global power of markets and wanting to create a "theory" (or "critique") of what was going on, Marx was more successful, as Stedman Jones observes, "precisely in the area for which he affected to have least regard." His worldly writings connected capitalism's historical roots in the rise of industrial production and the emergence of finance capital to its international spread and globalized resistance. He was better, Stedman Jones argues, at sketching the contours of an economic system's global history than he was at managing his crystal ball. Marx may well be the first global historian, a finer diagnostician of the past than a prophet of the future.

What Happened to the Real Marx?

No wonder Marxists cornered themselves. They sought a theory of revolutions drawn from a work that was born when capitalism was going through one of its growth pains rather than suffering from a death spiral. The habit of confusing transitions with collapses became a stubborn habit; Marxists have made careers out of predicting free falls that never happened.

For this, Marx is partly to blame. In the preface to the *Critique*, notes Stedman Jones, Marx "appeared to open himself up to a much more determinist view of man than had been evident before." For starters, there was no politics; matters of state were left for *Das Kapital*. Then, when he turned to his "fat book," some of the vital pieces got kicked down the road—to future volumes he would leave to Engels to remake into a version of what the latter thought Marxism should be after Marx.

Marx knew that *Das Kapital* was unable to realize its explanatory ambition. It was weakest on the matters about which Marx had been agonizing since the late 1830s: group consciousness and community membership. But he kept this to himself. Instead, he receded and let Engels to do more and more of the talking—and publishing. Why? Stedman Jones points to a number of reasons. Tired of his ranting about reactionaries in France and Russia, the editors of the *New York Daily Tribune* cut him off. This made Marx even more dependent on Engels's subsidies.

There was also a political problem, which was never Marx's strong suit. Populists were better at inspiring the masses than communists; nationalism, not internationalism, was gaining ground. Tussy was among the millions who swooned when Garibaldimania swept Britain in 1864. Then the movement upon which Marx pinned so much hope, the Paris Commune, ended in horrible bloodshed. There were also the bruising duels with another exile, Mikhail Bakunin, the Russian firebrand and Marx's truest rival for the spiritual leadership of radicalism, whose finger was better placed on the pulse of popular politics. It was Bakunin who warned against the authoritarian strain within the communist movement.

During the 1870s, Marx wrote a lot but published little. In public, he "was prepared to allow Engels to act for him," notes Stedman Jones, which only widened the gap between an ambivalent Marx and certainty-seeking Marxists.

The final chapters of *Karl Marx* are not only essential readings in global intellectual history. They also reveal just how much Marx was pulling away from class struggle as a "nature-driven necessity" and returning to themes of an earlier age, when he wondered about humans as social creatures seeking recognition and membership. But all this Marx kept to himself. The idea of Marx's fascination with Darwin and evolutionary thinking, for instance, is a myth peddled by Engels. Marx was "respectful of" Darwin but not "excited by" him, Stedman Jones tells us.

What did excite Marx, by contrast, was news of village life, German primeval *Mark* (feudal community), Henry Maine's work on ancient law, and, most surprisingly of all, studies of Russian peasant communities and the Slavic popular spirit as captured by Nikolai Chernyshevsky. For years, Marx had disparaged primitive accumulation and the "idiocy of rural life" (as he was famously translated in *The Communist Manifesto*—though there is a debate about whether Marx meant *isolation*, not *idiocy*) as despotic, explaining in part his disdain for almost anything Russian. Captivated by ethnographies and early world history and struck by the populist appeals of rural communities fighting to resist capitalist development, Marx filled his notebooks after 1873 with musings about alternative collective responses to globalized capital.

He later tried to erase the tracks of some of the views of capitalism he had offered as the general leading the *marche generale*. In the first edition of *Das Kapital* (1867), there is a famous line in the preface: "The country that is more developed industrially only shows, to the less developed, the image of its own future!" The exclamation mark leaves little room for doubt about Marx's original certainty. In the second German edition, of 1873, the exclamation mark is gone. In the French translation of 1875, in chapter 26, on "The Secret of Primitive Accumulation," Marx tinkered with the prose to imply that the dispossession of the English peasantry might spread only to some parts of Western Europe. Private letters reveal Marx admitting that people didn't all have to go through the same sausage maker. The would-be poet forged in a pre-1848 world of classical literature, ancient mythology, and idealism turned to anthropologists, ethnographers, and studies of communitarian outposts to imagine free people resisting the homogenizing machinery of capitalism. In his last and largely forgotten writings, Marx saluted the American anthropologist and student of Iroquois villages, Lewis Henry Morgan, for anticipating "the revival, in a higher form, of the liberty, equality and fraternity of the ancient gentes."

Everyone remembers this line in the first chapter of *The Communist Manifesto*: "All that is solid melts into air, all that is holy is profaned, and man is at last compelled to face with sober senses his real conditions of life, and his relations with his kind." Meant to evoke the ways in which the bourgeoisie was turning all aspects of social life into the commodity form, it is one of the most haloed lines in modern "theory." What's often forgotten is the line before it: "All fixed, fast-frozen relations, with their train of ancient and venerable prejudices and opinions, are swept away, all new-formed ones become antiquated before they can ossify."

A quarter century after it was written, Marx must have wished he could take it back. As he grew increasingly ill, and with Jenny's death in late 1881, whatever faith he had in the *marche generale* gave way to a fascination with forces he had once denounced: gods, myths, and efforts to humanize nature—quietly forsaking the assumption about inevitable dehumanization.

Remembering Marx

While Jenny was dying, Marx wrote a letter to the Russian Group for the Emancipation of Labour in Geneva on the question: Was communal property good? Stedman Jones ends *Karl Marx* with a story about the fate of these pages. Many years after Marx penned them, the first editor of the *Marx-Engels-Gesamtausgabe*, the largest collection of the works of Marx and Engels in any language, David Riazanov (who would later perish in Stalin's purges) was curious: did any of the Russian exiles receive the letter? He went to the survivors, including Plekhanov. They all said no. And yet Riazanov could recall, having passed through Geneva in 1883, that there had been an exchange. There was even talk of a charged confrontation between Plekhanov and Marx, with Marx defending village communal property. The letter disappeared into the voluminous papers of the Russian Menshevik Pavel Axelrod, denied and forgotten, and only turned up in 1923 thanks to Riazanov's sleuthing. Riazanov was left to wonder about the "extraordinary deficiencies of the mechanisms of our memory."

Was it just forgetting? As an orthodox, self-described Marxist movement was bolting its fortunes to urban workers and the imminent collapse of capitalism, the airing of Marx's last thoughts would have been trouble, threatening an already fragile group. Stedman Jones implies that the followers covered up the divide between Marx and Marxists instead of accepting that History could not be so easily mastered. The cover has now been lifted. Separated from the *ism* attached to his name, the Marx that Stedman Jones wants us to remember is a man more aware of his limits than most of his followers; for all Marx's bravura, this portrait admits more room for doubt.

Doubt is not a word that comes to mind when we picture Marx, much less Marxists. Are we being reintroduced to an ambivalent Marx for a skeptical age? Since it has generally been the Right, not the Left, that has successfully mobilized discontent, the portrait of a doubtful Marx is fitting for a Left that must once again find its coordinates. Marx the doubter, the rethinker, the worrier may have more to say in our uncertain global times than does just a voice of conviction from another, forgettable, age.

NOTES

1. Francis Wheen, *Karl Marx: A Life* (New York: Norton, 2001); Jonathan Sperber, *Karl Marx: A Nineteenth-Century Life* (New York: Liveright, 2013).
2. From late November 1877, translated from the French by Donna Torr, in *Marx and Engels Correspondence* (New York: International Publishers, 1968).
3. Tristram Hunt, *Marx's General: The Revolutionary Life of Friedrich Engels* (New York: Metropolitan, 2009), 185.

WHO SEGREGATED AMERICA?

DESTIN JENKINS

R ecently long-listed for the National Book Award for nonfiction, Richard Rothstein's *The Color of Law* is an accessible and powerful account of how metropolitan America became racially segregated during the twentieth century. Rothstein contends that whenever the government recognized, certified, protected, tolerated, supported, or ignored discriminatory practices—by money lenders, private businesses, tax-exempt institutions, or housing developers—it effectively produced and reproduced racial segregation.

But Rothstein doesn't convincingly explain *why* the government remained committed to racial residential segregation for decades. If government was the tool by which segregation was created, who—or what—was the hand that wielded it?

Curiously, *The Color of Law* ignores the obvious answer: capitalism. The book's focus on law and policy shifts attention away from surplus value and patterns of extraction and exploitation, instead of focusing on these dynamics as an integral part of America's democratic, law-making system. We might well view residential segregation as the domestic expression of the racial capitalism of the twentieth century.[1]

Viewing residential segregation as a pivotal chapter in the global history of racial capitalism permits—indeed, demands—a critique of government policy and the state more generally. This perspective recasts the "private" as more than individual choice, belief, and action, allowing us to explore the racial character of the relationship between the state and private capital. It also forces us to attend to what that relationship meant to real estate agents, white homeowners, local law enforcement, black public-housing tenants, and insurance-company executives.[2] With government as the vehicle and capitalism in the driver seat, suddenly the racial segregation of the past century makes dreadful sense.

▪ ▪ ▪

Rothstein claims that the role of government in residential segregation has been "forgotten." If in the 1970s "the truth of *de jure* segregation was well known," today, he laments, "we have suppressed our historical memory." Although government complicity in producing racial segregation across the United States might be forgotten by some, a deep roster of urban historians has certainly told it.[3] Hip-hop is littered with similar accounts that attribute inequality to the government. As Rakim declared in the 1992 song "What's Going On?":

> My neighborhood don't look so good
> I'll find a way out . . . yeah, I would if I could,
> But the government is doing a project . . .
> So I live in the projects.

Indeed, we might ask, of both Rakim and Rothstein, what is the ideological work achieved through pinning inequality solely on government?

In *The Color of Law,* "government" becomes a neat container, a broad catchall term. All told, Rothstein argues that up until 1975 or so, "racially explicit policies of federal, state, and local governments" were deliberately, systemically, and forcefully designed to segregate black from white. We learn that the Federal Housing Administration (FHA) was the national amplifier of previously *local* racial zoning ordinances and restrictive covenants. Through the nation's public-housing program, moreover, local and federal governments purposefully sought "to herd African Americans into urban ghettos."

His argument rests on a contrast between private action and "government" action. In this narrow schema, antiblack racism articulated by white families and real estate agents, the purportedly objective language of risk used by bankers to deny African Americans mortgages, and the supposed cultural preferences of black Americans all fall into the category of "private practices," only "a small part" of a more multifaceted and consequential government project.

However, emphasis on the government alone, much less on individual personalities and sheer expediency, does not adequately address the question of *why* the government segregated metropolitan America. Government policies were essential to residential segregation, but largely because it chiefly relied on a crucial phase of American racial capitalism.

The racial capitalism of the twentieth century was partially founded upon contractual restrictions and public-private partnerships, both of which were permeated through and through, to paraphrase Cedric J. Robinson, by racialism.[4] The racial capitalism that underlay residential segregation was expressed at two levels.

The first was at the level of ideas, specifically, ideas concerning the asset values of blackness and whiteness. During the 1920s, the

National Association of Real Estate Boards published zoning manuals and circulated a code of ethics that instructed realtors to abide by the idea that different racial groups living together were "detrimental to property values," as Rothstein correctly notes. Scholar Jennifer S. Light has pointed to a concept of race that included nationality, but the association between blackness and lower property values remained a durable pattern of racial thought among government officials and real estate brokers.[5] Frederick Ecker, who led the Metropolitan Life Insurance Company for much of the twentieth century, felt ethics and zoning ordinances were insufficient: shared ethics should be supplemented by deed restrictions limiting sales to African Americans.

Ideas flowed between government and private capital. Amy E. Hillier has shown how the Home Owners' Loan Corporation (HOLC) built on the antecedent ideas of lenders and realtors to effectively institutionalize the "common practice" of refusing loans to areas with African Americans.[6] The remarkable "Mapping Inequality" project further reveals how HOLC recruited local real estate agents in the 1930s to create color-coded maps that graded neighborhoods to determine which areas were safe bets and least fit for housing loans.[7] Black people living in or near white neighborhoods were understood by FHA officials and real estate brokers as diminishing property values, a serious concern because white property owners who experienced diminished property values might increase the FHA's losses in the event of a default. FHA officials proclaimed that such decisions were objectively rooted in "the cold facts and the elements of risk," to quote one official.

But the agency either did not have the evidence to confirm the link between integration and property values or else ignored evidence that property values sometimes increased when black people moved into neighborhoods in transition.

That the ideas concerning blackness and property were similar among government officials and private capital can be attributed to the sort-of revolving door between government and the private sector. The federal government recruited developers and approved their loans to finance construction of racially segregated suburbs. During the 1940s, the FHA contracted with brokers to facilitate the resale of repossessed property—but only if they refused to sell to African Americans. By the early 1960s, Erle Cocke brought his experience as the former president of the American Bankers Association to bear on his role as chairman of the Federal Deposit Insurance Corporation. Speaking in defense of the asset value of whiteness, Cocke deemed it appropriate for federally insured banks to deny mortgages to upwardly mobile African Americans on the grounds that, as neighbors, their presence would diminish white property values.[8]

Where ideas concerning race and property were insufficiently implemented, law enforcement defended the asset value of whiteness. During World War II Culver City's air raid wardens went door to door to remind white suburbanites not to sell to African Americans and to seriously consider becoming party to racially restrictive covenants. The legal eclipse of restrictive covenants in the 1948 Supreme Court decision *Shelley v. Kraemer* meant that law enforcement would have to defend the asset value of whiteness through other means. Indeed, the late 1950s saw entanglements between local police, the FBI, and the U.S. attorney general. Together, they investigated how an African American teacher managed to move into the Elmwood district of Berkeley, California. When no crime could be conjured, the FHA did the policing work itself: it restricted the white owner who had rented the house to his African American colleague from obtaining government-insured mortgages in the future.

■ ■ ■

The second level at which racial capitalism was expressed was government guarantees. Relations between the state and private capital were not always cordial. During the 1940s, the real estate lobby fought intensely against public housing. Though it lost when Congress passed the Housing Act of 1949, providing for up to 810,000 additional public-housing units, the real estate lobby did win strict income restrictions on eligibility.

Those limits set in motion concurrent processes of racial capital accumulation. The real estate industry continued to provide homes for white middle-class Americans. Meanwhile, municipal bond financiers invested in racial inequality by purchasing and reselling debt tied to the construction and operation of public-housing projects. Many insurance companies also refused to issue mortgages in integrated neighborhoods, but as the major purchasers of public housing bonds, that refusal did not stop them from collecting tax-exempt interest income.

Segregation restricted housing options, a fact to which landlords responded by greedily overcharging African American tenants. As whites continued to move to the suburbs and African Americans searched for inner-city housing, landlords and absentee owners—crucially, white and black alike—fit African Americans like sardines into subdivided rental properties.[9] The racially inflected housing shortage allowed landlords to "wax fat off the poor," as San Francisco's leading African American newspaper put it in July of 1960.[10]

Real estate agents willing to sell homes at inflated prices on installment plans to African Americans profited from the exclusion of a precarious black middle-class from public housing projects and suburbia. Though lacking guarantees in a conventional sense, in the event that black owners missed a payment, contract sales ensured that brokers could seize the asset and repeat the process.

By midcentury, the nexus of racial ideology, state power, and private capital produced a vexing problem for municipal officials and property owners. Black people were seen as detrimental to white property values. The continued denial of housing opportunities to black people throughout American cities and suburbs often meant the spatial compartmentalization of poor, working-class, and middle-class African Americans in select corridors, often in close proximity to downtown business districts.

Urban renewal offered a solution: cities could use federal financial tools to clear out dense segregation. Absentee owners were promised fair market value as compensation for the expropriation of their blighted rental property, and the peddlers of debt profited from the monthly sales of bonds and short-term notes offered by redevelopment agencies from around the country. Indeed, what James Baldwin called "Negro removal" was profitable in more ways than one.

In short, codified protections for white homeowners betrayed the durable ideological belief that black people diminished white property values. Developers of, and lenders on, white suburban property were guaranteed against loss. Government guarantees for landlords, bankers, real estate brokers, wealthy individuals, and institutional investors made excluding African Americans from the single-family housing market safe and profitable.

Richard Rothstein concludes by answering a number of frequently asked questions, one of which concerns the case for reparations or, as he prefers it, "*remedies*." He hopes the book will help create "a national political consensus" on how segregation occurred, without which no remuneration is possible. He maintains that pinning segregation on the government might allow interest groups to build a legal argument to push governments to "adopt equally aggressive policies to desegregate." Remedies might include, but are not reducible to, monetary payments.

In these ways Rothstein goes further than journalist Ta-Nehisi Coates, who essentially conceives of reparations as a largely symbolic historical reckoning with the afterlives of slavery.[11] Still, Rothstein stops short of groups such as the Black Youth Project 100, which has called for budgetary line items at all levels of government "to include cash, land, and economic development," among other forms of payments for "generational oppression."[12] Rothstein proposes guarantees and subsidies to African Americans and calls for negating restrictive ordinances to improve black access to housing, education, and employment. There are differences in what reparations could look like, but undergirding the case is the assertion that the government is guilty and must pick up the tab.

■ ■ ■

And yet the prevailing discussion around reparations drives home the limits of blaming government and excluding capitalism from accounts of residential segregation. We might reasonably resist the gravitational pull of analyzing reparations in monetary terms, but to the extent that reparations take the form of government expenditures, we should reckon with how the government would generate enough revenue to finance those expenditures. Governments do so by taxing and borrowing. However, recent work by Sandy Brian Hager has shown how the 1 Percent has waged a successful tax revolt since the 1980s. Moreover, the federal government perpetually borrows at a time when debt is perceived as bad and austerity the antidote.[13]

If government is responsible for funding reparations, who would ultimately pay for it? When the rapper Nas mused in the song "Black Zombie," "We run and we ask for reparations, then they hit us with tax," he brilliantly implied that poor, working class, and middle-class African Americans might be the ones paying for their own reparations.

The point is not to let government off the hook. Instead, we might learn from groups like the Reparations at UChicago Working Group who have demonstrated the direct links between slavery and private institutions.[14]

As part of the case for reparations, we might ask which mortgage banks, nonprofit trade organizations, and insurance companies demonstrably profited from segregating America? Which corporate descendants denied black applicants? Which tax-exempt private institutions actually promoted segregation and bankrolled the defense of restrictive covenants? To obviate regressive compensation and working-class rage among non–African Americans, those serious about securing reparations as redress for residential segregation might first locate this history in the annals of racial capitalism.

NOTES

1. Cedric J. Robinson establishes the indispensable interpretation of the intertwined processes of race and capital in *Black Marxism: The Making of the Black Radical Tradition* (Chapel Hill: University of North Carolina Press, 2000). Capital does not accumulate without relations of racial inequality and, as historian Peter James Hudson has recently explained, racism is "contingent on the shifting regimes of capital accumulation." See Hudson, "Racial Capitalism and the Dark Proletariat," in "Forum I: Race, Capitalism, Justice," special issue, *Boston Review*, January 13, 2017.

2. The outlines of such an approach can be found in Walter Johnson, "To Remake the World: Slavery, Racial Capitalism, and Justice," in "Forum I: Race, Capitalism, Justice," special issue, *Boston Review*, January 13, 2017.

3. There are too many outstanding works to cite, but to start see Thomas J. Sugrue, *The Origins of the Urban Crisis: Race and Inequality in Postwar Detroit* (Princeton, NJ: Princeton University Press, 1996).

4. Robinson, *Black Marxism*, 2.

5. Jennifer S. Light, "Nationality and Neighborhood Risk at the Origins of FHA Underwriting," *Journal of Urban History* 36, no. 5 (2010): 634–71.

6. Amy E. Hillier, "Redlining and The Home Owners' Loan Corporation," *Journal of Urban History* 29, no. 4 (2003): 396–98; Paige Glotzer, "Exclusion in Arcadia: How Developers Circulated Ideas About Discrimination, 1890–1950," *Journal of Urban History* 41, no. 3 (2015): 479–94.

7. Robert K. Nelson, LaDale Winling, Richard Marciano, Nathan Connolly, et al., "Mapping Inequality: Redlining in New Deal America," *American Panorama: An Atlas of United States History*, ed. Robert K. Nelson and Edward L. Ayers, https://dsl.richmond.edu/panorama/redlining/ (accessed August 28, 2017).

8. "Erle Cocke Sr., Headed FDIC, American Bankers," *Washington Post*, October 9, 1977, https://www.washingtonpost.com/archive/local/1977/10/09/erle-cocke-sr-headed-fdic-american-bankers/732c7fa8-32b9-401a-b861-dfb4c59c166a/.

9. N. D. B. Connolly, *A World More Concrete: Real Estate and the Remaking of Jim Crow South Florida* (Chicago: University of Chicago Press, 2014), 163–80.

10. "Goodbye Slums, Hello Corruption," *San Francisco Sun-Reporter*, July 23, 1960.

11. Ta-Nehisi Coates, "The Case for Reparations," *The Atlantic*, June 2014.

12. Black Youth Project 100 (BYP100), "Agenda to Build Black Futures," 13–17.

13. Sandy Brian Hager, *Public Debt, Inequality, and Power: The Making of a Modern Debt State* (Berkeley: University of California Press, 2016), 6–7.

14. Caine Jordan, Guy Emerson Mount, Kai Parker, "A Case for Reparations at the University of Chicago," *Black Perspectives*, May 22, 2017, http://www.aaihs.org/a-case-for-reparations-at-the-university-of-chicago/.

THE INVENTION OF THE "WHITE WORKING CLASS"

ANDREW J. PERRIN

A s liberals came to terms with what happened on Election Day 2016, early press reports focused on the so-called white working class (WWC). We'd seen these folks highlighted at Trump rallies; Trump himself valorized them as real Americans, ignored by the powers that be, forgotten by establishment politicians more concerned with social issues than bread-and-butter working-class jobs. On November 8, it seemed, these "real Americans" had tipped the Electoral College to an unexpected Trump victory. More recent analysis suggests the WWC's role was less pivotal than all that, but the narrative has remained consistent.

The victorious candidate and commentators alike cast the election as the revenge of real America: the return of the repressed "Joe the Plumber." But who are the members of the WWC? What do they believe? How can they be at once so familiar—the "real" America—yet so distant that their political choices come as a shock?

Who makes up the WWC and what makes them tick is the subject of at least six popular books—most written before the election of Trump, some after. In each, the author tells readers that unraveling the mystery of this group is essential to understanding the populist movement that gave rise to Trump's candidacy and presidency. They imply, if not overtly say, that there is a single WWC culture and character, monolithic and unchanging. But the WWC is neither, and by treating it that way these books at once miss the diversity within the WWC and reinforce the myth that the WWC is more authentically American than the rest of the country.

The key move a populist such as Trump must make to succeed is to split one group of Americans off from the others, glorifying that group as more "real," more "true" than the rest of the populace. This is a point political scientist Jan-Werner Müller makes in his recent book, *What Is Populism?* Seen in this light, the Trump campaign was, in an important sense, an extended exercise in creating and valorizing the WWC at the expense of all others. Every person who isn't part of the WWC is presumed to be less American while the WWC is the favored group: made up of real Americans, living in "flyover country," distant from coastal elites, victimized by political correctness, and the only ones left behind by globalization, experiencing falling wages and rising economic insecurity.

Once he pulls that off—prioritizing one "real" slice of the populace above the whole, transforming this slice into the whole—Müller's populist can use that group to build power. And, crucially, the power will be in the name of "the people," though this is a rhetorical sleight of hand. In the process, the populist sets whole segments of the people off to the side as unworthy of representation or, at least, of as much representation as the chosen group. Populists, Müller teaches us, rule in the name of the people by promoting only *some* of the people to sovereign status. Those outside are treated as not fully part of the people. They are not sufficiently authentic.

We've been here before. Writing in the aftermath of World War II, the German philosopher and sociologist Theodor W. Adorno diagnosed what he called a "jargon of authenticity" in German culture. Shallow claims to authenticity were weaponized as justifications in and of themselves for otherwise inexcusable or unexamined ways of thinking, talking, relating, and behaving. Faced with the struggle and conflict of the modern world, authenticity was not so much found as strategically *deployed*. Jews, cities, "sinful intellectuality" were all deemed inauthentic, and as a result the jargon could serve to provide people with substitute templates that would reflect it instead of their real character: it would offer "patterns for being human . . . which have been driven out of them" and a mode of "reflected unreflectiveness."

The similarities are eerie: Adorno identifies German authenticity language as "a trademark of societalized chosenness, *noble and homey at once—sub-language as superior language.* . . . While the jargon overflows with the pretense of deep human emotion, it is just as standardized as the world that it officially negates." Then as now, the simple and old-fashioned—the "authentic," the "real"—are held up as noble and timeless, in contrast to the soulless, dangerous, diverse complexity of the modern city. The jargon that Adorno identifies is a fake authenticity imposed from outside. Culturally conservative, rural, pure character is a product of the jargon, which people are led to accept as authentic. Importantly, these are the same traits the authors of the books reviewed here ascribe to the WWC, thereby forming their own jargon of authenticity.

Many liberals, shocked and dismayed by the 2016 election, also seemed to understand the populist revolt in this way. How did it happen that "authentic" Americans—working-class ones, even— were so pivotal to the success of the divisive Republican campaign of a multibillionaire? How to understand this exotic culture next door? These six books try to answer that question, and in the process reify the WWC's authenticity.

The most recent among them is Joan C. Williams's aptly titled *White Working Class*, which is an expanded version of an essay she addressed to urban, liberal elites. Williams, a law professor at the University of California Hastings College of the Law, in San Francisco, acts here as more of an anthropologist. A self-described "silver spoon girl," she claims direct knowledge through her marriage to a bona fide "class migrant"—someone who moves between the working class and the wealthy—a position that recurs in several of the other books as well. Working from the premise that the 2016 election was about "populist, anti-establishment anger that welled up," she presents a caricature—a sympathetic one, to be sure, but still a caricature—of working-class views, values, and experiences.

Consider the imagery here: something that "wells up" was previously lying dormant but essentially the same. Perhaps it had been building natural pressure or just waiting for an opening to erupt. The anger must have been there all along, lying in wait for a sympathetic candidate to provide opportunity for its expression. The implication is that the properties of the thing welling up (in this case, the WWC's antiestablishment anger) are fixed, not subject to change. That's why it takes a class migrant—someone with personal experience on both sides of the divide—to certify the authenticity of those on the other side.

Williams's motives go beyond electoral strategy; she is explicitly "committed to social equality, not for some groups but for all," and is convinced that the working class (the "white" modifier mostly disappears after the title page, its conspicuous absence suggesting that Williams has written off the rest of the working class) is socially excluded, even insulted by the professional class. It's certainly true that the working class is *economically* excluded; wages have stagnated for nearly two decades and productivity gains have gone entirely to employers and stockholders, as have nearly all the benefits (though not the costs) of globalization. But, by and large, that's not what this book (nor the others reviewed here) is about. Rather, it is about what political theorists call *recognition*, not redistribution: "The working class . . . want[s] respect,. . . recognition,. . . dignity—and they deserve it," Williams writes. That desire for recognition is, apparently, what's welling up.

■ ■ ■

Such images—of the WWC as unified, honorable, genuine, and grounded but scorned and excluded by educated elites—run through several of these other books too. And that, of course, is the problem. Indeed, Williams draws heavily upon two of these texts, Arlie Russell Hochschild's *Strangers in Their Own Land* and J. D. Vance's *Hillbilly Elegy*, as evidence for her own argument. The way she uses them, as confirmation of the essential deep character of the WWC, suggests a kind of closing of the ranks. It's as if this small group of observers—who have successfully migrated across class boundaries in one way or another—share privileged access to the exotic tribe that lives next door. The figure of the class migrant is a critical part of establishing these books' claims to document the authentic WWC to outsiders and thus serves to reinforce the idea of that authenticity.

Hillbilly is a politically motivated memoir—heartwarming if, ultimately, unremarkable—of Silicon Valley finance lawyer J. D. Vance, another class migrant. Vance recounts his upbringing among "hillbillies" of Kentucky and Ohio. He credits his rags-to-riches experience to a unique combination of adoring grandparents, personal optimism, and military discipline.

Throughout the book, Vance presents a tale of two cultures: one, the Appalachian, authentic, rooted, poor, and unambitious; the other, the "Acela corridor," fancy, out of touch, rich, and ambitious. Crossings between the two are few and far between; periodically, an Appalachian kid escapes for college (good, but the kid should beware the lure of college's corrupting influences). Frequently, the outside world steps in with welfare (bad, of course), other government programs (bad, too), educational resources (you guessed it, bad), all of which serve mostly to convince genuine Appalachian folks not to work hard enough to actually succeed.

Vance, though, elevated himself through effort and optimism, joining the marines on little more than a whim then taking the self-discipline learned there with him to college at Ohio State and law school at Yale, all the while feeling utterly culturally alienated by the high-status world he'd entered. A compelling story, to be sure. Even authentic, from one class migrant's point of view. But hardly a definitive examination of WWC culture!

Vance's by-the-bootstraps theme plays contradictory roles in the narrative. Vance relies on it to be at once accessible and rare. The whole folksy description of the hopelessness of his hometown implies that it's difficult to escape Appalachia, hence, the vast cultural divide between where he grew up and the Acela corridor. It's that rarity that establishes Vance's authority as a class migrant. At the same time, though, he implies that if only others had sufficient discipline, optimism, and energy, they, too, could succeed as he has. He is nobody special; he is just a product of folksy discipline combined with his own personal optimism. The book's core argument can't stand without Vance being *both* rare and an everyman: a logical impossibility. And yet that's what he wants us to believe as he extrapolates from his admittedly extraordinary story a morality tale for the whole Appalachian region.

How does this extrapolation take place? How are we asked to move from Vance's own life out to an assured expertise in his native culture? Vance squares that circle by relying on the timeless, rooted authenticity of his people. They are who they are, the result of their Scots-Irish ancestry.[1] Since Vance claims, implausibly, that Appalachians are who they are *by nature*, the dysfunction he sneers at must be the result of outside influence: the very federal and state social and economic programs that provide needed support for the folks he grew up with.

Strangers in Their Own Land, the work of sociological giant Arlie Russell Hochschild, is in many ways very different from *Hillbilly*. But although it takes a different approach to identifying the authentic WWC, Hochschild's work shares the presumption of that authenticity. (Both books, remember, are used as insiders' evidence in Williams's *White Working Class*.) And yet this assumption threatens to undermine the success of both.

Hochschild seeks to "scale the empathy wall"—becoming, essentially, a temporary class migrant—to understand the lives and worldviews of rural white conservatives in southwestern Louisiana. Disturbed by the social divisiveness she saw in the Obama years, which, she argues, ultimately gave rise to Trump, Hochschild traveled to rural Louisiana, living among, interviewing, and, most importantly, listening to members of the WWC as they went about their lives, approached problems, and interpreted their experiences over the course of five years.

The area Hochschild investigated suffers from major environmental problems: the presence of toxic chemicals dumped in the bayou that kill wildlife, for example. And a giant sinkhole caused when a drilling company, relatively unfettered by regulation, punctured an underground geological formation. Why, then, did these WWC people—particularly harmed by and vulnerable to ecological disaster—so resist government environmental protections? The area also needs and benefits from federal programs to mitigate unemployment, poverty, and illness; why do its residents hold these very programs in such low esteem?

After hearing many of her subjects talk about the successes and failures of government—often in direct contradiction to their own previous claims—Hochschild synthesized their ideas into what she called the "Deep Story." According to that story, folks feel like they are in line for something. What that is seems unclear even to the people Hochschild talks to: Jobs? Education? Benefits? Money? Hochschild names it simply "the American Dream, the goal of everyone waiting in line."

As they wait, they feel that others are invited to jump in front of them: "You're following the rules. They aren't," as she summarizes the attitude. These others are, of course, African Americans, immigrants, women: all those whom they believe the government favors over them. Once she'd developed this story, Hochschild returned to her WWC sources to see if it reflected their views. It did; many of them saw themselves as trapped in a line for something better, waiting patiently as others were allowed to get ahead.

Strangers offers a contemporary vision of WWC people and voters learning from and reacting to current events, challenges, and media. But, paradoxically, it relates a story from nowhere. The identification of this story as "deep" (it is, of course, from the deep that things "well up") underscores its timelessness. But where did *this* story come from? What alternative stories were jettisoned in favor of this one? How does it distort the world (as all stories must)? How does believing in it, thinking with it, come to shape the taken-for-granted worldview of the WWC? What, in other words, is the jargon these WWC Americans adopt to claim authenticity, and where did it come from?

Hochschild scrupulously avoids addressing these questions. That's because for Hochschild (as for Williams and Vance), this is just how members of the WWC are. Becoming a temporary class migrant by scaling the empathy wall requires that we not ask uncomfortable questions about, for example, media, education, race, or wealth. The empathy Hochschild so admirably demonstrates (and that is a hallmark of her sociology more generally) backfires here because it obscures the tendentious political history of the deep story.

Political scientist Katherine J. Cramer also adopted temporary class-migrant status for her book, *The Politics of Resentment*. A professor at the University of Wisconsin–Madison, Cramer noticed a divide among her students between those from the state's urban and suburban centers and those from its vast, sparsely populated farmland. Like Hochschild, she ventured out to listen to WWC people talk about their lives and their relationships to government and politics.

What she discovered was "rural consciousness": the repeated idea that life is different—and more genuine, more authentic, more real—in rural areas. Cities like Madison and Milwaukee (her respondents call these the "M&Ms") are foreign: "We totally live differently than the city people live," says one subject. They imagine residents of the M&Ms as the line jumpers of Hochschild's deep story, people getting more attention and support from government than the pure, simple rural folks. We're tempted to ask, again, where these stories come from, but Cramer doesn't investigate further.

In fact, as Cramer points out, Wisconsin's rural areas receive disproportionately *more* state funding than urban areas, but so what? Rural folks are convinced the opposite is true or, at least (echoing *Hillbilly*), that this money is tainted by its association with the outside world. But her sources don't find that point convincing; rural consciousness, it seems, comes first, and political analysis follows from it. "Support for small government," Cramer argues, "is more about identity than principle."

Cramer names this feature "place identity," but as with Hochschild's Louisiana WWC, there's a strong temporal dimension as well. Rural consciousness depends on a wistful nostalgia for times past: a nostalgia short on specifics but one that is substituted for a real consideration of how rural consciousness and the WWC came to be as they are. Again, where is the source?

To fill that hole, we turn to historian Nancy Isenberg's *White Trash*, billed as a "history of class in America." *White Trash* sets out to retell American history through the lens of social class. Isenberg's entirely historical treatment is a step in the right direction: the category of white trash was *constructed* through repeated social, political, and cultural decisions that made the wall of social class seem impenetrable. The WWC as it existed in 2016, then, was fixed in time and culture by its own historical development.

The implication is that historians' recounting of inequality through the lens of race has obscured how social class formed and has driven American politics and culture since the founding of the republic. In that sense, the book is quite successful, demonstrating the ways in which wealth and income have structured not just life chances but also cultural identity and belonging.

As the book progresses into the twentieth century, it deals more and more with cultural representations of class—movies, television, etc.—and less with political and material inequalities. Class becomes, by the late twentieth century, mostly a matter of style, as Isenberg's discussion of Sarah Palin's daughter's pregnancy (relying on *Us Weekly* and the reality TV show *Sarah Palin's Alaska*) illustrates. This methodological shift implies that class has become culture and style: a misunderstanding that helps reinforce WWC authenticity.

The hard-and-fast distinction between class and race breaks down here at times, largely because the two have been so intertwined in practice. To understand "white trash" (and its many regional variations) as being mostly about the "trash" and not so much about the "white" is an odd choice for a book with such sweeping ambition. A new preface, added after the 2016 election, lays bare that choice: in it, Isenberg claims Trump's victory as the next step in the class-as-culture narrative, explicitly attaching the victory to the repressed reality of class in America.

By stressing this continuity, *White Trash* also contributes to the message of Hochschild, Vance, et al.: that WWC character exists as an independent phenomenon *and* that these authors offer a definitive portrayal of what the WWC character is like. Whether that character occurs because of Scots-Irish ethnicity in *Hillbilly*, the history of social class in *White Trash*, or just . . . because, as in *Strangers* and *Resentment*, these volumes are all invested in bolstering the WWC's authentic character.

What all these books—disparate as they are—share is their implication that WWC culture is fixed, static, and authentic: at once a cultural backwater cut off from urban and coastal progress and the noble expression of real America prior to the corrupting influence of, well, the twentieth century. A book that notably avoids that implication is the older, irreverent *Deer Hunting with Jesus*, by Joe Bageant.

A class migrant himself, Bageant returns to his hometown of Winchester, Virginia, to understand what has led to its residents' political conservatism and economic stagnation. He finds a town that has been left behind: manufacturing jobs are gone, national fast-food chains define the local diet, nationalized media provides the language the WWC uses to describe the world. Bageant offers a very sympathetic view of a proud people, duped into a comfortable stupor that is at once the product of corporate manipulation and of willing complicity on the part of the people themselves. *Deer Hunting* effectively, even sensitively conveys the sense of despair and loss of dignity in this community and locates the cause of these in patterns of national and global capital.

Bageant's Winchester is not so different from Vance's Jackson, Kentucky. Both authors grew up in poor, simple, honest, depressed towns. But in Bageant's hands it is a confluence of outside forces—economic fatalism; educational failure; cheap, unhealthy food; manipulative media—that have combined to make Winchester the miserable place it has become. This contrasts with Vance, for whom governmental programs at most exacerbate preexisting cultural dispositions.

Most importantly, that misery is not static but malleable. Take the case of Dot, a fifty-nine-year-old woman with many health problems. "Doctors tell us [Winchester residents] that we have blood in our cholesterol, and the cops tell us there is alcohol in that blood. True to our class, Dottie is disabled by heart trouble, diabetes, and several other diseases. Her blood pressure is so high the doctor thought the pressure device was broken."

Dot's neighbor, Buck, like most of their WWC compatriots, blames welfare bums, social programs for minorities, tax-and-spend liberals, and big government—but when Bageant asks Dot "if she would vote for a candidate who wanted a national health care program," she responds, "Vote for him? I'd go down on him!" "Voter approval does not get much stronger than that," Bageant opines. A Winchester resident like Dot lays blame on the government not so much because of her ideology as in response to "who she thought would actually help her."

Unlike the portrayals of the rest of these books, Bageant's WWC is dynamic and responsive to the world, even if those responses are disappointing. Driven by lack of educational opportunities, he writes, "my people . . . [have] an intellectual life consisting of things that sound right, a blend of modern folk wisdom, cliché, talk radio, and Christian radio babble." The other books ask readers to understand the WWC as essentially unchanging: authentically American, timeless, genuine, and static. That understanding plays directly into the populist move of elevating the WWC to be the authentic voice of real America, substituting its own American-ness for that of the rest of the country.

Bageant—writing over a decade ago!—offers a bleak picture, to be sure, but one based on television, petroleum, education, and economic opportunity. It is, therefore, susceptible to change. And that, in turn, means that the Trump project of elevating the WWC to privileged authenticity is a farce: a political maneuver resting on an empirical fiction.

There is, of course, nothing wrong with Acela corridor residents climbing the empathy wall, trying to understand better their fly-over compatriots. It is revealing, though, that each of these books aims to provide liberals with a sympathetic portrait of conserva-tives. In the context of a deeply polarized electorate, it is certainly helpful to cross political boundaries in the service of mutual understanding. But the traffic here is one-way; to my knowledge, there are no books offering earnest portraits of the Acela corridor to the residents of flyover country. Why not? Perhaps it's that lib-erals are more curious in general, more prone to guilt over not understanding their compatriots, or just bigger readers. But I think part of the explanation lies in the jargon of authenticity. To imag-ine red America as authentic is to label blue America inauthentic: fake, affected, an impostor. What would be the point of a class migrant explaining such people to the wholesome WWC?

The distinction between *Deer Hunting* and the books reviewed above throws into relief the danger of assigning authenticity or populist nobility to the WWC. That presumed WWC authentic-ity originated from somewhere—it's not actually fixed or static. Having voted, in the past, for Bill Clinton and for Barack Obama, the WWC's members were primed by the forces Bageant identi-fies, weaponized by economic desperation and media manipula-tion, and deployed by an opportunistic Trump campaign happy to trumpet their authenticity for its own electoral ends. The WWC was made, not found; deployed, not discovered.

Most people—members of the WWC and Acela liberals alike—hold contradictory views and ideas: fragments of experience, knowledge, and understanding they can use to interpret and respond to new situations as they come down the pike. Which of these fragments they piece together into an expression, an idea, a vote is not about static authenticity. It's about context, politics, threat, emotion, opportunity, connection, education. Grasping the WWC's role in American politics doesn't mean fetishizing their inner character; it means understanding what fragments are available to them and how new contexts, new campaigns, new environments lead them to piece them together into new, varied, and different stories.

This difference has huge implications. If the WWC is fixed and authentic, educated elites need to learn at least to compromise with its members. That could mean giving up some of the commitments to equality, diversity, and opportunity that these books imply alienate the flyover tribe. But if indeed it is dynamic, flexible, and responsive, that task is not compromise but engagement.

NOTE

1. The idea of a unified, meaningful "Appalachian culture," whether based on Scots-Irish ancestry or another origin, is an old saw. It's been repeatedly asserted and popularized by writers, filmmakers, and others since at least the nineteenth century. The academic literature shows that no such thing exists; the idea has been deployed, though, to describe, vilify, praise, and manipulate "Appalachia."

GOING DEEP

Baseball and Philosophy

KIERAN SETIYA

mong the iconic images that memorialize one of the greatest
moments in baseball history—Bill Mazeroski's walk-off home
run to win the 1960 World Series for the Pittsburgh Pirates—I
have a special fondness for George Silk's photograph for *Life* magazine. It shows a crowd of fans cheering over a blurry Forbes Field
from the balcony of the preposterous gothic skyscraper known as
the Cathedral of Learning. Built by the University of Pittsburgh,
the Cathedral houses the Philosophy Department, in which I
taught for thirteen years. I like to imagine the philosophers of 1960
watching baseball from its office windows, as I would have done
myself had Forbes Field not been replaced in 1970 by the concrete
cylinder of Three Rivers Stadium, itself replaced by beautiful PNC
Park in 2001.

It is not just imaginary philosophers who love baseball, and it
is not just me. The great John Rawls, who revolutionized political
philosophy, believed that "baseball is the best of all games" and
once recounted reasons why.[1] In 1982, Chicago philosopher Ted
Cohen expressed his love for the game by claiming to have found
a contradiction in the rules.[2] He petitioned the league to resolve
the matter, without immediate success. But the rules were silently
changed, removing the apparent inconsistency, in 2010.[3] Mark

Halfon, who teaches philosophy at Nassau Community College, has written two books about baseball, *Can A Dead Man Strike Out?* and *Tales from the Deadball Era*.[4] And now Mark Kingwell, a philosopher at the University of Toronto, has published *Fail Better*, which concludes, "Baseball is . . . the most philosophical of games." Finding improbable depths in the game of baseball has become an intellectual performance art. This review is my contribution.

Baseball is the most philosophical of games because, like philosophy at its best, it harmonizes meaning with meticulous analysis. There is no opposition between wonder at the double play, the home run, or the perfect game and the statistical dissection now known as "sabermetrics" (after SABR, the Society for American Baseball Research).[5] In fact, it is the arithmetic and geometry of the game that best disclose its truth. The highest aspiration of philosophy is to be both rigorous and humanistic, to place analytical thought in the service of human values. Baseball shows us that it can be done.

This is not what Kingwell claims in his wide-ranging book, a collection of philosophically inflected essays about the game. He writes well about his own experience as a player, his accidental baseball-card collection, the addictive qualities of watching games on television, and the magic of listening to them on the radio. But when he turns to the meaning of baseball, his principal theme is failure.

Most obvious: failure at the plate. Everyone knows that if you fail seven times out of ten to get on base with a hit—walks and struck-batsmen don't count, nor do sacrifices (bunt or fly)—you are a potential Hall of Fame hitter.

The idea that baseball is a game of failure is sufficiently commonplace now that you might think it has been around forever. It hasn't. As far as I can make out, the canonical source is MLB commissioner Fay Vincent's 1991 address, "Education and Baseball":

"Baseball teaches us, or has taught most of us, how to deal with failure. We learn at a very young age that failure is the norm in baseball and, precisely because we have failed, we hold in high regard those who fail less often—those who hit safely in one out of three chances and become star players."[6]

This thought was famously echoed in the opening monologue of Ken Burns's incomparable documentary series, *Baseball*: "And yet the men who fail seven times out of ten are considered the game's greatest heroes."[7] Pitcher R. A. Dickey makes the same point in his preface to Stacey May Fowles's new memoir, *Baseball Life Advice*: "In what other profession can you fail seven out of ten times and be a Hall of Famer!"

Commonplace or not, the idea is almost entirely wrong. To begin with, walks and hit-by-pitches count. Plate discipline is among the most valuable, reliable, and replicable skills a hitter can have. At most, you could say, the best hitters in the game fail six times out of ten, with an on-base average of .400. But even that is a grave distortion. It depends on the unit of analysis. What if we switch from the at-bat to baseball's atom, the individual pitch? In Major League Baseball, about 39 percent of pitches are thrown for balls: a win for the hitter, a loss for the pitcher. By my calculation, just over 6 percent of pitches end up base hits; the rest are foul balls, strikes, or outs.[8] So, on a given pitch, the *average* hitter, never mind the best, succeeds just over 45 percent of the time. Good hitters do better than that.

In any case, why look at things solely from the batter's point of view? Why doesn't Kingwell focus on the pitcher, and the seven at-bats in every ten in which the batter is out, declaring baseball a game of routine success? His approach reminds me of a friend who was so bored by his son's Little League games that he rooted for whoever was at the plate. (I wish I had been there to protest that every hit extends the game: he should have been rooting for the other team. I wish even more I could communicate to him base-ball's transformation of boredom into the stillness of unbearable suspense.)

These arguments illustrate my point: you can't divine the spir-itual significance of baseball without grasping its mathematics. If you get the math wrong, you miss the meaning. Leonardo da Vinci studied anatomy in order to paint the human figure. The inter-preter of baseball must study sabermetrics.

Kingwell is made anxious by this idea: "Can the free spirit of the game survive the noted fan obsession with the rigidity of sta-tistics and the 'money ball' approach, all of which seem to reduce poetry to mathematics?" What will happen when baseball is "dis-enchanted" in Max Weber's sense, when "we can in principle *con-trol everything by means of calculation.*"[9] What about the "intangibles"—grit, clutch hitting, "knowing how to win"—that are baseball's equivalent of magic?

It is true that baseball superstitions fade in the cold light of sabermetrics. The clutch hitter is a myth, debunked by meticulous studies, and hot streaks are statistical noise. But the disenchant-ment of scientific understanding does not entail disenchantment of another kind: loss of value or significance. Baseball means as much or more to the incorrigible stat-head as it does to anyone else.

No one should doubt that Keith Law—an ESPN analyst whose book, *Smart Baseball*, introduces readers to advanced statistical metrics—loves and appreciates the game every bit as much as Stacey May Fowles, who writes about her adoration for Adam Lind, Devon White, and David Price, and has a chapter that defends the baseball crush. Other chapters of her book devote informed, humane atten-tion to cheating, booing, and performance-enhancing drugs. Two themes recur: baseball's endemic sexism, which Fowles confronts with honesty and grace, and our intimate-distant relationship with individual players. On pitcher José Fernández, who died in a boating accident at the age of twenty-four: "There is no real road-map for dealing with the kind of inexplicable grief that comes with the death of someone we didn't know."

Keith Law's book is less emotionally charged but equally humane. He happily rejects the manufactured conflict between reductive number crunchers and old-fashioned scouts fostered by films such as *Moneyball*, with its infuriating portrayal of baseball scouts as ignorant hicks.[10] For Law, statistics don't extinguish meaning; they interpret it: "Every player's stat line tries to tell the story of his season, so if you want to get the story right, you have to use the right stats."

Law documents the failings of conventional statistics, such as pitcher wins, runs batted in (RBI), and saves and explains advanced statistics that are more revealing: weighted on-base average, fielding-independent pitching, ultimate zone rating (a measure of fielding ability). He predicts a future in which teams exploit the almost unfathomable wealth of data supplied by PITCHf/x and Statcast, which track velocity, break, and location for pitches, exit velocity and angle for hits, positioning, reaction time, and route for fielders, and more.

Law is less reliable when it comes to history. He blames flawed statistics on baseball's reverence for tradition, with its consequent inertia, tracing the problem all the way back to Henry Chadwick, "the father of baseball": "Henry Chadwick is credited with creating batting average (among many other common baseball stats) in the late 1800s, designing it along the lines of cricket's version of batting average, which is runs divided by outs."

Because batting average ignores both walks and extra-base hits, it is a poor gauge of offensive contribution, and there is no doubt it has been overemphasized. But the quotation above is multiply skewed. For one thing, Chadwick did not invent batting average: the blame for that must go to H. A. Dobson.[11] Nor does batting average follow the model of runs divided by outs in cricket, as Law suggests, since the latter incorporates the equivalent of extra bases. In fact, Chadwick originally focused not on batting average but on total bases per game, which is much closer to modern slugging percentage (bases on hits divided by at-bats) but improves on that statistic by including walks. Law should be singing Chadwick's praises.

Chadwick wasn't perfect. He was corrupted by batting average and seduced by the misguided RBI.[12] But he anticipated Law's perspective more than once. Take the fielding error, in which a fielder gets to the ball but is unable to make what would be, in the opinion of the official scorer, an expected play. Law is derisive about this: "The problem here is that you'd get an equally good measure of a player's fielding abilities if you rolled a pair of dice. Fielding percentage doesn't impart any useful information whatsoever." For Kingwell, errors are another way in which baseball is a game of failure: "In no other major sport is 'error' an official scoring category, feared and respected by fielders at every position." Again, he echoes Vincent: "Baseball, alone in sport, considers errors to be part of the game, part of its rigorous truth."[13]

But errors are to be feared only because they are a wildly misleading measure of fielding ability. Errors are the opposite of "rigorous," Law complains, since they rely on the subjective judgement of the scorer. Worse still, they victimize fielders whose greater range means that they attempt more difficult plays. In practice, errors are scored only for fumbling the ball, never for failing to reach it: "You can't mishandle a ball you never touch."

As Henry Chadwick argued in 1868, when we evaluate a fielder, "[it] is in the record of his *good plays* that we are to look for the most correct data for an estimate of skill."[14] Instead of errors, he tracked putouts plus assists per game, a statistic reinvented by sabermetric guru Bill James as "range factor," more than a hundred years later.[15] It is far from perfect, but it is a whole lot better than tracking rates of error, as in fielding percentage, or simply rolling dice. The lesson of Henry Chadwick is that, like philosophy, baseball is never done with its past. Everything old is new.

Some treat baseball as an allegory for life or for a perilous journey in which, if we are lucky, we make it safely home.[16] For me, it is an allegory for philosophy at its best: humanistic but rigorous, historically informed. We do not have to choose between humanity and rigor, between progress in solving problems and engagement with history. In fact, you can't have any of these without the others. Baseball's romance with advanced statistics is not a rejection of its past but a fulfillment, not an indifference to meaning but a better interpretation. That is a condition to which philosophy should aspire.

NOTES

1. I criticize Rawls's arguments here: http://ideasofimperfection.blogspot .com/2008/04/critique-of-rawls.html.

2. For the complete story, see here: https://philosophynow.org/issues/115 /The_Philosophy_Professor_and_The_Holy_Book_of_Baseball.

3. In fact, I don't believe the rules were inconsistent. According to Rule 6.05(j), "A batter is out when after a third strike or after he hits a fair ball, he or first base is tagged before he touches first base." According to Rule 7.08(e), "Any runner is out when he fails to reach the next base before a fielder tags him or the base, after he has been forced to advance by reason of the batter becoming a runner." According to Rule 6.09(a), "The batter becomes a runner when he hits a fair ball." See Ted Cohen, "There Are No Ties at First Base," *Yale Review* 79, no. 2 (October 1990): 316. If the runner touches first base just as it is tagged, the last two rules imply that he is out; the first rule does not. But silence is not contradiction. The rules would be inconsistent if Rule 6.05(j) said that the batter is out *only if* first base is tagged before he touches it, not if both things happen at the same

time. But it does not say that. A philosopher should mark the difference between *if* and *only if*.

4. Mark S. Halfon, *Can a Dead Man Strike Out? Offbeat Baseball Questions and Their Improbable Answers* (Solana Beach, CA: Santa Monica Press, 2005); Mark S. Halfon, *Tales from the Deadball Era: Ty Cobb, Home Run Baker, Shoeless Joe Jackson, and the Wildest Times in Baseball History* (Lincoln, NE: Potomac, 2014).

5. On the role of wonder in scientific discovery, see Philip Fisher, *Wonder, the Rainbow, and the Aesthetics of Rare Experiences* (Cambridge, MA: Harvard University Press, 2003).

6. Francis T. Vincent Jr., "Education and Baseball," *America* 64 (April 1991): 373.

7. *Baseball*, dir. Ken Burns (PBS, 1994).

8. Here are the numbers: 17.5 percent of pitches are foul balls, 9.5 percent are swinging strikes, 15 percent are called strikes, which leaves 19 percent batted balls. Thirty-five percent of batted balls are fly balls and just under 10 percent of fly balls are home runs, which comes to about 0.65 percent of pitches. The remaining batted balls are put in play. Since batting average on balls in play hovers around .300, 5.5 percent of pitches are put in play for hits. Hence the figure of just over 6 percent. The data come from baseball website Fangraphs (https://www.fangraphs.com).

9. Max Weber, "Science as a Vocation," in *The Vocation Lectures* (Cambridge, MA: Hackett, 2004), p. 13. For a serious attempt to make this argument about modern sports, see Allen Guttmann, *From Ritual to Record*(Columbia University Press, 1978), p. 55: "When we can no longer distinguish the sacred from the profane or even the good from the bad, we content ourselves with minute discriminations between the batting average of the .308 hitter and the .307 hitter." For a response, see A. Bartlett Giamatti, *Take Time for Paradise: Americans and Their Games* (Summit, 1989).

10. *Moneyball*, directed by Bennett Miller (Columbia Pictures, 2011). The original book by Michael Lewis, *Moneyball: The Art of Winning an Unfair Game* (New York: Norton, 2004), is less cartoonish but still seriously flawed. See Allen Barra, "The Many Problems With 'Moneyball,'" *The Atlantic*, September 27, 2011, https://www.theatlantic.com/entertainment/archive/2011/09/the-many-problems-with-moneyball/245769/.

11. My information about Henry Chadwick derives from chapter 1 of Allan Schwarz, *The Numbers Game: Baseball's Lifelong Fascination with Statistics* (New York: St. Martin's, 2004).

12. Schwarz, *The Numbers Game*, 22–25.
13. Vincent, "Education and Baseball," 373.
14. Schwarz, *The Numbers Game*, 239–40.
15. Schwarz, *The Numbers Game*, 10.
16. See Giamatti, *Take Time For Paradise*, Chapter 3, "Baseball as Narrative."

THE WORLD SILICON VALLEY MADE

SHANNON MATTERN

A repairman at the Shenzhen electronic bazaar treks from stall to stall, gathering inexpensive camera modules, casings, glass displays, batteries, and motherboards and then, with only a screwdriver and his fingernails, he pieces it all together to produce a tiny talisman capable of channeling the world's intelligence. To consumers, the iPhone can seem hermetic, consummate, all-of-a-piece—an exquisite palantír hatched from a pristine white box. Those Shenzhen repairmen, meanwhile, work with the gadget's guts, revealing its mortality and mundanity (not to mention Apple's infuriating profit margins). Following their activities can also explode the device's mythologies.

Demystifying today's magical machines, like the iPhone, is the goal of two recent books, Brian Merchant's *The One Device* and Adam Greenfield's *Radical Technologies*. Each aims to dismantle the aura and ambition undergirding such machines' promises of constant connection and algorithmic efficiency. They start by showing how our smartphones and sensors and artificial intelligences are engineered, networked, and programmed—how they're made and how they work. Ultimately, though, the more difficult task is to demonstrate how these tools serve as vessels of contemporary mythology. While storing the photostreams and soundtracks of our lives, they also encapsulate all the fantasies and phantasms of the many agents who've contributed to their making. Even critical authors like Merchant and Greenfield can occasionally get caught up in the myths. But they also can help us think our way out of them.

This year marks the iPhone's tenth anniversary. Merchant, an editor at *Vice*'s Motherboard, uses the occasion to examine how the device came into being and rose to near-ubiquity. Apple designed and marketed the iPhone to appear as if it were an in-house miracle, the brainchild of Steve Jobs, but Merchant dismantles this "divine creation" myth. He reveals the iPhone to be the product of a vast network of people and ideas and things. Inventors, factory workers, designers, miners, engineers, and child laborers all contribute to its creation.

The technologies critical to its operation did not simply spring from the heads of geniuses in Cupertino but were the result of long processes of evolution, collaboration, and incremental developments in a variety of settings, from tiny start-ups to massive research institutions. The more we know about the complex mix of "work, inspiration, and suffering" that goes into this device, he argues, "the better we'll understand the world that's hooked on it."

To describe that complexity, Merchant takes readers on a tour of the world where the mining and inventing and suffering take place. In Chile, he and his entourage trek through the salt flats, a "barren, unearthly place" where miners harvest much of the world's lithium, an essential ingredient in our electronics' batteries. They descend into Bolivia's Cerro Rico mine, which yields the tin that solders our devices together. He and his companions find that "many of the iPhone's base elements are dug out in conditions that most iPhone users wouldn't tolerate for even a few minutes." Nor would they brook the long hours and draconian discipline at the Foxconn manufacturing facility in Shenzhen, which Merchant infiltrates through a bathroom.

He emphasizes his travails in gaining entry to these sites, as well as his discomfort and disorientation while there. "It feels stupid to have this fear after a brief jog into a tunnel where thousands of people work every day," he acknowledges at Cerro Rico, but "we didn't last half an hour down there." And at Foxconn: "We power-walk through a factory block, then another, and another. . . . My adrenaline is surging; I have no idea where we are going."

Such dramatic action serves to enliven a discussion of supply chains, a subject that can be quite dry, but Merchant's tale repeats elements of the geek-action-adventure hagiography common to much tech journalism. While his goal is to undo the commodity fetishism that Apple cultivates around its star product, his telling—emphasizing his own methodological mettle, the object's with-drawal from discovery, and its creators' often obsessive (and ego-maniacal) drive—at times serves to reinforce it.

Despite the lengths to which Merchant goes to organize his global tour of iPhone geology and genealogy, there's little new material here. "Inside Foxconn" has sort of become its own eso-teric genre of exposé.[1] His efforts also build upon recent scholarly and creative work that aims to "make visible the invisible" net-works and labor behind our digital technologies, to reveal their materialities and geographies.

For instance, Neal Stephenson, Andrew Blum, and Nicole Sta-rosielski have traced transoceanic fiber-optic cables around the globe.[2] Blum, Mél Hogan, Ingrid Burrington, and countless photo-graphers have infiltrated data centers.[3] Rob Holmes, Matthew Hockenberry, Jesse LeCavalier, Clare Lyster, and Ned Rossiter have mapped logistical networks, supply chains, and landscapes of extraction.[4] The Unknown Fields design research studio will even take paying explorers on a curated, several-week-long tour of the life cycle of a technological device or manufactured commodity; they've been to the electronic markets and lithium mines, too.[5] Filmmakers Ursula Biemann, Lucy Raven, and Steve McQueen have likewise followed the global pathways of copper and coltan and other "geological media" elements.[6]

The boon of reading Merchant's book lies in the way he illuminates the connections between those subterranean sites and the above-ground factories, labs, and studios where geology is transformed—via design, engineering, manufacturing, and marketing—into gizmos. He takes us to CERN, the European Organization for Nuclear Research, where Bent Stumpe and Frank Beck conceived of multi-touch technology decades before Apple purportedly "invented" it (multi-touch actually has multi-ple origin sites and stories). We meet the designers of Siri, Apple's intelligent assistant, who drew on years of research in artificial intelligence and speech recognition then decided to embody it in a warmly textured female voice. Merchant also acknowledges the deeper histories of fundamental technologies—transistors, gyroscopes, computer chips, and glass—that ultimately converged in the iPhone.

In what many Apple aficionados will likely regard as his greatest coup, Merchant introduces readers to several members of Apple's top-secret Purple Project team, who for years sacrificed personal health and domestic harmony to midwife Jobs's "revolutionary device." Repeatedly throughout the book we return to Cupertino to rehash their exhaustion and exuberance, their debates and divorces, their tenacity and triumphs (and Steve Jobs's role in fomenting fear and frustration). We ultimately learn that, while most team members relished the experience and recognize the significance of their accomplishment, they're also deeply ambivalent about the device they created and they recognize its ephemerality.

Merchant extends these themes of loss and limitation. As part of his global tour, he also takes us on a tramp through Ghana's Agbogbloshie dump, a massive toxic electronics graveyard where many such contraptions, scratched and desacralized, return to the earth whence they came. On the day of his visit, a boy was crushed by a dump truck, and the body lay there all day long. There are many deaths in Merchant's story: miners, cell-tower workers, failed start-ups, suicidal Foxconn workers, family members of work-tethered Apple employees, and even Jobs himself. It's hard *not* to feel ambivalent if this is the price of revolution. A revolution for whom or what though? While Merchant's fourteen-chapter odyssey examines the revolutionary ideas and engineering that generated the iPhone, he has relatively little to say about "the world that's hooked on it."

That's where urban technologist Adam Greenfield steps in. He, too, briefly catalogues the components and casualties of the smartphone. He describes the revolutionary insights and inventions that have given rise not only to the phone, but also to other "radical technologies" like the internet of things, augmented reality, digital fabrication (e.g., 3-D printing), cryptocurrency (e.g., Bitcoin) and the blockchain, automation, machine learning, and artificial intelligence—few of which have yet seen widespread implementation or adoption. Yet if the world were to get "hooked on" radical tech, that new "radical" world, Greenfield worries, could be quite regressive and oppressive, reinforcing existing hierarchies rather than promoting liberation.

These new technologies, their boosters argue, promise greater efficiency and equity. New manufacturing technologies promise a radical redistribution of the means of production. Blockchain-based economies promise the spread of incorruptible, distributed networks of trust. An internet of things–networked city promises perfect knowledge of its urban systems and its residents' habits.

Other monitoring technologies promise intelligent agents that can impartially predict crime, evaluate employee performance, and mete out opportunity.

This certainly isn't my utopia. Such visions can easily be interpreted as the vagaries of a Silicon Valley boys' club (Jasmina Tešanović, one of painfully few women referenced in either book, argues that these are the "project[s] of a technical elite that aspires to universality"). Yet Greenfield takes these scenarios seriously. He engages with them earnestly and then dismantles them, to show that "these allegedly disruptive technologies leave existing modes of domination mostly intact." Radical technologies pose little threat to the world of exploitative supply chains, punishing labor practices, and techno-fetishist dogma that Merchant explored.

The technologies are not only reproducing existing systems of exploitation; they are psychically dominating forces as well, Greenfield argues. They shape our experience of everyday life, prompting users to internalize their values, their epistemologies, and their politics. Jobs and Apple's exalted marketing department have, of course, constructed lifestyles and value systems around their products. Greenfield looks beyond the power of the Apple brand to examine these radical technologies as ecosystems, as materialized imaginaries and ideologies that reshape the world in their own image.

For instance, most of our interactions with our institutions—schools, banks, government agencies—are mediated through their information-management systems. Our interactions with the Internal Revenue Service, the mortgage lender, and the financial aid office are structured through idiosyncratic online forms and their databases, "none of which entirely agree, all of which contain a slightly varying representation of the underlying reality." Our smartphones, meanwhile, tailor the search results and maps they present to us based on our user histories and behaviors; each user thus sees a different map of the world, which "subtly erodes an experience of the world in common."

Self-tracking technologies, like Fitbits and Apple Watches, entice their wearers to monitor their behaviors and optimize their performance. Corporate surveillance technologies enable employers to monitor their charges' productivity. Workers adjust to this constant surveillance and internalize their supervisors' expectations. These technologies condition our behaviors. In the process, they shape our ideals and sense of purpose.

Those ideals, Greenfield finds, are rarely able to get past the logics of the market or to grapple with ethical nuance. Even the autonomous, trust-based communities envisioned for the block-chain—an often-baffling technology built on a distributed, verifiable ledger of transactions, which Greenfield explains lucidly here—still can't think beyond the concepts of property and ownership. Machine-learning systems, meanwhile, tend to embed and operationalize our own, and *their* own, biases and recast systemic risks as matters of individual responsibility. There's "no 'escape from politics' into the comfort of governance by math," Greenfield writes, echoing many others who've critiqued the rise of "algorithmic governance."[7]

Our technologies can serve as cultural mirrors, reflecting back to us our ideological priorities and the ways we distribute power. Yet many of our new, radical technologies are built with impenetrable, proprietary platforms, inscrutable algorithms, and, Greenfield proposes, systems that "operate at higher orders of complexity than any [that] our organic minds can encompass." What this means is that we sometimes can't even evaluate what logics and values these radical systems embody, or what their "radical" politics might be.

If only we could dig into the code and root out the bias. If only we could train our machines to be more empathic and tolerant. If only it were that simple. As Greenfield observes, we "barely under-stand anything about [these systems]: neither how they work, nor where they come from, nor why they take the forms they do." He quotes Tom Gruber, head of advanced development for Siri, who likewise acknowledges that, with machine learning, "no one really has any idea of what the models know or what they mean; they just perform in a way that meets the objective function of a training set."[8] Greenfield offers a manual to these often-inscrutable tech-nologies and their uncertain futures. He closes his book with a few speculative scenarios of technologized worlds, each representing someone's utopia and someone else's dystopia, prompting readers to ask which they might want, or reject.

Perhaps Merchant's and Greenfield's books aren't simply guides to understanding the power masked by machines. These books might also contribute to *readers'* training set: our means of test-ing inputs and outcomes, deducing our machines' functions and logics, assessing how agency is distributed, evaluating, as Green-field has it, "the effect on our lives of that which cannot be under-stood in isolation and cannot be determined in advance." Thus trained, perhaps we can intervene in their design.

We would also need to consider, then, the biases built into Mer-chant's and Greenfield's books, especially around gender and race. Very few women appear in these 784 pages, and most people of color serve in the background, as nameless child laborers and factory workers. When the Purple Project locked down an entire floor in one of Apple's Cupertino buildings, they hung a "Fight Club" sign to codify the protocol. Near the end of his four-hundred-plus-page tome, Merchant notes "the immense gender disparity on the project. For a time, there were no women at all working on the design, engineering, or development process."

A mostly white male coterie midwifed Jobs's baby. Eventually, women accounted for 10 to 15 percent of the team, which reflected their (paltry) proportional presence in the company as a whole, yet all the patents belonged to men. Apple (and any tech company, for that matter) could also be an inhospitable environment for the few minorities on staff. "It's hard to gauge the effect [of] any design biases exerted there," Merchant says, but it's not insignificant that "the design and development choices were made with men's hands on the screen."

The books' paucity of women simply, and sadly, reflects women's absence in the labs and conference rooms where such contemporary "radical technologies" were birthed and developed.[9] Yet even the theoretical frameworks and historical scholarship that serve to contextualize these industry narratives are again delegated primarily to men—which is a lost opportunity, given female and feminist scholars' and technologists' long-standing involvement in many areas of concern central to these books. Feminists' writing about the materiality of digital media, media infrastructures, environmentalism, collaborative design, gendered technical work, invisible labor, and care work could've added a valuable and more diverse critical dimension to Merchant's and Greenfield's histories and analyses. And giving these women voice would've helped to write them into the technological narratives from which they've so often been excluded.

Near the end of his book, Greenfield does draw from the work of bell hooks and Gayatri Spivak in advocating for subaltern and marginalized modes of resistance: we might resist technological domination, he suggests, by being clever, practicing concealment, or employing coded speech. He also acknowledges the work of diverse organizations like Deep Lab, the Radical Networks conference, and the critical engineering and making communities, which have some prominent females and people of color among their practitioners. Yet these voices come after three hundred pages of (almost exclusively) male inventors, visionaries, and theorists.

The two books may have helped to puncture the hype behind revolutionary devices and radical technologies, but perhaps not the hagiographies. As recent Silicon Valley and Hollywood scandals demonstrate, the boys' club, with the forgivably fallible visionary at the helm, still reigns.

NOTES

1. See, for instance, Pete Brook, "Inside Foxconn City: A Vast Electronics Factory Under Suicide Scrutiny," *Wired*, November 19, 2010, https://www.wired.com/2010/11/thomas-lee-foxconn/; James Fallows, "Inside Foxconn," *The Atlantic*, October 18, 2012, https://www.theatlantic.com/international/archive/2012/10/inside-foxconn/263791/; Dawn Chmielewski, "Where Apple Products Are Born: A Rare Glimpse Inside Foxconn's Factory Gates," *Re/code*, April 6, 2015, https://www.recode.net/2015/4/6/11561130/where-apple-products-are-born-a-rare-glimpse-inside-foxconns-factory. Monologist Mike Daisey shared a lengthy Foxconn story with *This American Life* in 2012; that story was later retracted because of factual errors.

2. Neal Stephenson, "Mother Earth Mother Board," *Wired*, December 1, 1996, https://www.wired.com/1996/12/ffglass/; Andrew Blum, *Tubes: A Journey to the Center of the Internet* (New York: Ecco, 2012); Nicole Starosielski, *The Undersea Network* (Durham, NC: Duke University Press, 2015).

3. Blum, *Tubes*; Mél Hogan, "Facebook Data Storage Centers as the Archive's Underbelly," *Television & New Media* 16, no. 1 (2015); Hogan, "Water Woes & Data Flows: The Utah Data Center," *Big Data & Society* (2015); Ingrid Burrington, all stories for *The Atlantic* (2015–17), https://www.theatlantic.com/author/ingrid-burrington/.

4. Rob Holmes, "A Preliminary Atlas of Gizmo Landscapes," *mammoth*, April 1, 2010, http://m.ammoth.us/blog/2010/04/a-preliminary-atlas-of-gizmo-landscapes; Matthew Hockenberry, *Supply Studies*, 2010–, https://supplystudies.com/; Jesse LeCavalier, *The Rule of Logistics: Walmart and the Architecture of Fulfillment* (Minneapolis: University of Minnesota Press, 2016); Clare Lyster, *Learning from Logistics: How Networks Change Our Cities* (Basel: Birkhäuser, 2016); Ned Rossiter, *Software, Infrastructure, Labor: A Media Theory of Logistical Nightmares* (New York: Routledge, 2016).

5. See Unknown Fields Division (http://www.unknownfieldsdivision.com/). See also Shannon Mattern, "Cloud and Field," *Places Journal* (August 2016), https://placesjournal.org/article/cloud-and-field/.

6. See Ursula Biemann, https://www.geobodies.org/; Steve McQueen's "Gravesend" (2007), http://stevemcqueen.schaulager.org/smq/en/exhibition /gravesend-2007.html; Lucy Raven, http://lucyraven.com/); Jussi Parikka, *A Geology of Media* (Minneapolis: University of Minnesota Press, 2015). See also "Lines and Nodes: Media, Infrastructure, and Aesthetics," Anthology Film Archives, New York, September 19–21, 2014, http:// anthologyfilmarchives.org/film_screenings/series/43191.

7. See, for instance, Kate Crawford and Meredith Whittaker's AI Now Initiative (https://artificialintelligencenow.com/); Cathy O'Neil, *Weapons of Math Destruction: How Big Data Increases Inequality and Threatens Democracy* (New York: Crown, 2016); and Frank Pasquale, *The Black Box Society: The Secret Algorithms That Control Money and Information* (Cambridge, MA: Harvard University Press, 2015).

8. Yet researchers are developing theories about how deep neural nets work and how their learning relates to our own. See Natalie Wolchover, "New Theory Cracks Open the Black Box of Deep Neural Networks," *Wired*, October 8, 2017, https://www.wired.com/story/new-theory-deep-learning/.

9. Women were routinely present in the labs of the early computer age. See, for instance, Jennifer S. Light, "When Computers Were Women," *Technology and Culture*, vol. 40, no. 3 (1999); Marie Hicks, *Programmed Inequality: How Britain Discarded Women Technologists and Lost Its Edge in Computing* (Cambridge, MA: MIT Press, 2017).

PART II

Think in Public

JILL LEPORE ON THE CHALLENGE OF EXPLAINING THINGS

An Interview

B. R. COHEN

Scholars who want to write beyond the academy often ask, where are the models for such a thing? Jill Lepore is often the answer. She is the David Woods Kemper '41 Professor of American History at Harvard University, a longtime staff writer at the *New Yorker*, an accomplished essayist, and a public voice for producing historical work that engages with audiences well beyond the classroom. Her publications have attended to technologies of evidence and writing, to the craft of historical writing itself, and to subjects as wide-ranging as Wonder Woman and board games. One recurring theme is the relationship between technology and progress. Benjamin Cohen, whose work addresses the intertwined histories of science, technology, and the environment, spoke with Lepore for *Public Books* about that theme and, more broadly, the challenges and meanings of writing for a broad public audience.

■ ■ ■

> **B. R. Cohen (BRC):** You address a remarkable range of historical subjects in your work. Among those, a theme in some of your *New Yorker* essays is the historical relationship between

technology and progress. Industrial efficiency, scientific management, the "disruption" mantra of business-speak, the ways we archive and understand the preservation of the internet (of information), to name a few. Have you intentionally sought to engage with this theme? Or does it just happen to come up often?

Jill Lepore (JL): I suppose, yes, that I have intentionally sought to engage with that theme, although it also occurs to me that each of the essays that you mention was an assignment I was given, with the exception of the last. ("The Cobweb," a piece about the Internet Archive, is a story I pitched.) But I've always been interested in the history of technology and arguments about progress. Much of my scholarship lies at the intersection of political history and the field known as the history of the book, a field whose very subjects—which include literacy and the printing press—are technologies. I have always been especially interested in technologies of evidence, communication, and surveillance, which would encompass everything from writing systems to lie detectors. I might add to your list essays on the histories of newspapers and magazines; we don't tend to think of those as "technologies" anymore, but of course they were and are.

BRC: As an essayist, do you hope to write more about newspapers and magazines *as* communication technologies? Or do you think your background at the intersection of political history and the history of the book is one you're moving past?

JL: Hmm. I don't have a plan like that. I wish I had a plan. Any plan. At the moment, I am trying to write a history of the United States from 1492 to the present, starting at the beginning and moving chronologically, so, honestly, all I can think about right now is what year I'm in and what I need to read to get to the year after that. I've been trying to weave a history of technology into an account of the origins of American political ideas and institutions, which is (A) not easy and (B) alarming. But, yes, I do think about things like the Constitution as having a vital relationship with the technologies of writing and printing.

BRC: You're right, too, and I didn't mean to skip past it, but popular discussions do treat the broader historical category of technology in an ever-narrowing sense. If we listen to students, it's often just computers or cell phones today. Admittedly, I asked about the more basic issue of technology and progress for a selfish reason—it's a theme of interest in my own work. But I also ask because putting the relationship into historical context makes it far more difficult to equate the two so simplistically. In other words, this is a topic especially ripe for better historical understanding. Does that seem fair or am I making too big a deal of it?

JL: Oh, no, you're not making too big a deal of it, though I think quite excellent scholarship on this subject already exists, even if it may not have reached the audience it deserves. Historically, of course, there are lots of critiques of the equation of technological change with moral and political progress: most of those critiques come from populists. What could be more important?

BRC: Well, and it's not just technology and progress, but the more cumbersome technological determinism. I thought your essay "Our Own Devices" offered a nice summary of that problem. How do you see the concept of technological determinism at play today?

JL: To be fair, it's difficult not to be susceptible to technological determinism. We measure the very moments of our lives by computer-driven clocks and calendars that we keep in our pockets. I get why people think this way. Still, it's a pernicious fallacy. To believe that change is driven by technology, when technology is driven by humans, renders force and power invisible.

BRC: Plus, that invisibility of power in visions of techno-progress keeps us from talking about how technological change requires us to understand, oh, something like gender relations or socio-economic conditions and the like. You've made that point in work that speaks to the oft-invisible labor of women in schemes for labor-saving or increased efficiency, like in the Progressive Era. It reminds me, I heard a phrase recently, "mom tech"; someone used it to describe Silicon Valley "disruptors" fashioning their ideas of a better future based on apps and on-demand digital services. The twenty-something, largely male coders are bent on inventing things to do what their moms used to do—wash their clothes, drive to the store, clean their dishes, buy their food. They invent apps to do it for them and then call it progress. This is weird, right?

JL: Good grief. "Mom tech"? Seriously? Siri, please send those boys copies of Ruth Cowan's brilliant book *More Work for Mother*, on how technological progress has made more work for women raising children, not less. (It will arrive by drone.) There's a freaky little passage in a book by Christopher Lasch called *The True and Only Heaven: Progress and Its Critics*, in which he quotes the English historian A. P. Taylor's quip that when academics start talking about decline, instead of progress, that means "only that university professors used to have domestic servants and now do their own washing-up." Leap ahead in time and over to California and . . . you get this nonsense. I realize I'm not taking your question seriously. It's just very hard to take app madness seriously. The heedlessness . . .

BRC: This seems like a good basis for an argument to understand historical context more fully. I've used your analysis of that much-discussed "disruption" mantra in class to show why the claims of Silicon Valley disruption only hold water if you don't actually check them against the evidence. But so many people do take them seriously, they do get wide-eyed at mom-tech innovations, and they don't think, "Oh, this is the current version of a common modern historical process—claiming to make life easier, when it shifts work to others rather than reducing it. And at less pay!"

JL: I once wrote a piece about the history of the breast pump. I was using a breast pump at the time, and every time I hooked myself up to that monstrosity I felt like I was in a Mary Shelley story and I wondered, "For God's sake, how on earth did it come to this?" So I looked into it. And do you know why we have breast pumps in the United States? Because we don't have maternity leave. Pumps are a very cheap and crappy substitute. *Freeze your eggs, freeze your milk, work like a man.* Phooey.

BRC: Part of that understanding is that there is political content *inside* the breast pump, as part of it, not just as a consequence of it. That's a hard thing to hold together in general conversation—the device and the politics—let alone for a broader audience. There's a good deal of literary skill in showing that. Do you intentionally seek to explain the political life of specific topics in your work—breast pumps, Wayback Machines, newspapers, nuclear bombs—or is it just how you think, sort of naturally? I'm trying so hard not to ask, "But how do you do it, bringing out the bigger political-historical issues in your writing without feeling like it's a staid lecture?"

JL: I had written three books before I started writing essays in any regular way, except for the many things I wrote, day after day, and shoved into a desk drawer, unread. Books are a separate case. But essays, it has taken me a long time and years of advice from my editor to learn how to put together an essay that does what I want it to do and that says what I mean. I have always been curious about the origins of things: how did this come to be? But how to deliver an answer to that question in an essay that a magazine reader would want to read, *that* I learned from my editor. I had a bat. I could swing it. I have a pretty good eye. Everything else—where to stand in the box, when to shift my weight to my front foot, whether to roll my wrists, which pitches to swing at, how to place the ball, when to bunt—good lord, I'm still trying to learn those things from him.

BRC: I think for many academics who want to write beyond the academy, the role of the editor, even that fact of editorial advising, is blurry. I'm curious, too, and this is a plain question, but how many drafts and revisions go into a typical published essay with the involvement of that editorial hand?

JL: Wouldn't it be interesting to write the history of the editor as a figure not in the history of literature but in the history of knowledge? One of the really staggering things to me about the great "newspaper death watch" of 2009 was the jeering jubilance of disruptors, their astounding confidence in the genius and efficiency of a new system of communication that, at the end of the day, did one thing above all: it killed the editor. Here's a way to think about that: what percentage of everything "published" in, say, 1952—that is, every radio and television broadcast, every magazine, newspaper, newsletter, book—was edited, in the sense that it passed through the hands of at least one person whose entire job was to consider the judiciousness and reasonableness of the argument and the quality of the evidence? Let's say—wild guess—more than 98 percent. And how much of everything "published" in 2017—every post, comment, clip—is edited? Who knows, but let's say, less than 2 percent. Doesn't that explain a lot about the pickle we're in? Anyway, to answer your question, when I set out to work on a topic, I read and read and take a gazillion notes and then I think for a while and then I write, headlong. Then I get notes. I could revise forever, except that I get restless to turn to something different, which is among the many reasons that I love a deadline. Then, if and only if I'm lucky enough to have something else to write, the whole thing starts all over again.

BRC: I'll go back to communications in general for a moment. Here we are, in 2017, and the constellation of social-media technology and politics is inescapable. Inescapable at the macro level, of course—voter alignments with news feeds, online community formation, the algorithms that help shape them. But inescapable at the micro-political level too, where people base the decisions they make in their communities on the ways they learn about the issues, on whom they talk to, on whom they believe and trust. This isn't a new thing, to be sure. But how do you think the new speeds and echo volumes of social media are different than (or similar to) prior historical eras, whether of newspapers, pamphlets, telephones, television?

JL: It's not new, in the sense that, as I once argued, realignments of the American party system tend to be made possible by revolutions in communications technologies. The question of the hour is whether the forms of communication that exist today make our frame of government unworkable, having thrown the system of checks and balances so far out of whack that it can't be hammered back into working order.

BRC: Do you worry that they have? Made our system of government unworkable? If only the tendency was for people—engineers, writers, publishers—to develop communications technologies that foster engagement and deliberation rather than, as you once wrote about Franklin's *Pennsylvania Gazette*, "entertainment, more frequent."

JL: Aren't a lot of people worried about that? That genuine political conversation is like a vinyl record, a retro collectible? Isn't there, out there, a whole *Black Mirror* theory of democracy? So, yes, I'm worried. The idea of representation is, in my view, what's really in crisis, as a matter of politics (everything in the culture swims against it, in favor of self-expression). Still, I do think there are lots of ways to adapt and, unlike in 2009, during the gleeful newspaper death watch, people who are engaged in developing new tools of communication are lately quite sober about the unintended economic, social, and political consequences of their work. Underneath the freak-out, something calming could be coming. It won't be an app. And I fear it will have the quality of a revival. But something . . .

BRC: As we talk about the historical trajectory of such things, of how things change and develop, I have a corollary question. How can we write about history in ways that don't come off sounding like what I think of as a tired mode: the academic translating obscure scholarship in smaller words and shorter sentences and calling that "writing for a broader audience." You don't take that approach. Did you evolve away from it early in your career? Or did you always know you would produce public (not just academic) commentary?

JL: I only ever wanted to be a writer. I love history, and I especially love teaching history, but I never intended to become an academic, and I'm baffled by the idea that reaching a wider audience involves using smaller words, as if there's some inverse correlation between the size of your audience and of your vocabulary. You don't talk about, say, technological determinism to a freshman the same way you talk about it to a colleague, right? Is it *easier* to talk to a freshman? No, it's harder. Is it more important to give that student a clear explanation of the concept than it is to chat with your colleague about it? I think so, though I suppose that's debatable. I love the challenge of explaining things to other people, in the same way that I love other people explaining things to me. I love being a student. Nothing is so thrilling as diving into scholarship I've never encountered before and trying to get my bearings, learning what so many scholars have been piecing together over a very long period of time and trying to figure out how to bring that learning to bear on a problem that I, like a lot of people both inside and outside the academy, happen to be struggling with. The hitch is getting the scholarship right. I always worry I've missed something or distorted something or failed to understand the big picture. That's the downside: missing something crucial. Nothing is more concerning or more discouraging than getting something wrong; there's no real way to right it. It's horrible; it kills me.

BRC: I've got to ask about the kind of boilerplate historian's op-ed (I've done it, we've all done it, so I'm not criticizing others), one that goes like this: "Look, here is a thing that journalists are reporting as new and shocking/surprising/stunning. Guess what, it isn't new. Let me show how it played out in [insert year here]." I'm not sure why it bothers me, maybe it's the ubiquity of it, I don't know.

JL: It's not going away, the false analogy. It's a journalistic move that journalists really like, and they think readers really like it, too. Historians can't stand it, and it generally makes no sense to us. But you can see why it's all over the place. I used to find it more maddening than I do now. These are hard times, impossible times. People who are trying to contribute a sense of the past to this present are doing very hard work; God bless them, every one.

BRC: That's helpful, a kind of optimistic realism. It's got me considering metaphors and a sort of rolodex of pithy quotes about historical awareness. We've got Faulkner, "The past is never dead. It's not even past"; then there's the old standby Santayana, the condemned-to-repeat-it line; or we've got parallels, people love to write of historical "parallels"; and then one of the more elegant-sounding ones, that history does not repeat itself, but it rhymes (isn't it usually attributed, without citation, to Twain?). I don't necessarily have a critique of those, but do you prefer one over the other, or do you have a critique of their use in historical writing?

JL: I go to James Baldwin, in a letter to his fourteen-year-old nephew: "I keep seeing your face, which is also the face of your father and my brother. I have known both of you all your lives and have carried your daddy in my arms and on my shoulders, kissed and spanked him and watched him learn to walk. I don't know if you have known anybody from that far back, if you have loved anybody that long, first as an infant, then as a child, then as a man. You gain a strange perspective on time and human pain and effort. Other people cannot see what I see whenever I look into your father's face, for behind your father's face as it is today are all those other faces which were his." That's how I think of the past, face after face after face.

JAMES BALDWIN'S ISTANBUL

SUZY HANSEN

B aby, I'm broke, I'm sick. I need your help," James Baldwin said to a friend when he landed in Europe, looking for a place to rest. This time, his European city of choice wasn't Paris. It was Istanbul.

Many people might be surprised to learn that James Baldwin lived on and off in Turkey throughout the 1960s, the most dynamic and violent years of the Civil Rights Movement in America. Baldwin was one of the great literary and moral witnesses to the struggle of black Americans. Turkey, nearly destroyed by World War I, was by midcentury a poor, fledgling republic with a confused secular yet Islamic identity. It was a place that seemed to have little to do with Baldwin's main preoccupations or with America at all.

That, it turned out, was the point: Istanbul was Baldwin's escape. "I feel free in Istanbul," Baldwin told his friend, the Turkish writer Yaşar Kemal. "That's because you're American," Kemal replied. Baldwin loved the city. He combed through the *sahaflar*, the second-hand bookshops that line the streets around the Grand Bazaar, their dusty wares stacked on haphazard tables. He sat by the New Mosque, drinking tea out of tulip-shaped cups, playing backgammon, and watching the fishermen's wooden boats launch into the dirty waters of the Golden Horn. Then, as now, shouting hawkers pushed wooden carts piled with watermelons or onions; prostitutes and pimps hung around in dank doorways; groups of men drunk on *rakı* roamed the streets. Baldwin was delighted by the Turkish custom of holding hands—even men could be openly affectionate! It was easier to be gay in Istanbul than in America, easier to be black.

Baldwin's friends took him to the best *meyhanes*, or taverns, on Asmalımescit Street in old Pera, where the fin-de-siècle architecture still feels like Constantinople. The once glorious Art Nouveau buildings were rickety and full of soot, a memory of a lost empire and of the thousands of Jews, Armenians, and Greeks who had been forced to flee the city. Turkey, then, was a beautiful but sad, dark place; the detritus of its magnificent past collected at the bottom of Pera's many urban valleys. Baldwin must have found this postimperial atmosphere and its effect on Turks compelling. He believed the loss of empire meant a revolution of the soul.

Most of all, Baldwin was drawn to the northern neighborhoods around Boğaziçi University, which in his time was called Robert College. The campus was entirely unlike most of gritty Istanbul; it was lush, quiet, and green, a pristine oasis hanging over the twisting Bosphorus. It feels like a prosperous American university, with gray stone Gothic buildings like Princeton's, bright-eyed kids in Western dress, and expansive quads of grass, which were patrolled by broods of well-fed stray cats. The school had been founded by American Protestant missionaries during the waning days of the Ottoman empire. By the 1960s, even larger numbers of Americans were coming as part of a new, only slightly less holy mission: the Cold War.

Baldwin lived nearby in a red wooden *yalı*, a waterside mansion, once owned by Ahmed Vefık Paşa, an Ottoman-era intellectual and statesman. He also spent time at another multistoried home on the Bosphorus located near the fifteenth-century stone fortress Rumeli Hisarı, from which Mehmet the Conqueror launched his attack on the Byzantines. In those homes, Baldwin threw all-night parties and gave talks; he entertained Marlon Brando, Alex Haley, Beauford Delaney. According to his biographer David Leeming, attendees of his nightly salons also included "students from Robert College, young American teachers, a young Greco-Turkish love of Jimmy's, Turkish actors and writers," as well as Americans from the United States Information Agency, who may or may not have been spies. In one photograph from that time, Baldwin sits at his desk in front of a window overlooking the Bosphorus, whose color could change from brilliant blue to pewter gray in a matter of hours. From that window, Baldwin would watch U.S. Navy ships cut through the strait. "The American power follows one everywhere," he observed.

A couple of months ago, a friend of Baldwin's, the American writer John Freely, who had lived in Istanbul for fifty years and taught at Robert College, passed away. A memorial for him was held at the campus and was attended by many of the Americans and Turks from Baldwin's 1960s crowd. I met a charismatic elderly woman who said Baldwin hadn't been interested in Turkish politics, didn't learn Turkish. America was what consumed him, she said. From his perch on the Bosphorus, Baldwin saw that the United States was beginning to impose its unresolved racial traumas at home onto the rest of the world in the form of imperial ambitions. No one could escape America. Baldwin went home.

As I looked around at the last members of that 1960s Istanbul crowd, they and the campus seemed like a time capsule. Istanbul now sprawls as far as the eye can see. Very little green space remains. Istanbul has become a cacophonous, global metropolis of 15 million people. War, terrorism, and migration threaten to upend its fragile sense of order. But Robert College—with its towering, protective fir trees, precious quiet, and people who fondly remember a black American prophet—feels like a refuge, a reminder of a time when the country was left alone by both East and West, when it was a place anyone could go to live and feel free.

WHEN STUART HALL WAS WHITE

JAMES VERNON

I do not recall when I discovered that Stuart Hall was black. Growing up in Britain as neoliberalism first began to take shape under the rule of Margaret Thatcher, I found that Hall's work helped me comprehend what was happening to the world around me. I think I began reading him with "The Great Moving Right Show," an article published in *Marxism Today*, the ecumenical and "reform"-minded journal of the Communist Party of Great Britain, in January 1979. It is the piece now celebrated as having named "Thatcherism" as a new political formation. Thatcherism, he argued, represented a new type of politics, one that had mobilized a populist revolt to Make Britain Great Again by running it like a business and stopping immigration. It is strangely unnerving to read it again now. Later that year Hall became a professor of sociology at the Open University and began to appear regularly on its television programs designed (in the era before profit-seeking online classes) for their distance learning, nontraditional, students. It was probably on one of those superb programs, no doubt several years later, that I first saw and heard Stuart Hall.

In retrospect, it is not surprising that I had once assumed Hall was white. Growing up in the countryside as a white middle-class boy, people of color were almost completely absent from my life. I suspect that I was not the only person to imagine he was white. There has long been a way of narrating Hall's life and work that erases his formation in Jamaica as a colonial subject and a black man. It is a narrative that claims him as part of the British canon, as probably the country's most influential social and cultural theorist of the late twentieth century. It is a narrative that was rehearsed in many of the obituaries that followed his death in 2014.

In this telling, Hall's life begins when he arrives on the shores of Albion dressed like an English gentleman and goes up to Oxford University to study English literature. It continues with Hall, while writing a PhD on Henry James, beginning to forge, alongside other students there like Raphael Samuel and Charles Taylor, a New Left attuned to the changed social and cultural conditions of Britain in the 1950s. The big question for Britain's New Left was if or how culture mattered in shaping the working class. For Hall and many of his comrades, the urtexts for thinking through this question were Richard Hoggart's *The Uses of Literacy* (1957), Raymond Williams's *Culture and Society* (1958), and E. P. Thompson's *The Making of the English Working Class* (1963).

The received narrative then relates how he helped establish the *New Left Review* and, as its first editor, helped articulate the revisionist approach to Marxist theory that enabled a rethinking of socialist politics in postwar Britain. In the early 1960s, having worked as an activist in the Campaign for Nuclear Disarmament, he was invited to the University of Birmingham by Richard Hoggart to help establish what became the Centre for Contemporary Cultural Studies. It was there, under Hall's leadership, that the discipline of cultural studies emerged as new form of collaborative, interdisciplinary study of the contemporary world. After 1968 the CCCS, as it became known, was an important tributary for the flow of continental "theory" into Britain, challenging the still dominant presence of Anglo-Marxism among left intellectuals. In particular, Hall's discovery of the work of Gramsci, after the first translation of his *Prison Notebooks* into English in 1971, is seen as critical.

In many ways, this version of Stuart Hall's life and work culminates at the point I first imagined him as another white male intellectual of the left. His broadly Gramscian analysis of how Britain fell under the thrall of Thatcherism in "The Great Moving Right Show" was hugely influential. Hall insisted that the Left take seriously how Thatcher had convinced many that only a combination of anticollectivist, free-market economics and a return to both "law and order" and the primacy of the white heterosexual family could turn the country's fortune around.

In short, this narrative about Hall incorporates him within the familiar history of Britain's New Left and the arguments about the role of cultural analysis within Anglo-Marxism. It is largely a parochial story that rarely extended outside of England and only did so to grapple with events in the Soviet Empire or, at its most daring, to engage in the rethinking of Marxism across the English Channel. It is a story in which colonialism and the politics of race (to say nothing of feminism) were conspicuously absent because they were thought to have little to do with the reformation of capitalism and its class relations.

It was precisely this forgetting of empire during and after decolonization, this erasure of the politics of race and colonialism in British society, that became one of the central preoccupations of Hall's work. Indeed, by the time of his death, his life was widely celebrated as that of a black British intellectual, a postcolonial theorist of multiculturalism in Britain, and one of the postwar generation of migrants from the Anglo-Caribbean (a wave of immigration iconically associated with the arrival of the ex-German cruise ship *Empire Windrush* in London from Australia via Kingston in 1948). It was this version of Hall captured in John

Akomfrah's absorbing film *The Stuart Hall Project*, released just six months before his death. Some obituaries even described Hall as the "godfather of multiculturalism."

Hall, characteristically, refused such easy identifications, as either deracinated man of the New Left or postcolonial black theorist. Nowhere is this clearer than in Hall's own *ego-histoire, Familiar Stranger: A Life Between Two Islands*. The book will be posthumously published this spring as the third volume in a new series by Duke University Press collecting Hall's work, both published and previously unpublished, in themed volumes edited by leading scholars from across the world (many of them his former students).[1]

In *Familiar Stranger* Hall movingly writes that the iconic moments of European history—the Berlin blockade in 1948, the Soviet invasion of Hungary in 1956, or the revolts of 1968—were not those that made sense of his life. Instead he returned to the tense and tender ties of his childhood in Jamaica. It was a childhood structured by his mother's preoccupation with the family's color, class, and status in the late-colonial social order, as well as by the eruption of the labor rebellion of 1938, when he was six years old. Describing himself as the "last colonial," he knew that, despite his flight from Jamaica in 1951, the rest of his life in Britain would remain indelibly marked by and yet never simply reduced to his experience of colonialism.

Familiar Stranger, like the two volumes in the series already published by Duke, reminds us that for Hall thinking historically was essential to understanding ourselves and the conditions in which we live. The distinction between history and theory, like that between intellectual and political work, made no sense to him. Theory was not about arranging thought in abstract and systematic patterns; it was about engaging with the messy reality of the present. One could not understand the politics of the present without thinking both theoretically *and* historically. History ensured that the terrain of politics, and therefore of theory, were always changing. To be a historian and theoretician of the present one has to be a magpie.

This was not a position welcomed by any on either the old or the new Left who thought politics and theory were about adherence to unquestioned articles of faith. They accused him, mistakenly, of being a modish follower of fashion. Yet, Hall believed, the intellectual's task is to understand how each moment of our lives—each *conjuncture*, as he put it following Althusser and Gramsci—remains freighted by complex and contradictory combinations of old and new forms of capitalism, social formations, ideological forces, and affective relations. The ground we stand on is always shifting, so, he implored us, we must draw on every theoretical tool that helps us to make sense of each conjuncture and to build the politics necessary for its transformation.

Hall's capacity to remind us that it was no less possible to think Britain without its empire than it was the colonies without the metropolitan "motherland" was a product of the changing conjunctures in which he lived his life. It was the quickening pace of decolonization, together with the escalation of the commonplace racism and racial violence against people of color in Britain in the mid-1960s, that pushed the legacies of colonialism to the forefront of Hall's work. The last colonial could only slowly decolonize his own thought.

■ ■ ■

Hall was hardly the first Afro-Caribbean intellectual to make the transatlantic voyage to Britain. We often forget that it was common for the black colonial elite to move across the Atlantic world from Africa and the Caribbean to Paris and London. Britain's metropolis attracted students, artists, musicians, and writers from across the Black Atlantic. It became the center for a vibrant anti-colonial, Pan-African, and black-internationalist political culture before the Second World War. The litany of just the most famous names is remarkable: George Padmore, Marcus Garvey, and C. L. R. James from the Caribbean; Ladipo Solanke (Nigeria), Jomo Kenyatta (Kenya), and Kwame Nkrumah Ghana (Ghana) from British Africa. Afro-Caribbean women like the Jamaicans Amy Garvey and Una Marson provided black feminist perspectives on this predominantly homosocial world, where racially charged relationships with white women were not uncommon.

Oxford was not London. Nonetheless, moving to study there was also a familiar path to the aspiring black middle classes from the Caribbean. To again dwell on just the most well known cases: Twenty years before Hall made that journey, Eric Williams had arrived in Oxford from Trinidad to study history; his work at Oxford culminated with the PhD that brilliantly revealed the centrality of slavery to capitalism and Britain's early industrialization. Norman Manley, whom Hall remembered as a fellow pupil at the elite Jamaica College school in Kingston, studied law at Oxford. With the creation of the West Indies Federation in 1959 Manley became the premier of Jamaica while Williams became the first prime minister of Trinidad and Tobago when it left the federation in 1962 to become independent. The studies of all three were funded by scholarships designed to propagate a British-educated colonial elite. Manley and Hall were Rhodes Scholars, awards funded by the riches plundered from the mines of southern Africa by the archimperialist Cecil Rhodes.

It was no less difficult for Hall to think his way out of this colonial education than it was for Manley and Williams or Kenyatta and Nkrumah to build postcolonial nations. In a retrospective essay on the history of the New Left published in 1990, he remarked how, in the early 1950s, "there was no 'black politics' in Britain." By this he did not mean it was not possible to think of "black" as a category of politics. He pointed, instead, to the fact that the migrations that accompanied late-colonial rule and decolonization had only just begun.

If this was Hall's view from the cloisters of Oxford, it was not one recognizable in the more cosmopolitan world of London or in places like Cardiff or Birmingham, where mixed-race, working-class communities daily navigated an informal "colour bar." This bar ensured that people of color were kept effectively segregated from (at least respectable) whites and could only eat, drink, live, and work in particular places. Studying at Oxford was inconceivable for these Britons of color.

Hall stood out in a sea of white faces at Oxford but he managed to surround himself with a few fellow colonial students, white and black. To this group the Bandung conference of nonaligned and recently independent African and Asian states in 1955, the Suez Crisis of 1956, and Ghana's independence the following year were as important as the Soviet invasion of Hungary in 1956. Those events signaled the emergence of a new form of "Third World" politics that offered an alternative to the Cold War battles between Soviet-style communism and the welfare capitalism of America and its Western European imperial allies.

This reconfiguration of the world beyond Britain made little impact upon Hall's own early writings for the New Left. As racial animosity toward those who had migrated to Britain as Commonwealth citizens from across its empire escalated, Hall published an essay on the reformation of Britain's working class amid the relative affluence of 1950s welfare capitalism that had nothing to say of its whiteness. That essay was published in 1958, as racism turned to violence in a series of "race riots" that spread across several cities.

Even Hall's subsequent work as an activist for the Campaign for Nuclear Disarmament had little to say about colonialism. It did not register the testing of nuclear weapons in British colonial territories, and it was animated by the old imperial claim that Britain had a duty to show moral leadership to the world by being the first to unilaterally disarm.

It was on a CND march to the American nuclear base at Aldermaston outside Oxford in the early 1960s that he met his future wife, Catherine. The daughter of a Baptist minister in Leeds, Catherine went on to become an important figure in feminist politics and history writing (she is today the most eminent historian of modern Britain and its empire). When the newly married couple visited Stuart's family in a now-independent Jamaica in 1964, his mother, delighted to have a white daughter-in-law, was perturbed when she was chided by her for being condescending to the servants.

Being a mixed-race couple back in Britain had a different signification. This was especially the case in Birmingham, where they set up house on their return from Jamaica. In that city, in that year, a Conservative Party candidate ran an election campaign on the slogan "If you want a nigger for a neighbour, vote Labour." Four years later the city was also the place chosen by the Conservative MP Enoch Powell, a member of the Mont Perelin Society and an inspiration for Margaret Thatcher, to give his "Rivers of Blood" speech. In it, he infamously warned of further racial violence if tighter immigration controls were not imposed and Commonwealth citizens encouraged to take voluntary repatriation. One can only imagine the racism that Stuart and Catherine Hall encountered living in Birmingham during the 1960s.

It was at this time that Hall's work at the Centre for Contemporary Cultural Studies began to address the role of decolonization and the politics of race in the deepening crisis of welfare capitalism in the late 1960s and 1970s. There were glimpses of this in his essays on "Political Commitment" (1966) and "A World at One with Itself" (1970), republished in *Selected Political Writings*, the second volume of Duke's series. In these essays he respectively castigates Oxfam and the BBC for erasing the legacies of colonial rule in their treatment of world hunger and of Black Power protests in Trinidad.

We see this interest in race and colonialism emerging more clearly in the CCCS working groups that studied white and black youth cultures; *Working Papers in Cultural Studies* no. 7/8, coedited with Tony Jefferson, was first published in 1975 and later reissued as *Resistance Through Rituals* (1991). One of those initial working papers discussed the moral panic that surrounded the media's discovery of "mugging" and the forms of racialized policing and law enforcement it engendered. By the time *Policing the Crisis* became its own book in 1978 (it was reissued in 2013), the unraveling of Britain's social democracy was read as a crisis of the racial order. In an important anticipation of Hall's analysis of Thatcherism, and in an uncanny echo of our own times, the books' authors argued that the racialized contradictions of social democracy produced a new and alarming politics of security, aimed at people of color and in defense of whiteness.[2]

Oddly, there was no discussion in this work of the escalating violence against black men nor of the indifference, or even the complicity, of the police to it. By the late 1960s and early 1970s, racial violence against and police harassment of young black men—most infamously through the "Sus laws" that allowed police to stop and search "suspicious" persons—was an important rallying point for the growing number of Black Power activists and black feminists in Britain. Like Black Power movements in the United States and the Caribbean, activists in Britain connected the violent harassment of black men by white policemen and civilians

alike with the legacies of slavery and colonialism. Britain no longer had an empire in the 1970s, but the old forms of colonial policing, which had routinely legitimized racial violence and murder,
had come home.

The decolonization of Hall's thought was nonetheless gathering speed. His talk on "Race and Racism" to the British Sociological Association in May 1978 decried the way in which the history
of slavery and colonialism, let alone the violence and chaos of much
decolonization, had been erased from contemporary discussions
of race in Britain. White Britons, Hall wrote, had forgotten how
slaves and colonial labor had long entered "the blood stream of
British society. It is in the sugar you stir; it is in the sinews of the
famous British 'sweet tooth'; it is in the tea-leaves at the bottom of
the next 'British' cuppa."

He reminded his audience that those Commonwealth citizens
who began to arrive in Britain in the late 1940s had not done so
entirely of their own accord. They had been denied livelihoods in
the underdeveloped economies of Britain's late colonies. They had
been caught on the wrong side of violent "communal" partitions
or Africanization programs during decolonization. This erasure
of history enabled racism to become the mode of expression of a
white majority facing economic and political crises that decolonization had probably produced and certainly aggravated.

A few months after this talk a new working group on "race and
politics" was formed at the CCCS. Their work would culminate,
four years later, with *The Empire Strikes Back: Race and Racism in
70s Britain*. The publication of this book marked an important
moment. Four members of the group that coauthored it were
Afro-Caribbean, one was South Asian, and two of them were
women.[3] Their analysis of the historically specific forms of racism
and its contemporary relationship to the crisis of welfare capitalism and the formation of a new type of authoritarian security

state owed much to Hall. Yet they conceived of their work, in ways Hall had never articulated, as serving the black communities whose struggles antiracist groups and the British Left had failed to comprehend, let alone do justice to. Their attention to the gendered experience of race and the raced experience of gender appeared at a critical distance from both Hall's fidelity to Anglo-Marxism and the forms of white socialist feminism that arose in critical response to it.

In his 1988 essay "New Ethnicities," Hall looked back to this moment as one in which the political work of black politics in combating white racism began to give way to a politics attuned to the heterogeneity of "black" experience and thus to the inadequacy of the category. In that essay and in his subsequent work on multiculturalism, he turned to the work of cultural politics as the key arena in which identities, like the new ethnicities, were assembled in highly contingent and always provisional ways. While others saw the rhetoric of multiculturalism as signaling that white Britons had finally come to terms with the way colonialism and decolonization had generated diverse cultures and faiths in their midst, Hall demurred. He warned that when the advocates of multiculturalism insisted that all cultures were distinct and possessed the same relative value they reproduced the logic of empire. After all, "communalism" had long allowed Britain to rule its colonies by dividing and essentializing different groups as races, tribes, castes, or religious groups. Hall advocated for a different, postcolonial understanding of multiculturalism. It was one that both acknowledged and celebrated the hybrid and mongrelized nature of cultures that slavery and colonialism had both produced and displaced. Colonial history ensured that it was no longer possible to conceive of specific communities or traditions whose boundaries and identities were settled and fixed.

This was how Stuart Hall, the self-professed "last colonial" and Rhodes Scholar from Jamaica, eventually came to terms with living in Britain for over sixty years. He no more felt at home in Britain than he did on his occasional returns to postcolonial Jamaica. He lived in the space between Britain and Jamaica. Living there ensured that his greatest achievement was urging Britons to face the legacies of colonialism and to contemplate what decolonizing their politics and thought, as well as the institutions that police them, would look like.

■ ■ ■

In recent years the Rhodes Must Fall campaign—directed at statues of the scholarship's namesake first at the University of Cape Town, then at other campuses in South Africa, and subsequently at the University of Oxford—has become one of the key rallying points for universities in the former "British world" to recognize their complicity in slavery and colonialism and to decolonize their curriculum. Rhodes has not fallen. That may hardly be surprising, given that almost 95 percent of professors in Britain are white. Only 1.2 percent of all those teaching in UK higher education are black Britons of Afro-Caribbean descent (and the vast majority of those are men). Although almost 6 percent of Britain's student body are black, Oxford, Hall's alma mater, admitted just twenty-seven black students in 2014, less than 1 percent. Britain's first degree program in Black Studies will be launched next academic year in Birmingham, not at the university where Hall taught but at the neighboring and less prestigious City University.

British universities are not alone. That the British Left has yet to decolonize—to fully understand the entanglement of capitalism and colonialism or the intersections of class and race they have created—was painfully evident from its struggle to make sense of the resurgence of white nationalism unleashed by Brexit. It is, as Hall wrote of the Left at the height of Thatcherism, a hard road to renewal. Let's hope it is not also a long one.

NOTES

1. My thanks to Bill Schwarz, who as Hall's literary executor (along with Catherine Hall), completed the unfinished manuscript of *Familiar Stranger*, for allowing me to read it ahead of its publication.
2. Stuart Hall, Chas Critcher, Tony Jefferson, John Clarke, and Brian Roberts, *Policing the Crisis: Mugging, the State, and Law & Order*, 2nd ed. (1978; London: Palgrave MacMillan, 2013).
3. The authors were Hazel V. Carby, Bob Findlay, Paul Gilroy, Simon Jones, Errol Lawrence, Pratibha Parmar, and John Solomos.

AN INTERVIEW WITH FORMER BLACK PANTHER LYNN FRENCH

SALAMISHAH TILLET

Lynn French was a member of the Black Panther Party from 1968–1973, working in Chicago, Berkeley, and Oakland. In the party, she worked in newspaper circulation, labor, finance, breakfast programs, food and clothing giveaways and was instrumental in starting child-care centers in Berkeley and Chicago. Today, French serves as executive director of Hope and a Home, a transitional housing program for low-income homeless families, supporting efforts to develop affordable housing and equitable alternatives to gentrification. Salamishah Tillet spoke with French about the role of women in the Black Panther Party and about the party's contemporary legacy.

■ ■ ■

Salamishah Tillet (ST): How did you join the Panther Party, and what drew you to the Panthers in Chicago?

Lynn French (LF): When I graduated from high school in 1963 the world was so different from the way it is now. It seemed that the only options out there for African American women were cleaning someone's house, becoming a school teacher, or marrying someone who would take care of you. And none of those options embodied the vision I had for myself and my life. I come from a long line of women who knew themselves and spoke their minds, so it just wasn't my concept.

By the time I joined the Black Panther Party, I was living in Chicago. I was a student, and I met Bobby Rush and Fred Hampton when they were organizing the Illinois chapter. I'd been in a variety of organizations, but this was the first that I saw as saying, "We have a vision for ourselves in this world and we aren't asking for permission." I also saw that within the party women had equal status to men. It didn't even occur to me that this was a feminist action, just that we were asserting ourselves to build the world that we would want to pass on to our children.

ST: The fact that the Panther Party, by the time you joined in 1968, was over two-thirds women struck me as amazing. The dominant images that we still have of the party are of African American men with leather jackets and berets. What do you think causes this disparity between the reality as you lived it and the public imagination?

LF: We were considered a huge threat to the United States and to the status quo. The media never looked at us with any depth or complexity. And so the image that was reflected in the newspapers painted us as black men with guns who were going to wipe everyone out. But that wasn't how we saw ourselves. If you look through old issues of the Black Panther newspaper you see women very positively displayed in the art and in the articles.

ST: Another thing I've been thinking about based on what you're describing is state suppression of the movement during the Nixon presidency.

LF: Fred Hampton was murdered in his sleep in December of 1969, and a lot of people left the party because they were scared. The police were really not making any bones about lashing out at black men. There's a photo that I have—a powerful photo—of the policemen carrying Fred's body, under a blanket, out of the apartment. The police are laughing. To this day the Chicago PD has this photo mounted on the wall. So it's like they're still celebrating the good old days when they murdered Fred and really got away with it.

It's a very powerful, systemic thing they have going on in Chicago. Even today there is a place in Chicago where police will detain someone—mainly African American and Latino males—take them to this place, torture them, and try to beat confessions out of them. And because the police haven't yet officially arrested them there is no way to know where they are. So you could be looking for someone and call the Chicago police and say, "Do you know where Joe is?" And they'd say, "No, we don't know where Joe is." Meanwhile, Joe may be being held and tortured. This has been exposed, and yet it still goes on. To me it's a continuation from the time of the Great Migration, when people went from Mississippi to Chicago. The Chicago Police Department was like another KKK there, keeping people in place. I mean, what has changed?

ST: The Panther Party was also unique in its multiple programs: free-breakfast programs, the health clinic, etc. So many aspects of the party came out of a community of activists trying to think through what a family can look like—

LF: And what people's needs were. The breakfast program was our first big program. At that time there was no such thing as free breakfast for children in schools. That's one of the ways that we changed society. I hear from women who are young feminists, who say, "Well, serving breakfast, isn't that women's work?" But no, men and women were cooking up food and serving it to address the needs of children. From our perspective, you weren't doing "women's" work at a breakfast program because we all pitched in together. The same with the daycare center. Everybody, including men, shared in that responsibility.

ST: So even if the public image was heteronormative, the practice was really much more fluid.

LF: Yes.

ST: So I guess I have two additional questions. One is about black women who are also being killed by police officers—

LF: Like Sandra Bland.

ST: And then Rekia Boyd, who was killed by a police officer in Chicago in North Lawndale. Recently, Bland and Boyd have gotten attention, but usually when black women or black girls die at the hands of police officers it is rarely the catalyst for action. There's sometimes a lag between the incident and when the movement—even in Black Lives Matter—catches up to these women's deaths. How do you explain the time lag, even when these movements are primarily led by women and when the origins are feminist in impulse?

LF: I just read something in the *Washington Post* about a young woman who, as a very young teenager, was raped. She knew the person and went to the police. After a lot of this, that, and the other, she ended up being charged with lying to the police. She was taken from her family and put in foster care. It is being written about now because she is now independent. They forced a review of it, and the police chief had to admit that it was wrong and they are going to go back and reopen it. But when you think about the impact it all had on her life it is just horrifying. There was so much sexism within the police department that it was easy for them to say, "Oh, she's just lying." Or to buy into the idea of, "Oh, you can't believe what this girl says." That is troubling.

ST: And it's obviously a pipeline for the incarceration of young girls. And being sexually assaulted is actually one of the key indicators of incarceration. A report recently came out from the Ms. Foundation stating that sexual assault is a precursor to being incarcerated for black girls and girls of color.

Do you view your current work as an extension of your work in the Panther Party? There was a report a couple of years ago about African American men being pushed out of their homes due to disproportionate mass incarceration. But the report also said African American women are disproportionately evicted, too. So you have these two groups that constitute working-class African Americans being either part of the state, because of incarceration, or homeless because they're being kicked out of their housing.

LF: Yeah, that's why I do the work I do. My last job working in city government was as the city's homeless czar. That was during the period when the real estate market in Washington went crazy and property that had never been valuable before was suddenly worth a million dollars. Several nights a week there would be fires which I was sure had been arson. We have very strong tenant laws in Washington, so if the owner wants to change the use of the building, she has to give a certain amount of notice, give people money, and deal with various laws. So to avoid that, people are lighting up the buildings. I saw a disproportionate number of black women there with their children in what was once a functioning household. Invariably, if they didn't have many resources, they would end up in a family shelter. After having been in a family shelter between thirty to ninety days I could see a family lose all the fabric of their family life. They're living in substandard conditions and everything just deteriorates. That has become the norm in Washington now. And these are working women, women who work but don't make enough money to pay rent in the city. So what I work for now is equitable development.

ST: I'm a mother of a three-and-a-half-year-old girl and a four-month-old boy, and the other day I was listening to the radio in Flint and there was a mother who is an organizer there. She's been a community organizer for a very long time and now has to think about leaving Flint. She talked about giving her daughter a bath and how the ritual of giving your child a nightly bath is no longer possible.

LF: I hope this isn't offensive to people, but when things happened in Paris everybody said, "*Je suis Paris.*" Do you see anybody saying, "I am Flint?" And nobody has really yet come up with any solutions.

They're still talking about real estate value. The last thing I watched on Flint, they were saying the houses in Flint aren't worth as much as it would cost to replace the pipes in the houses. They don't think that it's a good investment to replace the pipes in Flint.

ST: It seems to me that this is where the Panther platform was so useful. It enabled us to think about the various ways in which families, individuals, and communities are impacted by systemic racial violence, gender inequity, and capitalism, then came up with different types of solutions and programs to address those issues. It's almost like a hydra with many, many heads. Today we have Flint, we have Chicago, we have Detroit, we have Baltimore. And yet to deal with these things honestly and sincerely requires so many different types of strategies, programs, and revolutionary belief. So I just want to thank you for that. This is why the Panthers are so important, because they gave us many answers.

LF: We were inspired by many things that are still happening. We felt that we should not accept them.

BLACK INTELLECTUALS AND WHITE AUDIENCES

MATTHEW CLAIR

Sometime last fall, I received an e-mail from a Harvard colleague inviting me to join a reading group of Ta-Nehisi Coates's *Between the World and Me.* "I just had an image this morning of a room full of white people discussing the book," she wrote, before clarifying in the next line: "I certainly don't mean to say, 'come explain what it's like to be black to us.'" But of course, in some way, that is precisely what she meant.

Amid protests against racialized police violence and debates over the limits of free speech on increasingly diverse college campuses, a good many (often white) progressives have been left scratching their heads. What explains the current upswell of black Americans' frustration, just eight years after the election of the nation's first black president? Black intellectuals like Coates—perceived to be authentic interpreters of the black experience—have been recruited to make sense of the disillusionment. That Coates is both black and a native son of Baltimore's restless inner city only heightens his authenticity in the eyes of a white liberal public searching for answers. But even I—the suburban-raised son of two black physicians—carry a certain racial authenticity, one seemingly much desired in predominantly white academic spaces.

Where does this belief in and demand for racially authentic explanations of black life come from? Far from unique to this contemporary moment, the notion of a racially authentic interpretation of blackness has been a mainstay of American understandings of the role of black intellectuals for more than a century. Through different routes, two recent books explore the centrality of racial authenticity in black intellectual practice—or the belief in a uniquely and authoritatively black knowledge produced by black scholars, writers, and artists. In his book *On the Corner*, Daniel Matlin considers how Kenneth Clark, a psychologist; Amiri Baraka, a writer; and Romare Bearden, an artist, variously navigated their designations as "indigenous interpreters" for white audiences in the 1960s. Similarly, in his book *The Scholar Denied*, Aldon Morris explores black intellectual practice but during a time when many white audiences expressed little interest in the insights of black intellectuals, even of the preeminent W. E. B. Du Bois. Placing these books in conversation illuminates the costs and benefits of racial authenticity in the production of knowledge about black America and, ultimately, in the struggle to alter the course of American racial inequality.

The 1960s marked a turning point in the position of black intellectuals with respect to white progressives, Matlin argues. The migration of African Americans from the South to major cities in the North and Midwest in the mid-twentieth century resulted in a massive geographic—and symbolic—relocation of black America. The terms "ghetto" and "urban" came to signify a population that had, for successive generations, been exploited and contained in the rural South. But migrants' lofty expectations of northern prosperity were tempered by the realities of dilapidated housing, a declining manufacturing sector, and more modern, less strident forms of racism. The cities grew restless. Various white audiences looked to black intellectuals—whom Matlin describes as racial "insiders" with "experiential knowledge"—to make sense of the emerging black ghettos and the attendant appeal of the Black Power movement's politics of racial separatism.

On the Corner opens during the Harlem riot of 1964. During a racist altercation between a white man and several young black students on Manhattan's Upper East Side, James Powell, a black boy, was shot dead by Thomas Gilligan, a white police officer. Protests lasted several days. As the summer progressed, similar protests against police brutality engulfed cities from Philadelphia to Rochester. To many observers, the perils of the northern black ghettos were fast eclipsing the promises of the southern Civil Rights Movement, which had dominated media coverage in the preceding decade.

It was "amid the riots" that cultural arbiters such as newspaper editors, theater producers, and policy makers sought out black intellectuals to interpret "black urban life to the white American public." For these cultural arbiters, the racial identity of black intellectuals—in addition to their intellect and disciplinary training—was fundamental to the legitimacy of their claims about and solutions to black urban crises. "The logic of racial authenticity," Matlin writes, "stipulates both that black intellectuals have a particular responsibility to *represent*, in both senses of that word, 'their' people, and that, as racial insiders, they are uniquely capable of doing so."

As much as it has been imposed by white audiences, the logic of racial authenticity has been articulated by black publics and intellectuals as well. Intellectuals as disparate as Du Bois and Baraka argued that blacks possessed not only intimate understandings of blackness but also the moral authority to speak first on the social problems facing black ghettos. In the 1960s white liberals imbibed these dual claims, fostering a veritable marketplace for the "pronouncements of those believed to possess both intimate knowledge of black life and the ability to articulate that knowledge to a broad white public." This marketplace boosted the careers of many black intellectuals of the time. Black scholars, writers, and artists were invited to the White House and regularly asked to provide their perspective on myriad black urban crises, large and small, in the form of interviews, essays, art exhibitions, and social science research.

But there were costs, too. Matlin reveals how Baraka, Bearden, and Clark each experienced ambivalence, at one point or another, toward their roles as indigenous interpreters. The story of Kenneth Clark paints the clearest portrait of what it meant for black intellectuals to feel "cornered" by the logic of racial authenticity.

Throughout his career, Clark would maintain that interpreting for white audiences was critical to social change. The psychologist who, with his colleague and wife, Mamie Clark, provided social science evidence undergirding the Supreme Court's assertion in *Brown v. Board of Education* that segregation was damaging to the psyche of black children, Clark witnessed firsthand the impact his scholarship could have on social policy. In his 1965 book *Dark Ghetto*, Clark sought to "lay 'the *truth* of the ghetto' before the white American public and to explain the meaning of the riots to white liberals perplexed and disturbed by this violent turn." Social change, he believed, would come about only by appealing to the compassion of the "ruling white majority" through the dramatization of the "injustices of segregation and poverty." While other black intellectuals, such as Ralph Ellison, criticized Clark for pathologizing the black ghetto, Clark found such an accounting to be not only accurate but also practical in the struggle for white sympathy.

But Clark would later grow disillusioned. The Johnson administration's War on Poverty ultimately failed black ghettos, and local politicians chose to treat urban unrest as a crime problem requiring police suppression rather than as a social problem requiring welfare-state intervention. Clark came to view white elites as unwilling to enact needed social reform. At the same time, he began to wrestle with his intellectual identity, struggling to define himself outside white audiences' expectations. When elected in 1969 to serve as the first black president of the American Psychological Association, Clark felt pressure to give a presidential address that spoke to general, as opposed to only black, psychological and social processes. The resulting address—which advocated for the use of psycho-technological drugs among political leaders to inhibit their potential to abuse power—proved disastrous. Clark would later lament that his address failed not necessarily because his ideas were anathema but, at least in part, because his colleagues expected him to speak only on issues of race or civil rights—the intellectual domain "reserved for blacks."

The ambivalence of 1960s black intellectuals about serving as authentic indigenous interpreters could, perhaps, appear overwrought, particularly when considered in contrast to the persistent marginalization faced by many black intellectuals prior to the urban crises of the 1960s. Indeed, Morris's book *The Scholar Denied* affords us insight into a historical moment when white audiences— especially within academia—often ignored rather than sought out the experiential expertise of black intellectuals. In particular, Morris details how white sociological and public audiences marginalized the scientific contributions of the sociologist W. E. B. Du Bois and other black social scientists working at the historically black Atlanta University in the early 1900s.

For Du Bois and his colleagues, their racial identity as black delegitimized their scientific scholarship on race rather than serving as proof of its authenticity. Even at the height of his sociological career, Du Bois faced numerous hurdles in his attempt to secure research funding from predominantly white institutions. For decades, he struggled to fund his *Encyclopedia of the Negro*—a project that was ultimately undermined by several white scholars, including the anthropologist Melville Herskovits, who served on the project's advisory board and expressed doubts to potential funders about Du Bois's scientific objectivity, given his blackness. Morris writes that Herskovits believed that "black scholars could not be trusted to conduct objective scholarship on blacks and race because they were too emotionally engaged with these topics and because they violated the basic scientific law not to mix activism with scholarship."

Du Bois's marginalization from sociology was a matter of racial politics as much as racial identity, as evidenced by the relative status of Booker T. Washington with respect to white audiences within and outside academia. A conservative educator, Washington was arguably the first "black public intellectual," serving as a "trusted informant to communicate to whites what the Negro thought, felt, wanted, needed."[1] Washington successfully courted white benefactors to fund the historically black Tuskegee Institute and even dined with President Theodore Roosevelt. Within the academy, his expertise was legitimated despite his lack of social scientific credentials. Telling is Morris's recounting of how the economist Walter Willcox once sought Washington's conjectural, unscientific confirmation of Willcox's data on black wealth over Du Bois's data-driven criticisms. Morris also devotes many pages to detailing Washington's close relationship with Robert E. Park, one of the central figures of the Chicago school of sociology, who worked as Washington's assistant at Tuskegee before moving on to the University of Chicago. Washington's conservative racial politics, as Morris reveals, both aligned with and shaped (through his tutelage of Park) white academic and public views on the wisdom of Jim Crow racial segregation. In contrast to Washington, Du Bois advocated for the social and political integration of blacks, based on his assessment that racial inequalities resulted not from biological inferiority but from white racism and concomitant black cultural deficiencies. With such politics, Du Bois and his colleagues were viewed by Washington and Park as "arrogant snobs who promoted their unwise abstract notions as the solution to the race problem."

While Du Bois's race, politics, and perceived elitism served to delegitimize his contributions to science, his insights, ultimately, had an important influence on the burgeoning racial politics of the mid-twentieth century. In reading Morris's account, it is often easy to forget that, despite his marginalization within the academy, Du Bois was well recognized as a social activist whose indigenous insights authentically articulated the experiences and desires of a certain segment of black Americans. Through his involvement with the Niagara movement and the NAACP, Du Bois and other intellectuals such as William Monroe Trotter and Ida B. Wells planted the then-radical seeds for the political activism of the Civil Rights Movement. Although such activism threatened to undermine Du Bois's scientific authority, white social scientists who believed their whiteness lent them greater objectivity in the study of race nevertheless relied on Du Bois's insights. For instance, Park, according to Morris, appropriated Du Bois's concept of double consciousness. Meanwhile, the Swedish economist Gunnar Myrdal's 1944 work *An American Dilemma*—often cited as a landmark study of American racial injustice—owes a debt, acknowledged by Myrdal himself, to Du Bois's *The Philadelphia Negro*.

For white social scientific audiences of the early twentieth century, authentic indigenous understandings of the black experience served merely to confirm or, at best, inform scientific research rather than functioning as legitimate forms of scientific knowledge in their own right. It was believed that racial authenticity amounted to scientific bias—in the case of Washington as much as in the case of Du Bois. Washington's relative success with white audiences—scientific and lay—says more about these audiences' willingness to accept his moderate politics of black humility than their legitimation of his scientific or intellectual expertise. Indeed, Washington's much-promoted separate-but-equal politics rests on a notion of distinct racial difference, similar to that which undergirds the logic of racial authenticity in knowledge making. In this sense, Washington's audiences were perhaps doubly prepared to legitimate his interpretations of blackness. Of course, the irony of white academics' framing of Du Bois as biased is that Du Bois was the first American sociologist to collect systematic empirical data on black social life, at a time when white social scientists found the empirical study of blacks largely unimportant. In his 1898 essay "The Study of the Negro Problems," Du Bois lambasts his contemporaries' thin investigations into black communities: "A college graduate sees the slums of a Southern city, looks at the plantation field hands, and has some experience with Negro servants, and from the laziness, crime and disease which he finds, draws conclusions as to eight millions of people, stretched from Maine to Texas and from Florida to Washington."[2] By contrast, Du Bois's multimethod approach to data collection while at Atlanta University was so pathbreaking, Morris argues, that it served as a model for later studies conducted by the U.S. Department of Labor in the early 1900s.

Thus, an important difference between the white audiences of the two time periods appears to be the purpose for which they sought the knowledge they understood to be authentically black. Matlin describes 1960s white audiences as seeking both to understand and manage the problems of the emerging black ghettos. White progressives, buoyed by the hope of the Civil Rights Movement and pressured by the radicalism of Black Power, were open to the politics and activism of racial progress. Or, at the very least, they were open to indigenous solutions for managing the black ghettos, whose welfare, it seemed, was beginning to impinge on their own well-being. But early-twentieth-century white audiences, as Morris describes them, were seeking neither racial progress nor the management of urban crises. For these earlier audiences, the race problem was a distant one, requiring not political or social inclusion but instead a good-faith effort on the part of the Southern black masses to uplift themselves through moral and industrial cultivation.

Since the 1960s, the logic of racial authenticity in the production of knowledge has blossomed both within and beyond the confines of black intellectual practice—with contradictory consequences. On the one hand, the belief in an authentic black form of knowledge has fostered inclusion. Workplaces recruit minority employees with the understanding that diverse perspectives are good for the bottom line, and the most rigorous white academics have come to interrogate the potential limitations and biases of their whiteness, particularly when documenting the conditions of the black urban poor. On the other hand, the belief in authentic black knowledge has also been the foundation on which new justifications for the exclusion of people of color have been built. Since the late 1970s, for example, affirmative action has become justified as a compelling state interest not because people of color face unique disadvantages or because integration is an absolute good but because minorities are understood to have inimitable perspectives to contribute—but only in certain contexts. Minorities' experiential knowledge has thus come to be valued only when such knowledge enlightens white audiences. Thus, in oral arguments in the latest affirmative action court case, the Chief Justice of the United States Supreme Court can legitimately ponder: "What unique perspective does a minority student bring to a physics class?"

For his part, Coates, one of today's most recognized black intellectuals, has expressed skepticism about writing for the enlightenment of white audiences. During a public conversation in New York this past October, he remarked that he never "set out to accumulate a mass of white fans," going on to observe that when black intellectuals have sought to interpret for white audiences, they have often, seeking not to offend, done so in a way that obfuscates more than clarifies their understanding of racial injustice. Coates's sentiment echoes that of a new generation of unapologetic black activists and intellectuals who, with their impenitent positioning of white supremacy as the root cause of racial inequalities, have garnered the attention and resentment of great numbers of whites. As history reveals, sympathetic attention does not always translate into policy. Even when it does, long-term social change can be elusive. It is disheartening how familiar the 1964 police killing of James Powell in Harlem appears to us today, in 2016, as images of police brutality dominate our daily newsfeeds.

For more than a century, black intellectuals from various disciplinary backgrounds and political positions have articulated their insights on racial injustices. Some have played their role as indigenous interpreters faithfully and with an unfailing optimism while others have grown wary of bearing witness, of explaining the array of emotions and events—from tragedy and rage to humor and brilliance—that constitute the black American experience. Matlin writes that depicting oppressed people "in a manner that both witnesses the extent and consequences of their suffering and simultaneously recognizes their dignity, resourcefulness, and agency remains an intractable problem for social scientists, artists, and historians." But the representation of black subordination—no matter how carefully constructed—must also find a receptive audience. So much black intellectual energy has been expended on convincing white audiences simply to care about the exploitation of the black poor and the alienation of the black middle classes. The receptivity of particular white audiences has fluctuated over time and, with it—in tandem, arguably—various indicators of racial inequality. Perhaps just as pressing, then, as interpreting blackness for white audiences is interpreting the causes and consequences of white attention for the rest of us.

NOTES

1. Adolph Reed Jr., "'What Are the Drums Saying, Booker?': The Curious Role of the Black Public Intellectual," in *Class Notes: Posing as Politics and Other Thoughts on the American Scene* (New York: New Press, 2000), 79.
2. W. E. B. Du Bois, "The Study of the Negro Problems" (1898), reprint, in *The Study of African American Problems: W. E. B. Du Bois's Agenda, Then and Now*, ed. Elijah Anderson and Tukufu Zuberi (Thousand Oaks, CA: Sage, 2000), 21.

CAN THERE BE A FEMINIST WORLD?

GAYATRI CHAKRAVORTY SPIVAK

The following is the lightly edited text of a lecture delivered on November 16, 2013, at the Columbia University Global Center in Amman, Jordan.

ıllıllıllıllıllıllıllıllıllıllıllıllıllıllıllı

I am pleased to be here at the Columbia Global Center in Amman. I lunched with the vice president for Global Centers three days ago and told him, only half in jest, that I was going to enjoy Amman more without him. I explained that I wanted to make new friends here, rather than be guided affectionately by him, by now an old friend.

Yet my experience in Jordan is not quite new. In the fall of 1980, I taught for three weeks at the Women's Section of the University of Riyadh. There were students from all over the area, and some of them were from Jordan. Those young women would be in their fifties now. I do not expect anybody from that group to be here today. Yet among my dearest memories from that outstanding experience are our conversations in the free periods on the rooftop behind the water tank, agitated and real, where we tossed around in urgent whispers the question raised for you today: Not just can, but *how* can there be a feminist world? Some of my dearest interlocutors were the young women from Jordan. Tonight I continue that earlier conversation, and I can only imagine the difference between those conversations and today's conversations.

(Between then and now, I have delightedly encountered one of those allies from the water tank! Moneera Al-Ghadeer, colleague, author of *Desert Voices: Bedouin Women's Poetry in Saudi Arabia*.)

And yet, for many women in our shared world, have things changed?

I am a teacher of the humanities. I do not directly influence state policy. Humanities teachers are like personal trainers in the gym of the mind. They believe that unless this work is done at the same time as agitating for merely legal change, generation after generation, persistently, supplemented by rearranging the desires of people, nothing can succeed. In the long run, if laws have to be constantly enforced on the majority, without any change in how people really think about rape, honor killings, gender discrimination in general––and I mean people, men *and* women—the laws become useless, ways of dodging them proliferate, and force takes over: not a feminist world. Short-term problem solving should not be stopped. There are too many problems. But the kind of work we do, silent work, quiet work, slow work, is the work that sustains everything. "Public awareness" preaches to the choir, at best makes the choir a bit larger. "Sustainable" is used only in the economic/ecologic sphere. We humanities teachers can be the sustainers because, generation after generation, we can produce the will to sustain. We can work toward being the long-term producers of problem solvers. We do not solve problems top-down, 24/7, with little result.

I learned to think this way during those deeply agitated conversations with those young women, behind the water tank on the rooftop, in 1980. I myself am from the world's largest democracy, with huge numbers of rural poor. I have engaged myself actively there doing the kind of persistent work I have outlined, and that work continues at Columbia. In order to say something useful here in Amman, I would have to know the dynamics of social stratification thoroughly. Since I do not have that knowledge, let me just say that the solution that I am going to talk about here will be a one-size-fits-all general solution, the humanities in general: ceaseless uncoercive rearrangement of desires, which must keep supplementing all the quick-fix leadership talk.

A leader is one who knows how to follow. Under Safwan Masri's leadership, we see this at work. As a leader, he has followed our suggestion that a global university should also involve its global centers in the central mandate of a university: learning and teaching. Not just top-down philanthropy. Indeed, my being here is the result of this. He knows well that I am bent on this kind of non-glamorous, persistent, generation-by-generation teaching—it is my fiftieth year of full-time university teaching in the United States—including those three weeks in Riyadh—and my thirtieth year of elementary school teaching and teacher training among the landless illiterate in India. This has taught me that you do not achieve social change by only changing the laws. It is good to change the laws. I am myself involved with that. Changing the laws, however, is not the same thing as teaching the general public to will the law, to want the law. As long as the law is predicated on enforcement, it is the same world, perhaps superficially changed, always observed, precarious, ready to revert any moment.

My work stands, then, in a spectrum, from theory, through the teaching of theory in the West and the elite schools of the world, into the practice of activism. I am not interested in the activism of literacy. When we send our children to school, we do not send them to learn literacy. I do not have different standards. My standards are the same at Columbia University and my rural schools. The Human Development Index, in order to measure a country's development, asks for quantity: how many years of schooling. When the team that put the index together look for their own children, they look for quality. As long as there is this difference between human beings, we will not have a just world. Superficial activists located in the international civil society make much of access to education. They do not have the time, patience, or yet preparation to realize that the wretched quality of education in the bottom layers of society, even when available to women, does not change internalized core values—rape and bribe as normal. (In fact, quality education without slow humanities training also does nothing much to change this. We will remember this as I go on with my words this evening.)

However impractical it might seem, I believe that for general long-term thinking in this area it is right to assume that there is the possibility of goodwill in women and men today, generally in the educated middle class, but not only, to wish for their children a future world where regulations will be socially just. (In the Jordan that I have seen, admittedly without reference to the dynamics of sociopolitical stratification, this assumption seems quite possible because of the enlightened sphere and the general level of education, women's involvement in feminism, and the sphere of the legal. The point I am making is that we have to believe this for the rest of the world as well. Otherwise there is no going forward.) Now, as to whether people can imagine what that is, is a different issue. Everywhere there are some vestiges of what I call "feudal benevolence" in the ethical section of the upper class and the motivated middle class. (The World Social Forum, when it comes to the global front, generally relates to such benevolent "feudal" folks, thinking that they are the ethnic heart of the Global South.) The task of the humanities is to teach literature and philosophy in such a way that people will be able to imagine what a socially just world should be. On the other hand, I think we should start from the assumption that they can. That is why the work of cooking the soul does not end.

For this brief talk, I broke my theory down into three. Theory by itself, which I outline above, psycho-analytico-social and ethico-political. Simply put, psychoanalysis deals, among other things, with ourselves before we become reasonable. When a child begins to develop a sense of self, "drives" in the mind are programmed to set it up. In the English of the Standard Edition of Freud, "drive" [*der Trieb*] is translated "instinct," certainly a possible translation, but it misses Freud's point. Like many neurophysicians today, and German classical philosophers since Immanuel Kant, Freud imagines the mind as also a machine, within which these drives begin to work before the time a baby has actually developed a sense of self. Psychoanalysis suggests that in this work, drives placed in the mind-machine, but not accessible to the child, relate the mind-machine to the openings in the body. The child gets a sense of the body in terms of its openings to the world, including eyes and ears and the reproductive apparatus, to give it a sense of a bordered whole that is our bodies and our selves. So we are wholes, but we are also bordered with permeable borders with the outside world. That is the first sense of what I am as the play of life begins.

Now I want to move on to a general word on gender. Gender is the tacit globalizer of the world before the globe could be thought by cartographers. Gendering embraces everyone. Both capitalists and communists are children of mothers. Being gendered is bigger than our beliefs. And the psychoanalytic insight is that being human begins with the coming-into-life of the bordered, gendered body. The female body is felt as permeable by the male. It is seen as permeable in perhaps the most basic gesture of violence. Yet, as the pathway to children, it is also in the benign service of humanity itself.

To assure respect for such a female body (and indeed also such a male), the short-term work is law. The long-term work is of imagining the borderlessness that attends to borders. To be borderless is also a pleasure for the female. We cannot deny this pleasure as we are working toward a feminist world, and I do not know what to say to this audience when I am also thinking of the queer. So it is attending to borderlessness rather than simply respecting it that is our first gender lesson. As you must know, there have been terrible rapes in India (in the rest of the world also, of course, but I am speaking here of what happened in my country), and there is a great deal of outrage in response. Yet it is not just a gender problem. Because there is such a class difference in education all over the world, rote teaching, learning prepared answers to prepared questions, the enforcers of the law, the lower ranks of the urban and rural police, cannot escape internalized rape culture and bribe culture, and this situation is feared and accepted by most women. The idea of attending to borders habitually rather than merely respecting them is thus difficult to teach. And, at the baseline of gendering, we enter the space of the incalculable, because part of this is worked into us before we become rational beings.

One of the things that needs to be done for the implementation of the Beijing Declaration and Platform for Action, twenty years after its adoption at the Fourth World Conference on Women in 1995, is to take every woman's suffering and assign it to a slot in that platform. If, however, we think that this is going to lead to a just world, we are wrong. That slotting is for the convenience of necessary and short-term problem solving. But even violence can be desired when we are in the arena of the incalculable. Attending to borders is a complex thing, as incalculable as life and death, subject to teaching that touches the spirit, rather than mere legal action or tabulation for convenience.

These theoretical speculations, relating to the outlines of human beings, can translate into the collective history of the world, by way of the understanding that gender is not only the first tacit globalizer, but also our first instrument of abstraction.

We are used to thinking that gender is the most concrete. But it is also the collective first instrument of abstraction. If you are working with information technology, you know that an entire system of meaningfulness is created with a plus and a minus. The plus and the minus that was immediately perceptible to human beings, long before the digital age, is sexual difference. It is in terms of that plus and that minus that the sacred and the profane arranged themselves into social values. Gender was thus our first instrument of abstraction, at the base of the formation of every society as a system of internalized rules.

I am not talking here only theoretically. I am not taking this only historically, either: as a story about how something named feminism emerges in the northwest European eighteenth century. I am asking us to remember this story, before theory and history: the idea of the bordered body as the first perception of the self in the gendered infant, leading on to the idea that it is with that perceived difference that culture, another name for deep social-meaning-making systems, is created.

By contrast, what we recognize as the social tells us that the gender division of labor and inequality of rights, which the deep social may tell us is natural, are in fact socially constructed. And therefore in our day, all over the world, the focus is on equality of rights, and in many areas of Asia, for communal gender equality. This is a tremendously good struggle, but it is necessarily centered on justified self-interest. I am not against this. But as someone who works for a just world, a personal trainer of the rearrangement of desires, I have to accept that this work is based on our self-interest, however justified, and try to push beyond. However against common sense or counterintuitive it might seem, those of us with a humanities focus, thinking of the long term, must remind ourselves that beyond the enforcement of the law is the creation of a society where the law becomes equal to a general social will. Our question today—"How can there be a feminist world?"—relates to the difficult and persistent effort of the establishment of this general will. And this is why the education that I do at both ends is to produce intuitions of democracy, not single-issue feminism alone.

I am either dealing with self-infantilized adult U.S. students who think their world is *the* world or with teachers and children who are so poor that they too cannot think of a world unlike their own. At both ends, it is the intuitions of democracy that must come through the philosophy of education. Anyone who is a parent here knows this. Talking *at* them is not going to change their minds. Therefore, a set of contradictions operates at each end: at the top, not claiming too much for ourselves yet seeing the way forward even as we learn to acknowledge complicity; at the bottom, combining the absence of competition with class struggle, equality for all combined with affirmative preference for the young girls, and female teachers. Contradictions will inhabit humanities work if you realize that work only for self-interest, however justified, is not going to create a just world in the long run.

Justified self-interest for groups at risk is the secret of human rights work, and that important struggle must go on. Yet the personal trainer for the gym of the mind, productive of future collectivities, must be mindful that such work will not produce a just world in the long run.

Democracy is not just "me," it is not just "autonomy," it is also other people. And equality is not sameness. The question of rights concerns both gender and class, women, servants, workers, those from whom duties have been expected by suggesting once again that it is natural or divinely decreed that it be so. I come from a country with a caste system. There again, changing the law is very good, but try working in the villages because on the ground, even my students and teachers with whom I labor think that I have some kind of private connection to divinity because I am "upper caste." We have done more harm to our people than colonialism. That complicity is something to think about in Africa, in India. I have nothing against Western feminism. After fifty-four years in the United States, I share in dominant feminism, international civil-society feminism.

Whatever we call ourselves in terms of national origin, we must remember that the problem is gender and *class*. And within class there is still homophobia, heterosexual violence, rape culture, bribe culture. We must remember that much of this comes because of class apartheid in education. Building school buildings, donating textbooks, free education does not mean much without human commitment to quality. And that work is as focused as teaching at a university in the United States. You do not teach at all the universities in the United States, do you? Therefore, this kind of focus is required. It is more difficult. If you are going to attend to quality among the very poor, below a certain class level, it is not money you need, it is time and skill. Fundraising is not education.

As a feminist, I am not ignoring the possibility of affection between men and women. But this affection, unintended consequence of social bonds, is transformed into the iron law of legitimacy and becomes a cruel imposition upon the freedom of women's spirit. Given the powerful work of feminist legal activists, I will say very little here, except once again to emphasize the importance, in this area also, of humanities-style education, imaginative training, the involvement with rearranging desires rather than consciousness raising or public awareness.

Education is not consciousness-raising. It is not public awareness. It is a change in how one wills. This is our long-term goal as concerns women, women given the preparation to will freedom, across class and gender, across nation and war, even as the shorter-term work of protection and keeping the peace necessarily goes on.

Now we come to the third point related to theory: the ethical and the political. The ethical is not just the moral, "Do the right thing." Ethics are unconditional. Morality, operating by rational choice, is fine. Yet, unless we learn to engage in the impractical and powerful call of unconditional ethics, nothing will last. There is no doubt about that at all because democracy is about everyone, not just for the nice self-selected moral entrepreneurs of international civil society. No social contract is self-selected. When we think of the ethical in a human being in general, we think of being directed toward the other rather than toward the self. It is not necessarily always doing good. This requires training. Because we are generally focused on saving ourselves, as we should be.

This creates a particular problem for us, as concerned women, because women in the underclass, as I said before, are socially obliged to care for others. Socially obliged. In the ethical, therefore, we have to learn to work within this contradiction. When we work with homeworkers, sweated labor inside the home without any workplace regulation at all, sometimes the women themselves say, "We are supposed to do all the work at home anyway, and here we are getting paid for it, so what's your problem?" This is the kind of contradiction—women willing their subjection as ethical— within which you have to work. If ethics is other-directedness, because women and servants have always been obliged to be directed toward others, we are obliged to work within this contradiction and take this practice away from cultural requirements into training for what I will call, in this brief talk, the *literary*— not *literature*, because what I am talking about is not identical with what is recognized as literature, which came into being, in terms of history, very recently, and which is also specific to certain areas of the world. What we define as the *literary* is that of which the reading, making sense, is for its own sake, necessarily requiring that you suspend yourself in what the writer or the speaker says, rather than using it for self-interest. This is classroom teaching in literature. In any kind of classroom teaching in literature, you know that the teacher who teaches you how to read what the writer means, rather than making the writer's text resemble what you yourself think, is teaching the literary. This is real literary teaching. This so-called training in reading is a practice of moving away from your self-interest into the other's interest. It is just training for unconditional ethics; it does not make you ethical. It is like going to the gym and training your body, which does not necessarily make you an athlete, but without it, you will not be able to do anything. It is training. So always "me," "my rights," and so forth is not going to produce a just world.

If at the bottom there is no training for intellectual labor because we have denied the right to intellectual labor, from within the caste/race/class/gender/colonial system, millennially, we have punished them for intellectual labor and trained them for nothing but obedience; then, at the top, intellectual labor is no longer understood or undertaken because of this untrained use of the digital, of so-called social media. I am not a technophobe, but the digital is like a powerful wild horse; you have to have a slow-trained mind in order to use it properly.

I am not against social media. I am not against any civil-society worker. To be against is to deny complicity. I am so much for the digital that I think people need to prepare for it. Otherwise cyber-crime, pornography. The *New York Times* reported that top Silicon Valley executives send their children to schools where there is no computer training. Why do they do that? Because they best of all know, they understand, that you cannot use this incredibly powerful and dangerous instrument with minds that are untrained.

Literary reading and philosophizing gives you practice in moving away from self-interest and going into others' interests. This is ethical practice. When servants and women have to work out constantly what the masters think, this is in fact a travesty or degradation of the ethical thing, required social obligation. It is within this profound social contradiction that we must work, so that so-called free women and indeed free men do not become completely self-interested. In the political, also, this contradiction is firmly present. If democracy is based only on my own rights, it is not democracy. Democracy is not just about us; it is also about others. The idea of democracy is based on the possibility of minorities. This contradiction is what makes it so hard. Democracy is a hard thing to work with, and I think we should try to translate this word—small *d*, not the Greek name for a certain kind of constitution—into many languages of the world to see what the difference is between several cultures, between Democracy as a Euro-style system of government, and democracy, which is caring about other people's children as your own, irrespective of race-class-gender, if you like, moving desires so that human beings, wherever placed, are capable of thinking of a world that is not self-interest and/or feudal benevolence.

I belong to the middle class, and I was born in 1942 in Calcutta, where and when the middle class had servants. Being humane and kind to servants is not a just world; it is feudal benevolence. The idea of democracy is where you think about other people not as things but as equal. That is different from feudal benevolence, which is a lot present both here, in my world, and in the rest of the world, transforming itself now to long-distance remote-control top-down philanthropy. There is no systemic instrument of social justice any more. In the 1980s, when I worked in Algeria, I would ask women in the so-called socialist villages, "What is it to vote?" The answers made it clear to me that voting had something to do with insights that the postcolonial state belongs to citizens, females and males. And then in 1991, after the Islamic Salvation Front came to power by democratic procedure in Algeria, I also saw the massive involvement of chador-wearing office-cleaning women, altogether underreported, in overturning an elected government, and the rest is history. Since 1986, my involvement with the landless illiterate, in the country of my citizenship and of my first language because you can only teach in a language you know well, has made me realize that the question we asked—"What is it to vote?"—is the presupposition for developing democratic intuition rather than only a test.

I come now to my very last point. Activism. I wrote it down in four points. One, work. Two, labor-movement work necessarily involving women. Three, ecological work. Four, theory and practice.

One. This is very different from Doctors Without Borders, who come in when there is a problem. They are wonderful people, but let me tell you a story. In 1991, there was a huge and destructive cyclone in the Bay of Bengal. I traveled to the area in a trawler with food aid from the EU. Over the ice-like, slippery mud came running perhaps twenty Bangladeshi women because they had heard that there were women on the trawler who spoke Bengali, saying: "We do not want to be saved, they are treating us like animals." Who was treating them like animals? Doctors Without Borders. Why? Because the local interpreters from Bengali to English, in that crowd, have nothing but contempt for these women. So whatever they were saying to the doctors was not what the women were saying. Public health Euro-U.S. institutions get million-dollar grants, and some of it is earmarked for translation, but one never thinks of the possibility of gender [contempt] and class contempt at the grassroots on the part of those who have access to the imperial languages. Paramedical work is different because you have to know the language. I began my activism in the early eighties in Bangladesh. Trying to transform the life habits of the rural poor, in order to save women from unwanted pregnancies and stop infant mortality and to provide good food habits, inoculation habits. Here I began to understand how much society depended upon their definition of women as the foundation. I call this "the training of the imagination of the rural underclass for epistemological performance"; in other words, constructing yourself differently. That is the "literary-philosophical" as I have described above.

I have no husband, no children. I am seventy-three years old. Not only in my country but in most places, the world is divided into childed and unchilded people, and to be such as me is considered to be a real misfortune. But my mother trained me, trained my imagination, in such a way that I think of it as freedom. I truly think of it as freedom. That is imaginative training in epistemological performance. The mother thinks honor; the daughter thinks reproductive rights. That is epistemological performance. Marx, in the only book that he wrote, *Capital*, volume 1, asked the working class to think of themselves not as victims of capitalism but as agents of production. Epistemological performance. Imaginative training for epistemological performance: that is something that was happening, for me as well, when I was traveling with the rural paramedics. That was my first training in activism.

Believe me, I was talking to these women, in their dialect, as if I were Muslim, acknowledging that even the very poor, the uneducated, have imagination. If you relate to them in the feudal version of love, top-down philanthropy, there is no solution, they know how to deal with that: automatic and effusive agreement followed by automatic forgetting. Why trust the ruling class, even when it smiles? As I have said, the task is to produce solvers of problems, not only solve problems.

To move to the labor movement in Bangladesh involves the permanent casuals, generally women, in the computer-assembly works, in the textile industry, in international subcontracting, and in the extension of micro-credit without imaginative training. I think micro-credit works sometimes; I am not against it. But far and wide, what did Women's World Banking say when they were talking to new graduates at the Columbia Law School, not necessarily feminists? That it was a vast, untapped commercial sector. Why did the Grameen Bank first begin to lend to women? Because women's record for repayment was 93 percent. This internalized gendering is something that has not gone away.

Women with little or no imaginative preparation do not deal well with income. I have to leave that statement hanging, with nothing more than a warning against positive responses in photo ops, or the manufacturing of statistics. If you spend time with me we can discuss these points.

The work I am describing can be called supplementing vanguardism. In any group, there will be two or three people who do all the work. If you have done any activism or, not even that, committee work, any work, you will realize that it always takes two or three people to actually get the work done and so they in fact do all the work. This is the vanguard. Most of the time the vanguard goes on to constitute itself as a Steering Committee. They begin to become more and more famous and get more and more prizes and awards. They begin to delegate and it becomes a classed endeavor: empowerment work, leadership work, micro-credit, consciousness-raising, backed by corporate fundraising.

If this structure is not persistently and forever supplemented by people doing the unglamorous slow work of producing problem solvers rather than having a vanguard constantly solving problems, we cannot imagine a just world, where feminism is the anchor of justice, because gender is global, and gender is the primary instrument of abstraction. You cannot do it globally, from the top. It is a collectivity we must produce not through interpreters. This is the sustaining policy preceding and following the global, embracing the global.

In conclusion, a summary: because I work in high theory in a very elite school, teaching this material to students, and also at the other end, teaching and training the very poor, trying to learn from below, because they are very different from us, the landless illiterate in the world's largest democracy, I am learning to share my experience at both ends in terms of a gender-just world. My theory is therefore one of supplementing, wherever one's own sphere of interest is universalized. I base social theory on gender. I say that ethical theory, a theory of unconditional ethics, can be practically taught through the literary-philosophical. I base political intervention on a performative contradiction that must presuppose what it wants to achieve. Supplementing work is persistent, I say, and define activism as imaginative training for epistemological performance: in labor movement work, ecological work, among the poor. The thing dearest to my heart is teaching the intuitions of democracy through an understanding of the meaning of the right to intellectual labor, on top as well as below. Thank you for your attention. Flesh it out for your own world.

THE STORY'S WHERE I GO

An Interview with Ursula K. Le Guin

JOHN PLOTZ

W hen did Ursula Le Guin last cross your radar screen? It could have been her memorable broadside at the 2014 National Book Awards ceremony, against Amazon and "commodity profiteers" who "sell us like deodorant." My favorite line: "We live in capitalism. Its power seems inescapable. So did the divine right of kings."[1]

If you have memories of Le Guin from before that day, they probably include Tenar in the tombs of Atuan and Ged, a goatherd turned wizard. Do you also recall a little boat called *Lookfar*, the wizards' school on Roke, and dragons who can't lie because they speak only the True Speech? Join the club, comrade: you're remembering Earthsea, realest land that never was.

Over six decades, the eighty-five-year-old writer has won a Newberry, five Nebulas, five Hugos, and a raft of other awards for adult and children's science fiction, fantasy, poetry, and essays. It was between 1968 and 1974, though, that Le Guin vaulted into the hearts of kids everywhere by publishing her first trilogy of Earthsea books: *A Wizard of Earthsea* (1968), *The Tombs of Atuan* (1970), and *The Farthest Shore* (1972). A second, equally compelling trilogy followed many years later: *Tehanu* (1990), *Tales from Earthsea* (2001), and *The Other Wind* (2001). It was also between 1968 and

1974—the Nixon administration had to be good for something—that Le Guin turned out a further three science-fiction master-pieces, in three distinct molds. *The Left Hand of Darkness* (1969) is a chilly quest in a world where gender is intermittent and muta-ble; *The Dispossessed* (1974), a thoughtful anarchist utopia/dysto-pia; and *The Lathe of Heaven* (1971) centers on a reluctant dreamer whose dreams can change the world, for better or worse.

This March I climbed toward Portland's West Hills to interview Le Guin. It was one of those days that begins foggy and rainy, then turns unexpectedly sunny by midmorning. I crossed a bridge over one of those mossy green gorges no doubt designed to remind us outsiders about Portland's effortless superiority to, say, frozen gray Boston. Built along a steep hillside, virtually all the houses in Le Guin's knobby neighborhood look back down across the flats to the gleaming Willamette River. It's the sort of place where you see an American flag with the fifty stars replaced by a giant peace sign and a local carpenter's hand-lettered placard reads: "By hammer and hand all things do stand." Her house and the crescent-shaped porch out back radiate permanence and comfort. Inside: Morris chairs and light-drenched rooms, blood-red Bukhara rugs, a cat who played intermittently with a ping-pong ball.

Over the course of a morning, our conversation ranged widely. Le Guin proposed that fantasy's power to free the reader's imagi-nation paradoxically increases when its descriptions are most painstakingly exact; she described her friendship with science-fiction great Philip K. Dick and how differently the two of them felt about the *I Ching*. She was eloquent on what she likes and what she distrusts in modern fiction, and she offered a fascinating way to think about the inescapable barrier between the actual and the fantasy realm. She also spoke movingly about what her work owes to anthropology, to science, and to her socialist and anarchist ide-als. Le Guin once ended a speech by asking, "Now that we're free, where are we going?" That's a question she knows each of her readers will have to answer alone. Still, I left feeling she had laid down a few cairns for us, the hint of a trail to trace.

1. Names Come First with Me: Fantasy's Exactitude and the Power of Maps

John Plotz (JP): When a writer creates an imaginary world, are readers traveling into the writer's imagination? Or is it more that the book activates the reader's own imagination?

Ursula Le Guin (UL): Both things happen, particularly with kids, which is why I think it's important that kids get imaginative literature. As a writer I feel I'm taking the reader with me into this world that I see and discover, but of course I discovered that the readers make that world their own, and it's sometimes quite, quite different from what I imagine. This comes out very clearly when I work with illustrators, and try to say, "No, no, that's not what a dragon looks like!" You know, not *my* dragon. There always has to be a compromise.

JP: So the imaginary is a very definite place to you, with its own set of rules.

UL: I'm very strong on accuracy and exactitude. You can't describe everything—that would be very boring. With an invented world, though, you have to describe more than a realist does. Of course, you have to leave out an enormous amount, too, and the leaving-out is half the art. There the reader is free to supply whatever they want to supply, to fill in all those white spaces that you leave.

I think sometimes in science fiction, more than in fantasy, the author wants you to see it just exactly the way the author sees it. Some people like to be coerced when they read, but I'd rather be given latitude. Tolkien is really such a master there. You know where you are, you know what the weather is, from what direction the wind's blowing. He tells you what he can about it—but the rest of it's up to you.

JP: I was reading a funny Tolkien letter recently. He was worried that the moon phases were working differently for characters in different parts of Middle-earth: Bilbo had a full moon the same night that Aragorn saw a crescent.

UL: That would be very distressing to me, too. Jane Austen apparently mapped out the rooms, and the Brontës always wanted to know distances. My kind of novelist thinks that way.

JP: There's a map at the front of the Earthsea books: you can find the Dragon's Run near Selidor, and Atuan far off in the East. Did that map come to you before you wrote the books themselves?

UL: I wrote a couple of short stories that took place on islands that had wizards. Then I was asked by a publisher to write—we didn't even have the word "young adult" then—to write a fantasy for older children. I thought, "Oh no, I can't do that. I've never written for children. I don't know how to do that." Still, I went home and thought about it; how does a wizard become a wizard? He goes to wizard school? Wouldn't that be fun? So there I went, and then I thought, "OK, where? Oh, it's those islands where those other stories are." But I needed to know more about them. So I did literally sit down and draw *a big map with lots of islands*, about which I knew nothing at that point. I named them, happily. For the rest of the six books I could just travel around and find out what they were like.

JP: I have such strong associations with the island's names: Roke, where the wizards' school is; Havnor, at the heart of the kingdom; Gont; Vemish . . . I could go on! Were all the names there to begin with?

UL: Names come first with me. I can't write about a character if he or she doesn't have a name. The right name. So I had to name all of the islands right away. Isn't that weird? I have no understanding what the process there is.

2. Blundering Toward a Transition: SF vs. Fantasy, Gender vs. Sex

JP: I think you once said, more or less, that fantasy is the inward life and science fiction the outward life.

UL: That's kind of crude, a bit judgmental, maybe, but I know what I meant. Fantasy tends to arise from somewhat unexplored sources within. Science fiction depends on what Chip [the science fiction writer Samuel R.] Delany called "what is known to be known." Meaning science, technology, various kinds of knowledge. It uses those imaginatively. So in that sense it is more outward.

JP: And has it always been clear to you which category your books fall into?

UL: Oh no. When I started it was all mushed up together! My first three novels are kind of science fantasy. *Rocannon's World* (1966) is full of Norse myth barely disguised. But I began to realize there was a real difference between these two ways of using the imagination. So I wrote *Earthsea* and *Left Hand of Darkness*. From then on I was following two paths.

In *Left Hand of Darkness* I was using science fiction to come at a problem that I realized was very deep in me and everybody else: What is gender? What gender am I? A question we just hadn't been asking. Look at all the answers that are coming out now. We have really deconstructed it. We really didn't even have the word "gender" back then. Just, "What sex are you?"

So in some respects we really have come a long way, and in a good direction, I think.

JP: You described feminism then as waking up from a very long nap. I guess it's really woken up now.

UL: Yeah, and there are a lot of people trying to put us back to sleep.

JP: I think you once wrote that while writing *Left Hand of Darkness* you would forget what gender your characters were.

UL: Well, I was trying to get inside the Gethenian body and viewpoint, in which gender happens once a month and is an event, and then they just go back to being human.

JP: Do you think that's true now, that gender is something that only intermittently matters?

UL: No, gender still is the first thing people want to know about the baby.

JP: In writing the later Earthsea books, did you feel that you needed to tell the story of gender in Earthsea in a different way from the earlier trilogy?

UL: I had been writing like a man. I was writing adventure fantasy in a grand old tradition, and it was all about men and what men did. I just needed to write like a woman, write *as* a woman. I was learning how to write as a woman in *Tehanu*, and it was very important to me to do so, to me personally, and for moral justice. I had been unjust to women in the books.

JP: And do you include *Tombs of Atuan* in that? As a kid, as a boy reader, I remember thinking that Tenar, the girl priestess, was a new kind of character for me.

UL: Her appearance of having power and being actually totally powerless is a paradigm of a woman's position. But I was still operating there in a man's world, and some of my feminist friends were cross. They say, well, Ged comes and gets her out. And I said, "No! He can't get out without her and she can't get out without him." And I do think that's true. So I was beginning to blunder towards a transition. But the next book is totally male.

3. A Rule of the Imagination: Moving the Boundary with Elfland

JP: Is *The Beginning Place* [a 1980 novel about two teenagers who cross back and forth between reality and a fantasy world] meant to be set in Portland?

UL: No. Actually, I had more like a middle-sized Midwestern city in mind. Cincinnati, possibly, I don't know.

JP: That book seems to have a lot of real-world problems in it: drugs, urban infrastructure. Very 1970s, American cities in trouble. I'm not saying that it sounds like a John Updike novel, but . . .

UL: Since then there's this whole genre of urban fantasy, as they call it, which has gone all sorts of different directions. One of the first ones I read was Megan Lindholm's *Wizard of the Pigeons*. It's a Seattle novel, a terrific urban fantasy, with street people. As I recall, the wizard is a guy who was damaged in Vietnam and is living on the street, as so many people were and still are.

In *Beginning Place* I was kind of trying to see if you could move the boundary between the real world and Elfland, as it were. And I couldn't. They could go down to the Beginning Place by the little stream, and go through, but the doorway is always there.

JP: You once said, "We have inhabited both the actual and the imaginary realms for a long time." But you're saying that the two have to be unmistakably separated? Like an atomic rule?

UL: Yeah, it's a rule of the imagination. I think you could possibly say, "If you break the rule, if you transgress, you are playing with insanity." You are allowing the unreal into the real in a dangerous way.

JP: *Lathe of Heaven* is a dangerous book in that way, isn't it?

UL: Oh yeah, there's dreams coming true. I'm totally with George, the protagonist of the novel, who fears his reality-altering dreams. I don't want it to happen.

4. Madness Is a Kind of Irresponsibility: Philip K. Dick

JP: Were you thinking about Philip K. Dick while writing *Lathe of Heaven*?

UL: Oh yeah. It's sort of an homage to him.

JP: Was it something you shared with him and discussed with him?

UL: We wrote letters back and forth some. We never met. I was rather scared of Phil. He was very heavily into drugs, and drugs do scare me. I had three kids at home and was not enthusiastic about having a real—not a pothead but a heavy drug user around. Phil went off the rails periodically, and so I was not really looking to meet him. But we did correspond, very friendly, for some while. We seemed to respect each other's writing, were interested in what each other was trying to do.

JP: I read you had gone to high school together. That's not true?

UL: That is so weird. Yes, we were complete contemporaries at Berkeley High School, but he's not in the yearbook. His name is in the yearbook, but there is no photograph. I think Phil dropped out before graduation.

I don't know many people anymore that were at Berkeley High with me. When there were more of us alive we tried to find out anything about him. Nobody remembers him. Not one person in this group remembered him physically. He worked at a store where I bought records when I had the money, so I might have met him there. But what he looked like then, as a teenager? [*Shrugs.*] He is absolutely the invisible man at Berkeley High.

JP: He clearly thought about you a lot.

UL: Yeah, apparently I shook him about women particularly. He realized his women were kind of odd creatures.

JP: He also invokes you when he's worried about his mental health.

UL: I didn't know that he ever admitted that.

JP: He thought of you as a person who worried that he might be mentally ill.

UL: Well, he wrote to me while he was having his visions and so on. Once he wrote to me very touchingly, because he was so happy. Was it a phone call? We did talk on the phone sometimes. He had been conversing with St. Paul in Greek, although he didn't know Greek, and he was just so happy about all this information he was getting from St. Paul. I think I just played along with it, but I suppose a certain amount of withdrawal or horror or something on my mind he might have felt. Because, yeah, I am afraid of madness. It's scary.

JP: I think that's something that comes through in *Lathe of Heaven*. . . . On the one hand, there's this immense power, imagination's power to reshape the world. But on the other hand, who *wants* that? That's terrifying.

UL: Right. And the thing is, with power comes responsibility, in my world. Just, they've got to go together, and once you separate them bad things are going to happen. And that's the trouble: to me, madness is a kind of irresponsibility. It may not be desired or wanted at all, but all the same. A mad person is irresponsible and is usually treated as such. So if he's got power, well, look at Stalin.

5. Make the Work Good Enough: Politics, *The Dispossessed*, and the Scholars

JP: *The Dispossessed* works through its political ideas very openly.

UL: It's my political book: anarchy, socialist anarchy, pacifist anarchism. The ideal is people can work freely together, can choose to work together. That's the anarchist ideal, such a lovely ideal. I know William Morris had it. Make the work good enough and people will want to do it and do it together.

JP: Were you tempted to write other books like that?

UL: That book took a long time to prepare for and get ready to write, and it was hard to write. I asked help on it from Darko Suvin [leading theorist and critic of science fiction as a genre and first editor of the journal *Science Fiction Studies*]. It is very rare for me to ask for any help. We were in moderately close epistolary touch at that point. And I rather nervously sent it to him, because . . . Darko can be very drastic.

JP: I was going to ask about him.

UL: Darko has a very, very warm heart and a very good mind. And he's a Marxist, and an anarchist needs a Marxist to remind them of certain truths. And vice versa. So Darko read the book in manuscript, and he said two things I remember. He said, "You've given it a closed ending. You can't do that, you can't close your circle. You're an anarchist!" And he said, "It has twelve chapters. It has to have thirteen."

JP: When I read Suvin or Fredric Jameson praising your science fiction, especially *The Dispossessed*, I feel them mobilizing you for a political cause.

UL: I would agree that I felt that a little and pulled away. And Darko would love to turn me into a Marxist, but there's no hope, and he knows it.

JP: Why is there no hope?

UL: Marxist? I'm a socialist, maybe, but . . . no, Marxism was tried and failed rather grandly, decisively.

JP: State power, is that what failed?

UL: The Soviet Union was a major experiment, and it went wrong from the start.

JP: What did you hope *The Dispossessed* would *do*? Change minds? Make anarchists?

UL: It's pretty much a thought experiment. "What if we did it this way?" What if we tried anarchism, and what if there was a place it could be tried? Which is not going to be on Earth because there's always a neighboring state.

JP: There'd be someone you'd need to dispossess?

UL: Or someone would come and invade you. They did try anarchism in Spain: kind of misguidedly, perhaps.

Otherwise, I don't think any of my other books are particularly political because the next big book I wrote after *Dispossessed* is probably *Always Coming Home*. It's a utopia of sorts, too, but not a political one. It's a social one.

JP: Do you see *The Left Hand of Darkness* as a political book because of what it does with gender?

UL: Yeah, well, you know, that was the old feminist slogan: the personal is the political. But only in that sense. The people [who are androgynous twenty-seven days of the month and then briefly assume either male or female characteristics before returning to androgyny] are physiologically enormously different from us.

6. Story vs. Plot, the Perils of the Present Tense, and Fantasy's Pitfalls

JP: You once wrote, "Actually I'm terrible at plotting, so all I do is sort of put people in motion and they go around in circles and they generally end up where they started out. That's a Le Guin plot. I admire real plotting, but I seem not able to achieve it."

UL: To me, the thing is the story. Story just starts here and goes there. The story is something that moves. Or maybe it starts here and ends up here. It has a shape, a trajectory.

And a plot is, to me, basically sort of complicating the trajectory. It's complications and additions and backtracks and all that. It is wonderful. You know, a good Dickens plot: We're reading *Bleak House* aloud, and watching him get that enormous plot into motion, wow! You know, I'm awed. But I can't do that. And all the same, it really isn't the plot of *Bleak House*, it's the story that is important to me. So OK, I'm not a plotter, and I cannot even follow a really complex plot, like some mysteries. I just get lost—who cares? But the story's where I go. So I just accept that. And people who want to read for plot are not going to read me.

JP: Not only does *Bleak House* have all of that plotting and backtracking, but it's also narrated half by an omniscient storyteller and half by the heroine, Esther.

UL: He's taking a real risk in doing that. Reading it aloud is very interesting, shifting those voices. Every now and then you can hear Dickens coming through Esther. But the other voice, the one that's always in the present tense—probably the first three times I read the book, I didn't even notice that.

That's very unusual in nineteenth-century writing. But it's become such a habit now. I'm sick of books in the present tense, which is a very restrictive tense. It's not as flexible as the past tense.

Writing in the past tense you have total freedom to move forward and back. I've thought about this a lot. Trying to think why the present tense, which never bothered me until it became a sort of habit of the modern novel, why it now bothers me so much.

My metaphor is it's a flashlight. It illuminates only a moment, and it moves with the moment, the present tense does. And the past tense is like sunlight, you can see everything all at once. And I think it's the focus that a lot of modern novelists love in the present tense: this tight focus, like a camera eye. But like a narrow-focus camera eye. I think this phenomenon of writing in the present tense is very strange, actually, a little unnerving.

JP: Does it connect to that weird phenomenon of writing in the second person? "You do this," "you merge onto the freeway." You're covering your face with your hands. That's bad, right?

UL: I've tried and tried to read second-person narrative, and it is so self-conscious. There was also—we're coming out of it now—there was quite a long time when poets used "you" when they meant "I," but didn't want to say so. "You walk down the street and you feel . . ." No, I don't! Talk about yourself! Don't dump it onto me.

JP: And how about modern fantasy? I gather that you distrust stories with angelic heroes and easy-to-spot bad guys?

UL: This whole battle of good and evil thing . . . oh, man, have they driven that into the ground! And all these Tolkien-derivative imitation things with the orcs against the elves. It's so simplistic, and it's so childlike—*childish*, rather.

JP: Kazuo Ishiguro recently remarked that fantasy is mainly about dragons and pixies. Your response was that you are on the side of the dragons but not really on the side of the pixies.

UL: There haven't been pixies, except maybe in Disney, for quite a while now, so what is he actually talking about? I don't go for pixies. They're sort of detestable.

JP: Because they're cute.

UL: They're cute, sentimental, yeah. Whereas dragons are kind of amazing because so many different cultures have some version of the dragon. And, you know, you have to take them seriously. I wrote that piece called "Why Are Americans Afraid of Dragons?," and they still are.

JP: Does that mean that you think that sweetness or sentimentality doesn't belong in fantasy?

UL: Well, sweetness and sentimentality are two entirely different things. Sentimentality to me simply means a false emotion, whatever it is. It's just sort of the sweet side of cynicism. But it's false, detached. But sure, it's the cute, sentimental, and trite thing that fantasy falls into so easily. That's not where I want to go. But I do want to go where the dragons are. And I'm not sure Mr. Ishiguro really does. [In his recent novel *The Buried Giant*,] his dragon never even woke up, the poor thing. It got its head cut off while it's asleep, which is kind of humiliating.

7. You Look for It Where You Find It: Growing Up Amid Anthropologists

JP: Your parents were the eminent anthropologist Alfred Kroeber and Theodora Kroeber, who wrote *Ishi: Last of His Tribe*. Can you talk about the influence of anthropology on your work?

UL: Well, it was sort of osmosis. I didn't read my father's kind of anthropology—what's often dismissed as "cultural relativism"—until I had been writing for some while. In Berkeley during the thirties and forties, though, I grew up in a household with refugees from Europe: intellectuals, anthropologists coming from exotic places to visit, and more

Indians than most little white middle-class girls would have seen in their life. It made a difference.

I also think I inherited some of my father's proclivities, as he might say. Some of his temperament. We're just interested. An interest in the way people do things. And if they're different from the way we do them, that's *fine*. It shocked me to realize that a lot of people don't want to know how other people do things, because it's wrong. "We do it right, and they don't." I just didn't get that as a kid.

JP: Isn't there tension between that kind of cultural relativism and your idea about the "true name of things" in the Earthsea books—the idea of an underlying order in the universe?

UL: Yes, there's a lot of tension. If you're completely culturally relativistic, what do you do with morality? Well, you do with it what you can. And you look for it where you find it. That's where I feel that I was given a genuine freedom of the intellect: I don't have to look in any particular place for what I want. I can look anywhere and hope to find what I want.

I became a Taoist in my teens because Lao Tzu's *Tao Te Ching* was in my father's bookcase. I saw him reading it—a beautiful little book. And I said, "What's that?" And he said, "Chinese stuff." I read everything—at thirteen, fourteen, or fifteen—so I read it, and thought, "Oh, this is wonderful!" From then on, I went back to that book, and all the different translations of it, which vary so much—eventually I made my own.[2]

JP: Is that book something you and Philip K. Dick talked about?

UL: As I think about it, looking back, I don't think Phil read Lao Tzu the way I did, with passionate interest. Phil was interested in the *I Ching*. He wrote *The Man in the High Castle* by throwing the yarrow sticks. And then he turned against it, and suddenly when he started talking to St. Paul, the *I Ching* became the Book of Evil. I think he had some sort of bad trip with it.

Well, I use *I Ching* a lot to make certain decisions. But I just threw the coins. I couldn't bother with the yarrow sticks.

JP: Six coins?

UL: With coins you need three, but with the yarrow sticks you need fifty, and it takes a long time, which of course gives you time to think about what's your right question. But with three kids I couldn't do the yarrow sticks. There were time constraints, you know?

JP: So you used the *I Ching* for writing?

UL: For practical decisions. Someone wants me to go speak somewhere. Should I do it or not? And it always gave me good advice because I was finding out what I wanted to do.

JP: But you were never tempted to use it in writing, like in a decision about writing?

UL: No, no, that was up to me. Kind of a matter of responsibility.

8. The Beauty of Science, Trying Not to Write Angry

JP: I think you have a soft spot in your writing for scholars and scientists.

UL: Oh yeah. I knew them. I grew up amongst them. Yeah, and I *love* science as a human undertaking, as much as I love art. Science rightly done is so beautiful. I can't understand math. I know it's probably the most beautiful, but . . . [*chuckling*]

JP: Yeah, my wife teaches math, so I have that experience a lot.

UL: I believe what they say, but I can't *see* it.

JP: I watch her eyes light up, but I'm not sure why they're lighting up.

UL: Thank you for telling me that. But geology, for instance, oh my Lord, it's all poetry. It's amazing. And I lived through that great revolution in geology where we discovered about plate tectonics. And that was so exciting to watch it happening, and the new article would come out, oh my God, look at that! Oh my God! It's right under Oregon!

JP: In your Earthsea books, the wizard school could become a site of evil—magicians as mad scientists—but it never quite turns out that way.

UL: Okay, but how come no women? How come no sex for the men? What's wrong? Something has gone wrong here. It ain't natural.

JP: But you're gentle on the all-male wizard school, aren't you?

UL: Well, people make mistakes, for heaven's sake. You can't get my age without realizing people make mistakes, and blaming them for it, what good does that do?

JP: Your writing is always willing to point out things that can go wrong, but it doesn't come across on the page that you're angry about things very much.

UL: I do get very angry, but I don't find anger a very . . . I think you have to get angry and be angry and not dwell on it, not nurse it. You have to get past it. So yeah, I would say I try not to write angry.

Since we talked about Taoism and anger, I should mention that later and much much later in my life I also have been fairly deeply influenced by certain forms of Buddhism. Buddhist thinking, not the practice, but the religion—by the Buddhist idea that if you deny suffering, you're denying everything.

9. Final Thoughts: Energy, Opportunity, and What Worked Out

JP: Are there any books that you could have written at some moment and didn't write? Or books you regret writing?

UL: No, neither one. I wish could have gone on after *Lavinia*, but I just didn't. It's just a matter of physical energy, really, I think. But I envy José Saramago, who wrote that lovely *Elephant's Journey*, like, oh my God, I think he was eighty-five, which is what I am now. Wow. Lucky him.

JP: What is the energy that writing takes?

UL: Oh, physical. Every . . . physical, mental, spiritual, you name it. It just calls upon one entirely. That's why I couldn't write when I was responsible for looking after my children. Because that is also a total commitment. And I just couldn't do two full-time things at once, so I had to get them to bed. They were really good about that.

JP: That's Virginia Woolf, isn't it? The room of one's own.

UL: Yes, my room of my own was only after nine o'clock, once the kids were in bed either asleep or reading. But it worked out. It does work out.

NOTES

1. For a transcript and a link to video of the speech, see " 'We Will Need Writers Who Can Remember Freedom': Ursula K. Le Guin at the National Book Awards," November 19, 2014, https://parkerhiggins.net/2014/11/will -need-writers-can-remember-freedom-ursula-k-le-guin-national-book -awards/.
2. Lao Tzu, *Tao Te Ching: A Book About the Way and the Power of the Way*, trans. Ursula K. Le Guin, with J. P. Seaton (Boulder, CO: Shambhala, 1997).

THINKING CRITICALLY ABOUT CRITICAL THINKING

CHRISTOPHER SCHABERG

A
t Loyola University New Orleans I teach a seminar on David Foster Wallace—a class I designed at the urging of several students. One day late in the semester we were tackling Wallace's very short story "Incarnations of Burned Children." Four students in the class immediately and enthusiastically declared that they had read and discussed this story in their Introduction to Creative Writing courses, several years prior. I asked what they had learned about it, and not one of them could produce anything beyond a rather equivocal answer: "I think it was supposed to teach us how to tell a story." I pushed them to recall the specific lessons the story held for beginning creative writers. I asked what sort of textbook this story had appeared in, and one student described the book, mentioning that it was "the kind of anthology with a list of *critical thinking* questions after each piece." My ears perked up. What sort of questions were these? No one could remember any of them, even in the most general terms.

I let it go, and we went on to have a lively discussion about Wallace's manipulation of time and the red herrings of symbolism in the story. But the spectral "*critical thinking* questions" stayed with me, aggravating a growing interest I have in this phrase. I had been reflecting on "critical thinking" for the ways it attained buzzword status on college campuses, signifying something important, even necessary—but something equally difficult to pin down or articulate. I find myself frequently repelled by how these two words are required to appear on certain syllabi or how they get trotted around as a transcendent sort of skill that students are supposed to learn in a paradoxically quantifiable way. How does this phrase function, and what do we want from it? To get at these questions, we have to approach the topic . . . critically.

Consider this two-tier explanation from the University of Louisville website:

> After a careful review of the mountainous body of literature defining critical thinking and its elements, UofL has chosen to adopt the language of Michael Scriven and Richard Paul (2003) as a comprehensive, concise operating definition:
>
> Critical thinking is the intellectually disciplined process of actively and skillfully conceptualizing, applying, analyzing, synthesizing, and/or evaluating information gathered from, or generated by, observation, experience, reflection, reasoning, or communication, as a guide to belief and action.

On the one hand, this elected definition would seem to be fairly airtight and straightforward: critical thinking is the application of information to shape decisions. Easy enough. On the other hand, this definition is so capacious as to nearly explain away the very thing it seeks to describe. Critical thinking is an "intellectually disciplined process"—overarching (or sidestepping) all disciplines per se. It involves a chain of "and/or" activities that can happen in so many contexts (including the most ordinary "experience") that one would be hard pressed to find a place where it *isn't* happening, on some level. It is a sort of mental Swiss Army Knife, able to unfold a range of analytic tools depending on the circumstances.

Closing out the citation, there is the suave conjunction of "belief and action." If only the connections between thought and action were so simple as to be causal. But as Marx once shrewdly pointed out, "one does not judge an individual by what he thinks about himself . . . but, on the contrary, this consciousness must be explained from the contradictions of material life." In other words, just because teaching is conducted under the explicit rubric of critical thinking, it cannot be taken as a given that expected actions will result. Rather, students' actions in the world will tell you if critical thinking has taken place. This might pose problematic parameters for assessment, to say the least. (Incidentally, this all-encompassing field of learning may begin to sound like more than college professors signed on for.)

If the stated imperatives of critical thinking do not necessarily render anything real in the world, anything remembered, then critical thinking can amount to mere mental exercise, a sensation that wisps away like the fading afterglow of a brisk walk or bike ride. The metaphor of a physical workout is more than simply convenient. In puzzling over the phrase, I asked my composition and rhetoric colleague Kate Adams for her suggested reading, and Kate directed me to John Bean's seminal work *Engaging Ideas: The Professor's Guide to Integrating Writing, Critical Thinking, and Active Learning in the Classroom*, first published in 1996 and republished in subsequent editions.

Bean's study launches from the basic assumption that humans are naturally problem-solving creatures: "Presenting students with problems . . . taps into something natural and self-fulfilling in our beings." Citing Ken Bain, Bean asserts that " 'beautiful problems' create a 'natural critical learning environment.' " As Bean goes on to claim, "Part of the difficulty of teaching critical thinking, therefore, is awakening students to the existence of problems all around them." The aesthetic terms and environmental rhetoric in these sentences are striking. They hint at a quasi-Nietzschean philosophy, with their overtones of self-fulfillment and awakening in a raw, natural environment. As if to reinforce this ambient attitude, Bean goes on to elaborate: "As Brookfield (1987) claims, critical thinking is 'a productive and positive' activity. 'Critical thinkers are actively engaged with life.' This belief in the natural, healthy, and motivating pleasure of problems—and in the power of well-designed problems to awaken and stimulate the passive and unmotivated student—is one of the underlying premises of this book."

Is this really what we are referring to when we speak of critical thinking in college? Can we so easily justify course design and instruction—not to mention the entire project of the liberal arts—with recourse to active engagement with life, to what is "natural, healthy, and motivating"? It sounds so . . . *romantic.* Unfortunately, these platitudes may fail to satisfy measures of "value-added" and "return on investment" that colleges are under growing pressure to determine and demonstrate. Nevertheless, "critical thinking" lingers as a nebulous skill and pedantic requirement on college campuses.

For instance: during a recent meeting for a strategic-planning committee I serve on at my university, one of my colleagues adamantly rejected the inclusion of an allegedly trendy catchphrase ("experiential learning") as part of our mission statement and insisted that we use "critical thinking" instead. My colleague was ostensibly rejecting the professionalization of college education in favor of the more properly academic priority of intellect. This preference, however, struck me as curious, as it revealed that "critical thinking"—whatever cluster of ideas or intellectual ideals hide behind the phrase—had become something for which we felt nostalgia. I had been in meetings before where *that* was the buzzword to be scoffed at. Now we pine for critical thinking, in its apparent recession, however elusive a definition remains.

The philosopher Margret Grebowicz has observed that "whatever is vernacular is what is most difficult to view from a critical distance." The phrase "critical thinking" would seem to be caught in a double bind, its first word trapped in the very vernacular mist that such mental effort is supposed to dispel. The most authoritative definitions are either vast beyond usefulness or brazen in their deferrals to romantic sentiments. Either way, critical thinking seems to point toward some immeasurable beyond: to a place where life is vibrant and rife with problems begging to be solved on the spot.

The Grebowicz line I quoted above is from a book called *The National Park to Come*, which ends up being surprisingly useful. At one point she analyzes historical constructions and critiques of "the scene of Nature" (with a capital *N*), suggesting that "what remains to be theorized is the wilderness hallucination, the postcard projection, the scenic backdrop, the wild as spectacle."

This is akin to the problem with the liberal arts broadly, the phrase "critical thinking" as a synecdoche of sorts. Higher education is increasingly expected to be a concentrated site for focused job training and career preparation; this comes with an attendant fantasy of a robust economy and ample employment opportunities. This is one kind of "hallucination," to use Grebowicz's term. On the other hand, college can be imagined as a fecund (or vivid, anyway) wilderness of sorts, life-generating and adventurous. This is the "scenic backdrop" behind Bean's formulation of critical thinking. It may be well intentioned and even *motivating* from a pedagogical (and learning) standpoint, but we would do well to recognize that these two governing fantasies are not only incompatible; *they are also both fantasies*, projections of something that can only be maintained as such. Critical thinking, in either context—as a practical skill or as a rugged comportment toward the ineffable—would seem to function as a second-order fantasy, hovering above the very thing that we cannot come to terms with in a satisfying way: the role of liberal arts in higher education. This is a problem worthy of critical thinking, a knot that won't be severed by any ready blade or mere mental exercise.

IF YOU'RE WOKE YOU DIG IT

William Melvin Kelley

ELI ROSENBLATT

William Melvin Kelley, the experimental novelist and filmmaker—who mastered and reinvented a kind of mid-century literary style crafted from a colorful array of language and perspectives—died in Manhattan on February 1, 2017, at the age of seventy-nine. For the past three decades, Kelley taught fiction at Sarah Lawrence College, where I enrolled in his seminar. We struck up a long dialogue about Jewish and African American literature and culture.

From his teaching and the dialogues that followed off and on for years afterwards, Willy inspired in me a self-reliance and will to originality, which seems to always pull me back to his surreal and carnivalesque view of American culture. Never predictable, Willy, when I asked him which novel might give my work a sharper, more distinct view of Jewish American culture, responded: Harriet Beecher Stowe's *Uncle Tom's Cabin*. That novel—in its Yiddish translation—became my doctoral dissertation's keystone. Kelley's work was always spiritual: he studied the Jewish tradition—as closely as he could without the benefit of an official conversion—calling himself a Child of Israel and a believer in the "True God." He often said that as a poor reader, there were only two books in his life that he had read end-to-end: James Joyce's *Ulysses* and the Hebrew Bible.

Willy, or "Duke" as he was known in his Harlem neighborhood, was born in Staten Island on November 1, 1937. His father, William Melvin Kelley Sr., was an editor at the African American newspaper the *Amsterdam News*, who tried unsuccessfully to start his own newspaper and ultimately became a civil servant. His mother, the former Narcissa Agatha Garcia, was a homemaker and devout Catholic.

Kelley was intimately involved in discovering a new African American aesthetic, one catalyzed by the history-shifting politics of the Civil Rights and Black Power era. In 1962, he published his first novel, the masterpiece *A Different Drummer*. The novel takes place in a mythical southern state that mysteriously loses its large black population in forty-eight hours. The literary critic Trudier Harris called the novel "a battleground of sorts," which rebelled against expectations by depicting African American characters with no narrative voice of their own. Instead, the narrators are taken from among numerous white characters, who each describe and analyze the actions of black characters for the reading audience.

Kelley was a late subject of the Harlem Renaissance photographer Carl Van Vechten and a young protégé of Langston Hughes, who in 1965 invited him to tour Europe under the auspices of the State Department. Kelley's imagination honored the legacy of the Harlem Renaissance by depicting the absurd inequalities that followed in its wake. He published prolifically throughout the 1960s, including a collection of short stories, *Dancers on the Shore* (1964), and the novels *A Drop of Patience* (1965), *dem* (1967), and *Dunfords Travels Everywheres* (1970). In that final novel, Kelley devised a Joycean creole: "*Dust, we may away ouSelfs from the langleash language for a Perusol o' so some Source matourial gleanered from dPages o' Dialy Citysun*"

"I would say there were two languages that were created by African Americans," he explained in one of his seminars. "One that is being created so that African people could communicate with European people and another language for African people to communicate with other African people. I imagine that at that point, English was the common language that we were using. So, OK, we would use English words, but we use them in an African way. That process takes a long time," he thought, "Yiddish is a language that can be considered a Creole language. It was a combination of Hebrew and German, and it was spoken by Jews in Europe. It's a question that African Americans will have to answer. Do we let it die out and learn standard English, or do we keep them both and develop a language and literature in both?"

Willy's assignments at once confounded and invigorated the Sarah Lawrence campus's avant-garde sensibilities. One recurring exercise, for example, was for seminar participants to write a romance novel collectively. Each of the fifteen students would be responsible for writing one chapter. At the culmination of the semester, the students came together for a charged reading that voiced a cohesive work with divergent points of view, styles, and levels of diction. Another involved writing five pages without the verb "to be"—a technique that Willy culled from the biblical narrators.

In 2014, the *Oxford English Dictionary* credited Kelley with coining the political term "woke," in a 1962 *New York Times* article titled "If You're Woke You Dig It; No mickey mouse can be expected to follow today's Negro idiom without a hip assist. If You're Woke You Dig It." The hashtag #staywoke later became a catchphrase of the new Black Lives Matter movement, after first passing serendipitously through Erykah Badu.

Kelley wrote intricate novels that identified with the rejection of dominant social orders while also penning incisive essays drawn sharply from his experience in the centers of power. In "The Ivy League Negro," which appeared in *Esquire* magazine in 1963, he remarked on African American men like himself enrolled at elite universities:

> In my class at Harvard, out of a thousand boys, there were ten Negroes. By the end of the first three weeks of the term, I had met them all. A Negro in a new situation will look, either consciously or unconsciously, for other Negroes. He will not feel really at home until he knows how many there are, their names, and where they came from. I always compare it to two spies in enemy territory dropping notes scribbled on matchbook covers as they pass one another on the street.

In his novel *dem*, an absurdist parable, a white woman gives birth to twins—one of whom, mysteriously, is mixed-race—only to discover that the mysterious baby is the result of super fecundation: the "fertilization of two ova by two separate sperm during two separate copulations." After the death of the white baby, her grieving husband Mitchell searches for the father of the brown baby and finds Calvin Coolidge Johnson in Harlem, who denies any responsibility for the child. A man who long held a "grudge" against whites, Coolidge reminds Mitchell of the countless slave owners who fathered children and denied their paternity, forcing black men into a false paternal role. Instead, Coolidge insists that Mitchell's time had come. When Mitchell asks, "Why me?" Coolidge replies, "Why [my] great-granddaddy?"

Kelley was an expert in the arts and theories of mixed metaphor. Of his childhood he wrote:

> I was not raised in a ghetto, but in the North Bronx, the only Negro boy on a predominantly Italian-American block.

Knowing this you must not immediately assume that I was unhappy, you must not assume I was always fighting on my way to school; this was not at all the case. On the contrary, being the only Negro gave me a wonderful advantage; I was always a very important part of the games my white friends and I played. When we played the Lone Ranger, I was always Tonto; when we fought the Japs, I was always the Friendly Native. This is because I was not so much "colored" as brown, and too good a friend to be one of the outlaws or the Japanese.

Kelley attended the Fieldston School and in 1957 entered Harvard College planning to be a civil-rights lawyer. Instead, he was drawn to the seminars of John Hawkes and Archibald Macleish and won the Dana Read Prize in 1960 for the best piece of writing in any Harvard undergraduate publication. Shortly thereafter he took a leave of absence to focus on his writing and left campus six months short of earning a degree. In 1965, in the moments after hearing of Malcolm X's murder, he detailed his decision to go into exile: "I wouldn't assign myself the task of announcing that our little rebellion had failed, that racism had won again for a while. Not with a young wife and a toddler depending on me and all this killing going on. By the time I reached the Bronx, I had decided to depart the Plantation, perhaps permanently." Kelly's time abroad brought him and his family to Rome, Ibiza, Paris, and Jamaica, where he taught at the University of the West Indies. In Europe, he joined other African American artists, writers, and intellectuals in self-imposed exile.

Besides his uncollected short stories, which have appeared in the *Saturday Evening Post*, the *New Yorker*, the *Negro Digest*, *Quilt*, and many anthologies, Kelley has a 1964 short-story collection, *Dancers on the Shore*, which won the Transatlantic Review award. In 1988, he wrote, produced, and starred in the rare experimental film *Excavating Harlem*. From 1989 until 1992, he kept a video diary, as a way to capture the beauty of his family and neighborhood that he felt could not be described in words. The resulting video, some of it damaged by years of storage, was collected and edited over the course of two years into another short called *The Beauty That I Saw*. The film debuted in the 2015 Harlem International Film Festival, where it won a Harlem Spotlight Award. In 2008, he was awarded Anisfield Wolf Book Award for Lifetime Achievement.

Willy Kelley was known for his enduring devotion to his family and his beloved Harlem. His acerbic and artful allegiance to the masses came through in a 1977 *New York Times* dispatch from Kingston, Jamaica, where he wrote of the political similarities between the island and his native land:

> The poor and the righteous can do anything they will, as they periodically and devastatingly show. But oftentimes (weary after years on a low-protein diet), they surrender the Authority to Do to some fatty ego with a megaphone and one ancient laugh in his script. Country people will stand quietly for hours listening to a fool. They grow the food the fool gets fat on, but after all the fool comes from the city.

TRANSLATING THE UNTRANSLATABLE

An Interview with Barbara Cassin

REBECCA L. WALKOWITZ

B arbara Cassin is a French philosopher, translator, and theorist of translation. Trained as a philologist and philosopher specializing in ancient Greece, she is the director of research at the Centre National de la Recherche Scientifique (CNRS) in Paris. She is the author, editor, and translator of many books, and for more than a decade she has been leading an international project devoted to the multilingual history of philosophical concepts. That project led to the 2004 publication of the *Vocabulaire européen des philosophies: Dictionnaire des intraduisibles*, which has been enormously successful in French and has been followed in the past decade by editions in Ukrainian, Arabic, and now English. The U.S. version was published earlier this year as *Dictionary of Untranslatables: A Philosophical Lexicon*. Edited by Emily Apter, Jacques Lezra, and Michael Wood, the 1,300-page *Dictionary* retains the original introduction, most of the entries, and an orientation toward Europe, but it has also been adjusted and supplemented for U.S. audiences. Apter's robust preface documents the enormous complexity and scale involved in translating *intraduisibles*.

One of the most provocative and important contributions of the *Vocabulaire* is its insistence that philosophical concepts, often assumed to be transhistorical and universal, in fact have a history in languages. The editions, adaptations, and translations of the project are important, too, however, because they show that philosophical concepts have a history in books as well. The *Vocabulaire* may be a multilingual project, whose entries collate and compare terms in more than a dozen languages, but the editions are not all multilingual in the same way and for the same reasons. Whereas the Ukrainian editors sought to expand the vocabulary and prestige of their language, their U.S. counterparts were more concerned to acknowledge and mitigate Anglophone dominance. The books are different structurally and economically as well as linguistically. The Ukrainian and Arabic editions have appeared only in parts, while the U.S. edition appears as a whole. In tongues with fewer readers and fewer resources, publishing one part helps to fund a subsequent part. That kind of funding is not necessary for most books published in English.

Readers interested in how the translation, adaptation, and circulation of the *Vocabulaire* has shaped the production of the *Dictionary* might begin by turning to the entry on "gender," which now includes a sidebar by Judith Butler that adds to and physically interrupts the original contribution by Monique David-Ménard and Penelope Deutscher. The text of Butler's sidebar—really a very large inset box—is in fact longer than the text of the entry proper. The U.S. editors gently describe the relationship between the two contributions as a "colloquy," but others might describe it as a kind of counterpoint. Butler's essay also stands out as one of the very few contributions in the volume to make reference to philosophical concepts in Chinese. As Cassin writes in her introduction, the *Vocabulaire* is focused on "the space of Europe" and, thus, on the languages of Europe. Of course, since the project's first appearance in 2004, the European Union has expanded to include a dozen additional countries, and, as the U.S. editors acknowledge, the distinction between European and non-European languages is not always clear. The *Dictionary*'s entry on "Europe" is worth considering for its approach to the history of that concept as well as to the history of European philosophies.

Finally, English-language readers interested in the politics of translation might want to consider the *Dictionary*'s references to English-language writing and intellectual traditions, which are often attributed to the "Anglo-Saxon world." Phrases such as this serve to remind U.S. audiences that they are holding a French book. *The Dictionary of Untranslatables* is a welcome arrival. It gives us the tools to think seriously about the history and politics of languages, about the relationship between philosophy and languages, and about how concepts not only reflect but also crucially shape the meanings of citizenship. And this is how the project started, as Cassin notes below: "It has always been linked with political ideas, with the crossing between philosophy and politics, from the beginning . . ."

1. What Animated This Book?

Rebecca L. Walkowitz (RLW): Did you imagine at the time that there would be translations of the *Vocabulaire* into other languages?

Barbara Cassin (BC): No, not really. I thought it was a gesture, not a closed book. And I've always thought that it could be increased in many ways. But the way I imagined it most often was just to augment the thing because, of course, there are many other important symptoms of the "untranslatable." I define "untranslatable" as a symptom of difference between languages. There are heaps and heaps of differences, and we chose the most significant ones that we were used to fighting with as philosophers and translators. Of course, we could expand online. But it is not so simple for the French editors. And it's a huge job to control. I didn't feel like doing that as a full-time job.

What was certain is that people who would translate or, better, make an adaptation of the original book were to be native [speakers of the target language] and very conscious of philosophical, linguistic, and political issues in their own country, such that the gesture could be continued one way or another with them. And the first one to propose a translation was the Ukrainian Constantin Sigov. We had both been invited to Citéphilo Lille, which is a big philosophy event held every November, and [while there] we spoke about the *Vocabulaire*, for which he wrote the entry on "Pravda," and about translation.

And he suddenly declared that he wanted to translate it [the *Vocabulaire*] into Ukrainian because he wanted to rebuild a philosophical language. He wanted to create a philosophical language in Ukrainian that was different from Russian and to bring together a kind of assembly, a community of philosophers that did not yet exist as such in Ukrainian. The Orange Revolution had just happened, and he hesitated for a while about whether to translate it into Russian or into Ukrainian, but after the Orange Revolution he was sure it needed to be Ukrainian. That was the point. So it has always been linked with political ideas, with the crossing between philosophy and politics, from the beginning, and from my beginning, too, because the idea was to make something for Europe. I wanted that kind of pluralistic Europe, neither globalizing, Globlishing Europe, nor what I call "ontologically nationalist," philosophically nationalist Europe. So that's why the idea for the book was also a political idea.

I have two enemies: the Heideggerian way of thinking, which roots language in nation and race or strain, and which imagines that some languages are better than others as they are nearer to, let us say, the language of Being—so Greek and German, more Greek than Greek. This hierarchy of tongues and ontological nationalism is what I didn't want. And I had been working with Heidegger. I'd been a pupil of Heidegger at one point in my life. Well, it was absolutely interesting. But I didn't want this kind of understanding, even of Greek, as an untranslatable, as something sacralized. This I didn't want.

And the other enemy was analytic philosophy, done badly in France, which says, for example, that we all think the same, that there is no problem of tongues, of languages, and no problem of time (Aristotle could very well be my colleague at Oxford), that the universal is universal and we are all human. So I didn't believe in this either, and I don't like the effects it has. So I wanted something else, and this something else is rephilosophizing words with words and not with universals. And these words are words in languages. Let us see what it means, how it can bring us to dwell a little bit on the difference between mind, *Geist*, and *esprit*. What happens if we look at the words, where they emerge and where they philosophize? Let us have a look.

RLW: Your project seems to have a kind of local ambition also, which is to remind readers in French of the significance and texture of foreign words.

BC: Yes. But when you translate you are always making footnotes, and these footnotes become the point of departure for our work. For example, when you translate, I don't know, *disegno*, and you say, "Of course it's *dessin* [drawing], but it is not exactly *dessin* because it's also *dessein* [design or intention], with an *e* and not only the *i*."

RLW: So in that sense it seems to be a kind of slowing down of language.

BC: Absolutely. And there are also questions of syntax. For me, I worked a lot on [Aristotle's] *Sophistical Refutations*, and the *Sophistical Refutations* contain many reflections about the ambiguities of syntax. There is a sentence of Lacan's I find very interesting, where he says, "*Une langue entre autres n'est rien de plus que l'intégrale des équivoques que son histoire y a laissé subsister.*" (A tongue [*or* a language], among others is nothing more than the integral of the equivocities its history left in it). It's absolutely precious to understand what is untranslatable. And going back, looking forward, looking backward, the entries we've chosen, for example the Russian ones, we become aware that they are all homonyms for us, and they are "*équivoques.*" But these multiple meanings, you see them from outside. You see them, as Deleuze would say, only when you are leaving the territory. It's from outside that you can say, "Oh! *Pravda* [justice/truth] is an *équivoque.*" And from Russian, you can say, "*Vérité* [truth/exactitude] is an *équivoque.*" The point is, how do you manage with the *équivoques*, both syntactic and semantic?

2. Philosophy and Language

RLW: Can you say a little bit about what the globalized version of the *Vocabulaire* would have looked like? How would that have been different from the one you produced?

BC: The idea of taking into account the difference of languages as such is in itself not a globalized idea. You know, language is more than a flavor. If you look at Google, they say, "We have linguistic flavors!" That's not the point. We have a linguistic constitution of ideas. And we don't speak with concepts; we speak with words. And we philosophize in languages. So that's the point. That was my point of departure.

RLW: How do you take account of words moving across languages, at the same time that you take account of the history of the word within its own language? It's very hard to keep both going at the same moment because the horizontal comparison requires at least a provisional moment of stasis in which you say, "Okay, I'm going to hold it here. It's this in French," so that you can get to Japanese. But you may also want to say, "Well, today it is this in French, but a hundred years ago it was this other thing in French."

BC: It depends. You can choose moments. And symptoms of the history [in which a word has been used] are also welcome. The first key is to think that it's not a concept, it's a word. And the second key is to think of everything as symptoms. So let us speak of this moment because it's very symptomatic of the difference between, say, French and English. And then let us take this other moment and see that it's another way of languages being combined or different. But you have to reconstruct things and not derive the whole thing from one point of departure.

RLW: When you use the word *symptom*, are you trying to keep your readers from imagining that they are in direct contact with the meaning of the word or that the word exists the same way in every moment?

BC: We have been more cautious than that. No, we are in Europe and within the European languages; we don't compare with Japanese or Chinese. Judith Butler completed [the entry on] "gender" because "gender" was maybe not worked up enough for the United States. But she compares it with the words for "gender" or "woman" in Chinese. This will be one of the very few articles like that because such a comparison is something else entirely.

RLW: So it seems it's hard to draw the line between what is a translation and what is a new edition, where there is translation and where there is recontexualization and reinterpretation . . .

BC: Adaptation. In the case of the Arabic edition—the first volume is already published in Arabic—they chose to make it as faithful as possible a translation. They didn't add anything. But their choice is already interesting in itself: they chose to translate the political vocabulary, in order to see how it might interact with existing Arabic terminology. They wanted to add [material], but it was too difficult. They ought to have added some words. *Sharia*, for example, was treated in the entry on "*Torah*." It's difficult . . . I do hope there will be a new and longer article [on *Sharia*], but it has not yet been done. But for now I think they want to make their version whole, and I am not sure they want to make it the same whole as the French one.

RLW: I could imagine that translators would feel that they wanted to register their own sense of Europe from their space.

BC: That's why there is such a need for a preface. It's very important to say what gesture is being made. I ask that my own preface always be present [in the various editions], but with another one.

3. Why Translate? And How?

RLW: It often seems to me that we assume translation is a consistent political gesture, either nationalist or cosmopolitan. But what I think is very interesting, particularly in the Ukrainian example, is that for them translating the *Vocabulaire* involved both cosmopolitanism and nationalism since they are enriching the language by absorbing new ideas and also bringing new status to their language through the translation of a distinguished text.

BC: Absolutely. You know, it just continues what happened with the translation of the Bible, for example. It's the formation of vernacular language. So it's a kind of philosophical vernacular language. That's the point. There are a lot of interlocking strategies. One consists of fixing the right term [a single term], the term you can find. The other is to make readers conscious that there are problems of translation and that there is a Ukrainian language that is able to deal with it but in several different ways. And then you choose one because you think it's better for now and for people who need to use that language. And then you have to add terms, other symptoms, which are very important for the language, [in this case] for the Ukrainian language, for the Ukrainian philosophy, for the Ukrainian intersection between philosophy and theology, between philosophy and politics, or between philosophy and literature. And with this they [the translators] conquer their right to be actually philosophical, in a sense.

RLW: It sounds like you imagine the *Vocabulaire* changing.

BC: That's even the point. That's why I didn't imagine it was closed but rather a gesture, an *energeia*. But I couldn't imagine immediately how the gesture could be transposed into another language's gesture. But it was possible.

4. Translating the Untranslatable

RLW: I want to return to the idea of the untranslatable because, in English, the untranslatable sometimes makes one think of irreducible singularity, the idea that a word cannot be translated or really should not be translated because to translate it is to violate it in some way or to violate the culture from which it comes.

BC: This is the Heideggerian way of thinking.

RLW: The term *untranslatable* is itself difficult to translate. I might translate it into English, as—this is not a real word—"untranslated-able," that is, unable to be finished being translated. And obviously, there's no word like that.

BC: Yes, yes, that's what I call, *ce qu'on ne cesse pas de (ne pas) traduire*: what never stops being (not) translated.

RLW: And I think that right now in the United States there's a real conversation about what it means to say that something can't be translated. And about those two meanings of "can't be translated": mustn't be translated, or—

BC: Is difficult to—

RLW: Is difficult to, or—

BC: Will never be—

RLW: Or will never be perfect, as if there could be a perfect translation, but you can't get to it. And that gets back to the question: How do you translate in a way that registers the incomplete nature of the process of the translation? Expanding the paratext seems to be one way.

BC: Yes, but explaining the difficulties is the other one, and that's what we have chosen. We have always been in the metatranslation.

NOTE

Interview conducted (mostly in English and occasionally in French) and edited by Rebecca L. Walkowitz. Interview transcribed and translated by Jennifer Raterman.

MY NEIGHBOR OCTAVIA

SHEILA LIMING

For years, I knew Octavia E. Butler, the famed African American science-fiction and fantasy writer, by her first name only. That was the way she introduced herself when I first met her back in the fall of 1999. Butler had just purchased the house across the street from my parents' and joined the ranks of our rather conventional suburban community in Lake Forest Park, WA, located just north of Seattle. A spate of rumors had attended her arrival on the block: "Octavia" wrote novels (about *aliens*!); "Octavia" had one of those "genius" grants; "Octavia" lived alone and was a reclusive artist type. An interview with Butler appeared in the *Shoreline–Lake Forest Park Enterprise*, our humble (and long-since defunct) local weekly, explaining that our new neighbor was, indeed, the author of a dozen novels and a MacArthur Fellowship recipient.

At the time, I was a high school junior who, like many my age, counted my recently minted driver's license among my most prized possessions. My new neighbor, meanwhile, did not have a driver's license—had never driven or owned a car in her life—and this disparity soon became the basis of our neighborly dealings with each other. I would often pass Butler on her walks to and from the grocery store and would stop to offer her rides, which she didn't always accept; she was an inveterate walker, and walking had even factored into her house purchase. She told me as much on one of the days that she consented to being driven the rest of the way up the hill. She said that she desired only that a grocery store, a bookstore, and a bus stop be located within walking distance and that the neighborhood should grant her access to the city without actually being *in* the city.

This was Butler's motivation for moving to Lake Forest Park, a setting that I, at sixteen, viewed as insufferably unimportant. I never learned her general motivations for moving to Washington in the first place, but I have since glimpsed some of them in her fiction. Butler grew up in Southern California, remaining in the greater Los Angeles area until the age of fifty-one. In the 1990s, prior to her relocation to Washington, she wrote her award-winning Parable novels. Both *Parable of the Sower* (1993) and *Parable of the Talents* (1998) describe a not-too-distant dystopic future in which the main characters, initially residents of Southern California, flee northward to escape the growing water crisis there and in the hopes of finding "any job that pays money." "We're going to Seattle," proclaims the character Natividad, who, along with her husband and six-month-old, form part of a "broad river of people" flowing north from California toward the Pacific Northwest in *Parable of the Sower*.

Butler's Parable novels—like almost all of her novels—portray California as a site of postmodern exodus and ruin. Butler's decision to leave California in the late 1990s seems, accordingly, to have hinged on the realization that it was becoming increasingly difficult to remain an optimist in such a setting. In a 2005 appearance on *Democracy Now!*, for instance, Butler explained that writing the Parable books, which she saw as "cautionary tales," had left her "overwhelmed" and depressed, yearning for something more "lightweight." Much like her characters in *Parable of the Sower*, she imagined that the Pacific Northwest might prove to be a more constructive setting for thinking about the future.

Nonetheless, I imagine that the move to our neighborhood constituted a dramatic change for Butler. She couldn't help but stick out among the mostly white, unvaryingly middle-class residents of Lake Forest Park, the majority of whom tended to structure their lives around the very things that she lacked—namely, cars and children. But Butler, it is clear, was no stranger to the experience of being a stranger. "I'm black. I'm solitary. I've always been an outsider," is the way she put it in a 1998 *Los Angeles Times* interview.

Given such a statement, it is tempting to read Butler's oeuvre through the lens of isolation; her novels ask us, time and again, to reflect on the terms of ordinary outsider-hood. At the same time, though, they also examine the complications and the rewards associated with social belonging. Solitude requires strength and self-assuredness, sure, but so does the trust that social belonging entails. As Walidah Imarisha recounts in her introduction to *Octavia's Brood*, a recently released collection of "visionary fiction" dedicated to the author's memory, Butler never sought to claim the title of "the solitary Black female sci-fi writer. She wanted to be one of *many* Black female sci-fi writers. She wanted to be one of thousands of folks writing themselves into the present and into the future."

For instance, in *Kindred* (1979), Butler's best-known and most canonized work, the main character, Dana, travels back in time and winds up on a pre–Civil War plantation in Maryland. There, Dana encounters a variety of characters who are, in one way or another, "kin" to her: both Rufus, who is white, and Alice, who is black, are her distant ancestors, and Dana also gains an appreciation for the ties that establish her fictive kinship with the other slaves on the Weylin plantation. In spite of these overt references to formal systems of kinship, though, *Kindred* also advances an argument for the ties that exist between creative laborers in the postindustrial economy. Butler's protagonist, who is black, is married to Kevin, who is white. Rather than foreground the subject of racial difference, Butler describes Kevin as being "like [Dana]—a kindred spirit crazy enough to keep on trying." Trying to *write*, for what unites these characters is a bond of creative perseverance that grows and deepens in spite of their personal fears of futility.

Back when I was sixteen, I, too, wanted to be a writer. If I wasn't a full-fledged "outsider," the time that I spent in the company of books meant that I didn't resemble anything close to an "insider," either. Which brings me back to the subject of my driver's license: my anxieties about being an outsider-in-training (among other things) meant that I tended to skip a lot of classes back in high school. In my own, very small and very narcissistic way, I had come to rely on escape and subterfuge to combat the discomfort of social isolation. I didn't know it then, but, just across the street, my neighbor Octavia was also struggling with similar feelings of isolation and anxiety (in addition to depression and writer's block, as a *Seattle Post-Intelligencer* article explains) during that time.

One day, I blew off an entire day of school and instead drove to the remote mountain town where my family had lived and owned property when I was very young. Upon my return to Lake Forest Park, I met Butler coming back from the grocery store. "Aren't you supposed to be in school?" she asked me when she got in the car. I told her that I hadn't felt like going, skirting the deeper complexities of the issue, and said I'd been in Darrington. She responded that she had never visited the town, which is home to fewer than 1,500 people and located more than sixty miles from Lake Forest Park, but that she had seen it on maps. She asked me a variety of questions about the place before concluding our conversation with a remark that, for all its severity, still struck me as well intended:

"You should probably just go to school and stop screwing around," she said.

I left for college in Ohio in the fall of 2001 and, to my very great regret, did not stay in touch with my former neighbor. Butler, for her own part, eventually conquered her writer's block and went on to produce a final novel. *Fledgling* (2005) centers on a group of vampires who occupy a commune of sorts located "a few miles north of Darrington." I was still in Ohio at the time of its publication, but I bought a copy and read it that winter. I imagined that, upon my next visit back in Lake Forest Park, I might be able to talk to Butler about the book and about Darrington. That conversation, however, did not come to pass: Butler died in February 2006 from what is believed to have been a stroke. My mom called to tell me the news, and it was from her that I learned that Butler's body had been discovered by the two young girls who lived next door to her. I knew them well; once upon a time, I had been their babysitter.

Now, when I look back on the few years that I spent in close proximity to Butler, I find that I cannot do so without experiencing a kind of concomitant regret. I ask myself how I might have succeeded in being a better neighbor or friend to a person whose celebrity status seemed, to me, to mean that she needed neither. And I dwell on the memory of my missteps, marveling, for example, at the naiveté that led me to invite Butler, a Hugo and Nebula winner, to join my friends and me at our science-fiction book club. Even worse, I cringe to think about the wasted opportunity that resulted from my failure to follow up on the invitation (which Butler actually accepted). I remember that we were reading Mary Doria Russell's *The Sparrow*, and Butler said she knew it. *Of course she knew it*: she'd appeared alongside Russell at a sci-fi symposium held in North Carolina that same spring.

This year marks the tenth anniversary of Butler's death, a fact that has been observed by news media tributes and by the

Huntington Library in California, which acquired Butler's papers in 2008 and has hosted a year-long series of commemorative events. In literary circles, then, it's clear that Butler's reputation has continued to rise over the last decade. But a recent trip back to Lake Forest Park prompted me to ask the question: Did the neighborhood remember, too? I was curious to see what, if anything, might form the basis of the community's recollections of Butler and to know the extent of its residents' acquaintance with her works and literary legacy.

I spoke to Terry Morgan, who still lives in the neighborhood and remembers passing Butler on the street and giving her "the black nod." "I was the only other African American artist/musician living in the area, and Butler was kind of a mystery to me. You almost never saw her," he said. As our conversation progressed, I learned that Morgan's relationship with Butler in fact had the same foundation as my own: "I used to offer her rides," he told me, explaining that, in exchange for this service, Butler invited him inside her house one day and presented him with an autographed copy of a book. The moral that emerged from our conversation was also similar: Morgan and I both wish that we could have known our neighbor better, and we both regret that feelings of intimidation and awe prevented us from doing that.

This regret finds its echo in Butler's fiction, where characters are often forced to alter their expectations of independence in the wake of catastrophe, to venture to know and to trust their neighbors in ways that they previously believed to be impossible or implausible. I squandered much of the opportunity that I had to know Octavia as a neighbor, but I have relished the process of getting to know Butler as an author, builder of worlds, and archivist of life in America at the dawn of the twenty-first century.

STOP DEFENDING THE HUMANITIES

SIMON DURING

Whatever things the humanities do well, it is beginning to look as if promoting themselves is not among them. I say this after having read widely across the rapidly accumulating literature in defense of the humanities, to which this book loosely belongs. Strictly speaking, *The Humanities and Public Life* is a record of a seminar on the ethics of reading organized by Peter Brooks at Yale, but whose participants (all of them well known and formidably accomplished scholars) often found themselves moving into exactly the "defense of the humanities" mode that enabled someone—I assume the publisher—to present the book under a slightly misleading but presumably marketable title.

It turns out that the humanities' defensive accounts of themselves have some rather curious features. In particular, they tend to pass quickly over what we tacitly know about them as a matter of fact, turning instead to the sermonic. And in insisting on the humanities' value for society and culture as a whole, these accounts routinely fail to confront their own interest in making this case.

What do we tacitly and neutrally know about the humanities? We know that they exist as a combination of different academic disciplines, which, at least in the United States, are often housed in university departments and thereby bound to the university system's larger bureaucratic/professional structures.

We know that each discipline has its own history, its own mix of instrumental and noninstrumental purposes and functions, its own methods and topics, its own set of values, its own tolerance (or lack thereof) of positivist methods and knowledge.

It is important to remember what is obvious—that the humanities contain many disciplines—to forestall arguments that promote practices that belong just to one discipline as definitive of the whole. So that, for instance, neither close reading (as here argued for by Peter Brooks) nor ideology critique (as here argued for by Judith Butler in a subtle essay that asks us to ask "what is the value of our values," as if such exist) nor the deployment of paradigms of interpretation and meaning nor even creative openness to the contingencies and surprises of encounters with others (as here invoked by Jonathan Lear) can be used to define and defend the humanities as they exist as a whole. Indeed the humanities are not the kind of thing that can be defended by reference to a single practice or even set of practices, a single value or set of values.

We know, further, that the humanities in their modern Western form were established quite recently—around the end of the nineteenth century. They are only very loosely connected to those older humanisms that appeared in the ancient, early-modern, and Enlightenment eras. And we know that the modern humanities have taken different forms in different nations: it is a matter of some argument whether the academic humanities as they have developed in Anglophone nations have strict equivalents even in France, Spain, Italy, and Germany, let alone in China or Japan.

We also know that the Western humanities expanded at the beginning of the second half of the twentieth century under a regime we can call social capitalism. Especially after World War II, many states subsidized the humanities as they sought to make higher education available to a larger proportion of the population in an effort to increase social mobility. And we are becoming increasingly aware that this element of the social-capitalist compact is fraying under neoliberalism, as a humanities education comes to be viewed just as a private rather than as a public good. One example: in 2010, in a sobering move few saw coming, the UK Tory government, in deregulating university fees, simply stopped funding undergraduate teaching in the arts, humanities, and social sciences while maintaining support for engineering, the sciences, technology, and math. Partly as a result, applications for the humanities fell by over 11 percent the following year, although in some disciplines the position has stabilized since.

We also know that the humanities' borders, both internal and external, are loose. Internally, each discipline contains within itself not only subfields but a variety of schools or methods (theory, Marxism, ethnography, close reading . . .), some of which contest others and many of which are shared across disciplines. Externally, at least some humanities disciplines—history, say—fade more or less peaceably into the social sciences. But it is widely supposed, I think, that three or four disciplines—philosophy, history, literary studies, and maybe the classics—lie at the modern humanities' heart. And we know that, nonetheless, new disciplines or postdisciplines (which lack the institutional infrastructure of a full discipline) are continually being created, whether in response to new technologies or genres (TV studies, the digital humanities) or to new social, cultural, and political movements (gender studies, postcolonialism) or to new career opportunities (museum studies) or to new service relations with other disciplines (professional writing) or just to new demand (creative writing). So that, although, at least in the United States, the humanities' share of the total undergraduate population has not significantly declined since the 1980s, it is likely that fewer students proportionally study the core humanities in their traditional modes than in social capitalism's heyday. It would appear that it is this (overdetermined) shrinkage of certain core humanities disciplines that has sparked the outbreak of sermonizing in defense of the humanities as a whole.

Furthermore, different disciplines have different relations to the world outside them, some being more parasitic on external forms than others. Thus, for instance, while philosophy generates itself more or less continuously out of ancient impulses, history interprets and uncovers the past by way of the archives as the past continually and self-recordingly flows into the present, and English depends on literature, past and present, usually as written at some distance from the academy, just as film studies, say, depends on film, commercially produced or otherwise.

These externalities matter, first, because the humanities as a concept can denote both the academic disciplines and their subject matter in the outside world where such exist. So, for instance, the often adduced argument that literature departments encourage empathy (here put by Elaine Scarry) gestures more toward literary texts themselves than to their academic study. Even if you buy Scarry's argument for empathy (as few in this collection do), it is literature that increases our capacity to engage and imagine otherness rather than studying it according to academic English's protocols, including close reading, which anyway, right or wrong, is in decline.

And, second, these externalities matter because the parasitic nature of many humanities disciplines means that they are unlikely to disappear so long as their objects persist. They are not under present existential threat. Further: their shrinkage, were it to accelerate, is likely to be less culturally significant than many of us believe. For instance, academic literary criticism could fade while literature itself (and its effects on the world) prospered.

The humanities join the wider world in other ways. They belong to an economy of prestige that helps prop up class and ethnic hierarchies. Forty or so years ago, Pierre Bourdieu presented a complex, evidence-based theory of how this economy then worked in France. His findings may now be partly out of date, but surveys since have routinely found that those who study the academic humanities disproportionately belong to the white upper-middle class, i.e., those with significant inherited cultural and economic capital. In this situation, those humanities disciplines that have emerged in relation to newer technologies and social movements tend to have less status and to be taught in different kinds of institutions and through different methods and theories than the core humanities, part of whose purpose remains to reproduce certain bourgeois sensibilities and cultural capital.

The humanities' rather complex use in maintaining class hierarchies may be one reason why, as we are now learning all too well, they are unpopular. Especially in the United States the "liberal intellectual" is more than a stereotyped figure of fun: he (less often she) is the target of political resentments that help sustain conservative politics. This negative stereotyping takes wing, in part, from the sense that humanities academics and the students whom they send into the professions acquire their privilege too easily, exempt from the hard scrabble of working in small business, farming, factories, supermarkets, and so on. Worse still: liberal intellectuals and humanities academics use their privilege in their own interest to promote unworldly politics and tastes that undercut or lie aslant values and lifestyles that help sustain many of those with less privilege. Seen like this, the humanities' unpopularity is not irrational, even if from inside the neoliberal university any sense of our effete privilege may seem misguided. At any rate, scorn for the humanities cannot simply be discounted: it, too, demands understanding and empathy. Certainly, it is one reason why the humanities are so vulnerable politically: outside their own spheres, they find it hard to make friends.

Where does it leave us in thinking about the humanities?

I would suggest that it leads us to picture the humanities as something like a form of life or, better, because vaguer still, as something like a *world*, an institutionalized world. A world that contains smaller worlds. A simultaneously beleaguered and privileged world whose members typically belong to other, somewhat ontologically similar worlds, too.

The main reason to think in such terms is to avoid betraying what is central to the humanities: that they cannot be properly defined in terms of their parts, in terms, for instance, of their instrumentalities or avoidance of instrumentality or of the dispositions they nurture or of the interests they nourish and serve or of the knowledge and techniques they produce or of the professional/bureaucratic protocols they enact or of the ethics perhaps still installed within them. They cannot be limited to their constitutive rules or methods or personae or models or "values." Those who join them can find their own paths through them and the rule-bound institutions they are based in, outside of essences and definitions, making their own connections and alliances, as in a world. And they don't share a single project, if indeed they have projects at all.

To help us better grasp this way of thinking (which I have loosely borrowed from Michael Oakeshott's *Experience and Its Modes*) it may be useful briefly to name other such worlds adjacent to the humanities: The world of theater. The world of music. The art world. In some ways better still, because less apparent: the world of sport. Like these other worlds, the humanities are not only or even primarily projective or instrumental (they are probably more instrumental than sports, though, even if they are economically less important). And for that reason, like these other worlds, the humanities seem to be simultaneously deeply embedded within, and peripheral to, society as a whole.

The key consequence of seeing the humanities as a world alongside other broadly similar worlds is that the limits of their defensibility becomes apparent, and sermonizing over them becomes harder. If people stopped watching and playing sports, how much would it matter? The question is unanswerable since we can't imagine a society continuous with ours but lacking sports, even though one such is, I suppose, possible. We do not have the means to adjudicate between that imaginary sportless society and our own actual sports-obsessed society. The same is true for the humanities. If the humanities were to disappear, new social and cultural configurations would then exist. Would this be a loss or gain? There is no way of telling, partly because we can't picture what a society and culture that follow from ours but lack the humanities would be like at the requisite level of detail and partly because, even if we could imagine such a society, our judgment between a society with the humanities and one without them couldn't appeal to the standards like ours that are embedded in the humanities themselves. The humanities would be gone: that's it.

Of course, those of us in the humanities who love and breathe them, whose institutional (but not just institutional) lives are formed in relation to them, who would like more people to join them and so become more like us, to think and feel and talk like us, who may even find the "meaning of life" articulated from within them, find the prospect of their fading insupportable, heart-rending, unimaginable. But that offers no substantive public reason to maintain them, just as it turned out in the end to be no reason to maintain all the more or less similar worlds that have disappeared over the centuries, before and after modernity: the worlds of the aristocratic honor code; the world of older humanisms and the "republic of letters"; the worlds of industrial working-class solidarity; the world of Scholasticism and the trivium; the worlds of old Anglican rural, parochial, and liturgical life; and so on.

But, as I say, the humanities are not now under existential threat, and so the last two paragraphs present merely a thought experiment. To repeat, their point is to put a brake on our sermonizing, on our confusion of self-interest and public interest, and on our various reductivisms and to make us stop regarding ourselves as necessary to any future healthy society whatsoever. Applying these brakes may help us make our case for the humanities in more modest terms that are more narrowly directed to those who most matter in this context.

Those who matter most to the humanities fall, I think, into two classes. The most important is that relatively small group of eighteen-year-olds (disproportionately few from poorer families) who are inclined to study the humanities. Our immediate future rests primarily with them. And in regard to them, surely, we support the humanities best by teaching well whatever it is that we teach and then by inviting them further into our world by presenting ourselves as its fit and welcoming members (*not* exemplars).

The second group who matter are the policy makers and politicians who control public research and education funding and those who may influence them. This is tricky terrain. But one caution seems apposite. It is true that the humanities are socially instrumental in various and not unimportant ways, but pointing that out is, in the end, a vulnerable policy argument since the social uses the humanities do have could probably be achieved more cheaply by means that don't require the humanities as a whole. After all, most of what the humanities do has internal, not external, use value, where it has use value at all.

It is also true, for instance, that the humanities will remain vibrant and socially accepted to the degree that they continue to attract members from outside the white upper-middle classes and that this requires state support. But that, too, is not an especially politically effective argument, partly because it is so tinged by self-interest.

The case needs to be more minimal: it needs to show that restricting access to the world of the humanities by those who wish to engage them (for whatever reason) but find it cripplingly difficult to afford them is a form of social injustice. It is discriminatory. And that is another argument that doesn't need a sermon. Otherwise put: the humanities may form a world more than they provide a social good, but that does not mean that access to them should be determined by money. After all, they constitute a world substantive enough for lack of access to it by those capable of seriously engaging it to be a form of deprivation. But if barriers to entry to the academic humanities are not to be primarily financial then they require state support.

Let me briefly return to *The Humanities and Public Life*. It brings together a set of excellent and at times brilliant essays, each of which, however, proposes its own linchpin for the humanities and none of which wholly avoids the sermonic mode. As I have said, I believe the humanities now would be well advised to use a different rhetoric, one more attuned to their actual institutional conditions. One moment in this collection where this something different appears is in those sections of his essay where, leaving theory and rousing rhetoric aside, Jonathan Lear reports on his meetings with Crow Indians after the publication of his *Radical Hope: Ethics in the Face of Cultural Devastation*. In that book Lear reported on the widespread belief among the Crow that, after being placed in reservations in the nineteenth century, "nothing happened" to their culture again. (Lear's book focused on a systemic loss not unlike that which some in the humanities now seem to anticipate for themselves.) But after his book appeared new understandings were reached between Lear and his Crow friends. Things did indeed happen again to both, and unexpected things, too: Lear believes that a poetic and creative spark across divides was ignited, one capable of building new alliances. In recounting his social and intellectual adventure, then, he implicitly invites newcomers to follow his lead and become engaged in the humanities on their own terms. It is not an invitation put in terms that all of us will find attractive (it belongs to the America of romance, not of realism), but, still, that kind of universalism is exactly what the world of humanities cannot offer since they are just *a* world, and a manifold world, too.

PAINTING WHILE SHACKLED TO A FLOOR

NICOLE R. FLEETWOOD

W hat does it mean to make art with limited resources, under constant surveillance, when incarcerated in some of the most restrictive and punitive institutions in the modern American prison system? Two exhibits currently on view in New York City pose that question by bringing paintings, drawings, and sculpture out from behind the bars of death row and Guantánamo Bay and displaying them in galleries at the John Jay College of Criminal Justice and the Columbia Law School, educational institutions that in many respects reproduce the carceral state. Such schools help to define what is a crime and who is a criminal by shaping laws and policies of policing and confining. They train lawyers, police and parole officers, and correctional employees in the ever-expanding landscape of policing, detention, and imprisonment.

Art and law converge in both exhibits not only through the status of the artists as prisoners and the locations of the galleries but also in how the works on display engage the impact of imprisonment on aesthetic practices and art making. Some of the artists in these shows painted while shackled to a floor. Others were not allowed pens, pencils, or pallet knives.

Ode to the Sea: Art from Guantánamo Bay at John Jay College of Criminal Justice comprises more than thirty paintings, drawings, and miniatures from detainees at the infamous prison camp. In one, Muhammad Ansi's watercolor painting of a storm at sea, the crest of purple and white waves submerges a capsized boat, splintering its frame. Ansi renders the ferocity of the storm and the despair of the wreck through aggressive strokes and jarring colors. The show's title comes from the proximity of the camp to the Caribbean Sea and the visions that emerge in the artwork of the detainees. While they are held close to the water, detainees are not allowed to see it, as part of their punitive captivity. Tarps block their view, except for a few days in 2014 when the tarps were removed in preparation for a hurricane. During that brief time, anyone who made art drew the sea.

Surveillance, punishment, and scarcity of materials are the conditions under which the art in *Ode to the Sea* was produced. Erin Thompson, Charles Shields, and Paige Laino, the curators of the exhibit, note that the works had to go through many levels of clearance before receiving approval; faintly visible on many of them is the stamp, "Approved by US Forces," described by the curators as "a ghostly mix of art and authority."

Lighthouses, bodies of water, and idyllic pastoral scenes are common symbols of freedom in prison art, and so they appear here, though the sea in these works is multivalent. It promises and obscures. It is a passageway and a barrier.

Ansi's paintings stand out among the works of the eight current and former detainees featured in the show. In his *Untitled (Statue of Liberty)*, dark waters merge with an evening sky in a moody distillation of blues and a gray-obscured figure of democracy. In another painting by Ansi, a brown body has washed ashore. "If the wind enrages you, your injustice is obvious. / If the wind silences you, there is just the ebb and flow. / O sea, do our chains offend you? / It is only under compulsion that we daily come and go"—so read verses on the gallery wall written by former detainee Ibrahim al-Rubaish, part of a poem whose title gives the exhibit its name. In later verses, the poet gestures to Cuba as a witness, indicating the island where the military prison is located but also the inability of the nation of Cuba to serve as a refuge. Many of the detainees whose works are in the show have been held there for years without formal charges. Because of this status, they have been called the "forever prisoners."

To access the John Jay exhibit, one passes through a permanent installation, *Memorial Wall*, honoring law officers and other emergency personnel who died in the September 11 attacks. It is worth pausing here to take in the photographs and text memorializing the many lives lost and to consider the escalation of violence, surveillance, and indefinite detention that the "War on Terror" continues to produce.

After viewing *Ode to the Sea*, I returned to *Memorial Hall* to consider the connections between policing and notions of public safety, to absorb how local sites have been transformed under the auspices of national security and global terror threats, and to observe the links between law enforcement working a crime scene and law enforcement producing criminal suspects, as tensions animating the space between the memorial and the art of the detainees.

Windows on Death Row: Art from Inside and Outside the Prison Walls, an exhibit in the corridors of Columbia Law School, displays art by current and former prisoners on death row alongside pieces by well-known political cartoonists. Interspersed on the walls are data charts and text about capital punishment, sentencing, and racial disparities in the U.S. prison system. The touring exhibit was organized by Swiss journalist Anne-Frederique Widmann and Lebanese Swiss political cartoonist Patrick Chappatte, who work together investigating capital punishment in the United States, and involves several partnering organizations.

Like water in *Ode to Sea*, light in this exhibit is complex: a symbol of opening, visibility, freedom, as well as interrogation, surveillance, and judgment, as with the glaring lights of the execution chamber. Bars, slumped shoulders, and a blinded figure of justice gesture to experiences that viewers can only imagine, as penal time and confinement are beyond the imaginative capacity of those who have never been imprisoned.

Just as the curatorial statement for *Ode to the Sea* takes a strong stance against detainment without due process and the targeting and profiling of "terrorist suspects" without just cause, the organizers of *Windows on Death Row* use the artwork of death row prisoners to critique the racial and economic inequalities that lead to the harshest sentences in the U.S. prison regime, especially to capital punishment, rather than focus on the events that led individuals into the judicial system in the first place.

But the issue of wrongful convictions also arises. Kevin Cooper's painting of a black man screaming from his cell, called *Free Me!* (2011), is part of a greater effort to bring awareness to Cooper's case as an innocent man on death row in San Quentin State Prison. He has been the subject of several op-eds and petitions to California governor Jerry Brown to grant clemency.

Another featured artist, Ndume Olatushani, spent twenty years on death row for crimes he did not commit. Appearing with his defense team at a recent panel for the show, he told the audience that he turned to art to cope with despair and helplessness after the death of his mother, who was his primary support in the first years following his conviction. During his two decades on death row, he painted in his cell. His art eventually led to him meeting his wife and later brought attention and a new defense team to his case. He was eventually released, but after having served twenty-seven years in prison. When he states, "Art literally freed me," no one in the audience dismisses his words as an empty platitude.

Olatushani is an exception, though, among the artists featured in these shows. Most of them remain confined, as people awaiting death in domestic prisons or as those forced to stay alive—through rectal feeding and other methods used to manage detainees—in occupied territories, black sites, and military camps. Ahmed Rabbani and Khalid Qasim, two artists in *Ode to the Sea*, have been on hunger strikes since 2013; both are suffering from debilitating complications. While art provides creative and expressive outlets, their bodies are bound in punitive time and space. Freedom for them is a longing for the expanse of the sea, to return home to wherever or whatever that might be, to be transported from enclosed cells of isolation and rightlessness.

The power of the two shows, seen in tandem, is the emotional force and sheer existence of art produced within brutal practices of punishment, practices that have become endemic to domestic and military prisons. As Angela Davis has observed, "The everyday tortures experienced by the inhabitants of domestic prisons in the U.S. have enabled the justification of the treatment meted out to prisoners in Abu Ghraib and Guantánamo."[1] Davis and other scholars of the prison-industrial complex have brought attention to how punishment is more the result of increased surveillance, in particular toward racialized communities, than of crime.

Death row and military camps might appear to be anomalies in the American prison regime. Yet they are only the most extreme aspects of an entire United States culture of excessive punishment, one that has been unleashed on the rest of the world, with its retributive practices of deprivation, isolation, and even death. *Ode to the Sea* and *Windows on Death Row* complicate facile notions of justice by highlighting aesthetic practices that emerge from, not despite, systems of punishment. Some of the artists are condemned to death and know the dates of their executions. Others remain indefinitely detained. The only freedom any of them now know, the only sea they can ever reach, is in their art.

Postscript: November 20, 2017

Due to the attention Ode to the Sea has received, the U.S. government now says it owns prisoner art and proposes to destroy it. Although works in the show by detainees at Guantánamo Bay had been reviewed by state and military officials before being approved for display, their policy has suddenly changed. According to a Pentagon statement: "Items produced by detainees at Guantánamo Bay remain the property of the U.S. government."[2] Art by detainees will no longer be allowed to leave the prison. The current proposal is to incinerate it.

NOTES

1. Angela Davis, *Abolition Democracy: Beyond Empire, Prisons, and Torture* (New York: Seven Stories, 2005), 65.
2. Carol Rosenberg, "After Years of Letting Captives Own Their Artwork, Pentagon Calls It U.S. Property. And May Burn It." *Miami Herald*, November 16, 2017, http://www.miamiherald.com/news/nation-world/world/americas/guantanamo/article185088673.html.

PART III

Read in Public

TO TRANSLATE IS TO BETRAY

On Elena Ferrante

REBECCA FALKOFF

The stunning fortunes of Elena Ferrante's Neapolitan novels in the United States have only recently begun to affect their reception in the author's native country, giving rise to competing theories and occasionally ugly polemics: Are Italians simply unable to recognize greatness in one of their own? Are American readers uncritically falling for sentimental "women's" novels? Is the real Elena Ferrante actually a man or even a collaboration among several writers? Should a pseudonymous author with no public profile be eligible to compete for Italy's most prestigious literary award? Then, just last month, came the apparent unmasking of the author's identity. What should we stateside sufferers of "Ferrante fever" make of it all?

In 1991, on the eve of the publication of her first novel, *Troubling Love*, Elena Ferrante sent a letter to her publisher explaining her decision to use a pseudonym and make no public appearances to promote the book. The letter set out a theory of the author with the declarative texture of a manifesto: "I've already done enough for this long story: I wrote it. If the book is worth anything, that should be sufficient."[1] Ferrante continues, comparing literary texts to gifts from the Italian Santa Claus, the Befana: "True miracles," she writes, "are the ones whose makers will never be known."[2]

It's a metaphor I find troubling, one that Marx might have glossed as follows: the magical quality of the commodity—in this case, the literary text—is the result of an erasure of labor. Is this really what Ferrante means? I don't think so. Such an interpretation is challenged throughout her oeuvre by an unwavering interest in work. Perhaps the theme emerges most vividly in the third volume of the Neapolitan tetralogy, *Those Who Leave and Those Who Stay*, which chronicles the savage working conditions in a sausage factory and the brutality with which efforts at labor organization are crushed.

But more relevant than factory work for a consideration of the Befana metaphor is the labor of writing (and, more broadly, working with words), which recurs in each of Ferrante's novels. *Troubling Love* is about a comic-strip artist who struggles to find language to accompany the images of her childhood, and its very title is indebted to the labors of translation.[3] *The Days of Abandonment*, published ten years later, is about a woman who begins writing as her marriage collapses. *The Lost Daughter* is about a professor of English literature.

The Neapolitan novels tell the story of a friendship formed around the pleasures of fabulation. Essential to the story's progress are a series of texts that result from negotiations between spontaneous brilliance and laborious revision. The first volume begins with a telephone call to the narrator, Elena Greco, announcing that Lila, the eponymous brilliant friend, has disappeared without a trace; "The Blue Fairy," the dazzling tale written by Lila as a schoolgirl, is present not through direct quotation but through the narrator's description, and it is consigned to a pyre long before the present of the tetralogy's narration.

In the second volume, *The Story of a New Name*, Elena receives a letter from Lila that seems to effortlessly embody the easy rhythm of speech in writing; we later learn the letter is the result of a torment of drafting and revision. The volume opens with Elena throwing the writing entrusted to her by Lila into the Arno River, a gesture whose significance would be clear to any Italian reader: Alessandro Manzoni, author of *The Betrothed*, famously wrote that he had moved to Florence to rinse his rags in the Arno, that is, to Tuscanize his manuscript, purging it of linguistic traces of his native Milan.

In the final volume of the tetralogy, *The Story of the Lost Child*, the brilliant work Elena imagines Lila to be writing—one that would reinvigorate the form of the novel and revive Naples, condensing all its passion and violence into a language as literary, as Italian, and as visceral as dialect—fails to materialize. Such a book, Elena imagines, would be her undoing: "The book would become— even just for me—the proof of my failure. Reading it, I would understand how I should have written but was never able to. . . . My whole life would be reduced to a petty battle to change social class."[4] The Neapolitan novels (according to their fiction) are only a shadowy approximation of the work of true genius. Lila's masterpiece—were it to be written—would reveal Elena's books to be mere translations into a language capable of signifying outside the neighborhood. Instead, Lila leaves no trace, save for her presence in the pages of the Neapolitan novels. The novels, then, seem to perform the Italian aphorism "*tradurre è tradire*": to translate is to betray. They *translate* by rewriting Lila's lost pages, along with the Neapolitan dialect that is continually alluded to but virtually excluded from the tetralogy. They *betray* not only by dulling Lila's expressive force or by rendering the experience of the neighborhood in a language with the potential to grant Elena access to a different social class but also by their very existence, as Elena had promised Lila never to write about her.

■ ■ ■

If the metaphor of the Befana is at odds with Ferrante's interest in the labor of working with words, it is compatible with Roland Barthes's seminal 1967 essay, "The Death of the Author," which heralds the liberation of the literary critic from the oppressive shackles of authorial intent. Barthes writes: "We know that to give writing its future, it is necessary to overthrow the myth: the birth of the reader must be at the cost of the death of the Author."[5] Barthes's claim drew on and contributed to a body of theory dedicated to an idea that now seems obvious: that language itself is overdetermined, bursting with intentions and implications that no author could call his or her own.

However fundamental the death of the author remains to literary criticism, no less so is Michel Foucault's response, "What Is an Author?," published two years after Barthes's essay. For Foucault, to make the author disappear, it is not sufficient to simply state that the author has done so. Pointing to the influence that authorship continues to exert, he instead proposes the category of the "author function," distinct from the real individual who inhabits the role. In the case of Ferrante, it seems clear that the "author function" is robust, despite—or, as some have argued (see below), because of— the writer's physical absence. Building on Foucault's work, Italian literary critic Carla Benedetti has coined the term "authorialism" to describe how, in the modern system of artistic production, having an author is the very condition of possibility for a work of art. She dismisses the debates that followed from the interventions of Barthes and Foucault, which divided authors between real and implied, empirical and ideal: "Someday these distinctions will appear as byzantine as a disquisition on the sex of angels."[6]

I note the death and resuscitation of the author largely to justify my prurient interest in the identity of Ferrante, my guilty participation in the scandalmongering media obsession. It's an interest that requires particular justification because it has been judged politically repugnant—complicit with Berlusconismo—by Ferrante herself. In her most recent interview, she explains that while she first chose anonymity because of her shyness, she remained committed to the choice because of her disgust with the incessant self-promotion and banal chatter required of authors.[7]

Until recently, the fact of Ferrante's pseudonymity played a fairly small role in the reception of her work. When *Troubling Love* originally appeared, in 1992, it generated a small but devoted readership and garnered the attention of a handful of literary critics in Italy and the United States, particularly those interested in gender and sexuality and Italian feminist theory. Three years after the publication of *Troubling Love*, Mario Martone adapted it for the cinema, introducing Ferrante to a broader audience. In 2005, her second novel, *The Days of Abandonment*, was the first to be translated into English, followed by *Troubling Love* in 2006. Both were "Briefly Noted" in the *New Yorker*, and Daniel Soar reviewed the former for the *London Review of Books*.[8] Ferrante's third novel, *The Lost Daughter*, was published in 2006 in Italy and in 2008 in the United States. With three novels in translation, she had a considerable readership in Italy and beyond, but it wasn't until the 2012 publication of the first of the Neapolitan novels, *My Brilliant Friend* and James Wood's glowing 2013 *New Yorker* article that we could really speak of the "Ferrante phenomenon" or "Ferrante fever."[9]

Ferrante's ascent, in the United States, to the status of "literary rock star" has changed the conversation about her in Italy, which now seems polarized into two camps, the self-flagellating and the snidely condescending. The self-flagellating insist that Italy is unable to recognize and retain its native talent. This is the subject of much public concern in Italy and of Marco Mancassola's recent *New York Times* op-ed, "Embracing the Other Italy."[10] Ferrante herself addresses this problem insofar as, by the fourth and final Neapolitan novel, Elena's grown-up daughters live outside of Italy:

"They consider Italy a splendid corner of the planet, and at the same time, an insignificant and inconclusive province, livable only for a short vacation."[11]

The snidely condescending faction may best be illustrated by Paolo di Paolo's October 2014 *La stampa* article, which credits the success of Ferrante in the United States to well-oiled plots, a solid narrative hand, plain language, and a touristic rendering of Naples.[12] He attributes the praise offered to Ferrante by venerated Italian cultural critics like Goffredo Fofi, on the other hand, to her facelessness. Cristiano de Majo offers a somewhat more perceptive reflection on the topic by comparing the Neapolitan novels to Paolo Sorrentino's Oscar-winning film *The Great Beauty*, which was derided—or worse, slept through—in Italy.[13] Both works, de Majo notes, feature Neapolitan protagonists who have emigrated north and achieved success as writers. He asks whether the nostalgia for a lost Naples of childhood poverty might resonate not just with American descendants of Neapolitan emigrants but with the kind of longing that guides touristic sensibilities. In a short "Central Park West" video for RAI (Italy's national public broadcasting company), Antonio Monda proposes that the excitement about Ferrante coincides with a tendency in American universities to all but ignore nineteenth-century greats like Ugo Foscolo, Manzoni, and Giacomo Leopardi in favor of mystics and other women writers. Mirroring the dichotomy he laments, the video cuts from Monda, seated in front of a wall of bookcases and solemnly addressing the camera, to what appears to be softly lit stock footage of a young woman curled up on a cushioned bay window seat, sensuously turning the pages of a book.[14]

A friend of mine, perhaps imagining such a scene of cloistered reading reverie, recently asked me over what became a contentious dinner, "But are the Neapolitan novels *political*? Or are they about *women*?" The a priori exclusion of women from the political, presupposed by my friend's question, is often implicit in speculation about Ferrante's identity. Some who dismiss her writing as plot-driven and sentimental seem to accept that she is a woman. Others, noting an epic sweep of historical and political significance, attribute the works to a man. *Those Who Leave and Those Who Stay* engages directly with these positions, as Elena begins writing about the sociopolitical turmoil of the so-called Years of Lead and reflects on both her own insecurity in handling such material and her envy of male writers who seem to do so with an arrogant ease.

Academics tend to remain aloof from speculation about Ferrante's identity; for these readers her work is most certainly that of an implied writer textually constructed as a woman.[15] And I. too. might be happy to repeat that the author is dead and the Befana's gifts delivered, were there not so much evident sexism in the speculations about the gender of Ferrante and were such sexism not also addressed explicitly in the novels.

I must also confess that, as a reader impassioned by "Ferrante fever," I found it unbearable to imagine her as a man. And yet as an equally passionate reader of Judith Butler, I was unsettled by my emotional investment in essentializing gender. And so I set about trying to hedge my bets: to come to terms with the possibility that she might be a man or, as one rumor has it, a collaboration between the husband-and-wife founders of Edizioni E/O, Sandro Ferri and Sandra Ozzola, and an intimate circle of friends. This possibility holds a certain appeal insofar as it both presents a challenge to the "authorialism" identified by Benedetti and evokes another recent Italian literary phenomenon: the Bologna-based collaborative writing group Wu-Ming, founded in 2000. (When I first heard the collaborative-author theory of Ferrante, I figured it was a rumor started by members of Wu-Ming to bring attention to their own "Unidentified Narrative Objects" and "New Italian

Epics.") Despite the interest that collaborative authorship would thus hold, the idea still seemed somehow insulting to the reader: as though the novels were cooked up by focus groups bent on exploiting our narrative desire and producing escapist diversions. Like my resistance to the possibility of Ferrante being a man, my discomfort with the idea of collaborative authorship revealed some hypocrisy. Am I really so committed to the ideologies of individualism and artistic genius, despite all my Barthesian, Foucauldian, and Benedettian posturing? Why should a work by one author be any more authentic, sincere, or true than a collaboration?

■ ■ ■

These digressions, which I undertook in order to justify my interest in Ferrante's identity and my emotional investment in her gender and number, have become superfluous in the last month. There was a great deal of excitement leading up to the publication of the spring 2015 issue of the *Paris Review*, which features the first-ever in-person interview with the writer. Presumably, such an interview would have revealed that Ferrante is one individual, a woman. The importance of this interview, however, was somewhat diminished by the fact that the in-person interview was conducted by Ferri and Ozzola, the very editors rumored to be Ferrante, and by their daughter, Eva Ferri.

In Italy, as the deadline approached for nominations for the country's most prestigious literary award, the Strega Prize, concerns about the possibility of a pseudonymous awardee escalated into front-page news and scathing polemic. Raffaella de Santis's February 16 article in *La repubblica*, "Who's Afraid of Elena Ferrante for the Strega?," described and stoked the controversy. She reported that Sandro Veronesi, a past Strega winner and thus a member of the association of literary elite known as the Amici della domenica that forms the prize jury, threatened to resign if Ferrante was nominated, declaring: "If you decide not to exist, don't participate in the most important literary competition in Italy!"[16] As de Santis and many others have noted, Ferrante was nominated for a Strega in 1992 for *Troubling Love*, but her candidacy attracted little attention at the time because there was little chance of her winning. (Popular belief, supported by history, is that Strega recipients alternate—by design—between the nominees of the two largest publishing houses, Edizioni Mondadori and Einaudi.)[17]

On February 21, Roberto Saviano, Strega Prize–winning author of *Gomorra*, the enormously successful exposé of organized crime in Naples, wrote an open letter to Ferrante, published in *La repubblica*:

> Dear Elena Ferrante, I write not as someone who knows you in person but as a reader, and I believe this is the kind of acquaintance you prefer. I have never been interested in uncovering who hides behind your name, because since I was young I have always had your pages available to me, and that was enough—and still is enough—for me to believe I know you, to know who you are: a person close and familiar to me.[18]

Saviano continues to make a case for her participation: "It would add fresh water to the long stagnant swamp" of the Italian literary establishment. Ferrante responded three days later with a letter in the same publication:

> I am glad that you read one of my books and wish to make it the banner of a small cultural battle, but it's useless to ask my permission. No reader writes to me for permission to use *My Brilliant Friend* to prop up a table with a broken leg. . . . I completely

share your opinions about the Strega, which in my view is one of a great many tables in our country whose legs have been devoured by woodworms. . . . The use of my book will serve only to prop up an old worm-eaten table for another year, as we wait to see whether to restore it or to throw it away.[19]

Over the next week, at least two more letters from Ferrante—quickly revealed by Edizioni E/O to be fakes—appeared in Italian newspapers, as did a fake interview that made Ferrante a dialect-speaking, bearded old lady hitting on her young Neapolitan interviewer. Amid this cacophony, devoted readers chimed in on Twitter and beyond to obsequiously repeat the metaphor of the Befana, urging everyone to read the novels and to stop worrying about Ferrante's identity.

My curiosity endured.

In response to de Santis's article, published later on the same day, February 16, the gossip blog *DagoSpia* declared the debate about the possibility of Ferrante's nomination for a Strega ridiculous, because "Even the stones know that Elena Ferrante is Anita Raja."[20]

I wouldn't always be so quick to believe the words of a disreputable gossip blog, but the more I read about Raja the more convinced I become that she is indeed Ferrante. Raja is among those long rumored to be Ferrante. (As is Raja's husband, the Strega Prize–winning Neapolitan novelist Domenico Starnone.) But more importantly, she is the translator, for Edizioni E/O (which has published all of Ferrante's novels), of the East German writer Christa Wolf. Raja translated Wolf's *Medea* (1996), a novel that, like *The Days of Abandonment*, which it must have in some part inspired, sets the myth in modern times. Stefania Lucamante, a professor of Italian and comparative literature at the Catholic University of America, finds a critical precursor in Wolf's *Medea*:

It is not until Christa Wolf's version of the myth . . . that we see Medea's torment suddenly appearing in the garb of an "everyday" life experience: being left by your beloved husband for another woman. Wolf speaks often of the usefulness of myths to represent the present in the process called in German *Vergangenheitsbewältigung*, or "the process of getting over the past."[21]

Another Wolf title translated by Raja is *The Quest for Christa T* (1968). Like *My Brilliant Friend* and the rest of the Neapolitan tetralogy, Wolf's novel is the story of a woman who becomes a writer by piecing together the traces of a lost friend—one who seems sometimes to disintegrate into and become indistinguishable from the narrator herself. While *My Brilliant Friend* opens with Lila's disappearance without a trace, *The Quest for Christa T.* begins with the following reflection: "Christa T. was timid. Mainly it was the fear that one might vanish without a trace, a frequent enough event in those days. She compulsively left traces, hasty and careless ones."[22] The premises may be reversed; the influence seems clear.

After Wolf's death, in 2011, Raja wrote a short essay to commemorate her dear friend, inspiration, and mentor:

The assiduous study of the words of an author generates affinity, closeness. If the person writing is a great writer, translating becomes an experience that profoundly enriches she who translates. Her work of verbalization acted upon my poorer and more common work of welcoming into my language. Her work strengthened mine, leading me to paths I never would have thought of taking. To the point that I had the impression that the texts of Christa were expressing me, that I would have liked to write them just as they were written, that Christa wrote them thinking of me. But translating Christa Wolf I also—and above all—came to understand that the relationship between two languages ends up developing though the relationship between two people: and Christa, whom I met in 1984, revealed herself from the very first moment to be a model of humanity, closeness, concreteness, curiosity, attention, generosity. Always, right up to the end, when we heard from each other, she would first of all ask questions about children, family, health, work, about politics and vacations, about common and quotidian things, at length and with real attention, and then almost seamlessly we would be talking about books or problems of translation.[23]

The complex relationships between the narrator of *The Quest for Christa T.* and Christa T., and between Elena and Lila, are echoed in the relationship Raja describes between herself and Wolf. The Italian feminist Luisa Muraro—who has interviewed and influenced Ferrante—has developed a theory of *affidamento*, a practice of "putting faith in" or "entrusting" between women that would be the basis for a new symbolic order to counter patriarchy.[24] The relationship Raja describes between herself and Wolf—one of apprenticeship and friendship—seems like an *affidamento*. But it is also a *tradimento*, for it is the relationship between translator and translated, betrayer and betrayed. This is the horrifying ambivalence of friendship and of working with words.

NOTES

This article was originally presented in slightly different form to the fellows of the New York Institute for the Humanities, Deutsches Haus at New York University, March 13, 2015.

1. Elena Ferrante, "'True Miracles Are Those Whose Makers Will Never Be Known' (Letter to Her Publisher, 1991)," in *Fragments: Elena Ferrante on Writing, Reading, and Anonymity*, ed. Eva Ferri, trans. Ann Goldstein (New York: Europa Editions, 2012), 1. The publication cited here is an

abridged version of a collection of interviews and letters originally published in Italy as *La frantumaglia* (Rome: Edizioni E/O, 2003).

2. Ferrante, " 'True Miracles,' " 2.

3. In the essay "La frantumaglia" (not included in the abridged translation of the eponymous collection), Ferrante explains that the title, *Amore molesto* in the original, was inspired by a reading of the Italian translation of "Female Sexuality," where Freud—or rather, his translator—describes the father, for the pre-Oedipal girl, as merely "a troublesome rival," "un rivale molesto." *La frantumaglia*, 133.

4. Elena Ferrante, *Storia della bambina perduta* (Rome: Edizioni E/O, 2014), 437; my translation.

5. Roland Barthes, *Image, Music, Text*, trans. Stephen Heath (New York: Hill and Wang, 1977), 148.

6. Carla Benedetti, *The Empty Cage: Inquiry Into the Mysterious Disappearance of the Author*, trans. William J. Hartley (Ithaca, NY: Cornell University Press, 2005), 57.

7. Elena Ferrante, "Art of Fiction No. 228," interview by Sandro Ferri, Sandra Ozzola, and Eva Ferri, *Paris Review*, no. 212 (Spring 2015).

8. Daniel Soar, "Wiggle, Wiggle," *London Review of Books*, September 21, 2006, http://www.lrb.co.uk/v28/n18/daniel-soar/wiggle-wiggle.

9. See James Wood, "Women on the Verge: The Fiction of Elena Ferrante," *New Yorker*, January 21, 2013, http://www.newyorker.com/magazine/2013/01/21/women-on-the-verge.

10. Marco Mancassola, "Embracing the Other Italy," *New York Times*, March 10, 2015, http://www.nytimes.com/2015/03/10/opinion/embracing-the-other-italy.html.

11. Elena Ferrante, *Storia della bambina perduta*, 435; my translation.

12. Paolo di Paolo, "Il caso Ferrante, il romanzo italiano secondo il New Yorker," *La stampa*, October 13, 2014, http://www.lastampa.it/2014/10/13/cultura/il-caso-ferrante-il-romanzo-italiano-secondo-il-new-yorker-k6z6crdyRB5A6Z4ycRUrIO/pagina.html.

13. Cristiano de Majo, "La narrazione esotica italiana all'estero," *Rivista studio*, January 21, 2015, http://www.rivistastudio.com/editoriali/libri/la-narrazione-esotica-italiana-allestero/.

14. "Central Park West e il caso di Elena Ferrante negli Stati Uniti," RaiNews, January 30, 2015, http://www.rainews.it/dl/rainews/media/Central-Park-West-e-il-caso-Elena-Ferrante-negli-Stati-Uniti-7cf51161-aad4-42e3-bbe6-4d619c6d0ad3.html.

15. Stiliana Milkova's superb article "Mothers, Daughters, Dolls: On Disgust in Elena Ferrante's *La figlia oscura*," for example, begins: "Elena Ferrante

is the pseudonym of a contemporary Italian writer who has kept her identity a secret over the past twenty years," in *Italian Culture* 31, no. 2 (September 2013). Milkova does not engage in any speculation about the identity of Ferrante, and the arguments set out in the article would remain unaffected by any revelation about the gender (and number) of the writer.

16. Sandro Veronesi, "Chi ha paura di Elena Ferrante allo Strega?," *La repubblica*, February 16, 2015, http://ricerca.repubblica.it/repubblica/archivio /repubblica/2015/02/16/chi-ha-paura-di-elena-ferrante-allo-strega48 .html; my translation.

17. Einaudi, historically associated with the left and still generally considered the most prestigious publishing house in Italy, was acquired by the Berlusconi-controlled Arnoldo Mondadori group in 1994.

18. Roberto Saviano, "Cara Ferrante, ti candido al premio Strega," *La repubblica*, February 21, 2015, http://www.repubblica.it/cultura/2015/02/21/news /roberto_saviano_cara_ferrante_ti_candido_al_premio_strega-107829542/; my translation.

19. Elena Ferrante, "Accetto la candidatura allo Strega," *La repubblica*, February 24, 2015, http://www.repubblica.it/cultura/2015/02/24/news /elena_ferrante_accetto_la_candidatura_allo_strega-108043390/; my translation.

20. "Lo Strega di Pulcinella—Si può dare il premio a una scrittrice dall'identità misteriosa? Peccato che lo sanno anche i sassi che Elena Ferrante è Anita Raja, moglie di Starnone (che rosica mica poco)," *DagoSpia*, February 16, 2015, http://www.dagospia.com/rubrica-2/media_e_tv/strega-pulcinella -si-pu-dare-premio-scrittrice-94606.htm.

21. Stefania Lucamante, *A Multitude of Women: The Challenges of the Contemporary Italian Novel* (Toronto: University of Toronto Press, 2008), 86.

22. Christa Wolf, *The Quest for Christa T.*, trans. Christopher Middleton (New York: Farrar, Straus & Giroux, 1970), 33.

23. Anita Raja, commemoration of Christa Wolf, Goethe-Institut Italien, December 2011, http://www.goethe.de/ins/it/lp/prj/lit/gelit/it8590177.htm; my translation.

24. An interview with Ferrante by Luisa Muraro and Marina Terragni, entitled "Il vapore erotico del corpo materno. Risposte alle domande di Marina Terragni e Luisa Muraro," is included in a more recent, expanded edition of *La frantumaglia* (2007). In her doctoral dissertation, "Italian Female Epistemologies beyond 'The Scene of the Crime,'" University of California Berkeley, 2013, Leslie Elwell uses Muraro's concept of *affidamento* to produce an incisive reading of Ferrante's *The Lost Daughter* and its relation to Sibilla Aleramo's 1906 *Una donna*.

WHAT GLOBAL ENGLISH MEANS FOR WORLD LITERATURE

HARUO SHIRANE

G lobalization is one of the great issues facing universities today, particularly in humanities departments. It means different things to different people, but most agree that globalization pluralizes. In the words of Jonathan Arac, globalization "opens up every local, national or regional culture to others and thereby produces 'many worlds.'"[1] However, this rapid pluralization is occurring in the age of English, when a single language has achieved a dominance hitherto unknown in world history. As a result, the many worlds opened up by globalization are increasingly likely to be known through that single language alone.

The combination of globalization and "Globlish" paradoxically tends to flatten foreign cultures even as it enhances their accessibility. Minae Mizumura's recent book, *The Fall of Language in the Age of English* (skillfully translated from the Japanese by Mari Yoshihara and Juliet Winters Carpenter) reveals the various consequences of that flattening from the perspective of a prominent writer working in a non-European language. For those living in the Anglosphere, no barrier seems to stand between their world and the many other worlds that now appear at the push of a button. But for those outside that world, particularly in non-European countries, the literary and linguistic consequences of globalization in the age of English can often be severe.

Mizumura's book met with fierce hostility in Japan when it first came out in 2008. The original Japanese title means literally "when the Japanese language falls: in the age of English." Largely because of the provocative title, which suggests the imminent demise of Japanese, it caused a furor and became an internet sensation in which legions of bloggers gave their opinions, sometimes without even bothering to read the book. Mizumura was attacked from both ends of the political spectrum. On the right she was criticized as anti-Japanese and antinationalist for implying that the Japanese language had weakened in the face of English. In the book, she advocated returning to the great Japanese novels of the late nineteenth and early twentieth centuries, which she considered the peak of modern Japanese literature and a means to revitalizing literary Japanese and Japanese language education as a whole. This stance caused her to be attacked on the left as reactionary and elitist, as a writer who harked back to the dark pre–World War II days and the country's imperialist past.

The fierce argument across digital media helped make *The Fall of Language in the Age of English* a national best-seller (a rare phenomenon for such an academic book), with over 65,000 copies sold to date, and stirred a national debate about the weaknesses of both Japanese and English education in Japan. Despite the book's title, Mizumura does not actually believe that the Japanese language is about to collapse; instead, she is concerned about the diminishing quality of literary Japanese and the fate of contemporary Japanese literature in an era of English.

Why was Mizumura's book translated into English? What can this book teach those who know little or nothing about Japanese literature and will probably never read Japanese? The book challenges us to reconsider global literature in an age of English, and it reminds us of the value of reading literature in the original, whatever that language may be. Mizumura traces the rise and decline of modern national literatures, using the example of Japanese literature. In the process she raises key questions about the relationship of local vernaculars to what she calls "national language" and the complex relationship of that national language to the new "universal" language (English), particularly as these concern a writer working in a non-Roman script or nonphonetic writing system.

By "national language," Mizumura means a local spoken language that has become a standardized, written, print language bound up with the identity of a modern nation-state; it differs from "local language" in that it takes on many of the important functions of "universal language," particularly by translating into the national language the advanced knowledge carried by the universal language. In the medieval and early-modern periods, transnational languages such as Latin, Arabic, or literary Chinese served as the language of high culture and technology; in the modern period, "national languages" have taken on that role. However, unlike the premodern period, when there were multiple "universal" (transnational, cosmopolitan) languages, or the modern period (late nineteenth and the first half of the twentieth century for Japan), in which national languages and national literatures flourished, the present age has seen a single tongue become the one and only universal language. English's dominance in all spheres from science to literature is far greater than that of the earlier cosmopolitan languages such as Latin in medieval Europe, literary Chinese in East Asia, Arabic in the Middle East, or French in nineteenth-century Europe. Because there are now more literate people than at any other time in world history and because of new technologies that create global simultaneity on an unprecedented scale, English now penetrates every sphere.

Much has been said recently about the growth of world literature in the age of globalization, but this has overwhelmingly come
from those writing in English and/or dealing with literatures in
the Romance languages. For example, Pascale Casanova's *The
World Republic of Letters* ([1999] 2004) traces the rise and dominance of French language and literature; David Damrosch's *What
Is World Literature?* (2003) examines the ways in which literature
travels around the world, either in translation or from one language to another, often following trade routes.[2] In secondary and
higher education in the United States, the traditional canons of
national literature have been expanded or broken up to include a
larger corpus of literature from around the world. However, almost
all of the literature dealt with in these studies is based on European languages, and these representatives of "world literature" are
read almost entirely in English translation.

The assumptions of this Anglophone view of "world literature" are reflected in the genres and texts that have been chosen
by Anglophone critics and scholars to represent "world literature." Franco Moretti, for example, in his attempt to draw up a
"world literary" map, ends up focusing on such modern European-
based themes and genres as the "rise of the novel."[3] In most of
Asia, the so-called novel was a minor genre, not even considered
serious literature until the nineteenth century, mostly under the
impact of the European novel, while poetry (particularly the
lyric), historical writings (chronicles and biographies), and philosophical writing were central. Compared to educated Europeans,
until the modern period, elite East Asians (especially Confucian
literati) had a very low view of fiction, at least on the surface,
and almost all canonical literary genres were thought to be direct
reflections of individual or historical experience. In other words,
the very notion of "world literature" that has emerged in English
largely reflects the modern European notion of literature as

imaginative narrative, with particular emphasis on the epic, the novel, and the short story.

In *The Fall of Language in the Age of English*, Mizumura, a leading contemporary Japanese novelist who was educated (from high school through graduate school) in the United States and returned to Japan to become a writer, asks a fundamental question: What is the position of non-English-language writers (particularly non-European writers) in a global world so thoroughly dominated by English that no writer can escape its weighty impact? In the opening chapter, which describes her experience at an International Writing Program at the University of Iowa, she points to a hierarchy among literary languages, in which languages at the bottom are dying at an unprecedented rate, like animals and plants affected by severe environmental change, with English overrunning and homogenizing what had been a highly diversified linguistic landscape.

What Mizumura calls a "universal language" is not determined by the number of its speakers of that language but by the number who depend on it for their survival. Outside of the Anglo-European sphere, a linguistic and cultural hierarchy has emerged in which English, with its access to the latest knowledge and technology, stands at the top while national and other local languages stand below; most nonnative English writers strive to be bilingual, but it is a severely asymmetrical relationship. Historically, in Mizumura's words, "the universal [now English], which society places above the local, is assigned the heavy responsibility of aspiring to the highest excellence, not only aesthetically but also intellectually and ethically. In contrast, even if it has a writing system, the lower-ranking local language is primarily intended for only uneducated men and women."

The equation of English with elite status may account for the influx of Chinese students into American private and public universities. These Chinese students, whose parents have made it into the top economic strata in mainland China, pay exorbitantly high tuition in order for their children to acquire the "universal language" of science, business, statistics, and other fields. Today, there are more speakers of Mandarin Chinese in the world than of English, but their native tongue is far from the "universal" language. English is now the lingua franca of East Asia, an area that saw less occupation by European powers than did Latin America, Africa, the Middle East, or South Asia, and where—with a few exceptions such as Hong Kong, Vietnam, and the Philippines—the European colonizers left much less of a linguistic imprint.

Having existed for most of its recorded history in a bilingual culture that depended on the reading or translation of the cosmopolitan literary Chinese for its survival, the Japanese have long been adept translators. From the late nineteenth century, in the race to catch up with modern institutions and technologies of Europe, the Japanese feverishly translated European languages into modern Japanese, introducing key Western terms and ideas, usually using Chinese graphs. In the pre-WWII era, Chinese and Korean students came to study in Tokyo—then the Asian metropole—and this practice transferred key words and ideas to China and Korea. Japan remains one of the most prolific translating nations in the world, and many of the titles in its bookstores are in katakana, the syllabary used for foreign words. But now Chinese and Korean students rarely bother to study in Japan (having no need for Japanese as an intermediary); instead, they come to universities in the global metropole, the United States. Today, when Japanese and Chinese tourists and businesspeople converse with one another, they do so in English.

At the heart of *The Fall of Language in the Age of English* is an extended debate with Benedict Anderson's classic account of linguistic nationalism in *Imagined Communities: Reflections on the*

Origins and Spread of Nationalism (1983). Mizumura agrees with Anderson's basic argument that national languages, the vernacular or local language employed by a nation-state, gave birth to national literatures, which in turn helped to build and solidify nation-states—the "imagined communities" for which millions of people have sacrificed their lives.[4] She lauds Anderson for showing how the rise of "print capitalism" was an integral part of the process by which vernaculars (especially spoken, local languages) become national (written and printed) languages.

Mizumura, however, sees two major flaws in Anderson's argument. First, Anderson acknowledges the role of the earlier "sacred languages" such as Latin, which created "religiously imagined communities" such as Christianity, Islam, Buddhism, and Confucianism—as well as bilingual writers who worked in both the universal and the local languages. However, he downplays the subsequent impact of "sacred languages" by describing them as essentially religious and elite and thus "arcane," in contrast to local vernacular languages, which for Anderson represent the masses. For Mizumura, the importance of a "universal language" lies in its ability to allow people speaking different vernaculars to pursue and accumulate advanced knowledge through a common language. It should be added that those "sacred languages," like the "universal languages" of the modern period (such as French and then English), were closely linked to empire building and were by no means limited to elite users.

Moreover, Mizumura underscores how Anderson fails to see the radical difference in status among vernaculars. Some vernaculars, such as English, French, Dutch, and German, became major print languages, with French reigning as the supreme literary vernacular (as Casanova has shown) before it was overtaken by English, which became the undisputed hegemon; other vernaculars were not so fortunate. This blind spot emerges, Mizumura argues, because Anderson (though a scholar of Southeast Asia) is working in that universal language. The stress that Anderson and other Anglo-European-based scholars place on "multilingualism" and on the vernacular mistakenly suggests that all vernaculars operate on a level playing field.

In the late nineteenth century, Japan followed the trajectory of many European countries in building a strong modern nation-state centered on the identity of its national language, but, as Mizumura points out, that national language did not directly emerge out of the vernacular. Japanese was not, like modern European languages, a written version of the local, spoken language. Instead, the national language of modern Japan depended on a long tradition of writing that mixed logograms and phonograms, a complex notational system that resulted in a rich literary tradition in which writing did not correspond directly with speech. As a written language, Japanese developed what Mizumura calls a "mesmerizing polyphony," a complex notation system that combines logographic and phonographic use of characters from Chinese with two different sets of native syllabary (kana).

To give a simple example, a name in Germanic or Romance languages may contain recognizable etymological stems, but there is only one reading: the way it is pronounced. A name in Japanese, however, can be represented in a myriad of ways, depending on the graph or graph compound. The name "Haruo," for example, can be represented by a range of different compound graphs, extending in meaning from "spring man" and "governing husband" to "clear brave male." The name exists on at least two levels: that of the sound and that of the semantic meaning of the graph. Furthermore, the same graph can be read different ways.

A single page of an English novel contains only the letters of the Roman alphabet, thus looking very plain in comparison with a single page of a late-nineteenth- or early-twentieth-century

Japanese novel, which is filled not only with letters from the two different syllabaries but also with Chinese graphs (carrying aural and/or semantic functions) and what are called *furigana*, small letters placed alongside the graphs that give those graphs a particular or alternative phonetic reading and meaning. The Japanese had access to printing technology as early as the eighth century and used moveable type by the late sixteenth century, but they chose to remain with xylography (engravings on wood), largely to accommodate this polyphonic writing and to enhance the aesthetic dimension of the book. Woodblock printing enabled the free combination of text and picture at low cost, spurring genres such as the modern manga, a sophisticated comic-book genre that is a major part of Japanese popular culture today. Traditionally, writing in East Asia has been an aesthetic phenomenon that gives equal weight to the imagistic and textual dimensions of writing. This is evident in the high place accorded to calligraphy, long considered the equivalent of poetry and painting. Word processing for a complex writing system like Japanese was initially time-consuming and slow, but once the technical difficulties were mastered, it led to such innovations as emoji (a Japanese word literally meaning "picture words"), with its smiley faces and other pictures (sometimes animated), a more three-dimensional form of writing that is potentially far more multisensory and polyphonic than the Roman script on paper.

From the nineteenth century onward, European imperial powers attempted to impose their own languages on the colonized or, at the very least, to enforce the use of the Roman script. Japan was no exception. As Mizumura points out, the Japanese writing system repeatedly faced the danger of Europe-based phonocentricism, in which repeated attempts were made in the modern period (from the late nineteenth century) to flatten Japanese into a European-style language, to make the Japanese written language a phonetic one, either by romanizing its alphabet (as happened in Vietnam) or by expunging the large number of Chinese-derived graphs embedded in its writing system (as is now occurring with Korean). Each attempt to romanize Japanese was defeated, but the adaptation of a new orthographic system during the U.S. occupation, which brought spoken and written Japanese into closer proximity, created a break between post-WWII Japanese writing and late-nineteenth- and early-twentieth-century literature. As a result, earlier Japanese literature has become increasingly difficult for Japanese high school and college students to read. The impact of English as a hegemonic language in Japan appears not just in the practical need to use English per se but in the phonocentric model that it represents.

In Japan, during the Meiji era (1868–1912), the vernacular novel became, at least for a time, the premier genre for the pursuit of knowledge. Japan produced a rich national literature, centered on authors such as Natsume Sōseki (1867–1916) for whom the novel became the ultimate vehicle for exploring the large questions of the day in ways that combined the local and the global. The specific example that Mizumura gives is Sōseki's *Sanshirō*, a novel "exemplifying *national literature* in which a character critiques his own country and people from a global perspective" (emphasis in the original).

Mizumura argues that Japan managed to produce a major "national literature" at the end of the nineteenth century against all odds. This modern "miracle" occurred for three basic reasons. First, as an island nation off the coast of a major civilization, Japan was both geographically close to the regional "universal" language of the premodern and early-modern periods (literary Chinese) yet far enough away from the yoke of the Chinese imperial examination system (which dominated the Korean peninsula) to establish its own literary tradition very early, in the tenth and eleventh centuries, at least two centuries before the development of vernacular literatures in Europe. Second, Japan enjoyed what Benedict Anderson calls "print capitalism" since the seventeenth century, during the Edo period, which created an infrastructure and market for mass publishing and the commodification of literature. Third, Japan escaped colonization at the peak of Western imperial expansion, avoiding a situation like that of the Philippines, which became an American colony where English thoroughly dominated the local language.

In my view, it should be stressed that Japan itself became a major imperial power in the first half of the twentieth century, closely resembling other imperial powers such as Great Britain, France, and the United States. In the process, Japan forced its colonies Korea and Taiwan to make Japanese their official language, and it made Koreans take on Japanese names. The imposition of Japanese as the national language on Taiwan and Korea was made possible in part because those countries were within the Sinosphere and already used Chinese graphs; the imposition also belonged to a larger imperial strategy that sometimes included banning English. The formation of Japan's "national literature" thus coincided with Japan becoming a modernized nation and a major empire intent on extending its geographical and linguistic reach, much like its Western counterparts; while Japan managed to escape linguistic colonization by the United States and European powers, it forced others into an asymmetrical, hierarchical bilingualism that ended only with Japan's defeat in World War II.

Given what she sees as the declining quality of Japanese language and literature, Mizumura advocates that young Japanese study the modern (late-nineteenth- and early-twentieth-century) canon of Japanese literature, which can provide the foundation for a vibrant contemporary literature. Taking such a position today in Japan, Mizumura points out, is regarded as politically incorrect;

in the post-WWII period, Japanese intellectuals, showing their "guilt" for Japan's wartime failings, moved en masse to the left and rejected the imperial past, refusing to view their own national language in any positive or rational light. In Mizumura's view, the deterioration of modern Japanese literature has been occurring over an extended period of time, but with the acceleration of globalization and the increasing dominance of English, a healthy recovery of the Japanese literary past may become very difficult. The danger is that young Japanese may not even bother to familiarize themselves with their own modern classics. At the same time, young Japanese students continue to struggle with speaking English since the separation of speaking and writing in Japan extends even to foreign-language education, which focuses almost entirely on grammar and written language.

The originality of Mizumura's book for Western audiences is that it raises the issue of national and universal languages from the perspective of a major non-European, non-phonocentric literary language that existed in a bilingual state both in the premodern past and in the present. To this broad frame Mizumura has added the critical dimension of the fate of "national languages" in the age of English and the role of the modern novel, which, at least for a limited time, became a vehicle for contemplation of the local in a larger global context. As a writer who was educated in the United States but who never left Japan linguistically, Mizumura has the rare advantage of examining the influence and power of the English language on the world stage even as she looks at it as an outsider, as a Japanese novelist. Through this broader perspective, Mizumura brings out features of literary Japanese that even scholars of Japanese language and literature, not to mention those outside Japanese studies, have hitherto failed to understand.

NOTES

1. Jonathan Arac, "Anglo-Globalism?," *New Left Review*, no. 16 (July–August 2012), 35, http://newleftreview.org/II/16/jonathan-arac-anglo-globalism.

2. Pascale Casanova, *The World Republic of Letters*, trans. M. B. DeBevoise (1999; Cambridge, MA: Harvard University Press, 2004); David Damrosch, *What Is World Literature?* (Princeton, NJ: Princeton University Press, 2003).

3. Franco Moretti, "Conjectures on World Literature," *New Left Review* (January–February 2000): 54–68, http://newleftreview.org/II/1/franco-moretti-conjectures-on-world-literature.

4. Benedict Anderson, *Imagined Communities: Reflections on the Origin and Spread of Nationalism* (London: Verso, 1983).

THE STRANGER'S VOICE

KARL ASHOKA BRITTO

T*he Sympathizer*, Viet Thanh Nguyen's riveting debut novel, is a chronicle of war wrapped in a spy thriller and tucked inside a confession. It is also a political satire, a send-up of Hollywood, and a scathing critique of mid-twentieth-century Orientalism. Nguyen juggles genres like so many flying AK-47s and to dazzling, often hilarious effect. At the same time, his play with narrative allows for a profound reflection on narrative itself: at its core, *The Sympathizer* is about power and representation, about stories that function to justify torture and murder, and about words that make abstract the bodies of people whose lives have been shattered by colonialism and war.

Published forty years after the end of the Vietnam War, *The Sympathizer* has already garnered considerable critical acclaim for Nguyen, who teaches English and American studies and ethnicity at the University of Southern California. The novel begins during the chaotic days leading up to the final departure of American forces from South Vietnam in April 1975, shifts to trace the establishment of the Vietnamese diaspora in Southern California, and then returns to early postwar Vietnam in its final chapters.

American literature about Vietnam has until recently been largely focused on the experiences of U.S. soldiers, and *The*

Sympathizer has rightly been welcomed for the different perspective it brings to the war and its devastating effects on the Vietnamese. And yet, while the novel has been praised for its "rare and authentic voice,"[1] what is most striking about Nguyen's unnamed narrator is how thoroughly he complicates any straightforward understanding of authenticity. Introducing himself as "a spy, a sleeper, a spook, a man of two faces," he signals from the novel's first sentence that his will be a story in which identity and truth are anything but clear.

Part of the novel's complexity arises from the density of its network of intertextual referents and resonances. Certain scenes, as well as the different moods that characterize particular sections of the novel, bring to mind the work of American and Vietnamese authors who have written about the war: Larry Heinemann, Duong Thu Huong, and Bao Ninh, among others. Many events within the narrative, and the narrator's reflections upon those events, directly reference or allude to a range of philosophers, theorists, and cultural critics, from Marx and Hegel to Frantz Fanon and Frank Chin. The narrator's own voice slips in and out of different registers and genres, both literary and cinematic. Consider the tone of this sentence: "The American Dream, the culture of Hollywood, the practices of American democracy, and so on can altogether make America a disorienting place for those like us who hail from the Orient." This modest piece of cultural analysis is offered by way of explanation for a markedly different kind of writing, the exuberantly hardboiled description of a woman's legs that appeared a couple of pages earlier: "Longer than the Bible and a hell of a lot more fun, they stretched forever, like an Indian yogi or an American highway shimmering through the Great Plains or the southwestern desert. Her legs demanded to be looked at and would not take no, *non, nein, nyet,* or even maybe for an answer."

The Sympathizer often wears its web of allusion lightly, and the novel's moments of intertextual reference and generic parody make for a lively and richly suggestive narrative. On a deeper level, Nguyen's engagement with Euro-American authors and texts concerned with imperialism and imperialist fantasies—Joseph Conrad and *Apocalypse Now*, Albert Camus, Graham Greene—contests a history of representation that, as Edward Said put it in *Culture and Imperialism*, "offers a profoundly unforgiving view . . . of Western imperialist illusions" while nonetheless arguing "that the source of the world's significant action and life is in the West, whose representatives seem at liberty to visit their fantasies and philanthropies upon a mind-deadened Third World."[2] At the same time, the prominence of intertextual reference in the novel also draws our attention—at times with humor, at times with anguish—to the mediated nature of any historical narrative.

The question of the narrator's authenticity is, of course, also complicated by his own story. The illegitimate son of a French priest and his young Vietnamese maid, the American-educated narrator works as a spy for the North Vietnamese, first in South Vietnam and then later in California, where he monitors and reports on the ongoing anticommunist nationalism of the refugee community. His two closest friends from childhood, Man and Bon, are situated at opposite ends of the ideological spectrum: Man becomes the communist official to whom he addresses his reports, written in invisible ink and encoded using a cipher based on a book of Orientalist, anticommunist propaganda; Bon is a former soldier in the South Vietnamese Army who believes the narrator to be committed to the struggle to win Vietnam back from the communists and who shares a squalid apartment with him in Los Angeles before returning to Southeast Asia to carry on the fight. The narrator's divided allegiance—his desire to protect his friend as best he can from the communist government for which he secretly works—pushes him to accompany Bon on this mission and sets in motion the events of the harrowing final chapters. His capacity to sympathize, "to see any issue from both sides," makes him both a compelling narrator and a vulnerable yet thoroughly complicit player in the theater of cruelty that shapes his life.

The bulk of the novel takes the form of a first-person retrospective account, though we learn early on that it is in fact a particular variant of this form: a confession, written in an isolation cell. In a striking formal gesture, the narrative continues beyond the end point of this confession, and the confession itself—that is, everything that we have read in the 295 pages that take us from the narrator's departure from Vietnam in April 1975 to his arrest on the banks of the Mekong a few years later—becomes the subject of his interrogation in the reeducation camp where he is imprisoned. The text he has written—the novel we hold in our hands—is mercilessly criticized by the commandant assigned to his case, as much for its style as for what may be lacking in its content: "It hardly seems like a genuine confession to me. . . . Confessions are as much about style as content, as the Red Guards have shown us. All we ask for is a certain way with words . . . you are a communist only in name. In practice, you are a bourgeois intellectual . . . your language betrays you. It is not clear, not succinct, not direct, not simple. It is the language of the elite. You must write for the people!"

Subjected to torture, the narrator makes a second confession that seems to fill a crucial gap in the first. Embedded in what is perhaps the most narratively complex passage in the text, this confession is written in the first person, transcribed from what we learn was a tape recording made while the narrator was being tortured, and of which he has no memory; furthermore, the chapter leading up to this moment has shifted into the third person, with the interrogation intermittently represented in a Q&A format:

Q: What did you do?

A: I watched.

Q: What did you see?

Later, sometime in the bright future, the commissar would play the patient a tape recording of his answer, though he had no memory of the tape recorder's presence. Many people who heard their voices on tape thought that they did not sound like themselves, which they found disturbing, and he was no exception. He heard this stranger's voice say, I saw everything.

This, then, is the authentic voice of the narrator: a voice that is strange to him and estranged from him, a voice that speaks from a place outside of memory, compelled to relate a scene of atrocious violence. The scene is deeply troubling not only for its manifest content but also for the way in which its horror seems to bring us, at last, to the heart of the war's darkness, even as we know that we cannot take this form of authenticity at face value. The confession, after all, has been extracted through torture. As the narrator has learned from a CIA operative, "Brute force will get you bad answers, lies, misdirection, or, worse yet, will get you the answer the prisoner thinks you want to hear. He will say anything to stop the pain." We also learn that the narrator is still imprisoned as he writes the pages that describe his interrogation and that the man who ordered his torture will read them.

Through this narrative complexity, Nguyen accomplishes something quite extraordinary: he represents the horror of war while never allowing us to forget the conditions out of which its representation emerges in the text. What is at stake here is not so much the objective truth of the scene described by the narrator but rather the novel's insistence upon staging his narrative as a confession, produced under constraint and compelled to exist in the service of a structure of power that sets the terms of representation itself.

Since farce and tragedy are deeply intertwined in *The Sympathizer*, it is hardly surprising that a double of the scene of atrocity appears much earlier in the novel, during an extended subplot in which the narrator is hired as a consultant—a sort of authenticity expert—on an overblown, *Apocalypse Now*–like Hollywood film about the war. While the darkly comic tone of this section of the novel would seem to distance it from the subsequent account of torture, a scene of violence in the film's screenplay clearly echoes the narrator's interrogation. Other details draw our attention to the link between these two parts of the novel: certain moments of dialogue during the narrator's interrogation appear in screenplay format, and the room in which the scene of violence recounted by the narrator occurs is called "the movie theater."

Nguyen's point here, of course, is not to equate the movie theater and the torture chamber but to remind us that power is always interested in shaping the raw material of traumatic history to its own ends. If *The Sympathizer* lays bare the corruption of post-1975 Vietnam and the coercive force underlying its national narrative, it is no less fierce in its critique of the goal of Hollywood, "the simultaneous lobotomization and pickpocketing of the world's audiences. The ancillary benefit was strip-mining history, leaving the real history in the tunnels along with the dead, doling out tiny sparkling diamonds for audiences to gasp over . . . I pitied the French for their naïveté in believing they had to visit a country in order to exploit it. Hollywood was much more efficient, imagining the countries it wanted to exploit."[3]

Caught within multiple structures of power, the narrator struggles to resist the forces that would produce the event as spectacle, to find a different way to comprehend the catastrophe of war. In this, he finds himself in the position of the angel of history described in the ninth of Walter Benjamin's "Theses on the Philosophy of History":

> A Klee painting named "Angelus Novus" shows an angel looking as though he is about to move away from something he is fixedly contemplating. His eyes are staring, his mouth is open, his wings are spread. This is how one pictures the angel of history. His face is turned toward the past. Where we perceive a chain of events, he sees one single catastrophe which keeps piling wreckage upon wreckage, and hurls it in front of his feet. The angel would like to stay, awaken the dead, and make whole what has been smashed. But a storm is blowing from Paradise; it has got caught in his wings with such violence that the angel can no longer close them. This storm irresistibly propels him into the future to which his back is turned, while the pile of debris before him grows skyward. This storm is what we call progress.[4]

Benjamin's figure resonates strongly within Nguyen's textual project both because it captures the narrator's anguish in the face of a disastrous past he is bound to witness and because it is, precisely, a figure: an allegorical representation in itself as well as a reflection on history mediated here through painting, another form of figural representation.

In *The Sympathizer*, the angel of history is first evoked at the end of the Hollywood section, almost exactly at the novel's midpoint. The narrator, having fallen out with the film's director over the scene of violence in the screenplay, is walking through the cemetery built on the set when an unexpected explosion sends him flying: "a blare of trumpets deafened me. In the silence, the earth vanished—the glue of gravity dissolved—and I was propelled skyward, the wreckage of the cemetery blazing before me, receding as I was blown backward, the world passing by in a blurred haze that faded into mute darkness." Here, Nguyen deftly embeds historical trauma within a heavily mediated narrative moment: the narrator is blown backward like Benjamin's angel, though by an explosion on the set of a movie meant to evoke *Apocalypse Now*—itself a representation of the Vietnam War mediated through Conrad's *Heart of Darkness*.

During his interrogation, the narrator takes up the position of the angel of history for a second time, just after narrating the scene of atrocity. Here, in a heartbreaking extended sentence that runs over two pages, he represents the history of Vietnam not as a series of chronologically unfolding events, but as a single utterance cast somewhere between supplication and yearning:

> if you would please just turn off the lights . . . if you could see that I have nothing left to confess, if history's ship had taken a different tack . . . if my father had gone to save souls in Algeria instead of here . . . if we acknowledged that we are all puppets in someone else's play, if we had not fought a war against each other . . . if the Americans hadn't come to save us from ourselves . . . if the Soviets had never called us comrades . . . if the French had never sought to civilize us . . . if the Chinese had never ruled us for a thousand years . . . if the Buddha had never lived, if the Bible had never been written . . . if the dragon lord and the fairy queen had not given birth to us . . . if legend's phoenix had truly soared from its own ashes rather than simply crashed in our countryside . . . if history had never happened, neither as farce nor as tragedy . . . if I saw no more of these visions, please, could you please just let me sleep?

This, too, is a form of authenticity: the counterfactual despair of a narrator with a story that can only be told through compromise and in full awareness of those left dead in the tunnels of history.

And yet the narrative continues, beyond the second confession, the interrogation, and the 354-page manuscript written in the reeducation camp. Having been released, the narrator waits for the boat that will take him away from Vietnam with other refugees from the revolution. He waits, and he writes, right up to the moment of his writing: "only a few more [words] need to be written by the light of this oil lamp." The final pages of the novel are produced outside of the confessional structure and are marked, significantly, by a shift in narrative voice to the first-person plural. The narrator has managed to secure copies of his manuscript and will carry it with him: "This manuscript [is] our testament if not our will. We have nothing to leave to anyone except these words, our best attempt to represent ourselves against all those who sought to represent us." For all of its shortcomings, gaps, and fissures, for all of its gestures of self-protection and self-annihilation, his manuscript is a part of Vietnamese history, just as the scene of atrocious violence that haunts it is no less a part of that history for being bound up in the structures of power that seek to govern its retelling.

NOTES

1. Robert Olen Butler writes that "Viet Thanh Nguyen bring[s] a rare and authentic voice to the body of American literature generated by the Vietnam War." http://vietnguyen.info/2014/sympathizer.
2. Edward W. Said, *Culture and Imperialism* (New York: Knopf, 1993), xix.
3. Nguyen has long been concerned with the power of Hollywood to produce dominant, Orientalizing representations. See his remarks on Oliver Stone's Vietnam trilogy in *Race & Resistance: Literature & Politics in Asian America* (Oxford University Press, 2002), pp. 112, 120. More recently, he has written in Fanonian terms of his own experiences watching Hollywood films about the war: "I watched 'Apocalypse Now' and saw American sailors massacre a sampan full of civilians and Martin Sheen shoot a wounded woman in cold blood. I watched 'Platoon' and heard the audience cheering and clapping when the Americans killed Vietnamese

soldiers. These scenes, although fictional, left me shaking with rage. I knew that in the American imagination I was the Other, the Gook, the foreigner, no matter how perfect my English, how American my behavior." See "Our Vietnam War Never Ended," *New York Times*, April 26, 2015, http://www.nytimes.com/2015/04/26/opinion/sunday/our-vietnam -war-never-ended.html.

4. Walter Benjamin, *Illuminations* (New York: Knopf, 1969), 257–58.

CAN'T STOP SCREAMING

JUDITH BUTLER

very line of Anne Carson's *Antigonick* is printed in boldface handwriting, emphatic, as if something urgent and excessive has to be loudly said. The title and the format suggest that this is a translation of Sophocles's *Antigone* with illustrations. From the start, however, contemporary elements intervene: stage directions are inserted within brackets, characters cite contemporary critics, and the scenes are referred to as "episodes," reminding us how even the contemporary television series has a precedent in ancient Greece. This translation is not wrestling with every word or phrase, trying to find felicitous English for the classical Greek, but skipping lines, adding some from contemporary discourse, distilling and dispersing the textual effects of this play for our time. In place of a loyal translation, a different kind of transposition and search for equivalence takes place here. Carson evokes something similar when, in 1999's *Economy of the Unlost*, she indirectly cites Mallarmé in describing thought's "best moments" as "vibrating" with the disappearance of the object of thought.[1] Something is passing by, in the process of vanishing, and yet, for a moment—or through an unexpected concatenation of moments—it is caught by language and in the nick of time.

Carson does not "rewrite" *Antigone*. Her text becomes the verbal and visual scanning of a prolonged scream or cry. Emphatic, elliptical, *Antigonick* is more transference than translation, a relay of tragedy into a contemporary vernacular that mixes with archaic phrasing, sometimes lacking commas and periods, a halting and then a rushing of words structured by the syntax of grief and rage, spanning centuries. The lines often stand alone, as if broken off from the original text, stricken monuments. Stanzas comprising twenty or thirty lines in the original are distilled into single words and staccato exclamations.

At other moments, the text becomes downright discursive. For instance, the sisters Antigone and Ismene self-consciously incorporate bits of Hegel, Beckett, and Freud into their famous standoff, knitting the reception of Antigone into the play itself, letting us know that our only access to this play is through this present time and yet showing that this time is still bound to that classical one.

Ismene and Antigone conduct a terse conversation about what Hegel might have meant when he said that Antigone had no "ethical consciousness" and that she acts from purely unconscious motivations. Antigone speaks up to refute his interpretation of the play: "Hegel says I'm wrong." Ismene responds, "But right to be wrong"; at which point Antigone makes a set of Freudian jokes: "Can a person be so completely conscious of being unconscious that she is guilty of her own repression, is that // what I'm guilty of?"

Separating "that" and "what I'm guilty of" is a page break and inserted there is one of Bianca Stone's stunning drawings, this one of a room with an empty chair, flowered carpet, window opening out onto oneiric stuff (maybe clouds or mountains or natural landscapes lacking clear contours), a radiator, a small china cabinet perhaps from New England and from some decades ago. What appears comes from some more modern time but one that is already vacated, as if some living character had departed the scene not long ago. Who lived there? It would probably be less right to say that this image interrupts the text as the unconscious does or that it *is* the unconscious in some symbolic sense. Rather, as the scene switches between the textual and the graphic, a temporal shift takes place between the past and the present: something is gone, and something is caught and vibrates still. The image is the nick of time.

Ismene is, of course, sullen and rejected as Antigone decides to go it alone in defying Kreon and burying Polyneikes against her uncle's orders.[2] Ismene pleads: "I want to row the boat with you"; "I'll be so lonely." After Stone's image cuts Antigone's sentence in two, the second part resumes on the left side of the next page along with Ismene's rejoinder. When Ismene speaks, nearly every word takes up its own line; the wide spacing that separates them opens up blank space time and again. The word is sometimes at the beginning of the empty line, sometimes at the end:

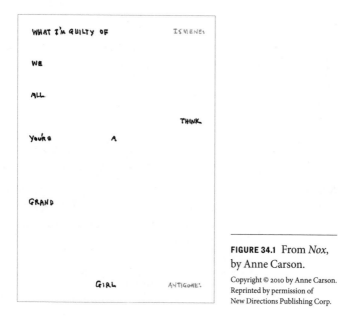

FIGURE 34.1 From *Nox*, by Anne Carson.

Copyright © 2010 by Anne Carson. Reprinted by permission of New Directions Publishing Corp.

The "girl" is followed by the announcement of Antigone's speech, but it is unclear what separates the locution of Ismene from the staging of Antigone's speech. Is she calling her, or is Antigone designated as the one whose speech follows her name? Do the two happen at once?

Sorrow, loss, and futility punctuate this page and many others, as if breathing has become difficult and the words of the sentence could only emerge from Ismene's mouth at stretched intervals. What we already know is that Antigone refuses whatever Ismene says, refuses her solidarity. Antigone's rejection settles into Ismene's speech, punctuating the latter's utterances with wide, empty space. Sometimes that emptiness is figured in Stone's spare and bold drawings; sometimes it structures the spatial organization of the page as in the case above. This emptiness is not an abstraction or philosophical trope. It is more like a sudden vanishing on the page that marks the prospective or retrospective vanishing of a life caused by unchecked rage, the distortions of grief.

When Kreon arrives to accuse, arrest, and condemn Antigone, he ushers himself on stage with "Here's Kreon, nick of time." Although Kreon seems to be saying that he is arriving in the nick of time, his syntax suggests that he himself *is* a nick of time or that he is about to nick away at the time of Antigone's life. After Kreon listens to Teiresias and recognizes his mad error in banishing Antigone to a cave to die, he rushes out of his abode and toward the cave in a race against time. The chorus then starts a list of ways to describe the sudden and urgent interval of time in which one life is endangered by someone in a rage, how reprieve can arrive just in time, or too late:

ANOTHER
AN HOUR

AN HOUR AND A HALF
A YEAR
A SPLIT SECOND
A DECADE
THIS INSTANT
A SECOND
A SPLIT SECOND
A NOW
A NICK
A NECK
KREON RUSHES OUT
ALL THE GUARDS RUSH OUT

The time in which life might be saved is surely a nick of time, but so we might say that a nick of classical Greek time becomes lodged in our own time, reopening the question of rage, grief, and loss within another idiom, often in short phrases from popular discourse. In Carson's free translation, the classical Greek terms transmute into contemporary and popular language even as some of the awkward, moving, and humorous archaisms are left there on the page (as always, in all capital letters): "The love in which to delete your own darling / The darling you dust / The dust you disperse." When Kreon learns that someone has buried Polyneikes against his will, he storms around, demanding that the guard find out who has done this deed. In Carson's rendition, the chorus then intervenes, "Many terribly quiet customers exist but none more / Terribly quiet than man / His footsteps pass so perilously soft across the sea / In marble winter." A moment in which the chorus interrupts the action to reflect on the nature of man (the famous "Ode to man") becomes somewhat ironic, if not hilarious, as the cosmos is figured as an awe-inspiring enterprise and this *Anthropos*, or human being, as a "quiet customer" of the divine, even "terribly quiet." This section relies on lines 332–364 of the original, where the human being is described as *to deinotaton*, or the most strange, wondrous, or terrible of beings. The Hugh-Lloyd Jones translation canonized in the Loeb Classical Library edition of *Antigone* brings the lines into English this way:

Many things are formidable [*polla ta deina*], and none more formidable than man [*deinoteron*]! He crosses the gray sea beneath the winter wind, passing beneath surges that surround him; and he wears away the highest of the gods. Earth, immortal and unwearying, as his ploughs go back and forth from year to year, turning the soil with the aid of the breed of horses.[3]

In the conventional translations, all that seafaring clearly references ships importing grain into classical Athens, creating new markets and amassing wealth for some Athenians. It refers as well to those more traditional forms of farming and plowing the land that take place to one side of that burgeoning harbor economy. In Carson's rendition, the divine takes form as an awesome business, and the human is described less as "formidable" than as "terribly quiet," suggesting an ominous obedience that belongs to the paying (or indebted) customer.

On yet other occasions, the associations move quickly among genres, decades, centuries, and media. For instance, Eurydike (mother of Haimon, wife of Kreon) introduces her own monologue in the third person, incorporating the didactic voice of someone who might be teaching the play or making comparisons between her and literary characters from the twentieth century. She has learned that her son, in love with Antigone and desperate about her fate, has died by his own hand:

THIS IS EURYDIKE'S MONOLOGUE IT'S HER ONLY
SPEECH IN THE PLAY. YOU MAY NOT KNOW WHO SHE
IS THAT'S OK. LIKE POOR MRS. RAMSAY WHO DIED //

Before the next page comes an image of a staircase ascending from
mountainous terrain into sky, at the top of which is a large human
figure on his back with only his bare legs showing. Then, on the
following page, the sentence continues:

IN A BRACKET OF TO THE LIGHTHOUSE SHE'S THE
WIFE OF THE MAN WHOSE MOODS TENSIFY THE WORLD
OF THIS STORY

The "girl," Antigone, like Mrs. Ramsay, is described as having "the
undead strapped to her back," after which the text breaks out into
hilarious associations in contemporary vernacular:

WE GOT HER THE BIKE WE GOT HER A THERAPIST
THAT POOR SAD MAN WITH HIS ODD IDEAS, SOME
DAYS HE MADE US SIT ON THE STAIRCASE ALL ON DIF-
FERENT STEPS OR VIDEOTAPED US BUT WHEN WE
WATCHED IT WAS NOTHING BUT SHADOWS.

Even Agamben and Derrida make brief and implicit appearances
in the discourse that comes next—musings on friends and enemies, the exception and the law—and though the humor is incontestable, so too is the pathos.

It is this polyvocal Eurydike who conducts the self-conscious
reverie on "the nick of time" toward the end of the play, asking first
whether "you" have heard this expression and forthrightly asking,
"What is a nick?" This is the question she has asked her son,

Haimon, who is now dead. What follows is less an answer than a graphic reformulation of the question—another image is then provided by Stone, a landscape of vast and shadowy mountains with diminutive and formless human figures, quiet customers, and two empty chairs in the foreground where the children, now lost, might have sat. Once Eurydike takes her own life ("she undid her eyes to the dark"), Kreon is left to consider that he is "too late." He did not arrive in any nick of time and could not save any of those lives—Antigone, Haimon, Eurydike—and so Kreon cries out, "I want Kreon's death," mixing first and third person in a way that continues to narrate the story it enacts. After all, it is a story, it has all happened before, and yet it is happening now. Stone's image intervenes: a barely discernible figure passes through a shadowy cavern, and we learn in a final line that only "nick" survives. Was that "nick" vanishing into that cavern? Who is nick?

"Antigonick" is a coinage that adds the problem of time to the character of Antigone but also produces another figure, Nick, in the wake of Antigone's death. The last line is a "bracket," not unlike the one in which Mrs. Ramsay dies in Woolf's novel:

[EXEUNT OMNES EXCEPT NICK WHO CONTINUES MEASURING]

The nick is the time of the line itself, the scan of poetic meter, but not as something that stays regular or predictable. It stops and starts, alters its pace and spatial form, breaks open white space unexpectedly, and registers a loss it can neither forestall nor redeem. We are left with the question, What kind of time is the time of tragedy? It is the time of the metrical and not so metrical line, to be sure, but also some graphic trace left from the time of life, something nicked away by some brute force, or perhaps the bracket within which life vanishes. The tone of the play does not become exactly wistful or reflective at such moments. The emphatic handwritten lines in all capital letters continue until the end, suggesting that something urgent and awful has taken place, is still taking place. In tragedy, Carson tells us in *Grief Lessons*, "through violence we are intimate with some characters onstage in an exorbitant way for a brief time";[4] what happened then keeps happening: these repetitions mark the continuing life of unconscious rage, explicit sorrow, unpredictable and winning humor, and new aesthetic forms that traverse the temporal distance between then and now.

So tragedy is neither very far away nor very foreign. It seems to be with us in the present, leaving its traces in the midst of popular discourse. In the preface to *Grief Lessons*, Carson makes clear that to understand tragedy, one need not come equipped with erudition (even though she clearly does). She answers the question "Why does tragedy exist?" by directly addressing her reader, as she had Eurydike do:

> Because you are full of rage. Why are you full of rage? Because you are full of grief. Ask a headhunter why he cuts off human heads. He'll say that rage impels him and rage is born of grief. The act of severing and tossing away the victim's head enables him to throw away all of his bereavements. . . . Perhaps you think this does not apply to you. Yet you recall the day your wife, driving you to your mother's funeral, turned left instead of right at the intersection and you had to scream at her so loud other drivers turned to look. When you tore off her head and threw it out the window they nodded, changed gears, drove away.[5]

Antigone rages forth from grief, causing new destruction, and so, too, does Kreon; they mirror each other in the midst of their opposition. So, too, do you, apparently, and everyone else as well, nodding and driving off, unless we catch ourselves in time. The reader is implicated in this recurrent alteration of grief and rage, subject to the destruction she or he is capable of inflicting, if there is no timely intervention.

Apparently "you" already know why tragedy exists. What Carson writes of Paul Celan's direct address to the "you" offers us a formulation that may well apply to her *Antigonick*: "But you, by the time we reach you, are just folding yourself away into a place we cannot go: sleep. Blank spaces instead of words fill out the verses around you as if to suggest your gradual recession down and away from our grasp. What could your hands teach us if you had not vanished?"[6] It is a cry of grief posed in question form, emphatic, handwritten, excessive, and abbreviated and, in this sense, a measured scream that gives us some sense of who or what lives on when it is all too late.

NOTES

1. Anne Carson, *Economy of the Unlost (Reading Simonides of Keos with Paul Celan)* (Princeton, NJ: Princeton University Press, 1999), vii.
2. I follow Carson's spellings of the characters' names.
3. *Sophocles II* (Cambridge, MA: Harvard University Press, 1994); my additions. In the Elizabeth Wyckoff translation (Chicago: University of Chicago Press, 1954), *to deinotaton* names the ambiguous status of the power of man more strongly: "Many the wonders but nothing walks stranger than man. / This thing crosses the sea in the winter's storm, / making his path through the roaring waves. / And she, the greatest of gods, the earth— / ageless she is, and unwearied—he wears her away / as the ploughs go up and down from year to year / and his mules turn up the soil." Is man "this thing"? The Robert Fagles translation (New York: Penguin, 1982) goes with "strange" as well. In the Richard Jebb commentary (Cambridge: The University Press, 1900), the order of things is perfectly clear: "Man is master of sea and land; he subdues all other creatures." But in the more recent, thorough, and nuanced commentary provided by Mark Griffith in the Cambridge Greek and Latin Classics edition (Cambridge: Cambridge University Press, 1999), the praise for man is "chosen precisely

because of its multivalence ('terrible,' 'awe-inspiring,' 'wonderful,' 'strange,' 'clever,' 'extraordinary')." Martin Heidegger dedicates an essay in 1935 to this "Ode to Man" in his *Introduction to Metaphysics*, translating the Greek *to deinotaton* as "das Unheimlichste," the most uncanny (unhomely) or the most strange. Ralph Manheim's translation of Heidegger's essay reads: "There is much that is strange, but nothing that surpasses man in strangeness" (New Haven, CT: Yale University Press, 1959). For Heidegger, the unsurpassingly strange is man, and yet for Carson, we find the terror and strangeness in the "quiet customer." Perhaps he is quiet from awe or because it is not clear what language, if any, can be spoken in this place where one feels out of place. If he is a customer, he occupies a different position from the seafarer or laborer, though exchange still remains key. He seems perpetually to be in someone else's store and, to be sure, feels some awe and disorientation in the face of the universe understood, perhaps, on the order of the multinational franchise. One does not have to look far from what has become daily life to find one contemporary meaning of the line. Carson, we might say, brings metaphysics into the mall.

4. Anne Carson, *Grief Lessons: Four Plays by Euripides* (New York Review Books, 2006), 9.

5. Carson, *Grief Lessons*, 7.

6. Carson, *Economy of the Unlost*, 9.

THE MODEL-MINORITY BUBBLE

JOSEPH JONGHYUN JEON

P erhaps the most famous shopping trip in American literature can be found in Don DeLillo's 1985 novel *White Noise*. Wounded by a colleague's unflattering assessment of his appearance, Jack Gladney turns to impulse buying as a form of self-help. "The more money I spent, the less important it seemed. I was bigger than these sums," he explains, "These sums in fact came back to me in the form of existential credit."[1] Leigh Claire La Berge has recently pointed out that an important context for Jack's feeling of expansiveness here is the rapid growth of the consumer-credit industry, which led to the explosive growth of personal banking and credit cards over the next three decades.[2] Jack's experience of "existential credit" updates the nineteenth-century linkage between creditworthiness and moral character for the 1980s.

The shopping that once made Jack and his ilk feel so good has far less salutary effects in Jung Yun's new novel, *Shelter*. We witness the protagonist, Kyung Cho, forced to stop on the way home from the hospital at a Walmart to buy clothes and toiletries for his father, who has been the victim of a brutal attack. Fumbling through his many maxed-out credit cards, Kyung finally selects his best hope and waits with bated breath. Much to his surprise, the purchase is approved. But even in this moment of relief, his terror is immutable. He and his wife have "refinanced their mortgage, borrowed from their credit cards, and transferred their balances over and over again—all in the name of staying current on their bills, but they can't keep up with this shell game much longer." Whereas Jack Gladney reveled in the ego-enhancing pleasures of a credit bubble, Kyung Cho experiences the mechanisms of personal banking in the shadow of debt that, since the 2008 subprime-mortgage crisis, has left people caught in what Annie McClanahan describes as "an endless cycle of discredit and dispossession."[3]

Shelter tells the story of Kyung, a middle-aged Korean American man married to a working-class, Irish American woman named Gillian, with whom he has a young son. Kyung's father, Jin, is an unusually wealthy university professor, who came to the United States as part of the white-collar Asian immigration boom facilitated by the 1965 U.S. Immigration Act.[4] Hidden behind the facade of a showpiece home in a prestigious Boston suburb is Jin's abuse of his wife throughout Kyung's childhood and adolescence, the memory of which haunts the adult Kyung's daily life. Adding to the trauma, his mother, Mae, took out her frustrations on Kyung as a child, until the day that Kyung, old enough to be credible, threatened to kill his father if he ever hurt Mae again, temporarily halting the family's violent cycle.

The novel's action begins years after this uneasy truce. As their real estate agent appraises Kyung and Gillian's house, which is saddled with an underwater mortgage that is forcing them into hoping for a possible short sale, she notices Kyung's mother emerging naked and injured from the woods beyond the yard. She has been the victim of a home invasion in which she and the couple's maid, Marina, were raped and assaulted, while the intruders plotted to extract as much money as possible from Jin.

Recovering from their wounds, Jin, Mae, and Marina move in with Kyung and his family, but the reunion recycles—rather than repairs—Kyung's childhood trauma. Already constitutionally aloof and further disengaged from family life under the pressures of mounting debt, Kyung fails to reconcile himself with his parents' abusive history and eventually causes the dissolution of his own family with a series of reckless, alcohol-fueled acts that cause his life to unravel even more.

Although it conjures familiar paradigms—as found in, for example, Chang-rae Lee's *A Gesture Life* (1999) and Sophie Kinsella's *The Secret Dreamworld of a Shopaholic* (2000)—one of *Shelter*'s more provocative features is to align immigrant trauma stories with contemporary debt narratives. If trauma repeats the past, debt makes for a present haunted by the future. In turn, the novel employs this synthesis in order to complicate the myth of Asian Americans as a "model minority," suggesting that the appearance of affluence may depend on both psychic and financial forms of specious credit.[5]

A surprising and compelling question emerges: what does it mean that the meteoric rise of Asian American literature from the 1970s to the present coincides almost precisely with the explosion of the U.S. consumer-debt economy? Reflecting the dark underbelly of the model-minority myth, Kyung is less a grown-up Asian American whiz kid than a burdened millennial faced with the realization that he will fall short of his parent's achievements but feels pressured to maintain the appearance of success. Much of the debt he and his wife have incurred is the result of buying a house or going on vacations they cannot afford. This comes to function in the novel as a perverse double of that stereotypical model-minority activity: in a contracting economy, *overachieving* becomes *overreaching*. If there is such a thing as a model-minority image, it was paid for in part by overleveraged credit, and the model-minority myth comes to function here as a kind of asset bubble.[6] Like other Asian American literary works, *Shelter* represents, to borrow erin Khuê Ninh's formulation, "the immigrant nuclear family as a special form of capitalist enterprise," bound to the economy it seems to double.[7] We might then place Yun's novel at the end of an arc that began with the irrational exuberance depicted in *White Noise*. Founded on unsustainably financed debt, the model-minority bubble awaits its inevitable bursting.

By transforming DeLillo's creditworthy personhood into a kind of racial indebtedness, *Shelter* sees the model minority as trapped in the emerging political economy from which it once seemed exempted.

NOTES

1. Don DeLillo, *White Noise* (New York: Penguin, 1986), 84.
2. Leigh Claire La Berge, *Scandals and Abstractions: Financial Fiction of the Long 1980s* (Oxford: Oxford University Press, 2015), 40–45.
3. Annie McClanahan, *Debt Pledges: Debt, Crisis, and Twenty-First-Century Culture* (Stanford, CA: Stanford University Press, 2016), 185.
4. See Min Hyoung Song, *The Children of 1965: On Writing, and Not Writing, as an Asian American* (Durham, NC: Duke University Press, 2013), 29–58.
5. The belief, in its most intense form, that Asian Americans are racially inclined toward socioeconomic success.
6. This formulation synthesizes critiques of the model-minority myth as, on the one hand, an inaccurate ideological gambit designed to break interracial political coalitions and, on the other, of the way in which Asian American culture enthusiastically absorbs the model-minority myth as part of an aspiration toward bourgeois achievement. The notion of a model-minority asset bubble, in short, accounts for both the aspiration and its unsustainability.
7. erin Khuê Ninh, *Ingratitude: The Debt-Bound Daughter in Asian American Literature* (New York: New York University Press, 2011), 2.

FREE IS AND FREE AIN'T

SALAMISHAH TILLET

Are novelists who write about slavery reminding us of its ongoing effects or using the past to illuminate problems specific to the present? Are they arguing that slavery never stopped shaping African American lives in the United States or helping us to imagine new grounds for African American feelings of national belonging?

In the weeks leading up to President Barack Obama's historic election in 2008, I, as a newly minted assistant professor, sat in my office trying to revise my dissertation for publication. My topic was the rise of African American narratives on American slavery in the post–Civil Rights era, and I would often stop mid-edit, plagued by concerns about syntax ("What verb tense should I use?") and temporality ("Has his election made my thesis passé?). Always guiding my research was the question, "Why, in this period of unprecedented legal and political gains for African Americans, marked by the Civil Rights Act of 1964, the Voting Rights Act of 1965, and the expansion of a black middle class, did African Americans feel compelled to remember slavery, that original site of exclusion and disenfranchisement?"

My answer was simple: American citizenship was never simply a matter of legal protections. It was also a matter of who did and didn't feel like a citizen, who was and was not treated like one. Citizenship included the feeling of belonging to the nation, of having your history and contributions recognized in the civic culture of the United States. Because slavery contradicted the myth that the United States was an unfettered democracy, the nation had to willfully forget the lives and histories of the enslaved. And for that reason, slave descendants were caught in a paradox of what I called "civic estrangement," in which we are simultaneously citizens and noncitizens, shaped by disillusionment, a sense of not belonging, and a yearning for civic membership.

Starting with Margaret Walker's 1966 novel, *Jubilee*, a generation of artists, white and black, who came of age during the Civil Rights and Black Power movements, turned back time. They reimagined the stories of those marked by slavery's lash. Octavia Butler's *Kindred*, Gayl Jones's *Corregidora*, Ishmael Reed's *Flight to Canada*, and, of course, Alex Haley's *Roots* continued this work into the 1970s; authors like Charles Johnson, Sherley Anne Williams, and, most famously, Toni Morrison carried it into the 1980s. By the 1990s, when I was an undergraduate, it felt like what Bernard Bell called a "neoslave narrative" appeared almost every year. Alongside the literature, visual artists like Glenn Ligon, choreographer Bill T. Jones, photographer Carrie Mae Weems, jazz musician Wynton Marsalis, and the young visual artist Kara Walker led this cultural preoccupation with slavery into the twenty-first century.

But by 2008, some artists had declared the topic of slavery dead. That year, in his essay "The End of the Black American Narrative," Charles Johnson wrote that the "unique black American narrative," which emphasized the experience of victimization in slavery and segregation, "despite being an antique," persisted, "denying the overwhelming evidence of change since the time of my parents and grandparents, refusing to die." At the same time, the U.S. House of Representatives issued an unprecedented apology to African Americans for slavery and Jim Crow. The Obamas became the first black family to inhabit the White House rather than just work there. African Americans finally saw themselves in the most powerful symbol of the land. As Michelle Obama put it, for the first time, we felt proud of the country, as if we finally belonged. In those days, my argument about civic estrangement suddenly seemed antiquated. Had the politics of recognition and that last rung of citizenship finally been achieved?

But something else happened in the days and years following Obama's inauguration. Other people grabbed hold of slavery: New Confederates and organizers of Secession Balls in the South expressed nostalgia for a better time before the South lost the Civil War by reclaiming "Dixie" as their anthem or engaging in reenactments that memorialize Lincoln, not Calhoun, as a traitor. Sometimes they acted to erase the slave past, as when House Republicans in 2011 excised any mention of slavery from their public reading of the Constitution—a shocking move from a party that tends to celebrate an "originalist" reading of the constitution. For these conservatives, slavery was both over *and* had never happened.

Whether slavery would reemerge as a dominant topic in American culture remained to be seen. But in the years to come, Hollywood responded: *Django Unchained* (2012) became Quentin Tarantino's highest-grossing film; director Steve McQueen won an Academy Award for *12 Years A Slave* (2013); and just over a year ago, Nate Parker sold his film on Nat Turner's slave revolt, *Birth of a Nation*, to Fox Searchlight for $17.5 million. By last summer, WGN's series *Underground* and A&E's remake of *Roots* were television sensations.

Critics repeatedly cast the success of these representations as the art of Black Lives Matter. James Poniewozik, in his *New York*

Times review of *Roots*, described it as "optimistic in focusing on its characters' strength, sober in recognizing that we may never stop needing reminders of whose lives matter." That comment stood in sharp contrast to scholar Stephen Best's warning in 2012 that to "articulate a sense of racial belonging rooted in the historical dispossession of slavery seems to be an unstable ground on which to base a politics."

In 2016, several black and white writers published novels that continue to compare the U.S. slave past and the contemporary moment. Of *The Underground Railroad*, Colson Whitehead's National Book Award–winning novel, *Vogue* asked, "Does the timing of the book feel uncanny, emerging at a moment at which shootings of unarmed black men crowd the newspapers, when we have the need to assert that black lives matter?" Ben H. Winters reportedly "kept thinking about Trayvon Martin, the black teenager who was fatally shot in Florida by George Zimmerman, and incidents of police violence against African-Americans" as he prepared to write *Underground Airlines*. A reviewer noted that Natashia Deón's *Grace* "takes place at a time in our history when the moral ledgers were never in proper balance"; the *Washington Post* said that Yaa Gyasi's *Homegoing* is "merely asking us to consider the tangled chains of moral responsibility that hang on our history."

History, like books and black lives, continues to matter. But these narratives are not only evidence of the long arm of slavery extending into our present. They also tackle the limits and possibilities of our present moment itself. Against our current backdrop of the U.S. carceral regime, global surveillance, and the ongoing erosion of civil liberties and reproductive rights, the question of freedom—who is, isn't, and never was free—has taken on increasing urgency. And these novels show that the concept of freedom is flawed because historically it has always been more available to some groups than to others, with some groups having something close to "perfect" freedom at the expense of others made unfree.

■ ■ ■

"Freedom was a thing that shifted as you looked at it, the way a forest is dense with trees up close but from outside, from the empty meadow, you see its true limits," marvels Cora, the fifteen-year-old protagonist of Whitehead's latest novel, *The Underground Railroad.* "Being free had nothing to do with chains or how much space you had." Cora's epiphany appears over halfway through the novel and far away from the Georgia plantation on which she was born and abandoned by her mother, Mabel, the only slave to escape their plantation without being returned. As a young girl, Cora is exiled to the Hob, quarters set aside for unfit women, during which she is brutally raped by four male fellow slaves. Her orphanage and alienation set her apart: "Somewhere, years ago," Whitehead writes, "she had stepped off the path of life and could no longer find her way back to the family of people."

When Cora is first approached by Caesar, a literate slave who plans to escape north on the Underground Railroad, she refuses him, invoking her West African grandmother Ajarry: "White man trying to kill you slow every day, and sometimes trying to kill you fast. Why make it easy for him? That was one kind of work you could say no to." But after being violently attacked by a plantation owner, she invokes her mother and opts to go, finding herself in an actual tunnel and on an Underground Railroad that Whitehead has quite brilliantly reimagined as an actual train line. Through this sleight of hand, the underground railroad is no longer metaphorical but a subterranean technological world that quickly indoctrinates Cora into a world where freedom, as the momentary suspension of her literal enslavement, cannot be separated from *unfreedom*, an inability to determine her fate: once on board the train, she doesn't know where she is going; once she gets off, she doesn't know when it will come back or where it will take her next.

The result is a panoramic portrait of the United States, each trip potentially taking Cora further and further away from her desired goal of freedom. Whitehead renders each state as having its own unique racial codes that flash forward to the racist violence that continued long after slavery had been abolished: sterilization, medical experimentation, lynchings. South Carolina seems to represent progress, with its skyscrapers and blacks and whites living and working alongside one another, but its white citizens are conducting a genocidal experiment in eugenics. North Carolina has banished all black people, sentencing to death those who, like Cora, happen into that state, sentences carried out in public executions that leave black bodies hanging from trees along a "Freedom Trail." Instead Cora boards another train, to Tennessee, and then yet another, to Indiana, all the while trying to avoid the traps laid for her by a slave catcher named Ridgeway as well as other bounty hunters, moles, and lynch mobs.

Each time Cora runs back to underground, she leaves more of her past behind, adopting a new name and inventing a new backstory for her newfound freedom. In North Carolina she spends over a year in hiding, peering through a hole in an attic crawl space that Whitehead adapted from Harriet Jacobs's autobiography, *Incidents in the Life of Slave Girl*, which described her seven-year escape to the nine-feet-long, seven-feet-wide, and three-feet-high crawlspace above her grandmother's porch. Jacobs's narrative, written in 1861, was a demand for abolition; hiding in that crawl space, she was imprisoned but not enslaved. Cora's fate reminds us that freedom is available nowhere; everywhere Cora goes, "America remained her warden."

As the novel progresses, Cora has to decide whether she will spend her life running away *from* the plantation and the man who seeks to return her to it, more likely dead than alive, or whether she is running *to* somewhere of her own choosing. That subtle distinction brings to mind political theorist Isaiah Berlin's 1958 essay "Two Concepts of Liberty," which defined negative liberty as the *absence* of an external constraint or barrier (like chains or a slave catcher) and positive liberty as the *presence* of something (like self-control or self-determination).

At novel's end, Cora, taking the train for perhaps the very last time, finds herself both driver and passenger, whizzing past the South and history itself, having a moment of full self-actualization that becomes the novel's apex of freedom. "On one end there was who you were before you went underground, and on the other end a new person steps out into the light," Whitehead tells us. "The up-top world must be so ordinary compared to the miracle beneath, the miracle you made with your sweat and blood. The secret triumph you keep in your heart."

Cora's fate may be hers, but Whitehead goes to great lengths to situate her freedom in relation to individuals and communities who help her. By contrast, the protagonist of Ben H. Winters's newest novel, *Underground Airlines*, who goes by the name Victor, is utterly alienated from those around him and even from himself. "I am not a slave," Victor confesses. "But neither am I man." Inverting Frederick Douglass's famous chiasmus in his 1845 slave narrative, "You have seen how a man was made a slave; you shall see how a slave was made a man," Winters situates his novel in a world so overrun by technology, bureaucracy, and slavery that almost all of its characters have come to lack inner lives or basic human connections.

This alienation stands out because, unlike in slave narratives or even in many post–Civil Right novels on slavery, like Toni

Morrison's *Beloved*, here it makes any pursuit of freedom mainly a matter of self-interest rather than a desire to be part of or advocate for a collective. Winters models *Underground Airlines* on hard-boiled detective fiction, which thrives on isolated, alienated protagonists. And he gives his novel a dystopic, counterfactual setting: though we meet Victor in present-day Indiana, these United States are a country in which Abraham Lincoln was assassinated *before* he could serve as president, the Civil War never happened, and, while most of the country has abolished slavery, the "Hard Four" of Louisiana, Mississippi, Alabama, and the reunited Carolinas still hold more than 3 million slaves. Externally, the United States is subject to global sanctions for its reliance on slave labor; internally, the nation is still getting over a war with Texas after its attempt to secede in the 1960s.

Victor plays a peculiar role in this alternate America; he is a tracker for the U.S. Marshals who recapture runaway slaves. Like Whitehead's slavecatcher Ridgeway, Victor is particularly adept at this job, having tracked down more than 209 escapees over the course of his career. His trick: he is black and was once a fugitive slave himself, caught by a U.S. Marshall who locked him in a basement and offered him the opportunity to work undercover as a "soul catcher."

Victor's liberty, his "miracles of freedom," requires that he deny those very same freedoms to others. We meet him in hot pursuit of a man enslaved on a textile plantation in Alabama owned by a vast corporation called Garments of the Greater South. Jackdaw has escaped with the help of the Underground Airlines, which "flies on the ground, in package trucks and unmarked vans and stolen tractor-trailers." As in any mystery, neither Jackdaw nor the corporation are what they seem.

Victor ends up a double agent and a potential agent provocateur, determined to redeem himself and perhaps even eradicate the institution of slavery along the way. The real mystery of the novel turns out to be the lengths that corporations like Garments of the Greater South will go to erase the distinction between laborers and the objects they produce. A critique of racial injustice becomes also an attack on globalization and on the environmental and economic exploitation of workers, at home and abroad.

■ ■ ■

"Free ain't never free," says Cynthia, a white brothel owner in antebellum Georgia. "Love is," whispers back Naomi, the runaway slave protagonist of Natashia Deón's debut novel, *Grace*. Naomi flees Alabama after killing her master with a fire poker to save her older sister, Hazel, from becoming a "breeder" like their mother. The fifteen-year-old Naomi gets as far north as Georgia and ends up with Cynthia, who offers her protection and anonymity in exchange for unpaid manual labor.

After being falsely accused of a crime, Naomi goes on the lam again—this time heavily pregnant with the child of Jeremy, a white man with a gambling addiction. She plans to travel west with him, until he explains that an interracial relationship would impair his freedom and social mobility. At seventeen, she finds herself in the Georgia backwoods, giving birth to her daughter, only to be immediately killed by slave catchers. Her daughter survives, but Naomi ends up in a new state of purgatory when she becomes a ghost haunted by her own inability to raise her daughter or save her from being brutally raped by a white man. "Tree roots, like dead fingers, have risen from the wet ground," Deón writes, "and press against her throat, crushing her windpipe." Naomi's postmortem suffering challenges the widespread belief that death was at least a relief from slavery.[1] Just as Cora's attic or Victor's basement do not represent freely chosen spaces of liberty, death in *Grace* is not a choice but another site of imprisonment in a long chain of unfreedom.

Unlike Whitehead and Winters, Deón does not present the Underground Railroad as a viable path to freedom. Instead, Deón offers human connection as the ultimate resistance to slavery's dehumanization, focusing on the bonds Naomi and then her daughter create with a host of characters and on how Naomi's love for her daughter, Josephine, in life and even in death becomes its own liberation.

"The British were no longer selling slaves to America, but slavery had not ended, and his father did not seem to think that it would end," explains James, a character in the Ghanian American writer Yaa Gyasi's sweeping debut novel, *Homegoing*. "They would just trade one type of shackles for another, trade physical ones that wrapped around wrists and ankles for the invisible ones that wrapped around the mind." By the time we meet James, we are already two generations into a story that opens on the coasts of Ghana's Fanti region in the mid-seventeenth century and centers on two Fanti half-sisters, his grandmother Effia and Esi, each half-sister unaware of the other's existence. The fifteen-year-old Effia is given to and lives with James Collins, a British governor who oversees the slave trade at Cape Coast Castle. Esi, also fifteen, lives just below her, trapped in a slave dungeon awaiting transport to the Americas.

Each of the novel's subsequent chapters is narrated from the point of view of one of the sisters' descendants, who now live on both sides of the Atlantic. By alternating bloodlines that eventually merge in the present day, Gyasi tells the long story of slavery, colonialism, segregation, Ghanaian independence, and the post–Civil Rights period. By crisscrossing the Atlantic, *Homegoing* gives us a long history of unfreedom. Even as each generation gains more and more autonomy over time, Gyasi tempers our optimism by revealing how their kin on the other side of the ocean might in fact be experiencing the exact opposite: a loss of rights or, worse yet, a life of increasing racial violence.

Quey, the son of Effia and James, is educated in England at the end of the eighteenth century and plagued by questions regarding his sexuality, his sense of cultural belonging, and, when he attempts to return home to Ghana, his family's engagement in the slave trade. Ness, Esi's daughter, is ripped out of her mother's arms, only to endure brutality on Alabama plantations not so dissimilar from what Whitehead's Cora and Déon's Naomi flee. She is whipped so often that "her scarred skin was like another body in and of itself, shaped like a man hugging her from behind with his arms hanging around her neck." While Effia's marriage to James enables her to protect her and her progeny from being enslaved, her grandson, James, will learn the cost of such calculations: he spends his life trying to redeem his grandfather's past, ends up abandoning his mother and fiancé, and reinvents himself as a local farmer, which puts his new wife and daughter at risk by association with a man void of clan or kin.

A few years ago, I was trying to teach Anglophone West African literature that explicitly dealt with the theme of slavery, but, as Laura Murphy's *Metaphor and the Slave Trade in West African Literature* tells us, with a few exceptions (Ben Okri's *The Famished Road*, Ayi Kwei Armah's *Fragments*, Ama Ata Aidoo's *Anowa*), this literary tradition has worked to forget slavery. Gyasi's crisscrossing in *Homegoing* enables her to achieve a rare literary feat: by reimagining the slavery from the perspectives of those who were collaborators and/or victims of the slave trade, she can depict the competing notions of freedom held by her characters. Notably, however, the threat of violence, familial and racial, hovers over all the characters, which ultimately makes their choice of whether to resist or accommodate a false one. For example, Gyasi's chapter on the Fugitive Slave Act depicts one descendant, Kojo, unable to move to a free state from Maryland because his wife is too pregnant to travel. "Baltimore still felt safe." But such safety matters little in a system when any free black person, like Anna, can be kidnapped and sold, despite her papers, reminding us of how arbitrary freedom has always been in a world, then and now, when the practice of capitalism requires the ongoing erosion of even the most basic rights.

NOTE

1. In *The Black Atlantic* (1995), Paul Gilroy reads Frederick Douglass as arguing that "the slave actively prefers the possibility of death to the continuing condition of inhumanity on which plantation slavery depends."

THE MIXED-UP KIDS OF MRS. E. L. KONIGSBURG

MARAH GUBAR

I magine that you are a children's book editor. An unproven writer who has only recently sold her first story sends you her second effort. The manuscript opens with a rich old lady's note to her lawyer; she is sending him a story, she explains, to help him understand why she wants to change her will. The climax of this narrative involves two children hunting for an archival document in a row of filing cabinets. Interpolated into it are long parenthetical remarks addressed by the elderly woman to the lawyer, although it is unclear until the end of the story how these two adults connect to the child runaways looking for the document.

As an editor, how do you respond? Most likely you urge the author to cut the strange framing device—"Too challenging for young readers!"—and to amp up the action: "Less research, more running!"

How fortunate we are that E. L. Konigsburg, who died a year ago, was not forced to dumb down her most famous story. Winner of the prestigious Newbery Medal, *From the Mixed-Up Files of Mrs. Basil E. Frankweiler* (1967) represents a glittering pinnacle in her remarkably long and ambitious career. For five decades, Konigsburg challenged readers by tackling subjects often avoided in children's books, from the undercurrent of hostility that runs through an interracial friendship to the domestic unrest generated by the stirrings of pubescent and parental sexuality. *The Mixed-Up Files* is no exception to this rule, since (as I will try to persuade you) it is essentially a meditation on what it means to be an intellectual, a lover of learning. Konigsburg was committed to depicting young people as capable knowers of what goes on in their own minds, homes, and the wider world they inhabit. Bad things happen in her novels when adult characters fail to respect this competence. At the same time, however, Konigsburg emphasizes that all knowledge is perspectival; the particular social position that each of us inhabits shapes what we know and how we come to know it.

Given her background, it is no wonder that Konigsburg was attuned to how a person's subject position affects her access to knowledge. Born in 1930 to Jewish immigrant parents who moved from Manhattan to a mill town in Pennsylvania, Elaine Lobl was the first person in her family to go to college. She majored in chemistry at what is now Carnegie Mellon University at a time when women in the sciences faced more barriers to advancement than they do today. After graduating, Elaine and her new husband, David Konigsburg, continued their educations at the University of Pittsburgh, respectively pursuing degrees in chemistry and psychology. (Since I am the director of the Children's Literature Program at Pitt, I was delighted to discover this connection—and even more excited when I found out that her manuscripts reside in our library. I'll share with you some of the secrets of this still uncatalogued archival cache later.) Mr. Konigsburg finished his degree and got a job in Florida; Mrs. Konisgburg disliked lab work and dropped out of her program, teaching science at a girls' preparatory school for a year before leaving work to raise their three children.

As a kid, Konigsburg had been bothered by the fact that her experience growing up in a heterogeneous community was not represented in the children's books that she read. When her first two children's novels won Newbery and runner-up prizes in the same year—a feat that remains unmatched to this day—she spoke about trying to fill that gap by providing "stories that made having a class full of Radasevitches and Gabellas and Zaharious [seem] normal." In 1965, Nancy Larrick used *The Saturday Review* as a bully pulpit to protest "The All-White World of Children's Books." Two years later, Konigsburg's first novel—the runner-up to *Mixed-Up Files* for the Newbery—treated ethnicity less as a problem or plot point than as one strand among many in a thick and sticky social web. Only Konigsburg's illustrations and a single word that appears halfway through *Jennifer, Hecate, Macbeth, William McKinley, and Me, Elizabeth* (1967) tip off readers that the prickly friendship shared by these girls is an interracial one.

(While I was working on this piece, Walter Dean Myers published a "Sunday Review" essay in the *New York Times* that gave me and others familiar with Larrick's lament a sinking sense of déjà vu. In "Where are the People of Color in Children's Books?" he cites a study showing that only 93 of the 3,200 children's books published in 2013 were about black people. Myers writes movingly about how he longed as a child to see people of color represented not just as victims of prejudice or idealized exemplars but as ordinary human beings like the ones "who made up an integral and valued part of the mosaic that I saw around me." This is precisely what Konigsburg did in *Jennifer*. If only more children's authors would follow her lead!)

Konigsburg's commitment to representing young people as enmeshed in diverse communities only intensified over the course of her career. In all four of her final novels, much of the action is set in the fictional county of Clarion, New York, allowing her to build up a richly detailed social world: a contemporary Northern counterpart to William Faulkner's Yoknapatawpha County.

Moving in and out of a city whose downtown has been leached of life by the closing of its glassworks factory and the opening of suburban malls are multiple generations of families who trace their ancestry back to Holland, India, Vietnam, and so on. Like Faulkner, Konigsburg returns to certain characters at different phases of their lives to illustrate how family history influences how they perceive the world. For instance, in the gripping mystery *Silent to the Bone* (2000), an adult named Margaret recognizes that a thirteen-year-old named Branwell has figured out without being told that his father has fallen in love again after his mother's death. She notices this because she has painful memories of a similar realization in her own youth, an incident chronicled in another late Konigsburg novel.

The plot of *Silent to the Bone* attests to the damage that can be done when adults assume that young people are incapable of knowing their own minds. Unable to believe that Branwell is excited—not jealous—about the imminent arrival of a baby half-sister, his grandparents not only refuse his request that he postpone his summer visit to them, they whisk him away on a Caribbean cruise without bothering to get his consent. Their insistence on segregating him from his new family helps precipitate the estrangement that leads Branwell to fall silent when he is later accused of injuring the baby. Given that the adults around him don't listen to him, it's no wonder that Branwell stops speaking, nor that his thirteen-year-old best friend is the only person who figures out how to communicate with him well enough to discover what really happened. No one age group has a monopoly on wisdom in Konigsburg's stories.

When *The View from Saturday* (1996), the first of her final four novels, won the Newbery, it made Konigsburg one of only five authors who had received the award twice. In this book, she borrows another technique from Faulkner by using multiple narrators to unfold the story of four children from different backgrounds who pool their expertise to win an academic quiz bowl title. When the same event gets recounted by two separate characters, the retelling invariably yields new information, thus reminding readers of the perspectival nature of knowledge. The social locations of the characters shape what they know. For instance, Ethan correctly answers a question about nineteenth-century American feminists partly because his "triple-great-grandmother" marched alongside Susan B. Anthony in the fight to secure the vote for women.

Konigsburg herself was an appealing advocate for feminism. From the start of her career, she represented women as potent and winning authority figures whose expertise extends into traditionally masculine realms. In *About the B'nai Bagels* (1969), for example, the witty and passionate Bessie Setzer successfully manages her son's baseball team, a premise that still seems radical today. Konigsburg's vivid portrayal of the various rituals, foods, and jokes shared by this tightknit Jewish family also prompts readers to notice that ethnicity is not something that only dark-skinned people have—a misconception she satirizes explicitly in *The View from Saturday.* Fresh from a workshop on multiculturalism, a pompous school official named Dr. Rohmer demands to know how Ethan and company were selected for the academic team. With an air of "hushed seriousness," their teacher and coach Mrs. Olinski replies,

"In the interest of diversity . . . I chose a brunette, a redhead, a blond, and a kid with hair as black as print on paper."

Dr. Rohmer was not amused. He gave Mrs. Olinski a capsule lecture on what multiculturalism really means.

"Oh," she said, "then we're still safe, Dr. Rohmer. You can tell the taxpayers that the Epiphany Middle School team has one Jew, one half-Jew, a WASP, and an Indian."

"Jews, half-Jews, and WASPs have nothing to do with diversity, Mrs. Olinski. The Indian does. But we don't call them Indians anymore. We call them Native Americans."

"Not this one," she replied.

"Mrs. Olinski," Dr. Rohmer asked, "would you like it if people called you a cripple?"

Not only does Dr. Rohmer forget about the existence of Indians from India, he also fails to recognize that people with disabilities "are a diverse group, and some make jokes." Konigsberg's inclusiveness as a writer extends to characters such as Mrs. Olinski, a paraplegic, and Branwell in *Silent to the Bone*, who seems to be on the high-functioning end of the autism spectrum, although Konigsburg declines to label him.

Konigsburg's goal in crafting such richly heterogeneous communities in her books is not just to allow various kinds of people see themselves represented in literature but also to emphasize that the process of knowledge gathering works better when all sorts of people participate in it. More than a decade before feminist epistemologists and philosophers of science articulated this point, she was already incorporating it in her earliest children's novels. (As for me, I first heard the word "epistemology" when I was earning my PhD in English at Princeton, but I never fully wrapped my mind around what it meant until I asked a ravishingly unpretentious philosophy graduate student to sum it up for me as clearly as he could. After thinking quietly for several moments before speaking—a habit so unusual in my milieu that it initially discomfited me—he replied, "How we know what we know." Reader, I married him.)

According to Nancy Hartsock, Sandra Harding, and other proponents of feminist standpoint theory, all of us who engage in intellectual inquiry approach our subject in a manner informed by our ascribed social identities, including WASP males. Growing up in a male body in a culture that attributes certain characteristics and powers to men influences how men in that culture perceive themselves and others. It can therefore affect the kinds of research questions men ask; how they go about answering those questions; the way they represent their findings to others; and how those findings get received.

Because of his gender, for example, a male anthropologist doing fieldwork might not think to investigate female kinship networks. Even if he does investigate this subject, his attempt might be hindered by that fact that his sex prevents him from getting access to particular social spaces. Reporting his findings, he might choose to adopt an emotionally detached stance because the milieu he inhabits has historically associated that mode with masculinity, and so the men who established his discipline privileged this cognitive style over others. His presentation might therefore be perceived as more convincing than that of a woman whose impassioned, self-revealing style is less in keeping with her culture's picture of what it means to be an intellectual.

Konigsburg's preoccupation with epistemological questions is evident from the opening page of *The View from Saturday*. "The fact was," an omniscient narrator notes, "that Mrs. Olinski did not know how she had chosen her team, and the further fact was that she didn't know that she didn't know until she did know. Of course, that is true of most things: you do not know up to and including the very last second until you do." "Something stronger than reason" dictates Mrs. Olinski's choice: she acts on a hunch, a sudden instinct that these four students have the right combination of strengths to make them a winning team.

It is no accident that Konigsburg names her principal fictional city "Epiphany": she aims to expand our understanding of how we know what we know to include intuition, a cognitive style often associated with women and dismissed as unreliable. Knowers, Konigsburg suggests, make judgments based not only on cold, hard facts but on fuzzy, incompletely articulated feelings that grow out of their relationships with other knowers. Indeed, the main point she wants to make about Mrs. Olinski's selection is that she shouldn't get all the credit for it. "Did I choose you," she asks her team, "or did you choose me?" Their answer is an emphatic "Yes!"

Perhaps because of her own experience trying to break into the male-dominated domain of chemistry, Konigsburg was already addressing epistemological issues in her second book. Like *The View from Saturday*, *The Mixed-Up Files* makes intellectual inquiry seem like the most exciting game in town. Trying to persuade her little brother Jamie to run away with her, eleven-year-old Claudia promises him that fleeing their suburban home will be "the greatest adventure of our mutual lives." But in fact, running away turns out to be something of a snooze. The two children have no trouble reaching their rather tame destination: New York's Metropolitan Museum of Art. They hoodwink the guards so easily that it's evident they can stay there as long as they like. No one comes after them, questions their presence, or forces them to leave—and when they do eventually head home, Konigsburg doesn't even bother to narrate their reunion with their family.

The Mixed-Up Files isn't really about running away. It's about how different people feel about knowledge. Soon after they arrive at the Met, Claudia and Jamie notice that a big fuss is being made over a small statue of an angel because experts suspect that it might have been sculpted by Michelangelo. Intrigued, the siblings decide to discover the truth about its origins. All the drama missing from the depiction of running away adheres instead to the act of doing research, which is described at length and portrayed as an emotional roller coaster.

First, they visit the local library, where Claudia experiences a sinking feeling familiar to aspiring scholars, that of being a latecomer to an already overcrowded intellectual scene. The siblings then experience excitement when they think they have unearthed a new piece of evidence and woe when it turns out that other investigators have already beaten them to it. And then there's the aforementioned race against the clock to find a key piece of evidence in the filing cabinets owned by Mrs. Basil E. Frankweiler, who sold the statue to the Met. The children are thrilled when they unearth a sketch of the angel signed by Michelangelo.

(I felt a similar excitement when I ventured into Pitt's Hillman Library to sift through our files on Konigsburg. What a thrill to find typewritten manuscripts full of penciled annotations and still-readable erasures that shed light on her writing process and the themes that mattered to her most! If you compare the manuscript passage reproduced in the online version of this essay with Konigsburg's final text, for example, you'll notice that she altered *Mixed-Up Files* to make it more feminist in its characterization of Mrs. Frankweiler and less condescending with regard to the children's capacity for knowledge.)[1]

Throughout the novel, Konigsburg stresses that Claudia and Jamie are very different kinds of knowers. In fact, Claudia is so much more emotionally invested in their research that it's tempting to argue that she's the real lover of learning and Jamie just goes along for the ride. Transfixed by the statue's beauty, she's the one who insists they make a last-ditch effort to solve the mystery by visiting Mrs. Frankweiler, saying "I feel that I've got to know." In contrast, skeptical, "businesslike" Jamie thinks it's time to give up: "If the experts don't know for sure, I don't mind not knowing."

A feminist epistemologist would say it's no wonder that Claudia is the more passionate knower, given that the siblings inhabit a culture that habitually aligns women with feeling, intuition, and narrative and men with reason, logic, and argument. When a society encourages males and females to comply with starkly different social norms, Hartsock points out, this state of affairs has epistemological consequences.

Konigsburg anticipates Hartsock's point that "material life structures understanding." Recall that Claudia decides to run away because she's aggravated by the "injustice" of the gendered division of labor in her traditional home; she dislikes having to do housework "while her brothers got out of everything," as well as being forced to subsist on the skimpy allowance doled out by her breadwinner father. Yet after the siblings hit the road, she reveals how thoroughly she has internalized these norms by putting her brother in charge of their money while she attends to domestic tasks such as sorting their laundry. "Although there is no real difference between boys' stretch socks and girls'," notes the narrator wryly, "neither ever considered wearing the other's. Children who have always had separate bedrooms don't." In other words, segregating bodies shapes how minds work.

Meanwhile, the strange way in which the story is told—long stretches that read like omniscient narration, interrupted by very personal parenthetical remarks—repeatedly reminds readers that accounts of what the world is like don't just drop from thin air; they come from specific sources, embodied human beings whose social position shapes how they interpret and arrange evidence.

Ways of knowing traditionally coded as feminine, Konigsburg shows, are often devalued. Jamie teases his sister mercilessly when she expresses a wish to hug the statue. Suddenly adopting a more coolly detached tone, Claudia explains that she hasn't yet decided who made the angel because "a scientist doesn't make up his mind until he's examined all the evidence." Her pronouns signal Konigsburg's awareness that these children inhabit a culture that views rationality and objectivity as masculine qualities. And, as Jamie's response indicates, it also links emotion to femininity as a trait that disqualifies you from having epistemic authority: "You sure don't sound like a scientist. What kind of scientist would want to hug a statue?"

To combat this androcentric view, Konigsburg makes a point of showing us that passion can produce knowledge. Claudia's caring stance toward the statue leads the siblings directly to a key piece of evidence. "Because anything associated with Angel [is] precious" to her, she stops to stare at its old pedestal and worries that the worker who moved the statue apparently set a can of beer down on its velvet-lined top: "What if he had spilled it on Angel?" She and Jamie then realize that the impression was made not by a can but by the sculptor's mark, an important clue.

Yet even as she validates Claudia's passion and intuition, Konigsburg does not privilege one way of knowing over another. Instead, she once again suggests that the best way to pursue intellectual inquiry is to team up with people who view the world differently than you do. Jamie's skepticism proves just as enabling as Claudia's passion. For example, his exasperation with his sister's obsession with good grammar—"Oh, boloney, Claude"—leads to their discovery that the sketch is filed under "Bologna, Italy." While Jamie is sometimes rude and dismissive, Claudia can be pedantic and pretentious. And both of them get so wrapped up in the life of the mind that they behave in an extremely uncaring way toward their family. Lovers of learning, Konigsburg suggests, are not always easy to love.

When Claudia pompously informs Mrs. Frankweiler that she should learn something new every day, Mrs. Frankweiler disagrees then shares *her* ideas about the nature of knowledge:

> "I think you should learn, of course, and some days you must learn a great deal. But you should also have days when you allow

what is already in you to swell up inside of you until it touches everything. And you can feel it inside you. If you never take time out to let that happen, then you just accumulate facts, and they begin to rattle around inside of you. You can make noise with them, but never really feel anything with them. It's hollow."

How fitting that a story about kids who move into a museum should conclude by characterizing knowledge as something you inhabit that in turn inhabits you. That E. L. Konigsburg was one brainy lady.

NOTE

1. The online version of this essay can be found at https://www.publicbooks
.org/the-mixed-up-kids-of-mrs-e-l-konigsburg/.

IN THE GREAT GREEN ROOM

Margaret Wise Brown and Modernism

ANNE E. FERNALD

When *Goodnight Moon* was published in 1946, no one predicted it would become a classic. Its sales began to take off in 1953, and now the book has sold over 14 million copies. I grew up with *Goodnight Moon*, and I raised my daughters on it. The text remains bearable, charming, and even compelling after many, many readings. I wanted to find out why.

When my children were still little, I went from reading *Goodnight Moon* at night to teaching Gertrude Stein to my college students in the morning. In the midst of talking with them about Stein's radical experiments, I was struck by how familiar they seemed. Instead of noticing Stein's break with tradition, I noticed how much her work had in common with the books I was reading at bedtime: a love of color, joy in ordinary objects, repetition with unexpected variation. This dovetailed with another observation: my students are not as puzzled by Stein as I expect them to be. Stein writes: "Glazed Glitter. Nickel, what is nickel," and my students recognize the moment of wondering. This habit of wonder is familiar in part because we have been raised on the lists of *Goodnight Moon*.

That similarity is no accident: Gertrude Stein was Margaret Wise Brown's favorite writer. Born into an affluent manufacturing family, Brown studied writing and early-childhood education—conventional pursuits for a young woman awaiting marriage—but she became neither a teacher nor a wife and mother. Instead, she combined her love of modernism and education to become a pioneer in the emerging field of children's literature.

Brown and Stein's sympathies both have their roots at Radcliffe College. Stein went to Radcliffe and studied with William James. One of her classmates there, a fellow student of James's, was Lucy Sprague Mitchell. Where Stein took James's lessons to Paris, Mitchell took them to New York, where she applied them to the task of educating children, founding the Bank Street School of Education. In 1935, Margaret Wise Brown entered the school, originally as a teacher in training, but, by 1937, she had become a writer.

Born in 1910, Brown was the second of three children in a conventional, upper-middle class family. Her nursery had a gas grate with decorative tiles depicting the Three Little Bears and the Cow Jumping Over the Moon. The young Brown had a menagerie, including many rabbits. When one died, she skinned it, kept the fur, and announced that she was going to be a lady butcher when she grew up.

Brown went to Hollins College, a women's college in Virginia, where she discovered Proust, Woolf, and Stein. After graduation, she moved to Greenwich Village and enrolled in a fiction workshop at Columbia. That fall, she reread Woolf and Chaucer, listened to Gertrude Stein on the radio, and went to BAM to hear Stein's lectures. That 1934 lecture tour followed the success of *The Autobiography of Alice B. Toklas* and marked the apex of Stein's fame.

As Brown worked to begin her hoped-for writing career, she also drifted toward teaching. A friend encouraged her to apply to Bank Street, and there she found a community inspired by the relevance of modern ideas to early-childhood education: welcoming immigrants and students of all faiths, emphasizing a pragmatic "here and now" curriculum that takes the child's experience and perspective as its foundation, and embracing the value of a hands-on acquaintance with science and the arts. Even so, Brown's start was rocky. Deeply interested in the individual child, she was indifferent to classroom management. One progress report notes that she "seemed to contribute a somewhat disorganizing influence to the class." Most damningly, she left the art closet messy, "with two pots of glue spilled."

While Brown struggled in the classroom, she excelled in Lucy Sprague Mitchell's language class. Mitchell recognized that a modern education called for new books. She also saw that she was not the person to write them. In keeping with Bank Street's emphasis on the here and now, Mitchell wanted children to read about the sights and sounds of their own world, unadorned with fantasy. She joked, in fact, that she was introducing the "spinach school" to children's literature. In Brown, she found the writer who could make her ideas palatable.

Brown continued writing for both adults and children, but it was a children's story that made her a paid author. When her first royalty check came, she cashed it, hailed a horse-drawn flower cart, bought every flower on it, and called her friends over for a party. By the fall of 1937, Brown was meeting regularly with Mitchell and others, forming the Bank Street Writer's Laboratory.

Soon thereafter, she met the painter Clement Hurd, just back from studying with Fernand Léger in Paris. On his return he and his friends had chartered a train car to Hartford to see *Four Saints in Three Acts*, an opera by Gertrude Stein and Virgil Thompson with an all-black cast. United in admiration for Stein and attracted to Hurd's paintings, Brown invited him to show his work at Bank Street. Hurd watched while the children looked at his art—a process as terrifying as any studio critique. When the teacher congratulated him on holding the children's attention for five full minutes, his career as an illustrator of children's books began.

At this time, Brown was also on staff at William Scott's new publishing house, W. R. Scott, working to develop children's books in keeping with the Bank Street philosophy. They invited contemporary writers, including Hemingway, Steinbeck, and Stein, to contribute manuscripts. Only Stein agreed, and the result was *The World Is Round*. Exciting as it was to have a reason to contact her hero, Stein's acceptance was clouded for Brown by the fact that, although she had drafted the correspondence, the male editors signed the letters. The two women never met. Moreover, Clement Hurd's illustrations notwithstanding, *The World Is Round* is not a good children's book. Over sixty pages long, it is too dense for a child to love or a parent to read aloud. Still, there are moments when one can see why people guessed Stein might be able to pull it off.

Brown continued work at Bank Street, writing a paper on books for five-year-olds. In it, she describes a child who "carries with him . . . the glamor of the two-year-old's own small self; the three-year-old's humor and love of pattern . . . and four-year-old's first playful flights into the humor of incongruous things . . . and, finally, the five-year-old's . . . careful watching of his own eyes and ears." We see, too, the strength of her conviction that writing for the very young could be great: "Here is an audience sensitive to the sheer elements of the English language. . . . Translate their playfulness and serious use of the sheer elements of language into the terms and understandings of a five-year-old and you have as intelligent an audience in rhythm and sound as the maddest poet's heart could desire."

In 1946 Brown wrote *Goodnight Moon* as a celebration of the objects in a wonderful, enormous nursery, including some features of her own childhood nursery. She asked Hurd, back from World

War II and looking for work, to illustrate it. In *Goodnight Moon*, objects are celebrated for themselves. The book's list is so perfect because it is so wholly from the child's perspective. Brown gestures toward an overwhelming feeling of smallness—"Goodnight stars / Goodnight air"—even the void—"Goodnight nobody"—but ultimately offers reassurance, in the final lines that cocoon our little sleeper in "noises everywhere." These noises, if not understood, are acknowledged. After all, misunderstood noises often keep us from sleep, and that final line seems to anticipate them, incorporating them into its lulling rhythm as if to reassure the youngest listener that the complaint she is about to make is unnecessary, that those noises are just another thing to placidly bid goodnight.

In November 1950, Brown's longtime partner, Michael Strange, died. Shortly thereafter, Brown fell in love with James Stillman "Pebbles" Rockefeller Jr., and they became engaged. She traveled to France but fell ill. Recovering from a routine operation, she was ordered to remain in bed. Unbeknownst to anyone, a blood clot developed in her leg. Demonstrating to a friend that she felt fine, she did a can-can kick. The blood clot dislodged. She died instantly. She was forty-two.

From 1953 onward, sales of *Goodnight Moon* grew, first steadily and then astonishingly. Brown left many, many unpublished manuscripts at her death; posthumous publications continue to this day. One of the first was *The Four Fur Feet*. There Brown wrote:

> And as he slept
> he dreamed a dream,
> dreamed a dream,
> dreamed a dream.
> And as he slept
> he dreamed a dream
> that all the world was round—O.

In writing for the very young, Margaret Wise Brown found the audience to delight in the imaginings of her mad poet's heart. And through her celebrations of the poetry of color, objects, rooms, Gertrude Stein's great imagination lives on, too.

AFROFUTURISM

Everything and Nothing

NAMWALI SERPELL

Whence the "Afro" in "Afrofuturism"? In the 1994 interview with Samuel R. Delaney that inaugurated the term, Mark Dery defines Afrofuturism as "speculative fiction that treats African American themes and addresses African American concerns in the context of 20th-century technoculture—and, more generally, African American signification that appropriates images of technology and a prosthetically enhanced future." This would suggest that the "Afro" in Afrofuturism is the "Afro" in the old-school census classification, "Afro-American" rather than, say, the "Afro" in the newer-fangled "Afropolitan," the word that Taiye Selasi coined in 2005 for "the newest generation of African emigrants . . . [with a] funny blend of London fashion, New York jargon, African ethics, and academic successes . . . ethnic mixes . . . cultural mutts . . . multilingual . . . Africans of the world."

Someone like President Barack Obama would seem to give the lie to any firm distinction between Africans of the Americas and Africans of the world. But in the 1990s, the lines of connection Dery drew in "Black to the Future" between speculative fiction and black culture—lines as tenuous and as striking as the puns he favors—were very much limited to a U.S. geography: "African Americans are, in a very real sense, the descendants of alien abductees. They inhabit a sci-fi nightmare in which unseen but no less impassable force fields of intolerance frustrate their movements; official histories undo what has been done to them; and technology, be it branding, forced sterilization, the Tuskegee experiment, or tasers, is too often brought to bear on black bodies."

Broadly speaking, none of this is limited to African American history. Abduction, intolerance, dismemberment, experiments, and weaponry have been inflicted on black bodies in the motherland, too. The resonance of this ancient nightmare with sci-fi was almost too perfect in Blomkamp's 2009 indie hit film *District 9*. But even a quick glance at the history of black science fiction shows that, however appropriative and naïve, Afrofuturism's reach back to Africa itself is a pervasive trope, from the ruins of an advanced Ethiopian civilization in Pauline Hopkins's 1903 *Of One Blood* to Sun Ra's Egyptian accoutrements to the inexhaustible polyvalence of the Middle Passage. And the recent swell of African American artists making music (Janelle Monáe), fiction (N. K. Jemisin), and art (Laylah Ali) within this rubric seems to have set off a wave of African artists—many Afropolitan in effect if not in name—intent on bringing the Afro back to Afrofuturism. As is often the case these days, this phenomenon has acquired a certain curatorial cachet for museums, conferences, festivals, listicles, and panels: the meme is mother to the making.

And what of the art being made? South Africa has been a particularly rich source, perhaps because its great wealth allowed it to build technology earlier and explicitly on the back of black labor. Apart from Neill Blomkamp's films and the best-selling novels of Lauren Beukes (author of the time-traveling murder mystery *The Shining Girls*), the pop-hip-hop-techno group Die Antwoord ("The Answer" in Afrikaans) has been dabbling in science fiction tropes for years. The rest of the continent is catching up. Much attention has been paid to the Ethiopian postapocalyptic film *Crumbs* (2015, dir. Miguel Llansó), the Kenyan science fiction short film *Pumzi* (2009, dir. Wanuri Kahiu), and *Afronauts* (2014, dir. Frances Bodomo), a surreal short film set in Zambia and directed by a Ghanaian American—the latter two debuted at Sundance. The last few years have seen the publication of *AfroSF* (2012), an anthology edited by Ivor W. Hartmann; *Omenana*'s issue X, ten flash fictions displayed at the African Future Lagos conference; *Jalada*'s Afrofuturism issue; and a volume of the scholarly journal *Paradoxa* devoted to "Africa SF." The Dark Matter anthology series, edited by Sheree Thomas and devoted to speculative fiction by people "of African descent," has a third volume forthcoming, subtitled "Africa Rising."

That most of the manifest literary output of African science fiction is in the form of the short story is not too surprising—the genre has always been catholic about length, as open to operatic trilogies as to stories (Bradbury and Asimov wrote both). But that it has thus far been a collection of little things poses a problem for considering "African science fiction" as a genre to be theorized rather than merely (repeatedly) heralded. Dery begins his essay on Afrofuturism with a "conundrum" about absence: "Why do so few African Americans write science fiction, a genre whose close encounters with the Other—the stranger in a strange land—would seem uniquely suited to the concerns of African American novelists?"

As Afrofuturism has begun to migrate back to the motherland in earnest, the same relative dearth continues to plague theorists and writers. Even Mark Bould, whose introduction to *Paradoxa*'s issue on African science fiction offers a comprehensive if nebulous syllabus, implies that it is nascent: "If African sf has not arrived, it is certainly approaching fast." The appearance of a deluge—a trend, a fad—is in effect a trickle. Is this just what happens when you cross blackness with futurity? As Dery asks of African Americans, "Can a community whose past has been deliberately rubbed out, and whose energies have subsequently been consumed by the search for legible traces of its history, imagine possible futures?" Or is this lack specific to African literature, where energies might seem to be better directed toward, say, political critique of corruption, poverty, disease, and unemployment?

Nnedi Okorafor, born in the United States to Nigerian immigrants, both bridges this breach and fills it. She appears on lists of black sci-fi on either side of the Atlantic. And while she says that she has "issues with [the label] Afrofuturism," she is one of the most prolific black writers of speculative fiction out there and has set several of her fantasy and science fiction novels on the continent. Okorafor, in other words, is Afropolitan *and* African American: she insists that her "flavor of sci-fi is evenly Naijamerican (note: 'Naija' is slang for Nigeria or Nigerian)." Yet in an essay on the Science Fiction and Fantasy Writers of America website, Okorafor herself bemoans the scant canon: "Here's my list of 'African SF.' It's really short . . . How do I define African SF? I don't. I know it when I see it . . . The main fact is that this list DOES exist. Africans ARE writing their own science fiction, contrary to what some may think. But the fact is that Africans need to also write more of it."

When building a canon, the question of inclusion becomes paramount. If the African v. African American debate seems unduly academic or divisive, just imagine when the question of race comes in: what does it mean, as Okorafor notes, that the first major African science fiction film, *District 9*, was directed by a white South African? In another essay, "Is Africa Ready for Science Fiction?," Okorafor cites two experts—a Nollywood director and a scholar of African fiction—who both essentially say no. Though she is more optimistic on the question, Okorafor explains: "In Africa, science fiction is still perceived as not being real literature. It is not serious writing. . . . African audiences don't feel that science fiction is really concerned with what's real, what's present. It's not tangible."

But to take the intangible, the unreal, the absent and make of them a world is precisely the mandate of science fiction. In his remarkable ur-Afrofuturist film *Space Is the Place* (1974), Sun Ra, adorned in Egyptian regalia, travels to Oakland, CA, to recruit black folk to colonize the planet Saturn. Like some kind of inter-galactic Marcus Garvey, he wants to "set up a colony for black peo-ple . . . bring them here through *transmolecularization* . . . or tele-port the whole planet here . . . through music." He tells dissipated hipsters at the local youth center: "I'm not real. I'm just like you. You don't exist in this society. If you did, your people wouldn't be seeking equal rights. You're not real. If you were, you'd have some status among the nations of the world. So we're both myths. I do not come to you as a reality. I come to you as the myth. Because that's what black people are, myths." Afrofuturism's insight is to elide the African diaspora with outer space as loci of blackness, roiling vats of inky, rich, infinite potential. The etymology of uto-pia, after all, is *ou* + *topos*, or *not* + *place*. Introducing himself to a wino, Sun Ra cryptically declaims: "I am everything and nothing."

Okorafor's most squarely science-fictional novel, *Lagoon*, both enacts and theorizes what it means to be ex nihilo, to emerge out of nothing—or rather the presumed nothing—at the heart of dark-ness. The prologue of the novel, entitled "Moom!," begins with a set of dark collisions that epitomize this conceit: "She slices through the water, imagining herself a deadly beam of black light. . . . She is aiming for the thing that looks like a giant dead snake. . . . She stabs into it. . . . It blows its black blood. . . . All goes black." This "she" turns out to be a swordfish—in her latest incarnation; her last form was a yellow monkey—penetrating the loading hose of an oil refinery in the "lagoon" from which Lagos takes its name.

Coincidentally, at the exact same moment, a space ship—"an enormous object, all shifting oily black spires and spirals and brown and yellow lights"—crashes into the lagoon. Its alien inhabitants grant the water spirit a new shape (eyes like the blackest stone, retractable spikes on her spine), triple her size, and double her weight: "Now she is no longer a great swordfish. She is a monster." Her metamorphoses continue apace when she emerges from the water onto Bar Beach on the occasion of another, more prosaic collision of humans: Adaora, a marine biologist in a struggling marriage; Anthony Dey Craze, a popular Ghanaian hip-hop artist; and Agu, a soldier whose conscience has just gotten him punched. They meet as the impact of the space ship in the water sends up a fist-shaped wave that almost drowns them and washes the water spirit ashore as a "naked dark-skinned African woman." They name her Ayodele.

A fascinating subject for Adaora's scientific gaze, Ayodele's metamorphosing powers are amped by the aliens into biotechnology. Her skin is made of tiny vibrating balls that atomize and rearrange at will, accompanied by a screech of marbles on glass, allowing her to assume any shape. It turns out she can do the same to others. When Adaora's home is swarmed by the army, the police, fundamentalists, protestors, and rubbernecking locals, Ayodele runs off, metamorphosing along the way like Daphne. When soldiers corner her and try to blow her to bits, she returns the favor:

> Where the soldiers had stood, heaps of raw meat wriggled . . .
> [Adaora] heard the sound of marbles again . . . the wet piles of
> meat, the scattered clothes, even the spattered blood, were gone
> as though they had never been there.

In their place was a plantain tree, heavy with unripe plantain . . . Ayodele had taken the elements of oxygen, carbon, hydrogen, nitrogen, calcium, phosphorus, potassium, sulfur, sodium, chlorine and magnesium that had been Benson and the other soldiers and rearranged them into a plant. *Does the soul transform, too?* Adaora wondered. She'd never believed in God but she was a scientist and she knew that matter could be neither created nor destroyed. It just changed form.

The terroristic tenor of the alien landing and Ayodele's explosions—Boko Haram hovers in the background of this novel—is offset immediately by the intimation of a new, green beginning. Suicide bomber as atomic gardener; out of nothing, everything. Like the birth of the planet Earth, a collision prompts an explosion, then a contraction back to stable form.

This dynamic movement of matter characterizes *Lagoon* as a whole. Lagos itself is presented as a throbbing, sprawling network of networks—an LGBTQ protest group called Black Nexus, an evangelical church, 419 internet scammers, the police, the army—whose members coincide at random as they try to account for the weird goings-on in their already anarchic city. One minor character, a visiting African American rapper, thinks: "If there is one city that rhymes with 'chaos,' it is Lagos." The city is said to give birth to itself, eat its young, eat itself. It becomes a monster populated by monsters as the aliens, who "pass for Lagosians," emerge from the water: "Some of them were dressed in various types of traditional garb, some in military attire, some in police uniforms, others in westernized civilian clothes. Most of them were African, a small few Asian, one white." Like Ayodele, who often uncannily mimics others when she transforms, the aliens reflect both the humans and the oscillation between "African Chaos" and "Black Nexus" already latent in Lagos.

This alternation between dilation and contraction is a pulse under the novel's skin. While we occasionally return to our initial A-team of four, a host of other characters proliferate in short chapters that skitter between perspectives and Englishes. In keeping with the novel's chaotic retroposthumanism, these characters range from animal to vegetable to mineral to spirit to various syntheses and collisions of these elements. There is a particularly memorable encounter between an alien passing as a Nollywood star—"there was a flicker of oddness about her . . . like a double-exposed photo"—and a native spirit said to haunt the famously dangerous roads of Lagos. This "Bone Collector" makes one road rise up "in a huge snakelike slab of concrete, the faded yellow stripes still in view," rippling "into a concrete wave" that sends cars and people to their doom. The confrontation between ancient spirit and futuristic alien is epic: "That woman, she was from outside this earth, yes. But . . . that thing that was haunting the road, it was from *here* and had probably been here since these roads were built, maybe even before then." It leads to a sacrifice as Hollywood as it is Nollywood: "'Collect my bones and then never collect again,' the woman said. 'I am everything and I am nothing. Take me and you will be free of your appetite.'"

Lagosians come to see the aliens as "agents of change," punning on their metamorphic capacities, which are keyed to reflective and political ones. Ayodele, on the run, a self-described "ambassador," becomes a hero for simply saying what she sees ("*Your land is full of a fuel that is tearing you apart*"), reflecting Lagos back at itself like the water from which she emerges. In a deeply disturbing climax, and in the tradition of black heroes both African and African American, her body is riddled with bullets. Her final transformation is to become a figure for transformation: she vaporizes herself into a white mist, "rolling like a great wave over all of Lagos . . . everyone was inhaling it."

Ayodele can broadcast herself on any communication device, and the aliens and the spirits are repeatedly aligned with the mutable and reflective and political affordances of media itself. While the novel adheres to print, it continually invokes other forms—television, newspaper, radio, the Internet, and film, including a "Deleted Scene" and a "Special Bonus Features" glossary of pidgin. The mobile phone is king, its portability matched by its mutability and ubiquity: "So many people in Lagos had portable chargeable glowing vibrating chirping tweeting communicating connected devices, practically everything was recorded and posted online in some way, somehow. Quickly. The modern human world is connected like a spider's web."

In *Lagoon*, mythos and technos intermingle. An italicized chapter announces, three-quarters of the way in, the novel's presiding spirit: "*I am Udide, the narrator, the story weaver, the Great Spider. I roll onto my back and place my hairy feet to the earth above me. I feel the vibrations of Lagos. This way, I see everything.*" The weaver of stories is presented here across several axes of symmetry—flipping underneath the city to listen, see, feel; roaming the roads to spin stories across the modern human world. This accords with the novel's imperative toward politics as reflection—"*change begets change*"—but it also hints at a fundamental and perhaps detrimental reliance on realism.

That might seem an odd thing to say about such a riotous speculative romp. But at its core, *Lagoon* seems to use science fiction as an occasion to reflect the cultural clashes and contradictions of Lagos, by far the most vivid character in the novel. In her acknowledgments to *Lagoon*, Okorafor says she was both inspired by and writing back to Blomkamp's incredibly popular and quite racist *District 9*. To center the locus of alien contact in Lagos instead of Johannesburg, to make the aliens benevolent eco-ambassadors: these are pointed political moves but essentially corrective ones, aimed at bettering our present-day reality. It is no accident that the novel begins with a swordfish destroying an oil pipeline, an incident Okorafor says she took from the headlines.

At its best, science fiction operates as the articulation of outlandish metaphors, even puns. Often, these resonances across ostensibly disparate notes—aliens and Africans, miscegenation and crossbreeding—produce eerie harmonies and genuine novelty. For all its plenitudinous variety, *Lagoon* sings a recognizable song, the old ditty that tells us Africa has always been sci-fi, that all this has happened before and all of it will happen again: "If anyone gon' be flying around, shootin' lasers outta they eyes or jumping in the water and making shock waves because they *can*, it would be a bunch of *Africans*." The notes of this chord may only be discernible to one audience (a readership familiar with alien contact stories) or another (a readership familiar with Afrodiasporic mythology). But even when they do chime—as when Ayodele's bullet-ridden body uncannily conjures Mike Brown's autopsy report or a character calls the alien spacecraft "the devil's *danfo*" (a rackety Lagosian bus)—the result is like one of those radio mashups that are so popular these days: more new flavor than original cover.

Okorafor recently appeared on a panel at the Black Comix Arts Festival in San Francisco. Asked about the future of Afrofuturism, she responded this way:

> I think that we'll see more Africans directly from the continent writing this kind of literature. I think that what they're going to write is going to have, like, a different flavor as well. And what I also would like to see in terms of "Afrofuturism" is just more diversity in the types of writing. I'd like to see female writers, writers with disabilities, just more variety *within* Afrofuturist writing. That's what I'm waiting to see. 'Cause right now it's so

small, you know, and it's slowly building, it's slowly building, and it's increasing and growing. But I'd like to see more of that. And I'd also like to see really . . . an extremely successful Afrofuturist writer—*extremely* successful as in like best-selling status—who's mediocre. I wanna see *that*.

Okorafor is already spearheading these efforts: Africanizing black sci-fi, diversifying it, making it popular. But as for this last, the kind of best-sellerish mediocrity she imagines for Afrofuturism—one that matches the thinness and flatness of a world wide web where, as the novel's epigraph says of Lagos, "*nothing works yet everything happens*"—well, maybe we should be careful what we wish for.

CHICK LIT MEETS THE AVANT-GARDE

TESS McNULTY

Ask the average critic, professor, or reader to name an experimental novelist and they will more likely name a man—Pynchon, DeLillo, Foster Wallace—than a woman—Tillman, Winterson, Lessing. Ask them to name the protagonist of an experimental novel and they will probably do the same. Though female authors write experimental novels about women—like Renata Adler's *Speedboat* or Sheila Heti's *How Should a Person Be?*—the avant-garde has long been associated with male authors and stories.[1] That association made Alexandra Kleeman's *You Too Can Have a Body Like Mine*, first published last August, seem doubly unusual.

The book was clearly experimental. Written in a postmodern style marked by parody, paranoia, and dispassion, it described a surreal version of our own world in which three semihuman characters, A, B, and C, grapple with technology and consumer culture. But unlike books by the most celebrated exponents of that style, Pynchon and DeLillo, *You Too* concerned itself primarily with the female experience. It even focused on the most insistently *girly* features of that experience, the blatantly feminine themes—diets, dating, cosmetics—that are typically consigned to the most trivialized literary genre: commercial women's fiction, or "chick lit."

Rather than efface her book's femininity, moreover, Kleeman flaunted it with pride. In interviews she framed her novel as an unconventional application of the "postmodern dystopian" style to the "female experience."[2] And though her career was just taking off, a super-saccharine femininity, knowing yet unironic, seemed already to be a trademark of her persona. Her website linked to a spread on her hairstyle in which, between pictures of herself posing coquettishly—holding up her hair, smiling over her shoulder, tugging at her tank-top strap—she earnestly adopted the idiolect of *Cosmopolitan*: "I carry a small hairbrush with boar and plastic bristles at all times—I use it for secret emergency teasings and sometimes to smooth over the surfaces of big tangles."[3] More recently, she's written an article for *Elle* called "The Slip Dress That Changed My Life."[4]

Following Kleeman's lead, media outlets promoting *You Too* emphasized its girly features. *Vanity Fair* embedded its discussion of the book in an interview with Kleeman about eye make-up, and *Vogue* followed her through the cosmetics aisle of a local drugstore, highlighting the clash between her obvious talent and intelligence and her enthusiasm for all things feminine: Kleeman "must have seemed like just another beauty junkie, right up to the moment she stopped browsing the store's goods and started disserting on their semiotics."[5] "*Fight Club* for Women," *Vogue* labeled her book, suggesting that this was an avant-garde novel for girls, a subversive sort of chick-lit, experimental fiction *for her*.[6]

The for-girls-only feel of the publicity surrounding Kleeman's book might have seemed a mere blip were it not for the fact that a number of books published in the past year—from Helen Phillips's *The Beautiful Bureaucrat* and Catie Disabato's *The Ghost Network* to Andrea Phillips's *Revision* and Sarai Walker's *Dietland*—staked out a territory at the intersection of experimental fiction and chick lit. Though spanning a spectrum from the predominantly literary (*You Too*) to the more clearly commercial (*Dietland*) all incorporated elements of both genres.[7] And all were publicized and celebrated as combinations of the two: the more literary works were lauded as experimental fiction for women; the more commercial, praised as chick lit with an edge.

The books' covers begin to suggest their hybridity, fusing the typical two-dimensional abstraction of avant-garde design with chick lit's girly signifiers: *The Beautiful Bureaucrat*'s foregrounds a hand with red-painted fingernails against a backdrop of gray-on-gray code, while *The Ghost Network*'s surrounds a heavily mascaraed eye with an illuminati symbol. Kleeman's, meanwhile, is predominantly abstract, with only a hint of eerie femininity about the Barbie-doll legs beneath its blue surface. *Dietland*'s cover might seem the most conventional—a cupcake plays a prominent role— were it not for the grenade pin perched atop the treat.

What the books' covers suggest, their blurbs more explicitly confirm: one of *Dietland*'s describes the book as "anti-chick-lit for smart chicks" while one of *Ghost Network*'s calls the book's author "Borges filtering Lady Gaga." None, however, could match that which appeared on Helen Phillips's first book: "'Brashly experimental'—*Elle Magazine*."[8] Or the sound bite that her editor provided, quoting a fan who claimed her latest book read like "Kafka with a vagina."[9]

Publicity schemes such as these can of course be misleading. Publishers have a reputation for trying to market almost any book written by a woman as chick lit, slapping a pink cover on it on the assumption that it will never attract male readers anyway.[10] In this case, however, the marketing campaigns don't entirely misrepresent the books. As one reviewer of *Ghost Network* puts it, "Imagine Thomas Pynchon possessed by the spirit of a teenaged girl."[11]

■ ■ ■

How, exactly, did this union come about? It's a story of boy meets girl, a narrative conforming to the classic structure of the romance novel, that fantasy of class mobility in which a high-status male and a socially subordinate female implausibly and yet predictably end up together. And, like any good romance, it begins with two figures divided by strong social forces.

For decades, experimental fiction has sat atop the literary totem pole. In keeping with its status as the most "serious" of "serious" literary fiction, it has been seen as probing, original, subversive, and inaccessible. Its exemplars, like David Foster Wallace's *Infinite Jest* or Tom McCarthy's *Remainder*, have been marked by an anti-realist or non-"lyrical Realist" aesthetic approach (to quote Zadie Smith).[12] And its subject matter has been mostly the male experience. That last fact should come as no surprise, given that its most celebrated authors are male.

Chick lit, meanwhile, has been lambasted as the most "trivial" of "trivial" commercial genres. Since its rise to prominence in the mid-1990s, it has earned a reputation as shallow, hackneyed, and conventionalizing. Its exemplars, like Candace Bushnell's *Sex and the City* or Helen Fielding's *Bridget Jones's Diary*, have been marked by a banal realist style ("There was a girl named Susan living in the city . . ."). And its subject matter has been unabashedly feminine. The classic chick-lit novel describes a young straight woman in her twenties or thirties, living in the city and spending time with her female friends and the occasional gay male sidekick while navigating a trifecta of concerns: diets, dating, and professional life. Needless to say, authors of chick lit are mostly women.

Lately, though, changes have been taking place in both genres, conducive to their union. Experimental fiction, on the one hand, has become more accessible. In recent years, it has produced a spate of remarkably well received novels, lauded for being less intimidating than their forebears. When Jennifer Egan's *A Visit from the Goon Squad* won the Pulitzer in 2011, it was praised as "Old School" avant-garde literature—or experimental fiction that didn't, as Egan herself put it, "drown out the story."[13] Ali Smith's *How to Be Both* was awarded Britain's Goldsmiths Prize in 2014 for proving "that formal innovation is completely compatible with pleasure."[14] The mainstreaming of the experimental novel has been aided by "for dummies" style guides, such as *Experimental Fiction: An Introduction for Readers and Writers*, which seek, ironically, to standardize experimentation and make it less off-putting.

Even as experimental fiction has been commercializing, chick lit has been heading in more literary and challenging directions. Since the 2008 recession, when chick lit of the classic mid-nineties variety was declared "dead," the genre has matured; in the words of *Publishers Weekly*'s editor in chief, Sara Nelson, it had to, like its heroines, become "a little more accomplished and grown-up."[15] That has meant embracing more serious themes, like motherhood and marriage, and becoming more "high-concept" so as to acquire more literary heft.[16] Its post-recession readers, agent Diane Banks explains, "want to be challenged by their reading as they are being challenged in other areas of their lives."[17]

Finally, pressures preventing female authors from fusing experimental form with chick-lit content have been weakening. As recently as 2013, critics saw the success of Rachel Kushner's *The Flamethrowers* as evidence for an accepted fact: that female authors of avant-garde fiction had to masculinize their manuscripts in order to succeed.[18] But that trend has been reversing in recent years, with experimental novels by and about women receiving more recognition. Jenny Offill's *Dept. of Speculation*, a fragmented tale of motherhood, was one of the *New York Times*'s top-ten books of 2014. A year before the Goldsmiths Prize was awarded to *How to Be Both*, it went to Eimear McBride's *A Girl is a Half-Formed Thing*.

Those books applied experimental styles to descriptions of female lives rather than to the far "girlier" sets of subjects associated with chick lit. But their successes paved the way for a far more radical fusion. With experimental fiction growing more accessible, chick lit becoming more serious, and the aesthetic approach of one converging on the feminine subject matter of the other, it was only a matter of time before the two would cross paths.

▪ ▪ ▪

And cross paths they have, though with less success than critics have suggested. What all of the books under review here have in common is that they apply experimentalism's antirealism to chick lit's girly topics. All portray "postmodern dystopian" worlds rendered surreal through the proliferation of technology and conspiratorial networks: *The Beautiful Bureaucrat*'s is populated by literally faceless drones; *Revision*'s is controlled by a website.[19] And most include some formal quirks: *Ghost Network* is encased in metatexts; *Dietland* includes footnotes. But all still focus, in classic mid-nineties chick-lit fashion, on city-dwelling young women juggling diets, dating, and jobs and obsessing over fashion and cosmetics: *Revision* describes a girl pining for her exboyfriend; *You Too Can Have a Body Like Mine* and *Dietland* treat body image; and *Ghost Network* centers on Molly Metropolis, "the world's hottest pop star."[20]

Indeed, many of the books' authors have publicly described their novels as unprecedented applications of experimental styles to feminine themes—*Dietland*'s author even proclaimed that she was trying to "subvert the form of a 'woman's novel.'"[21] To that degree, then, the authors were complicit with their publicists' schemes, encouraging reviews like *Flavorwire*'s celebration of *The Ghost Network*, which praised the book's elevation of "'girl' culture to its rightful status as a matter for thoughtful literary inquiry."[22]

That assessment, however overblown, defines the stakes inherent in the fusion of experimentalism and chick lit. The most celebrated works of "serious" fiction do in fact often exclude overtly feminine themes—a pattern to which the stigma in our culture equating femininity with triviality doubtless contributes.[23] And the genre to which those themes are so often consigned does often fail to subject them to "thoughtful literary inquiry." This isn't to say that all chick lit is bad. *Bridget Jones's Diary* deftly ironizes its heroine's travails. And *Twilight* and *Fifty Shades of Grey*, however poorly written, tap deep into the cultural bloodstream, satisfying itches readers didn't know they had. That, to be sure, is no simple feat. But most chick lit is less inspired, and reduces the experiences of twentysomething women to a set of tired tropes, neither accurately representing nor interestingly reinventing the everyday. And the genre often accepts its own banality with complacency, such that a fairly stale story can be seen as fully satisfying its aesthetic mandates.

If an experimental treatment of "girl culture" seems to promise to subject it to the "thoughtful literary inquiry" that chick lit so often does not, the books under review here do not deliver on that promise. Where chick lit often accepts its own banality, experimental fiction can court novelty for its own sake. And in the process it can lapse into its own type of formulism. Most of these books do little more than hang a few half-heartedly "experimental" forms on their frames like baubles. And most feel as if they were gleaned from *Experimental Fiction: A Guide for Readers and Writers*. *The Beautiful Bureaucrat*'s incessant wordplay, for example, falls flat: "Nobody. No Body. Oneself. One's elf."

But even if their experimental tactics were effective, the books would be marred by their inability to disentangle chick lit's themes from its typical hackneyed aesthetic, something that only the more ambitious among them even try to do. When *Ghost Network* turns to the world of female fashion, for example, it does so in accordance with the myth that clothing authentically expresses identity. Sentences like "[she] was also a trendy dresser, who spent most of the summer in long jean shorts and thin backless T-shirts" substitute for characterization. *The Beautiful Bureaucrat*, meanwhile, inadvertently crowds itself with stock chick-lit personae: "Joseph" is the guy who appears wearing a sign on his head that says "good boyfriend" and "Trishiffany" is the exaggeratedly silly woman who exists to make the protagonist look sensible.

■ ■ ■

Which brings us back to Alexandra Kleeman. From a stack of graceless blends of girly themes, formal quirks, and hackneyed styles, her book emerges as the only successful integration of the two genres. Stripping chick lit's topics of their mundane realist dress, Kleeman refashions them entirely in experimental forms. Viewed through the refracted lens of her stilted style, "girl culture" appears as something stranger than most of us had realized.

Take Kleeman's descriptions of cosmetics commercials. Each is a surreal little set piece, rendering the sort of ad one sees for Dove beauty cream or Bioré pore cleanser entirely alien simply by describing it in detail. In one faux advertisement for some sort of face cream, as plausible as it is bizarre, a woman peels off layers of her face, "smiling wildly at the camera" until "underneath is a video of the sea shore" and after that "a deciduous forest."

Or take her descriptions of A, the book's protagonist, interacting with her boyfriend, C. In one scene they exchange sexual fantasies, each an amusingly off-kilter caricature of gendered sexuality. In A's, all of her ex-boyfriends arrive at her door, bearing gifts. After they "sit around catching up" for a while, and A begins to feel a "tremendous sense of well-being," they suddenly start "stripping down and fucking . . . very politely." "The ratio of actual sex to chatting, joking, and eating snacks in this fantasy is about one part to six." C is horrified by that vision. His involves "five women, five different flavors of peanut butter, and a jungle gym."

But of all the surreal features of Kleeman's girl world, A's roommate B is by far the most inspired. In contemporary college-girl parlance, the B would stand for "basic." "If you reduced each of us to a list of adjectives," A thinks, "we'd come out nearly equivalent." B depends utterly on A for things like "companionship, interactivity," and "help [making] breakfast for herself." Throughout the book she performs a series of actions that, in their exaggerations of girly behavior, perfectly express its absurd quintessence. She bites people when she feels cornered. She photographs all of the doughnuts at the supermarket. She draws a painstakingly detailed portrait of her ex-boyfriend's head, "twenty percent larger than it would have been in real life." In sum, she is the bizarro everygirl. And Kleeman makes us feel that she is magnificent.

Which is why assessments of Kleeman's book have missed the mark. When *You Too Can Have a Body Like Mine* first came out, critics insisted that it was scathing. NPR called it "a takedown—chilly in its precision—of beauty standards, face creams," and so forth.[24] The *New York Times* lauded its gendered critique of "the society of the spectacle."[25] In so doing, they aligned it with a prevailing form of pop-feminist cultural critique that, though it accurately identifies the ill effects of "airbrushing" and "unrealistic beauty standards" on the female psyche, reduces feminist discourse to a set of fairly superficial complaints, as if the central problem with patriarchal control were the fact that it makes women feel un-pretty.

But Kleeman's book has little to do with that form of critique, and she resists applying cookie-cutter analyses to complex social realities. At the center of her book, for example, is a case of what we might call "anorexia," though defamiliarized to such a degree that we hesitate to apply the term. Rather than attribute it to a single social cause, Kleeman examines it from multiple angles. Consumer culture, to be sure, contributes to it—A's reluctance to eat has something to do with her desire to fuse with the women on the TV screen. But so, too, does a deep desire for spiritual purity, which predates the "society of the spectacle"—Kleeman claims to have based A's behavior on that of medieval mystics.[26] Furthermore, while A's motivations are at times intelligible, they are at others as inscrutable as real human actions often are. We may identify with her acceptance of the mantra *self-improvement is self-subtraction* but probably not with her urge to swallow a handful of her roommate's hair.

Rather than approach "girl culture" armed with a predetermined critical narrative, then, Kleeman approaches it as an anthropologist, holding it at a distance, looking at it askance, and recording its every detail before rendering any conclusions. So to reduce her book to an oversimple slogan—to say, for example, that it skewers the cosmetics industry or eviscerates consumer culture—is to rob it of the key to its success: the fact that it strips "girl culture" of all the clichés in which it has been couched, including shallow cultural critique.

NOTES

1. In her 2008 essay "Two Paths for the Novel," Zadie Smith identified Tom McCarthy as the sole inheritor of an experimental tradition whose practitioners were all male: "Barth, Barthelme, Pynchon, Gaddis, DeLillo, David Foster Wallace" (*New York Review of Books*, November 20, 2008,

http://www.nybooks.com/articles/2008/11/20/two-paths-for-the-novel). The 2012 *Routledge Guide to Experimental Fiction* has three chapters on "Experimental Fiction Today" (excluding a fourth that focuses on memoir); eighty-one of the ninety-two authors mentioned are male. Amy Hungerford has used Deb Olin Unferth's career to suggest that female authors feel pressure to make their protagonists male when they write experimental fiction (see Amy Hungerford, "McSweeney's and The School of Life," *Contemporary Literature* 53, no. 4 [2012]: 646–80, http://cl.uwpress .org/content/53/4/646.full.pdf).

2. E.g., Dan Duray, "Alexandra Kleeman's Debut Novel 'You Too Can Have a Body Like Mine' Charts New Dystopian Territory," *Vice*, August 25, 2015, http://www.vice.com/read/alexandra-kleemans-postmodern-debut -novel-you-too-can-have-a-body-like-mine-charts-new-dystopian -territory-0824.

3. Dan McMahon, "A Sixties Revival Comes Alive in This Sleek 'Do," *Refinery29*, August 30, 2011, http://www.refinery29.com/19479.

4. Alexandra Kleeman, "The Slip Dress That Changed My Life," *Elle*, September 25, 2015, http://www.elle.com/fashion/personal-style/a30704/the -slip-that-changed-my-life.

5. Rachel Tashjian, " 'You Too Can Have a Body Like Mine' and Our Obsession With Beauty Routines, Diet Diaries, and Chia Seeds," *Vanity Fair*, August 25, 2015, http://www.vanityfair.com/culture/2015/08/you-too-can -have-a-body-like-mine-alexandra-kleeman-interview; Maya Singer, "Alexandra Kleeman's 'You Too Can Have a Body Like Mine' Is 'Fight Club' for Women," *Vogue*, August 17, 2015, http://www.vogue.com /13295412/alexandra-kleeman-you-too-can-have-a-body-like-mine.

6. Singer, "Alexandra Kleeman's You Too."

7. *Dietland*'s blurbs and other promotional materials suggest its comparatively commercial status (it is the only book explicitly labeled as "chick lit," if of an off-brand variety); it also seems to have fared better than the other books with popular audiences. Unlike the others, it won a Goodreads Choice Award.

8. Helen Phillips, *And Yet They Were Happy* (Falmouth, MA: Leapfrog, 2011).

9. Celia Johnson, "An Interview with Helen Phillips and Editor Sarah Bowlin," *Slice*, August 17, 2015, http://www.slicemagazine.org/slice-and-dice /2015/08/an-interview-with-author-helen-phillips-and-editor-sarah -bowlin-by-celia-johnson/.

10. A recent Goodreads survey confirms the folk wisdom that women are more likely than men to read books by authors of the opposite gender (see Alison Flood, "Readers Prefer Authors of Their Own Sex, Survey Finds,"

Guardian, November 25, 2014, http://www.theguardian.com/books/2014/nov/25/readers-prefer-authors-own-sex-goodreads-survey).

11. As quoted on the publisher's website for the book, http://www.mhpbooks.com/books/the-ghost-network.

12. Smith, "Two Paths."

13. Lynn Neary, "Jennifer Egan Does Avant-Garde Fiction—Old School," *NPR*, July 25, 2010, http://www.npr.org/2010/07/25/128702628/jennifer-egan-does-avant-garde-fiction-old-school.

14. According to the Goldsmiths Prize's website, http://www.gold.ac.uk/goldsmiths-prize/prize2014.

15. Olivia Barker, "'Prada' Nips at Author Lauren Weisberger's Heels," *USA Today*, May 29, 2008, http://usatoday30.usatoday.com/life/books/news/2008-05-27-chasing-harry-winston_N.htm.

16. "What an Agent Wants: Week 2—Is Chick Lit Dead? Are Publishers Still Buying Chick Lit?," *Novelicious*, March 27, 2012, http://www.novelicious.com/2012/03/what-an-agent-wants-week-2-is-chick-lit-dead-are-publishers-still-buying-chick-lit.html.

17. Quoted in "What an Agent Wants."

18. For an account of the controversy surrounding Kushner's book, see Laura Miller, "Rachel Kushner's Ambitious New Novel Scares Male Critics," *Salon*, June 5, 2013, http://www.salon.com/2013/06/05/rachel_kushners_ambitious_new_novel_scares_male_critics. Miller and Adam Kirsch, whom she engages, disagree as to whether Kushner's book deserves the accolades that it has been receiving but agree that it has received them by virtue of its masculinity.

19. *Revision*'s author would be more likely than the others to call the experimental aspects of her work "science fiction"; in interviews, she labels them as such. But *Revision*'s description of a hyperreal world conforms to the pattern of the "postmodern dystopian" novel. And the categories of "science fiction" and "experimental fiction" are in any case increasingly interpenetrative.

20. For quote, see the *Ghost Network*'s publisher's page, http://www.mhpbooks.com/books/the-ghost-network. *The Beautiful Bureaucrat*'s plotline is less chick-lit-y than the others, given that its protagonist is married. But its frequent discussions of skincare and exaggeratedly effeminate characters (e.g., "Trishiffanny") give it a palpably feminine feel; *Ghost Network* deviates from the classic chick-lit formula in that two of its protagonists are gay. In most other respects (its emphasis on single life in the city, pop stardom, high-stakes sartorial choices), it is identifiable with more standard commercial women's fiction.

21. Sara Nelson, "Sara Says: I'm Binging On 'Dietland,'" *Omnivoracious*, May 21, 2015, http://www.omnivoracious.com/2015/05/sara-says-im-binging-on-dietland.html. Just as Kleeman framed her book as an application of the "postmodern dystopian" style to the "female experience," the authors of *Ghost Network* and *Revision* described their books, respectively, as a tale told by a female Murakami and an infusion of the anti-realist novel's science-fiction-like surrealism with "aggressive femininity" (Tom Houlihan, "Ten Questions for 'The Ghost Network' Author Catie Disabato," *Homewood-Flossmoor Chronicle*, July 23, 2015, http://hfchronicle.com/article/2015/jul/23/ten-questions-ghost-network-author-catie-disabato; Andrea Phillips, "'Revision': An Artist's Statement," *Deus Ex Machinatio*, November 5, 2015, http://www.deusexmachinatio.com/blog/2015/11/4/revision-an-artists-statement).

22. Moze Halperin, "Staff Picks: Petite Noir, 'The Ghost Network,' and 'Black Spider Memos,'" *Flavorwire*, May 13, 2015, http://flavorwire.com/518797/staff-picks-petite-noir-the-ghost-network-and-black-spider-memos.

23. For instance, a recent survey found that though women won major literary prizes like the Pulitzer, National Book Award, or Man Booker about 40 percent of the time since 2015, they almost never won for books about female protagonists (see Alison Flood, "Books About Women Less Likely to Win Prizes, Study Finds," *Guardian*, June 1, 2015), http://www.theguardian.com/books/2015/jun/01/books-about-women-less-likely-to-win-prizes-study-finds. For more on this see Hungerford, "McSweeney's."

24. Jason Sheehan, "Cults, Foam Heads, and Other Weird Things Thrive in 'Body Like Mine,'" August 27, 2015, http://www.npr.org/2015/08/27/434332419/cults-foam-heads-and-other-weird-things-thrive-in-body-like-mine.

25. Valeria Luiselli, "'You Too Can Have a Body Like Mine,' by Alexandra Kleeman," *New York Times Sunday Book Review*, September 4, 2015, http://www.nytimes.com/2015/09/06/books/review/you-too-can-have-a-body-like-mine-by-alexandra-kleeman.html.

26. Jane Gayduk, "You Too Can Have a Debut Novel Like Mine: An Interview with Alexandra Kleeman," *The Awl*, August 12, 2015, http://www.theawl.com/2015/08/you-too-can-have-a-debut-novel-like-mine.

FEELING LIKE THE INTERNET

MARK McGURL

W hat has the advent of the internet meant for the novel? Apart, that is, from its having opened a gaping time-sucking sinkhole at the center of culture? The sweet drip-feed of sentiment and savagery downloading to our devices is absorbing attention that might otherwise have been poured into books, but the effects of the internet on literary life have not been purely negative. Start with the fact that the internet now accounts, via transactions on Amazon, for more than half of the current U.S. sales of books. Add to that the array of opportunities it provides to discuss novels and to get them noticed, whether on Goodreads, the Amazon-owned social-media site for readers, or literary Twitter, or any one of the many web-based publications focused on culture. The adaptation of screen technology, via the Kindle and smartphone, to the needs of internet-connected readers has also been impressive, even as the printed book continues to hold its own.

Then there are the novels one suspects would not exist if not for the internet. They include works like Matt Beaumont's *e: a novel* and its sequels, in which the epistolary tradition is reborn as a long e-mail chain; Dave Eggers's dystopia of lost privacy, *The Circle*; M. T. Anderson's wonderful updating of *A Clockwork Orange* for the digital age, *Feed*; and more than a few mass-market thrillers that take a newly volatile networked world as their premise. Even more significant than these direct registrations of the internet as form and theme, however, are the countless thousands of self-published novels of various kinds that issue from Amazon's Kindle Direct Publishing apparatus, Smashwords, LuLu.com, and other purveyors of download- or print-on-demand literature. This is where works like *Fifty Shades of Grey* came from, vaulting from the precincts of online fan fiction into global ubiquity. Together these enterprises have lowered the up-front monetary cost of book publication and distribution to almost nothing, inaugurating an era of literary hyperabundance whose ultimate import for the life of literature has yet to be determined.

Jarett Kobek's *I Hate the Internet* is one of these self-published novels, having been put out by a microscopic LA-based publishing entity the author founded for that purpose called We Heard You Like Books. Approaching life in the age of social media analytically, it differs strikingly from the generic zombie novels, alpha-billionaire romances, and vampire erotica that dominate sales among Amazon's KDP offerings. And yet the boundary between "direct" publishing, as Amazon euphemistically calls it, and being published by others has always been blurry in the literary avant-garde, whose market is often not large enough to sustain the kind of impersonal relations we think of as underlying the feat of "getting published." Avant-gardes are among other things groups of acquaintances, friends, and lovers who publish each other and themselves.

The age of Kindle Direct Publishing has simply confused things further, making it difficult to separate the various meanings of "independence": from having the right to total delusion about your actual literary talents, to being free to misconstrue your dependent relationship to the giant corporation, Amazon, which saves you from exploitation (or more likely rejection) by traditional publishers, to staking out a space of genuine opposition to the reigning taste.

Kobek's novel, whose full title is *I Hate the Internet: A Useful Novel Against Men, Money, and the Filth of Instagram*, enters this interesting point in literary history firmly in the last camp, trailing a blurb from Jonathan Lethem. Kobek's previous works include *Atta*, brought out by the distinguished publisher of experimental writing Semiotext(e) in 2011, and a strange 2012 chapbook called *If You Won't Read, Then Why Should I Write?* The former inhabits the mind of the 9/11 terrorist ringleader up to the very moment of his collision with the North Tower, refusing to moralize about his murderous delusions while the latter is a hard-to-describe collection of fragmentary transcripts of moments from the ordinary lives of celebrities, bound with cardboard inserts detailing the trouble they have had with the law. You know, the usual avant-garde stuff.

Both of these works, especially the first, have their virtues, but the new novel is far more engaging than its predecessors. In fact, it is really good, which the reader of the novel soon learns is actually a grievous insult against it. But it *is* good, and even when it's not good it's interesting, a minor landmark in the field of contemporary literature, if only for the rare energy of its attempt to speak back to and against what is nonetheless admitted to be the condition of possibility of its own existence: the same capitalist world that gave us the internet it hates.

I Hate the Internet is often very funny, wending its way forward with the punchy rhythm of a stand-up routine, following a group of friends living in the supremely annoying San Francisco of 2013. In its humor and casually quick pacing it reads somewhat like Kurt Vonnegut, Kobek's acknowledged model, although without the dangerously cute dorkiness that leavened his predecessor's pitch-black assessment of our place in the universe. *I Hate the Internet* has no Billy Pilgrim figure, no holy innocent who throws the cruel absurdity of the world into relief, unless it is this novel's Ellen Flitcraft, a minor character whose life is arbitrarily destroyed when lewd pictures of her are posted online. What it does have is inexhaustible comic rage at the sea of "intolerable bullshit" in which its urbanely ironic characters are forced to swim.

At the novel's center is the friendship between a writer called J. Karacehennem, a last name we are told more than once is "Turkish for Black Hell," and his droll older friend Adeline, who was once a successful indie comic book artist working under a male pseudonym. Her connection to comics gives Kobek an opening to dilate on the history of corporate exploitation of individual artists in the comics industry, who earned almost nothing from their now multi-billion-dollar intellectual properties. A presumably milder version of this exploitation is what this book avoids by being self-published. It also enables Kobek to declare the symbolic alliance of his novel with gaudy popular culture over and against the dubious refinements of more respectable literature, the kind published by the likes of Farrar, Straus & Giroux, even as he stays well within the familiar bounds of social realism (no Tralfamadorians here, just techies).

When Adeline is recorded saying some outrageous things during a visit to a class taught by Kevin Killian (an actual person, one of the great avant-garde poets of our time) and those things are posted to YouTube and go viral, the internet suddenly gets personal. Having lived in lofty contempt of its incessant chatter, Adeline can't help herself—she opens a Twitter account. Complications ensue. In parallel to this, Karacehennem gets caught up in a controversy surrounding the gentrification of the Mission District of the city and finally decides to move back to LA.

But as is almost always the case in avant-garde fiction, the plot is not really the point here. Some versions of the avant-garde want to draw us into the mysteries of language and narrative structure, refusing popular demand for facile meanings. Those can be very boring, I guess deliberately. That's not what is going on in *I Hate the Internet*, which like a Vonnegut novel has a highly engaging, talky quality. The scaffold of plot is rather an occasion for the narrator to deliver a series of fragmentary disquisitions on various matters tied together by his titular hatred for the internet. Each hews to a recognizably contemporary left-progressive point of view but is uttered with unusually creative vitriol.

To hate the internet is, first of all, to hate the hateful men who congregate there to express their hatred for women like Adeline; it is, second of all, to hate racism, even as public discussion of race is understood as a screen for the more basic exploitations of capitalism, which is a third thing the novel hates, especially the hatefully self-adoring kind associated with the beautiful but hateful Bay Area. Finally, there is humanity, which is revealed as essentially a "bunch of dumb assholes," as is daily displayed (coming now full circle) on the internet. As it says on the first page: "The Internet was a wonderful invention. It was a computer network which people used to remind other people that they were awful pieces of shit."

This last is one of the techniques the novel uses frequently and to interesting effect: the deflating definition. Kobek gets it from Vonnegut, who got it from Ambrose Bierce's *Devil's Dictionary*, which got it from Dr. Johnson. It works really well in the context of the tech industry, where the tolerance for intolerable bullshit has always been very high indeed. Sometimes the deflating definition works by simple sarcasm; other times, by using the technical jargon of scientific truth. Most consequential for our experience of *I Hate the Internet* is the narrator's early redefinition of race as a misreading of a merely technical fact about human skin, which is that its color "is a visual byproduct of eumelanin's presence in the stratum basale layer of the epidermis." Thereafter in the novel, some seventy or eighty times, each character or group of persons is described not as belonging to one race or another but as having more or less "eumelanin in the stratum basale layer of the epidermis." It is Kobek's equivalent of Vonnegut's "So it goes," which follows each death in *Slaughterhouse-Five*; but whereas Vonnegut's version rides on its disturbingly fatalistic brevity, Kobek's point is to inject an unwieldy mouthful of scientific truth into every instance of racial identification. Although this becomes tedious and unfunny by about halfway through the novel, that is arguably the point.

Is it possible to make a good novel out of such ingredients? Apparently so, even if the very idea of the "good novel" was invented, according to this one, by the Central Intelligence Agency:

> This is not a joke. This is true. This is church.
>
> The CIA funded *The Paris Review*. The CIA funded the Iowa Writers' Workshop. The CIA engineered the 1958 Nobel Prize in Literature.
>
> A person would be hard pressed to find three other institutions with more influence over the development of the *good novel* and *literary fiction*.

Actually, truth is, the idea of the *good novel* Kobek references here was invented by Gustave Flaubert and Henry James if it was invented by anybody. And the CIA (fronted by the Congress for Cultural Freedom and other entities) funded jazz concerts, exhibitions of abstract expressionist painting, and a hundred other things during what is now called the Cultural Cold War, so picking on the *good novel* as the yield of the CIA's ideological engineering seems a little questionable. The CCF was willing to support pretty much anything that could be construed as advancing the cause of "freedom," and wasn't overtly communist. Too, the narrator's general account of postwar *literary fiction* is not exactly generous:

> For more than a half a century, American writers of good novels had missed the only important story in American life. They had missed the evolving world, the world of hidden persuaders, of the developing communications landscape, of mass tourism, of the vast conformist suburbs dominated by television.

Since he doesn't name names except, inevitably, the name Jonathan Franzen, it's hard to know what and whom exactly he has in mind here. For instance, say what you will about John Updike, who would seem to have been one of the central perpetrators of the postwar *good novel*, his fiction did not avoid the *vast conformist suburbs*. Neither did Richard Yates's *Revolutionary Road* or Evan Connell's *Mrs. Bridge* and *Mr. Bridge*, all "good novels" in Kobek's sense and all as deflationary in their day as he is trying to be in his. Although few would damn Thomas Pynchon or Norman Mailer or John Barth or Philip Roth or Don DeLillo with the faint praise of writing merely "good" novels, they and writers like them garnered a lot of attention and major awards in that span. Is Kobek excluding them from his charge of cultural blindness and irrelevance? And what about Vonnegut? As *Slaughterhouse-Five* tells you early on, it was written at the Iowa Writers' Workshop while Vonnegut was teaching there.

But so be it. Every literary generation will have its own claim to insurgent truth, whatever the cost to an accurate view of literary history. What's interesting to me, looking at the list of postwar literary big shots and bad boys I listed above, is how intensely *male* they are. And I have to say, this is a quality very much emanating from *I Hate the Internet*, too, despite its overtly and to all appearances sincerely feminist content.

From this perspective, *I Hate the Internet* looks not so much like a Vonnegut novel as a Philip Roth novel written by a young man not concussed by feminism, as Roth's generation of he-man liberals was, but raised by and within it. One can only welcome the new generation's ability to identify with female experience, and I for one (maybe not the best one to ask) found the character of Adeline convincing in her witty cynicism, which is her way of showing contempt for the patriarchal world without shouting it down. I feel like I've known a few women like her. But otherwise the rhetoric of male aggression continues unabated even as it turns on itself, meeting the challenge of the trolls with the erection of a counter-troll, a hater to hate the haters.

In other respects, however, *I Hate the Internet* is disarmingly savvy about its self-implication in what it critiques, pointing out how, for starters, it was created on a machine "built by slaves in China." As we read early on: "This bad novel, which is a morality lesson about the Internet, was written on a computer. You are suffering the moral outrage of a hypocritical writer who has profited from the spoils of slavery."

Bruce Robbins has memorably analyzed the potentially disabling perception of one's implication in a vast system of exploitative capitalism as the experience of the "sweatshop sublime," and part of what makes *I Hate the Internet* a good novel and not the bad one it purports to be is how intelligently it manifests the consequences of that implication. If there remains a blind spot in its lucid deflation of our bullshit balloons it would appear to be an emotional one. Whatever else we mean by the "internet" now we mean, by way of the rise of social media, a certain shared climate of feeling, an animated and sped-up hubbub of the discourse of human interest. By turns soothing and bruising, it is the very medium of what Lauren Berlant, correcting a longstanding tendency to think of emotions as internal and private, has described instead as *public feelings*. They are the affective substance of political life, the very thing, even more than political ideas, to which online citizenship has become attuned and by which it is increasingly deranged. While the tenor of our online exchanges runs the gamut from sympathy to snark and beyond, one of the internet's signature speech genres is surely the *rant*, the hyped-up rhetorical expression of mockingly contemptuous dismay. The novel as rant: in this way, too, *I Hate the Internet* is the internet it hates.

THE PEOPLE v. O. J. SIMPSON AS HISTORICAL FICTION

NICHOLAS DAMES

The location is wrong. The white Bronco is clearly weaving through traffic on the 710 South as it approaches its inter- section with the 10, on the eastern border of El Sereno, just by the Cal State LA campus. In June 1994, O. J. Simpson and Al Cowl- ings would have had no reason to venture that far into the Eastside; their legendary trip, between Encino, Orange County, and Brent- wood, was mostly played out on the 5 and 405, the region's major north-south arteries. In the context of a city notoriously opinion- ated about its driving routes, the substitution is disconcerting.

But the light is just right: the soft yellowish glow of a Califor- nia evening in early summer, the lingering brightness of the sky set against the shaded freeway. It's the light one remembers from the famous video footage of 1994, the lengthening shadows cast by both Bronco and police car in their parade-like procession toward Brentwood, watched by those to the east after their own nightfall.

Getting that light right is the key to understanding the version of history offered by *The People v. O. J. Simpson: American Crime Story*. The show's job, as its creators seem to have understood it— and at which they succeed remarkably well—is not fidelity to his- torical detail but evocation of a vanished era in its most intimate aspects: the moment-to-moment feeling of being alive then, the sensory and affective horizons of a time still within living memory, seen through the slight parallax of the present. Big narrative resolutions, like guilt and innocence, are beside the point. Instead, small things get magnified: the peculiar valence of scenes watched over grainy videotape and cathode-ray-tube televisions; the bright colors of print tabloids, hidden on desks and in drawers like samizdat; the quality of light playing on a police chase. The nuances of personal interaction between genders and races are part of this minutely observed world as well, although the tension and simmering resentments they display—despite the different haircuts and outfits—are much more immediately familiar.

What this means is that, allowing for all of its early-twenty-first-century savvy and its very different medium, *The People v. O. J. Simpson* bears a surprising resemblance to a Victorian novel. It was one of nineteenth-century fiction's most subtle inventions: the idea that realism's gaze was sharpest when focused on the recent past, neither beyond living memory nor quite like the contemporary world. Thackeray's *Vanity Fair* starts thirty-five years prior to its writing; Dickens's *Little Dorrit*, thirty years; Eliot's *Middlemarch*, slightly more than forty years; Hardy's *Tess of the D'Urbervilles*, roughly twenty.

The slight but decisive gap created by a shift back two, three, or four decades, into the youth of the writers themselves, was a way of thinking about present dilemmas through the tension these narratives created between nostalgia—the simple, irresistible longing for what is gone—and identification, the recognition of how much of that past unhappily persists. It was a way of producing a realism that felt the weight of time: a realism of incremental change, equivocal and uneasy, aimed at a middle distance where the past hasn't yet hardened into myth, where its seams still show.

It's a compromise more often associated with novels than film or television, which oscillate between a bleeding-edge fascination with the present and the spectacular indulgences of period drama, with its lovingly reconstructed Edwardian drawing rooms, ancient Roman atria, and Civil War battlefields. Television in particular, however, seems to be waking up to the power of the slight historicity of Victorian realist technique. There is, of course, the immense popularity of *Mad Men*'s portrayal of imperial America's 1960s belle époque; more recently, the adventures in late–Cold War historiography of *The Americans* or *Deutschland 83*, and the Carter-administration shabbiness of *Fargo*'s second season. Artists resurrecting the era of their youth—like *The People v. O. J. Simpson*'s directors, Ryan Murphy (born 1965), John Singleton (1968), and Anthony Hemingway (1977)—with the nuanced psychology and novelistic intimacies usually reserved for the present: this is more neo-Victorian than any Julian Fellowes adaptation, despite the surface dissimilarity between the show and any Victorian novel. At the same time, these shows manage a complex double address, partially nostalgic, aimed at those old enough to recall the period firsthand, and partially exoticizing, aimed at those young enough to find this recent past a slightly foreign country.

It's not easy to do well. At their best, such narratives can uncover possibilities and dilemmas in the recent past that we have not resolved, however much we have become sensitized to them. At their worst, such narratives are complacent, mythologizing the past with seductively nostalgic allure while smugly lecturing us about what we already all agree were its shortcomings.

The intelligence of *The People v. O. J. Simpson* is rooted in the deftness with which it avoids the latter trap. First, it is not quite "prestige TV." The critics that initially ridiculed it have clearly become used to the super-tasteful sheen and emotional earnestness of that genre. *The People v. O. J.* is candy-colored pulp, not above playing for jokes, and has no glamour. The taupes and pastel pinks of its sets; the lime-green and pale-yellow shirts; the wide, baroquely patterned neckties; the beige-toned sofas, bloated French Country furniture, and boxy, disposable-looking cars—all of that mid-1990s ephemera seems cheap even when it's expensive, and more than a little embarrassing, a bottle of Zima instead of Don Draper's Old Fashioned.

Its actors, who seem positively gleeful in their reanimation of the trial's iconic figures, reflect the show's inclination toward kitsch. There is David Schwimmer's Robert Kardashian, a middle-aged ingénu among sharks, Alyosha Karamazov in a polo top; Connie Britton's Faye Resnick, suggestively munching carrot sticks as a way of chewing scenery; John Travolta, out-Heroding Herod like never before as the beetle-browed Robert Shapiro; even Larry King, as surreally ageless as Queen Bess, playing himself. The two standout performances, Sarah Paulson's Marcia Clark and Courtney B. Vance's Johnnie Cochran, are figures of pathos and humor both; rather than riding history, they're clinging to its flank for all they're worth, hoping to end up on top rather than trampled.

By refusing to take itself seriously, by not seducing us with solemnity, the show manages to be far more adept than its peers. It doesn't traffic in grand secrets or tragic revelations but in a world of crazy happenstance, tangled contingencies, ridiculous impostures. That, as it happens, is its second virtue: the focus on the small scale, the fidelity to slippery feeling over narrative momentum. It isn't too much to say, in fact, that Simpson's guilt or innocence is the show's MacGuffin, the ultimately irrelevant plot motivation that occasions the narrative's truly important business. What emerges into a sharp foreground isn't any tantalizing mystery but what we now call microaggressions: the places where structural inequities lurk under behavioral norms. The camera lingers on cruelly appraising glances and wounding offhand remarks, on a cashier's comments as Clark buys tampons, on a traffic cop's impassive face as he handcuffs Cochran for a minor violation. No small part of the show's visual wit is its emphasis on fences, doors, barriers between bodies. Each of the major characters—Clark, Cochran, Chris Darden—has an essentially private understanding of what it means to live in their skin, one that they can share with others only indirectly.

They are much more capable of sharing their senses of incomprehension and incommensurability. The look of shock on Clark's face when Darden tells her "a lot of black people think he didn't do it" in the third episode is one of the show's many stagings of incompatible realities—entirely different truths, coexisting at the same moment. Often that clash of realities is delivered through the show's cunningly disrespectful choices of period music. When Mark Fuhrman (played with calm menace by Steven Pasquale) enters the courtroom for the first time, what ushers him in is the famous cimbalom of Portishead's 1994 early trip-hop masterpiece "Sour Times." More than just a witty verbal comment, this is a brilliantly perverse juxtaposition—the downtempo theme music to countless lounge bars of the mid-nineties and the confident strut of the trial's famous racist cop. It's thrilling and verges on uncomfortably erotic. It's also just weird, the idea that two such things, two such worlds, coexisted, unaware of each other except in the collision staged by the show. A heavier hand might have inserted a riff from "One in a Million," Guns N' Roses' notorious late-eighties white-boy anthem, instead, but the show is interested in collisions, not confirmations. Careful historical reconstruction of interiors and costume and music is a difficult art that usually has a simple rationale: to seduce you with the past's allure or to underline characterizations. Not so here, where the reconstruction exists to unsettle, to ironize.

A "history of the lights and shadows," George Eliot called it—the almost impossible-to-conceive collectivity of distinct lives and perspectives, which only becomes apparent in retrospect. One thing *The People v. O. J.* suggests as the lesson of its history of lights and shadows is that its moment wasn't, as has often been said, when a common culture frayed; it was instead the collective moment when everyone began to realize there never had been a common culture. If we've inherited that realization, we certainly know no better what to do with it.

KAFKA: THE IMPOSSIBLE BIOGRAPHY

JAN MIESZKOWSKI

The prospect of a new Kafka biography is like an invitation to a party that is bound to be entertaining but may end badly. Situating Kafka's writing within the cultural and political landscape of European modernism and the late Austro-Hungarian Empire is a worthy if daunting endeavor. Less certain is whether such efforts to contextualize his corpus actually garner insights into it. Kafka's readers are intrigued by virtually any anecdote about him, but few would allow that the abiding mysteries of his texts will be resolved by learning that he lived in Prague, was the son of a fancy goods merchant, and enjoyed going to the beach. Nor does history provide a reliable key to unlock his works, which have dates but do not date. If they are decidedly not a product of our time, there appears to be little chance of them ever going out of style.

Although Kafka's importance is incontestable, scholars and casual fans alike fiercely debate every feature of his corpus. Each plot twist or curious turn of phrase calls for clarification, yet customary interpretive practices are seldom up to the task. To read Kafka is to lurch back and forth between the uncannily familiar and the abjectly foreign. To reread a favorite story is to risk seeing any exegetical progress made the first, second, or third time through evaporate. Given these challenges, learning more about Kafka's life may be a good opportunity to win new perspectives on his writing, but it may also be the furthest thing from it.

Some two decades in the making, Reiner Stach's three-volume biography of Kafka confronts these difficulties head-on, acknowledging from the start that like virtually any discussion of this author, it is bound to be found wanting on many fronts. If anything, Stach is too self-deprecating. There is much to appreciate in the vast compendium of information he assembles, which fleshes out the stories about Kafka and his associates that have been in circulation for decades while introducing a host of new ones. Even better are the moments when Stach lets go of his skepticism about his project's viability and allows himself to enjoy the conundrums that arise when one tries to coordinate Kafka "the man" with Kafka "the oeuvre."

Intimidating in its thoroughness, this study is a major scholarly achievement whose comprehensive research is unlikely to be rivaled for decades to come. Stach chose not to avail himself of the biographer's elementary crutch, chronology, and waited until he had access to key documents from the estate of Kafka's friend Max Brod before writing this last volume, which covers the first part of Kafka's life. With the appearance of *The Early Years* in English, we now have translations of all three books, over 1,800 pages to analyze 41 years that were by most accounts far from epic.[1] Raised in a middle-class family in Prague, Kafka studied law and went into insurance, where he was rapidly promoted. He was spared the horror of fighting in the First World War, in part due to tuberculosis, an illness that ultimately forced him to give up his job and spend a large part of the last years of his short life in sanatoriums. Writing was something Kafka did in his spare time. He published relatively little, and at the time of his death, he was far from commanding a wide readership.

All three volumes of Stach's biography have been ably translated into English by Shelley Frisch, who has won prizes for the first two. Her style betrays none of the aloof awkwardness that can characterize English renditions of German academic prose, and she deftly captures modulations in tone. Frisch's preface to *The Early Years* helps the prospective reader orient herself within the larger study. This is no small matter, because coming to this trio of books for the first time, one may well wonder where to start. *Kafka: The Decisive Years*, which was written and published first, deals with the middle of the author's life. It opens, however, with Stach's thoughts on the nature of biography and on the unique problems encountered in tackling this particular writer, all of which are extremely clarifying for anyone picking up either *The Early Years* or *The Years of Insight*, the second volume published that deals with the end of Kafka's life.

At the opening of *The Decisive Years*, Stach writes: "This biographer seeks to experience what was experienced by those who were there. What it was like to be Franz Kafka. He knows that this is impossible."[2] The very fact that "the biographer" is discussed in the third person foreshadows Stach's ongoing dialogue with himself about the nature of his "impossible" enterprise. Stach observes that it is easy enough to identify Kafka's "issues," most prominently a vexed relationship with his father, struggles with sexual intimacy, and an uncertain engagement with Judaism. The problem is that when we chart these dynamics across four decades, the results are remarkably static, with little in the way of progress or regress. There also appears to be no clear way to prioritize the forces that informed Kafka's experience of any given anxiety or event because cause and effect can fluidly swap places depending on how a particular story is told. As a consequence, any persona one constructs will prove highly changeable. Look once and you see a fearful, neurotic young man; look again and you see a handsome dandy who was a successful investigator of industrial accidents and spent his leisure time cavorting in bars and nightclubs.

Stach never resolves the basic question of how a biography can best assist in the study of a literary corpus. He repeatedly introduces facts about Kafka's life, explains in what respects they illuminate general themes or the details of well-known texts, and then declares that proceeding in such a manner is reductive. By the tenth time we are thrown an exegetical bone only immediately to have it yanked away, we are understandably puzzled about precisely what is being demonstrated. Adding to the confusion, at other junctures Stach pursues similar lines of interpretation but does not retract them, leaving us unsure as to why this kind of analysis is only intermittently impermissible.

Given these difficulties, we could be forgiven for feeling that we were reading *Kafka: The Impossible Biography* or *The Biography That Is Not One*. One reviewer of *The Decisive Years* observed that it appeared to have been written "by a Kafka character called, to borrow the words of the book's promotional materials, 'the definitive biographer.'"[3] Hopelessly worn down by his Sisyphean task, this beleaguered individual alternately blames himself and others for his ills as he spars ineffectually with the mysterious forces imposing themselves upon him. Uncharitable though this assessment may be, it reminds us that as much as we may want to read Kafka's stories and novels through the lens of his life, it is equally tempting to understand his life through his fiction, as if any story about him laid claim to being a weighty parable worthy of sustained scrutiny. Stach tells us that Kafka's personality was shaped by "the feeling that he was standing outside of life and had to find his way in." This may also serve as a description of the biographer's—or reader's—experience of his inability to find a way in to Kafka's universe, where, as Theodor W. Adorno remarked, "each sentence says 'interpret me' but none will permit it."[4]

If ambivalence about the ultimate value of his research is present in all three volumes of Stach's biography, the stakes are higher than ever in this final book, on Kafka's early years. A psychological profile of the renowned author must necessarily be based in information about his family and childhood. Even here, however, Stach is consistently inconsistent. On the one hand, he appears to endorse psychologically or psychoanalytically informed analyses of Kafka's diaries and letters while maintaining that such interpretive practices are out of their depth when it comes to the literary texts. On the other hand, he rarely respects this distinction between the private and public Kafka, particularly when he is discussing Kafka's own opinions about how his writing should be understood. Stach also makes contradictory observations about Kafka's views on psychology. In the same breath as he describes Kafka's ambition to improve his relationships with others through mutual self-betterment, he reminds us of Kafka's scorn for "therapy" and the very notion of self-development.

As is the case with most literary biographies, there is a relative paucity of texts with which to make sense of Kafka's formative years, whereas we have all manner of documents from the later decades of his life, written by him and by those who knew him. The first part of *The Early Years* thus broadens the focus to provide a rich social and cultural history of the city of Prague and the Austro-Hungarian Empire. This includes an illuminating account of class and ethnic strife and a detailed picture of the economic situation of the Kafka family and other similarly situated merchants.

For more personal early source material, Stach relies heavily on Kafka's infamous "Letter to Father," a forty-five-page document that he wrote when he was thirty-six and gave to his mother to pass on to the *pater familias*, only to have it returned to him with the ostensible addressee none the wiser. The self-referential twists and turns of such a text are formidable, and the accounts it offers of events that took place decades earlier, in some cases when Kafka was barely old enough to have remembered them, must have undergone many degrees of revision, to say the least. Written in full awareness of these factors, the "Letter" itself may be as much a critique of the very possibility of autobiography as it is a basis for drawing any conclusions about the life of its author.

Stach's analyses of specific sections of the "Letter" are, in any case, disappointing. In one of the best-known passages in the text, Kafka's father puts the two- or three-year-old out on the balcony in the middle of the night because he would not stop whimpering for water. Stach declares that this was "a key event in [Kafka's] psychological development" that "sheds stark light on the three interdependent motifs in [his] world: power, fear, and isolation." Whatever one may think of such a sweeping conclusion, it is not based on a careful reading of the scene, not least since Kafka's opening line is that he was asking for water "not because [he] was thirsty, but probably in order to be annoying and to amuse [himself]."[5] The duplicitous, even sadomasochistic status of amusement in Kafka's work is a vertiginous topic, as is the irony with which he relates this information to his father by stating that this is "probably" why he was behaving so abominably. Where the power in this scenario lies and to whom feelings of fear or isolation are to be attributed is far more complex than Stach's brief gloss allows.

When Stach throws caution to the wind and embarks upon more creative lines of interpretation, the results can be perplexing. Having observed that Kafka loved the beach, Stach announces: "Swimming is an archaic activity that taps into deep, preponderantly unconscious realms of experience. It is an exceptionally intense and multilayered, yet easily achievable physical and mental state of being, comparable only to sexuality.... People can swim freely, and even swim their way free. Once this movement is ingrained as a physical technique, it provides lasting narcissistic satisfaction." Without pausing to substantiate or clarify these claims in any way, Stach moves on to confirm the importance of swimming to Kafka by citing a description he gave of his cousin Robert, who swam "with the power of a beautiful wild animal, shimmering in the water, with sparkling eyes . . . it was magnificent." Stach's conclusion is that for Kafka, being in the water was the "most persuasive metaphor for the fear-infused thrill surrounding [sexual] intimacy," a bedeviling mix of freedom and constraint.

The story of Cousin Robert, however, is not quite complete. For the final sentence of Kafka's description of his relative, Stach offers the pithy shocker: "And six months later [Robert] was dead." Having introduced this startling new detail, Stach hurriedly adds that Kafka is implying that it is difficult to imagine that such a strong swimmer could be mortal. A glance at the source for this tale reveals that Kafka actually ended his account: "And six months later [Robert] was dead, tortured to death by doctors. A mysterious disease of the spleen which they were treating principally with injections of milk, in the consciousness that it was no use."[6] One could envision various ways to link Stach's reflections on sexuality and swimming with death. Still, this additional material introduces a host of new motifs that will require considerably more discussion, especially if the story is to serve as evidence for the transcendently liberatory powers of swimming and their importance for understanding Kafka's psychosexual life.

As we follow a maturing Franz through his education, we learn a great deal about the Austro-Hungarian school and university systems. Some of this terrain will be familiar to those who have read Kafka's letters, which contain ample information about his trials and tribulations in the classroom. When it comes to Kafka's personal consumption of art and literature, Stach snobbishly judges his tastes to be middlebrow or worse. At times, our biographer sounds almost parental in his disapproval of the fledgling author's late-night escapades, which rarely saw him attend the theater, concerts, or academic lectures. Stach also has some amusingly unexamined assumptions about what famous writers like to read. He seems to feel genuine astonishment that someone with such creative potential could have spent so much time devouring travelogues, in particular "Indian, Eskimo, and animal adventures," although a quick review of the reading habits of Kafka's contemporaries would reveal this to be nothing out of the ordinary—one thinks of Joyce's love of cartoons or of Brecht's passion for detective stories.

For yet another perspective on the cultural environ in which the young author came of age, Stach details his encounters with "great men." We hear about Kafka's single consultation with Rudolf Steiner, after which he declared to Brod that the famous philosopher and social reformer had not understood him. We also hear about the occasion on which Kafka and his friends attended a popular science lecture by Albert Einstein, who taught in Prague from 1911 to 1912. Stach un-self-consciously strains to make more of the latter event than his sources warrant. Acknowledging that there is no evidence that Kafka ever met the famous physicist, Stach observes that Brod did socialize with him, so "it is highly likely that [Kafka] was at least introduced to Einstein." This impulse to embellish is telling. A life story of the sort Stach is relating will be rife with contingency, unambiguous cause-and-effect relationships at best taking shape only sporadically. In another biographer's hands, this fact could be a source of anxiety, if not a realization to be dissimulated at all costs, but Stach embraces it and savors the opportunity to see his discussion shade into fiction as he speculates on a quasi-hypothetical encounter between two people, one already famous, one destined to be.

At another point, Stach describes Kafka and Brod at an air show. The two men documented this experience in writing, and, improbably, their accounts are substantiated by a photograph discovered decades later, which appears to show Kafka from behind as he stands in a crowd watching the plane of a famous French aviator fly by. Chance has given us proof that Kafka and Brod's stories of this event are not just stories, although, looking at the photo, it seems less like corroborating evidence of their narratives than an image from a dream, whose power lies precisely in how it threatens to unsettle the border between fact and fiction.

In the end, *Kafka: The Early Years* may be most compelling at precisely such junctures, when its wealth of information about the young author fails to concretize in definitive assessments of his personality or cultural milieu and instead offers a glimpse of something inchoate and fleeting that does not need to be ascribed paradigmatic import. One might object that these flashes of contingency are symptomatic of the degree to which the different strands of Stach's project never entirely come together, but Kafka's fans are likely to be the last people who would imagine that they could.

NOTES

1. *Kafka: The Decisive Years*, dealing with Kafka's life from 1910–1915, appeared in German in 2002 and in English 2005. *Kafka: The Years of Insight*, which covered 1916–1924, appeared in German in 2008 and in English in 2015.
2. Reiner Stach, *The Decisive Years*, 15.
3. See Marco Roth, "Franz the Obscure," *New York Times*, January 1, 2006, http://www.nytimes.com/2006/01/01/books/review/franz-the-obscure .html.
4. Theodor W. Adorno, "Notes on Kafka," in *Prisms*, trans. Samuel Weber and Shierry Weber (Cambridge, MA: MIT Press, 1983), 246.
5. Kafka, "Letter to Father," cited in Stach, *The Early Years*, 65.
6. Quoted in Max Brod, *Franz Kafka: A Biography* (De Capo Books, 1960), 206–7. (The English translation of the Brod text actually begins: "And half a year later.")

SHIRLEY JACKSON'S TWO WORLDS

KAREN DUNAK

S tarting in the late 1970s, Revlon (in)famously peddled its fragrance Enjoli to working women by asserting a woman wearing this scent could not only "bring home the bacon," but also "fry it up in a pan." The celebration of the woman who "had it all"—that is, a personal *and* a professional life—seemingly represented the fruits of 1960s- and 1970s-era feminist activism, which had resulted in a reconsideration of men's and women's roles and, theoretically, a restructuring of American life, both public and private.

Except, of course, it was never so easy, and there were plenty of women in America who could have testified to that fact. Even before the Second World War brought a flood of women into the workforce, nearly 25 percent of American women worked full- or part-time jobs. That number climbed to almost 38 percent by 1960. By the time that Arlie Russell Hochschild named the problem of the "second shift" in 1989—the likelihood that working women would follow their professional workday with an evening of domestic labor, a "second" job that they shouldered no matter how much bacon they brought home—it was the lived experience of generations of American women.

Long before the Second Wave, as Ruth Franklin's biography of Shirley Jackson, *Shirley Jackson: A Rather Haunted Life*, demonstrates, working women struggled to balance their domestic tasks with their careers or creative passions. Jackson wed Stanley Edgar Hyman in 1940, gave birth to the first of her four children in 1942 and the last in 1951, and died in 1965. It was during these childbearing and child-raising years that Jackson, the family's predominant breadwinner, produced six novels, two memoirs about childrearing, four children's books, and dozens of short stories. Jackson's life sheds light on the longer history of working women's often undocumented efforts to balance domestic and professional demands, as well as the challenge that this attempted balance presented in the face of narrow conceptions of appropriate embodiments of American womanhood. The difference for women of Jackson's era is that there were virtually no voices suggesting that her domestic responsibilities should be anyone's but hers (and certainly not her husband's).

Franklin chronicles Jackson's emergence as a writer, going back to her California youth, when she voraciously read fantasy tales and penned multiple diaries as she tried on different personas. After her family's move to upstate New York and a false start at the University of Rochester, Jackson came into her own at Syracuse University, where she met Hyman, who, for all his failings (chronic cheating and sometimes staggering insensitivity, to top the list), championed Jackson as among the greatest writers of her time and place. The bulk of Jackson's writing came in short-story form, appearing in publications as diverse as *The New Yorker* and *Story* and *Good Housekeeping*. The stories toyed with the darkness of domestic life, the petty cruelties allowed (and often endorsed) by convention, and, occasionally, the pull of the surreal or supernatural.

It was the 1948 publication of "The Lottery," argues Franklin, which put Jackson firmly on the map of esteemed contemporary American writers and ushered in the era of sustained critical consideration of her work. The story infamously unfolds in a small, seemingly idyllic town, before revealing that the friendly-seeming townspeople ritually stone to death one of their own each year, a victim chosen by drawing lots. But what did Jackson mean with this story? Readers sent letters to the *New Yorker* en masse (the most the publication had ever received to a work of fiction, to that time), demanding an explanation. While most readers (and most critics) admired it, the primary result was that audiences were deeply unsettled by the story.

The same was true of much of Jackson's fiction. While Franklin sees "The Lottery" as a commentary on a community's proclivity for casual violence and humankind's capacity for grave inhumanity, she balks at Jackson's own claim that she chose the target of the story's lottery at random. The fact that Tessie Hutchison, a wife and mother, was the lottery's victim, Franklin suggests, was "a parable of the ways in which women are forced to sacrifice themselves: if not their lives, then their energy and their ambitions." This is Franklin's overarching estimation of the central theme not only of Jackson's body of work but of her life and the lives of so many women at midcentury. Franklin suggests the longer arc of this theme in noting "how contemporary" she found the "intersection of life and work" tenuously negotiated by Jackson.

But for all of the darkness of Jackson's stories and novels, she didn't live in a world of darkness. Writing was one world; her marriage, her family, and her home provided her with another. It was a world that often filled her with delight, as evidenced by her chronicles of her children's antics and misadventures, immortalized in stories published in ladies' magazines of the age and, most famously, in *Life Among the Savages* (1953) and *Raising Demons* (1957). These collections were a tremendous success, among Jackson's best-selling works. But these tales in no way put Jackson or her children upon a pedestal. Jackson's mother—a constant critic—bemoaned her daughter's penchant for airing the family's dirty laundry and representing her household in such a chaotic light. The vision of Jackson painted by Franklin is of a loving and attentive and creative parent but one who also was busy with other things. Multiple reminiscences indicated a house that, while not filthy, was not clean (and a perfectly kept home in one of Jackson's stories often signaled something was amiss). The image of the happy housewife, trim and beautiful and dedicated to domestic tasks performed to perfection, peppered the pages of the ladies' magazines for which Jackson sometimes wrote. But while Jackson was aware of this figure, it was not one she attempted to embody.

And yet that model, famously identified in Betty Friedan's *Feminine Mystique* (1963), was there. Jackson was not immune to the cultural expectations of the world in which she lived. When she arrived at the hospital to deliver her third child and was asked her occupation, she responded "writer." The nurse taking her information responded, "I'll just put down housewife." In interviews and publicity, she often framed herself as a wife and mother who also wrote. Money earned from her writing often went to domestic ends: new kitchen appliances, a washing machine, an outdoor playhouse for the children. Her hospitality was famous, and one friend, remembering being entertained at the Hyman-Jackson home, noted, "She did everything as though it was not the least bit of trouble." Until the end of her life, Jackson endured her mother's ongoing criticisms of her appearance and especially her weight. She endured the double standard that enabled her husband as a skirt chaser and left her wondering about her inadequacies.

But while Friedan critiqued writers like Jackson for publishing stories in women's magazines that suggested they were "just housewives," Jackson was hardly paralyzed by Friedan's "problem that has no name." As Franklin notes, the imperfection of Jackson's family tales, in pulling back the curtain and allowing for a view of domestic dysfunction, served a subversive function. Jackson was not perfect, and her stories suggested other women likewise were not and need not be. The world would not end were a floor unscrubbed or a dish unwashed. Children, while a joy to her life, were not made to be the center of the Hyman-Jackson universe. As for her appearance, Jackson suffered from insecurity, but not enough to stop her from indulging in drink and all the "beautiful and lovely and fascinating foods mankind has devoted himself to inventing." Women could be aware of the ideal, they could feel its pressure, but as demonstrated by Jackson, they could accept and reject elements to fit their individual proclivities.

Beyond eschewing the vision of womanhood celebrated by media and critiqued by Friedan, Jackson also serves as a representative of the many working women that Friedan's evaluation failed to consider. By 1960, after all, a significant minority of women were engaging in paid labor. But while many women had jobs, part time or intended as supplemental to their husband's income, Jackson had a career. And it brought her tremendous satisfaction. When she hired domestic help, she reveled in the freedom it allowed. She took great pride in her writing and loved to talk about her trade. In Jackson's life, there is little evidence of the guilt working women were assumed to have.

Was she less guilty because the nature of her work kept her at home? It bothered her that people assumed writers sat down to a blank sheet and began to write or type and that was how writing took place. When raising four children, Jackson conceived of her stories as she cooked a meal or washed the dishes or did the grocery shopping. Characters developed and plotlines emerged as she fulfilled her domestic duties. The sitting down to type was merely about getting the physical words on the page. Until her children were school age (and even then), Jackson had to find the time to sit down to type. Hyman provided virtually no support to domestic endeavors. Jackson, rather than facing a clearly delineated second shift (with household and professional tasks obviously demarcated), often fashioned makeshift moments for work whenever she found a respite from household responsibilities. In that sense she fits in a long line of "scribbling women" (in Nathaniel Hawthorne's dismissive phrase) from the eighteenth century onwards.

Where Jackson channeled different parts of herself to fulfill her domestic and then her professional responsibilities, she seemed also to possess different voices in her craft. Just as Jackson engaged in both public and private life, performing domestic and professional tasks, so too did she balance very different kinds of writing. And this befuddled literary critics. How, they wondered, could this woman write a story as masterful and unsettling as "The Lottery," suggesting the darkest impulses lurking in the minds of humankind, and then write a light-hearted story about a family's Christmas morning? Male critics, in particular, wondered why someone so skilled in her craft, capable of nearly perfect prose and sophisticated plotlines, wasted her time with domestic drivel or "ephemeral fluff." Jackson's skill, of course, remained the same. The topics are what varied. One world was valued; the other, not. Jackson insisted on writing about both.

Jackson lived very fully in two worlds, one of writing and agents and deadlines and publicity and another of children and dinners and boarding schools and trumpet lessons. She was one woman but of at least two minds. *The Bird's Nest*, Jackson's 1954 novel, chronicled a woman suffering from multiple personalities. Jackson balked at reviews that focused on Elizabeth, the main character, as insane or schizophrenic. Elizabeth's splintering, Franklin assesses, "is an exaggerated form of a universal condition" and an especially universal condition for midcentury women, expected to satiate themselves with domestic mundanities even as they longed for—or, like Jackson, lived—something more.

READING TO CHILDREN TO SAVE OURSELVES

DAEGAN MILLER

All those things for which we have no words are lost.

—Annie Dillard, "Total Eclipse"

M y youngest son's favorite book, this month, is called *Little Blue Truck*. If you read as much children's literature as I do, you are well acquainted with the book's parent genre, which descends from *The Little Engine That Could*: a small, underpowered vehicle is called upon to do something big and scary and seemingly impossible, and either the vehicle gathers its courage, scales the mountain, and saves the day (moral: trust yourself), or else it calls on its friends and together they chug their way to victory (moral: it takes a community).

My wife and I have two children, two boys, three and seven, and every day, for the last 2,558 days, I've read them somewhere between ten and thirty books. Most of the individual titles have dissolved into the blur of type—besides truck books, there are train books and construction books and family books and forest books and farm books and friend books and city books and country books and bathroom books and bedroom books and emotion books and eating-your-vegetables books and books for every other occasion, time, and situation you could think of; but the realization that's bubbled to the surface during my immersion is that most of the books are really about the same three things: love yourself; love all the other children; love every living thing.

There are outliers in the children's lit world, of course. The National Rifle Association has published a story called "*Little Red Riding Hood (Has a Gun).*" And I'm sure that the white supremacists have their own version of Dr. Seuss's *The Sneetches*, where those with stars on their bellies herd those without onto cattle cars.

We read to our children for all sorts of reasons. Books calm my boys down, dazzle their minds, tease their tongues with twisting sounds, show them people and animals and places from all over the world. We read to our children to bond. When my boys sit in my lap, wrapped in my arms, transfixed by word and image, it's an excuse for me to nuzzle my nose deep into their feral, tangled curly hair and breathe of innocence and health. We read to our children to teach them something about the world. My oldest son loves to try out Spanish, loves to read about different religions, loves tales of friendships that bridge boundaries while my youngest only wants to read stories that highlight camaraderie and mutual aid.

At some point—I'm not sure when—I began to take the books I was reading my boys as seriously as the books I read for my PhD advisors. I began to think about their meter, started paying attention to how narratives rose and fell, started taking seriously the ethics and philosophies and ideologies that scurried around each sentence. And then, the other day, a new book, by a British duo, Robert Macfarlane and Jackie Morris, called *The Lost Words*, came into our house.

Macfarlane is one of the most beloved living English-language nature writers at work today, and Morris, an artist and children's book author, has earned wide acclaim for her slightly surreal art that focuses on the natural world. *The Lost Words* was originally Morris's idea and stems from her sadness that, beginning in 2007, the *Oxford Junior Dictionary*, whose audience is my oldest son's age, began removing words like "bluebell," "acorn," "heron," and "kingfisher" from its pages because, in our tech-obsessed world, those words are thought not to matter as much as "broadband," "cut and paste," and "block graph." Morris approached Macfarlane with the idea for a book made up of these culls; Macfarlane, it turns out, had long since been bewitched by the power nature words have to summon forth a world. It was a perfect match.

The Lost Words is physically arresting. Nearly eleven by fifteen inches, printed on the heavy, glossy, peculiarly smelling stock that is reserved for art books, with highly stylized, large-face font, it is immersive and wild: Morris's art threatens to spill from the frame, gesturing to the wide-open world lying beyond the book's covers, while Macfarlane's words twine, skip, and trace their tracks across white expanse.

The book is composed of twenty lost words, from "Acorn" to "Wren." Each is introduced by a two-page watercolor—a cowlick of meadow grass, a single downy feather, a thicket's prickly brambles—through which a seemingly random scattering of letters is strewn. But look closely and you'll see certain letters highlighted, which together spell out the word to be regained. Flip the page, and, on the left, you'll find Macfarlane's poetic invocation of the word, matched, on the right, by Morris's spare art: the thing itself in translucent watercolor set off by an enormous, depthless field of gold leaf whose unpredictable, crinkly folds, tiny peaks and valleys, fill the image with a shimmering vitality.

Macfarlane's acrostic poems are lithe acrobatics of sound, which demand, and reward, close care. Here's "Newt," which had my seven-year-old giggling with glee over the words' sheer whimsy:

"Newt, oh newt, you are too cute!"
Emoted the coot to the too-cute newt,
"With your frilly back and your shiny suit
       and your spotted skin so unhirsute!"
"Too cute?!" roared the newt to the
       unastute coot. "With all this careless
       talk of cute you bring me into
       disrepute, for newts aren't cute:
       we're kings of the pond, lions of the
       duckweed, dragons of the water;
       albeit, it's true,"—he paused—"minute."

There's a gentle anthropomorphism reminiscent of *The Wind in the Willows* at work in a handful of Macfarlane's poems, as with "Newt" and its all-too human characters, but more often his poems are vivid in their evoked ambience, as in "Kingfisher," where the feathered thing materializes out of a tightly bundled explosion of sense impression:

Kingfisher: the colour-giver, fire-bringer, flame-flicker,
      river's quiver.

Ink-black bill, orange throat, and a quick blue
      back-gleaming feather-stream.

In a brief prelude, Macfarlane writes that his poems are really "spells," "for conjuring back these lost words," and he casts them with visual adjectives, quickening verbs, and, especially, shape-shifting metaphors—the kingfisher as the quick flicker of a flame. He's working in a very long Romantic tradition of nature writing and swaps descriptive scientific precision for something more eco-mimetic: sensuous metonym and synecdoche embody an animal or plant (an otter is "a shadow-flutter, bubble-skein" and "an utter underwater thunderbolter"), words that vibrate with action, come alive, and launch into flight.

There's a sonic mimicry, as well, in the way the lines flit or rattle or clomp across a page, in the way that sounds trip from the tongue. Take "Raven," whose opening line, "**R**ock rasps, what are you?" sounds like the bird's guttural "caw! caw!" These are poems that announce themselves as pure essence, an essence, one senses, that the book's audience can possess, not in order to gain control but to "unfold dreams and songs." That is, there's a surprising inwardness to Macfarlane's poetry; his spells are aimed at changing not the outer world but the reader's own intimate imagination.

There are two exceptions. Both "Conker" (better known to Americans as either the horse chestnut or the buckeye) and "Willow" are marked by a gentle, though boldfaced refusal to summon:

> **We** will never whisper to you, listeners, nor speak, nor shout,
>   and even if you learn to utter alder, elder, poplar, aspen,
>   you will **never** know a word of willow—for we are willow
>   and you are not.

When my seven-year-old heard these lines, he didn't laugh. He was quiet and meditative, and I, who know him so well, couldn't begin to know what he thought, other than that think he surely did.

It's a similar focus-compelling refusal that characterizes Morris's extraordinary golden images. She's a precise water colorist, and, to my eye, there's something of Roger Tory Peterson, whose works have illustrated thousand of pages of bird identification guides, in her pictures—only not quite. Whereas Peterson's birds are artfully generic representatives of a species, meant to aid the birder, Morris's watercolors reach beyond the empirical plumage, pelt, or bark to something more subjective and seemingly intrinsic to her subject. Whereas Peterson's birds are illustrations, standing in a one-to-one likeness with those of the field, I'm not sure that Morris's are meant to represent anything. They are simply themselves, immediate and arresting. And because she backs her subjects with gold leaf, there's no pretension to naturalism.

The longer I looked with my sons at Morris's paintings, the more I became convinced that what she's painted is an animist revision of the Christian religious icon, and her work is similarly radiant with devout passion. There's no hint of anthropomorphism nor even of naturalistic ecomimesis, and the point of convergence for Macfarlane's prose and Morris's art is that refusal of conker and willow to signify. While Morris's other images—the scenes set in fields or woods—gesture at an outside world, these gold-toned ones reside in a space of inner conviction, and to watch the way they lit my children's faces was to witness the spreading of a sublime feeling of reverent mystery.

Perhaps one of the most pressing reasons we read to our children is to teach them how to be good, and *The Lost Words* was made for parents like me, I think: its unstated root proposition is that we care for the things we know, that we know the things we name, that those things with no name are lost. And yet I have found myself wondering if it wouldn't be better for the world if the words "acorn" and "otter" and "newt" disappeared forever, if real acorns and otters and newts became invisible to humans, if in their invisibility, they became safe from humans.

After all, generations of children grew up saying "passenger pigeon" and "great auk," just as they now say "whooping crane" and "mountain gorilla" and "Great Barrier Reef" for those things that everyday are pushed closer to extinction. It would be nice if books mattered as much as we literary, intellectual people think they do. In other words, I have very recently found myself reconsidering why I read to my children.

The evening my wife and I first became parents, March 10, 2011, my nightmares took on a new ferocity, one that leaves me exhausted at the break of every day. I began dreaming of all the things that could happen to my child: the suffocations, the car wrecks and fires and illnesses and guns and drugs and swimming-hole accidents, all the ways that innocent lives are lost. But there is one recurring nightmare that surpasses all the others for its pure cold panic: it's the one where my boys simply vanish. There's no narrative to the dream, no cause, no mysterious trace to be sleuthed out, nothing that I can do. Just the emptiness of agony where once was the music of laughter.

There are many ways to lose a child. Ever since the Electoral College voted Donald Trump into the presidency, I have logged long daylit hours thinking about my nightmare. About the many ways to vanish. How did Trump become Trump? I desperately want to believe that today's proud predator had once been a sweet, funny, inquisitive little boy with wild hair but that his father didn't love him enough, didn't nuzzle him, didn't wrap him in his arms and read him the right books with the right words, the way I hope I do for my boys, that, in the absence of care, the once-wonderful child simply disappeared. But another way to vanish is to become unrecognizable to those who know you best, and I'm terrified that Trump lost his way all by himself, despite the efforts his father made.

The Lost Words won't save the world any more than 10,000 more books will save my sons—but, as I read it over and again with them, I realize that's neither the book's point nor its promise. And in scanning Macfarlane's poems and Morris's paintings, it dawns on me that there's a reason to sit before a book with one's children that I've so far missed. What if the millions of words that have crossed my tongue were also meant for me? What if we parents took children's literature as seriously as we take philosophy, history, politics, economics?

What if we adults read *Frog and Toad Are Friends* and learned that consensual love is always to be treasured, wherever and between whomever it burns? What if we took to heart the lesson of Dr. Seuss's Lorax, that one person's profit will always impoverish the entire world? What if we lived our lives with the conviction of *The Lion and the Mouse*: always help those in need, no matter how much they differ from us. Or sat with Ferdinand the Bull, smelling the flowers, refusing to fight for the entertainment of those in power? What if, I think *The Lost Words* is really asking, my children and I are simply meant to cuddle and to be and to learn together? Perhaps that's all we can do.

And so tonight, after work and school and daycare are over, after the dinner dishes are cleared, teeth brushed, and pajamas zipped, I'll call out my children's names, and we'll gather for the ritual that has helped to define every day of their lives. We'll welcome this new book into our family, we'll speak the words that are not yet lost, we'll gaze in rapture at the still-living icons. We'll read those concluding lines from "Conker"—

> *Realize this* (said the Cabinet-maker, the King, and
> the Engineer together), *conker cannot be made,*
> *however you ask it, whatever word or tool you use,*
> *regardless of decree. Only one thing can conjure*
> *conker—and that thing is tree.*

—and think our separate thoughts, together. I'll sit with my two boys to confront, if never to quite conquer, the nightmares of extinction, and who knows what tomorrow will bring but another pile of books, another evening to read, another chance to conjure.

CONTRIBUTORS

JEREMY ADELMAN is the Henry Charles Lea Professor of History at Princeton University. He is the author, most recently, of *Worldly Philosopher: The Odyssey of Albert O. Hirschman* (2013).

NAJWA AL-QATTAN is professor of Middle Eastern history at Loyola Marymount University in Los Angeles. Her areas of research include the Jews and Christians of the Ottoman Empire, the Ottoman *sharia* courts, and Syria and Lebanon in the Great War. Her articles have appeared in several journals and edited volumes, including *IJMES* and *CSSH*.

STACEY BALKAN is assistant professor of environmental literature and humanities at Florida Atlantic University. Her teaching and research focus on postcolonial ecologies, landscape aesthetics and counterpastoralism, and environmental justice. Recent articles for *The Global South and ISLE: Interdisciplinary Studies in Literature and Environment* examine the material legacies of uneven and combined development in Nigeria and India. Her current book projects include a monograph entitled "Rogues in the Postcolony: Developing Itinerancy in India" and an essay collection entitled "Oil Fictions: World Literature and our Contemporary Petrosphere," which is similarly committed to examining aesthetic registers of imperial violence.

KARL ASHOKA BRITTO is associate professor of French and comparative literature at the University of California, Berkeley. He is the author of *Disorientation: France, Vietnam, and the Ambivalence of Interculturality.* Britto's current work considers the body as spectacle in colonial and postcolonial literature.

JUDITH BUTLER is Maxine Elliot Professor in the department of comparative literature and critical theory at the University of California, Berkeley. She is the author of *Notes Toward a Performative Theory of Assembly* (2015).

MATTHEW CLAIR is a sociologist and a postdoctoral fellow at the University of Pennsylvania Law School. In summer 2019, he will join Stanford University as an assistant professor of sociology with a courtesy appointment at Stanford Law School. He received his PhD from Harvard University.

B. R. COHEN is an associate professor at Lafayette College in Easton, Pennsylvania; author of *Notes from the Ground: Science, Soil, and Society in the American Countryside* (2009); coeditor (with Gwen Ottinger) of *Technoscience and Environmental Justice: Expert Cultures in a Grassroots Movement* (2011); and cohost of the podcast *Various Breads and Butters.* His book *Pure Adulteration: Cheating on Nature in the Age of Manufactured Food* is forthcoming.

N. D. B. CONNOLLY is the Herbert Baxter Adams Associate Professor of History at the Johns Hopkins University and author of the award-winning book *A World More Concrete: Real Estate and the Remaking of Jim Crow South Florida* (2014).

NICHOLAS DAMES is Theodore Kahan Professor of Humanities in the Department of English and Comparative Literature at Columbia University. His most recent book is *The Physiology of the Novel: Reading, Neural Science, and the Form of Victorian Fiction* (2007). His current project is a history of the chapter from late antiquity to the modern novel. He has written on contemporary fiction, novel reading, and the humanities for *The Atlantic*, *n+1*, *The Nation*, *New Left Review*, the *New Yorker*, and the *New York Times Book Review*.

KAREN DUNAK is associate professor of history at Muskingum University in New Concord, Ohio. Her book, *As Long as We Both Shall Love: The White Wedding in Postwar America*, appeared in 2013. She currently is working on a book about Jacqueline Kennedy Onassis and American media.

SIMON DURING is at the University of Melbourne. His books include *Against Democracy: Literary Experience in the Age of Emancipations* (2012) *and Modern Enchantments: The Cultural Power of Secular Magic* (2002).

MATTHEW ENGELKE is a professor in the Department of Religion and director of the Institute for Religion, Culture, and Public Life at Columbia University. He is the author of *How to Think Like an Anthropologist* (2018); *God's Agents: Biblical Publicity in Contemporary England* (2013); and *A Problem of Presence: Beyond Scripture in an African Church* (2007), which won the Victor Turner Prize for Ethnographic Writing and the Clifford Geertz Prize.

REBECCA FALKOFF is assistant professor of Italian studies a New York University. Her research—rooted in psychoanalysis, gender and sexuality studies, and new materialist thought—focuses on possession and perversion in modern literary and visual texts. She is completing her first book, which argues that the hoarder of contemporary discourse is not exceptional figure but a personification of the economic, environmental, and technological conditions of modernity.

ANNE E. FERNALD is professor of English and women's, gender and sexuality studies at Fordham University. She edited

Mrs. Dalloway for Cambridge University Press and is the author of a book on Woolf as well as articles about women, feminism, and modernism.

NICOLE R. FLEETWOOD is a professor of American Studies at Rutgers University, New Brunswick. Recently, she completed a book on art and mass incarceration. Her previous books are *Troubling Vision: Performance, Visuality, and Blackness* (2011) and *On Racial Icons: Blackness and the Public Imagination* (2015). She is also co-curator and contributing editor to Aperture Foundation's "Prison Nation," an exploration of the role of photography in documenting mass incarceration.

PHILIP GORSKI is professor of sociology and religious studies at Yale University, where he is currently concluding a major project on the philosophy of the social sciences. His most recent book is *American Covenant: A History of Civil Religion from the Puritans to the Present* (2017).

MARAH GUBAR is an associate professor of literature at MIT. Previously, she directed the Children's Literature Program at the University of Pittsburgh. Her book *Artful Dodgers: Reconceiving the Golden Age of Children's Literature* (2009) won the Children's Literature Association Book Award. She is currently working on a book project entitled "How to Think About Children: Childhood Studies in the Academy and Beyond."

SUZY HANSEN is an American journalist and editor. She is a contributing writer for the *New York Times Magazine* and has written about foreign affairs for publications such as the *London Review of Books*, *Vogue*, *Bookforum*, and *The Baffler*. Her first book about America's role in the Middle East, *Notes on a Foreign Country*, was published in 2017 by Farrar, Straus and Giroux. The book won the Overseas Press Club Award for Nonfiction and was a finalist for the Pulitzer Prize.

MAX HOLLERAN is lecturer in sociology at the University of Melbourne. His work focuses on urban development for tourism in the European Union, and he has written about architectural aesthetics, postsocialist urban planning, and European nationalism for anthropology, sociology, and history journals. His work on cities and politics has also appeared in *Boston Review*, *New Republic*, and *Slate*.

LILLY IRANI is an assistant professor of communication and science studies at the University of California, San Diego. She is a cofounder of the Mechanical Turk worker-activism tool Turkopticon. She writes on the cultural politics of globalized innovation and development. She has a PhD in information and computer science from the University of California, Irvine.

DESTIN JENKINS is the Neubauer Family Assistant Professor of History at the University of Chicago. His research centers on the linkages between racial capitalism, inequality, and the built environment in twentieth-century America.

JOSEPH JONGHYUN JEON is professor of English at the University of California, Irvine. He is the author of *Vicious Circuits: Korea's IMF Cinema and the End of the American Century* (forthcoming) and *Racial Things, Racial Forms: Objecthood in Avant-Garde Asian American Poetry* (2012).

SHEILA LIMING is an assistant professor of English at the University of North Dakota, where she teaches classes on twentieth-century American fiction and digital media.

SHANNON MATTERN is a professor of media studies at the New School. She is the author of *The New Downtown Library* (2007), *Deep Mapping the Media City* (2015), and *Code and Clay, Data and Dirt* (2017). She contributes a regular long-form column about urban data and mediated infrastructures to *Places Journal*.

MARK McGURL is professor of English at Stanford University. He is the author of *The Program Era: Postwar Fiction and the Rise of Creative Writing* (2009) and is currently working on a book on Amazon.com as a protagonist of contemporary literary history.

J. R. McNEILL teaches environmental and global history at Georgetown University. His books include *Something New Under the Sun: An Environmental History of the Twentieth-century World* (2000) and *Mosquito Empires: Ecology and War in the Greater Caribbean, 1620–1914* (2010). He has authored several papers in scientific journals but, alas, not *Geophysical Research Letters*. In 2019 he will be president of the American Historical Association.

TESS McNULTY is a PhD student in the English department at Harvard, working on contemporary literature and digital culture.

JAN MIESZKOWSKI is professor of German and comparative literature at Reed College. He is the author of *Watching War* (2012) and *Labors of Imagination: Aesthetics and Political Economy from Kant to Althusser* (2006). His new book, *Crises of the Sentence*, is forthcoming from the University of Chicago Press in 2019.

DAEGAN MILLER is the author of *This Radical Land: A Natural History of American Dissent* (2018), and his essays and criticism have appeared in *Aeon*, *Bookforum*, the *Los Angeles Review of Books*, and *3:AM Magazine*, among other places. He and his family live in Madison, Wisconsin.

FRANCES NEGRÓN-MUNTANER is a filmmaker, writer, and scholar. Among her books are *Boricua Pop: Puerto Ricans and the Latinization of American Culture* (2004) and *Sovereign Acts* (2017). Her films include *Brincando el charco: Portrait of a Puerto Rican, Small City*; *Big Change*; and *War for Guam*. She is the founding curator of Latino Arts and Activism, founder of the

Media and Idea Lab, and former director of the Center for the Study of Ethnicity and Race (2009–2016) at Columbia University.

ANDREW J. PERRIN is a professor of sociology at the University of North Carolina, Chapel Hill. His most recent book is *American Democracy: From Tocqueville to Town Halls to Twitter* (2014).

IMANI PERRY is the Hughes-Rogers Professor of African American Studies at Princeton University, where she is also affiliated with the Programs in Law and Public Affairs and Gender and Sexuality Studies. She is the author of *More Beautiful and More Terrible: The Embrace and Transcendence of Racial Inequality in the United States* (2011) and *Prophets of the Hood: Politics and Poetics in Hip Hop* (2004) as well as numerous articles in the fields of law, cultural studies, and African American studies. She has a forthcoming book on the history of the Black National anthem from Oxford University Press and another on gender, neoliberalism, and the digital age from Duke University Press. You can follow her on Twitter at @imaniperry.

KIM PHILLIPS-FEIN is a historian and associate professor at the Gallatin School of Individualized Study at New York University. She is the author of *Fear City: The New York City Fiscal Crisis and the Rise of Austerity Politics* (2017) and *Invisible Hands: The Businessmen's Crusade Against the New Deal* (2010).

JOHN PLOTZ is professor of Victorian literature at Brandeis University. His books include *The Crowd: British Literature and Public Politics* (2000); *Portable Property: Victorian Culture on the Move* (2008); and *Semi-Aesthetics of Virtual Experience Since Dickens* (2018). His *Public Books* pieces on Doris Lessing and Ursula Le Guin are early pieces from a monograph in progress, "Nonhuman Being: Post-Darwinian Naturalism, Fantasy, and

Science Fiction." He and his partner Lisa live in Brookline with two children and three chickens.

ELI ROSENBLATT is a fellow at the Frankel Institute for Advanced Judaic Studies at the University of Michigan, where he is working on a book about Jewish literature and racial politics in four urban complexes: Paramaribo, Kiev, Johannesburg, and Chicago. He has taught at UC-Berkeley, where he received his PhD, and at Georgetown University. He lives in Chicago.

CHRISTOPHER SCHABERG is Dorothy Harrell Brown Distinguished Professor of English at Loyola University New Orleans. He is the author of *The Textual Life of Airports* (2011), *The End of Airports* (2015), *Airportness* (2017), and *The Work of Literature in an Age of Post-Truth* (2018).

NAMWALI SERPELL is a Zambian writer and associate professor of English at the University of California, Berkeley.

KIERAN SETIYA is a professor of philosophy at the Massachusetts Institute of Technology, working mainly in ethics, epistemology, and the philosophy of mind. He is the author of a self-help book, *Midlife: A Philosophical Guide* (2017), and is one of the most highly ranked players at Diamond Mind Online, the leading historical baseball simulation game.

HARUO SHIRANE, Shincho Professor of Japanese Literature and Culture and chair of the Department of East Asian Languages and Cultures at Columbia University, is the author and editor of over twenty books, most recently, *Japan and the Culture of the Four Seasons* (2012); *Reading the Tale of Genji: Sources for the First Millennium* (2015); and *Monsters, Animals, and Other Worlds: A Collection of Short Medieval Japanese Tales* (2018).

GAYATRI CHAKRAVORTY SPIVAK is University Professor and a founding member of the Institute for Comparative Literature and Society at Columbia University.

FRED TURNER is Harry and Norman Chandler Professor of Communication at Stanford University. He is the author, most recently, of *The Democratic Surround: Multimedia and American Liberalism from World War II to the Psychedelic Sixties.*

SALAMISHAH TILLET is the Henry Rutgers Professor of African American Studies and Creative Writing and associate director of the Price Institute of Culture, Ethnicity, and Modern Experience at Rutgers University–Newark. In 2018, she became the founding director of the Public Arts and Social Justice Initiative at Express Newark and is a contributing Culture Critic at the *New York Times.* She is the author of *Sites of Slavery: Citizenship and Racial Democracy in Post-Civil Rights America* and two forthcoming book projects, "In Search of *The Color Purple*" and "All The Rage: 'Mississippi Goddam' and the World Nina Simone Made." In 2003, she and her sister, Scheherazade Tillet, cofounded A Long Walk Home, a nonprofit that uses art to empower young people and end violence against girls and women.

JAMES VERNON teaches at the University of California, Berkeley. He is the author, most recently, of *Distant Strangers: How Britain Became Modern* (2014) and *The Cambridge History of Modern Britain: 1750 to the Present* (2017).

REBECCA L. WALKOWITZ is professor and chair of English and affiliate faculty in Comparative Literature at Rutgers University. Her research focuses on transnational and multilingual approaches to literary history. She is the author of *Cosmopolitan Style: Modernism Beyond the Nation* (2006) and *Born Translated: The Contemporary Novel in an Age of World Literature* (2015) and the editor or coeditor of several additional books, including, with Douglas Mao, *Bad Modernisms* (2006) and, with Eric Hayot, *A New Vocabulary for Global Modernism* (2016).